PRAISE FOR THE

Best Food Writing

SERIES

"There's a mess of vital, provocative, funny, and tender stuff...in these pages." —*USA Today*

"Some of these stories can make you burn with a need to taste what they're writing about." —*Los Angeles Times*

"The essays are thought-provoking and moving...This is an absolutely terrific and engaging book ... There is enough variety, like a box of chocolates, that one can poke around the book looking for the one with caramel and find it." —*New York Journal of Books*

"What is so great about this annual series is that editor Holly Hughes curates articles that likely never crossed your desk, even if you're an avid reader of food content. Nearly every piece selected is worth your time." —The Huffington Post

"Stories for connoisseurs, celebrations of the specialized, the odd, or simply the excellent." —*Entertainment Weekly*

"This book is a menu of delicious food, colorful characters, and tales of strange and wonderful food adventures that make for memorable meals and stories." —*Booklist*

"This collection has something for connoisseurs, short story fans, and anyone hungry for a good read." —*Library Journal*

"Browse, read a bit, browse some more, and then head for the kitchen." —*Hudson Valley News*

"The finest in culinary prose is offered in this new anthology…these pages delight and inform readers with entertaining and provocative essays…This book ultimately opens readers' eyes to honest, real food and the personal stories of the people behind it." —*Taste for Life*

"Longtime editor Hughes once again compiles a tasty collection of culinary essays for those who love to eat, cook, and read about food…A literary trek across the culinary landscape pairing bountiful delights with plenty of substantive tidbits." —*Kirkus Reviews*

"A top-notch collection, Hughes brings together a wonderful mix that is sure to please the foodie in all of us." —*San Francisco Book Review*

"An exceptional collection worth revisiting, this will be a surefire hit with epicureans and cooks." —*Publishers Weekly,* starred review

"If you're looking to find new authors and voices about food, there's an abundance to chew on here." —*Tampa Tribune*

"Fascinating to read now, this book will also be interesting to pick up a year from now, or ten years from now." —*Popmatters.com*

"This is a book worth devouring." —*Sacramento Bee*

"The cream of the crop of food writing compilations."
   —*Milwaukee Journal Sentinel*

"The book captures the gastronomic zeitgeist in a broad range of essays."
   —*San Jose Mercury News*

"There are a few recipes among the stories, but mostly it's just delicious tales about eating out, cooking at home, and even the politics surrounding the food on our plates." —*Spokesman-Review*

"The next best thing to eating there is." —*New York Metro*

"Spans the globe and palate." —*Houston Chronicle*

"The perfect gift for the literate food lover." —*Pittsburgh Post-Gazette*

best
Food
WRITING
2017

best
Food
WRITING
2017

edited by
Holly
Hughes

Da Capo
LIFE
LONG

Da Capo Press
Hachette Book Group
1290 Avenue of the Americas, New York, NY 10104
DaCapoPress.com
@DaCapoPress

Printed in the United States of America

First Edition: October 2017

Published by Da Capo Press, an imprint of Perseus Books, LLC, a subsidiary of Hachette Book Group, Inc.

The Hachette Speakers Bureau provides a wide range of authors for speaking events. To find out more, go to www.hachettespeakersbureau.com or call (866) 376-6591.

The publisher is not responsible for websites (or their content) that are not owned by the publisher.

Print book interior design by Jeff Williams.

Library of Congress Cataloging-in-Publication Data has been applied for.

ISBNs: 978-0-7382-2018-5 (paperback), 978-0-7382-2019-2 (e-book)

LSC-C

10 9 8 7 6 5 4 3 2 1

Contents

WHOSE FOOD IS IT ANYWAY?

FOODWAYS

HOW MY CITY EATS

UPDATING THE CLASSICS

SOMEONE'S IN THE KITCHEN

THEY ALSO SERVE

DOWN THE HATCH

PERSONAL TASTES

Introduction

The showstopper of the evening—the "ta-da!" course—was no doubt meant to be the lobster. The waiter presented it with a flourish, in a shiny copper vessel on a pillow of tangled seaweed, atop gleaming coals. The concept (there's always a narrative) was an homage to the New England shore dinner. The dainty lobster nuggets that landed on our plates were succulent indeed, and yet . . . well, I was still marveling over the previous course, the ecstatic silkiness of thin-shaved scallops marinated in leek and potato. Another new wine was being poured, and, perched on our banquette—more like theater seats than the setting for a romantic tête-à-tête—my husband and I were still trying to figure out which of the bevy of servers was officially "our" waiter. We were on gourmet overload.

Granted, I knew what I was getting into. I asked for this for my Christmas present, after years of jonesing to try out Eleven Madison Park. We'd been saving it for a special event, and then realized the meal itself should be event enough. We lucked out, as it happened; only a couple months later, the restaurant closed for renovations, coincidentally (or not?) just after it won the 2017 title of Best Restaurant in the World. And while I secretly hoped that the storied Dream Weaver (see *Best Food Writing 2016*) would deliver some soupçon of special treatment, I respect the fact that we got NO extra treatment that night. My husband and I had an exquisite meal. We came home with EMP's trademark jars of granola, just as promised. Done and done.

And yet . . .

I asked myself, am I too jaded to be thrilled by an experience like this? I'm not a professional dining critic; I cook at home more often than I eat out. While I've been editing this culinary anthology for eighteen years, I don't exactly haunt New York City's dining hotspots. So when I finally do visit a temple of gastronomy, I should be easily wowed, right? Or is it because I *don't* dine out for a living that I can't completely enjoy an experience so over-the-top expensive? In today's politically charged economy, do I really want to embrace the dining habits of the 1 percent?

Truth to tell, if I could point to one transcendent meal I've had this year, it would probably be a one-pot dish I cooked last summer, a real clean-out-the-refrigerator special. That night, I threw together a random bunch of vegetables with the right spices and a long slow simmer—and the result was orgasmic (and alas, irreproducible). I sat in my own kitchen and marveled at how the marriage of ingredients worked. No recipe, no meal kit, no Food Channel video—just a knife and a pot and a low flame. Magic.

That high-low dialectic—that contrast between gourmet palates and elemental appetites—informs *Best Food Writing 2017*. Because here we are, in 2017, struggling to define our national food conversation. In some weird way, all bets are off. While restaurants at the culinary forefront generate plenty of buzz, the chatter around artisanal and casual and regional restaurants is more robust than ever. Trophy dining has somehow mutated, with under-the-radar finds scoring more cachet than the entrenched four-stars. Meanwhile, even though home cooking is said to be in serious decline, the domestic kitchen has been cast as a battlefront, with no-fuss convenience warring with the imperative to show off mad culinary skills. After all, if Gwyneth Paltrow can do it so effortlessly, why can't we?

In an era where the 24-hour news cycle keeps our heads spinning, culinary trends change so often, and so quickly, it's hard to keep up. Avocado toast supplants pork belly, which supplanted kale; the meal-in-a-bowl will soon enough go the way of foraging and foams. Consider some of the fringe-ier elements profiled in "The Way We Eat Now" (starting on page 1): The meatless hamburger (J. Kenji Lopez-Alt, page 13) and kelp greens (Rowan Jacobsen, page 20).

On the other hand, heightened political sensitivities make food justice more relevant than ever, from Jane Black's profile of a chef bringing whole-food dining to an underprivileged community (page 40) to Greg Rosalsky's breakdown of the glaring price gap between the haves and the have-nots of New York City's restaurants (page 33). The vexed topic of cultural appropriation has roiled the food world this year, just as it has in the fields of film and literature. In "Whose Food Is It, Anyway?" (beginning on page 49), the debate over America's ethnic cuisines ranges far and wide, including African-American cooking (John T. Edge and Tunde Wey, page 50), Mexican-American cooking (Gustavo Arellano, page 88), and Asian-American cuisine (Luke Tsai, page 71, and Tim Carman, page 82). Sometimes it seems there's quicksand everywhere.

Why should things be so tricky? Food, after all, is one of our most basic needs; the simple act of breaking bread together has always bound families, friends, communities. But over the past decade, our food choices have also become a matter of personal identity. From Appalachian down-home meals (Ronni Lundy, page 94) to Vietnamese pho (Rachel Khong, page 102) to South Carolina barbecue (Kathleen Purvis, page 114), several writers in this year's book drill down on the food traditions they hold dear. And if these foods provide roots, it's only natural to try to bring them along when we're transplanted to another time and place. Witness Julia Moskin's attempt to re-cast the chicken potpie of her childhood (page 199), or Joe Yonan's repurposing of his mother's Texas Salad (page 204)—and John Kessler's dogged quest for authentic Southern eats after being uprooted from Atlanta to Chicago (page 193).

Not so many years ago, the badge of foodie sophistication was a global outlook, a world traveler's ease with foreign cuisines. Nowadays, you score bragging rights for how well you've navigated the regional American food map, the blue highways of local dining. Several of this year's writers do a deep dive into the essence of their hometown food culture, trying to pin down why Nashville hot chicken (Danny Chau, page 157), Maryland crab (Bill Addison, page 147), the Reuben sandwich (Elizabeth Weil, page 126), Seattle teriyaki (Naomi Tomsky, page 135), or San Francisco Mission burritos (John Birdsall, page 140, and Anna Roth, page 188) so potently convey an ineffable sense of place.

Meanwhile, the essays in "Personal Tastes" (beginning on page 301) focus on the central role food played at crucial points of the writers' lives. It might be the birth of a child (Eric LeMay, page 307), the death of a beloved parent (Bethany Jean Clement, page 329) or grandparent (Elissa Altman, page 322), or the emotional limbo of a child lost in a family crisis (Floyd Skloot, page 332). And then there's Paul Graham's book excerpt (page 302), a poignant elegy of sorts for food itself, or at least a certain type of food he can no longer eat.

Of course, gifted chefs have always been able to buck/drive the trends, as amply demonstrated by the pieces in "Someone's in the Kitchen" (beginning on page 209). Here, you'll read about newcomers like Kyle and Katina Connaughton (profiled by Tienlon Ho, page 236), scene-setting star chefs like Sean Brock (profiled by Brett Martin, page 216), and past masters like Michel Richard (memorialized by Todd Kliman, page 245). But these days, it's not all about the culinary elite—so why not revise our view of TV personality/chef Guy Fieri (Jason Diamond, page 210)? In our drinks section, "Down the Hatch" (starting on page 273), there's a similar underlying sense that all bets are off, with the craft beer scene getting downright weird (John Wray, page 281) and the wine scene going off script, with stratospherically priced bottles now being poured by the glass (Ray Isle, page 286). Anything goes.

Which brings me back to the gifted chefs and high-end wines of Eleven Madison Park. That evening, I didn't fully appreciate the ultimate act of hospitality—the fact that the tab had already been paid by credit card weeks ago, tactfully bypassing the awkward ritual of check-paying and gratuities. (We couldn't have figured out which waiter to tip, anyway.) I also wasn't aware that the EMP geniuses were also soon to open the much lower-priced Made Nice, a casual counter-service spot with the same creativity and focus on quality. Another act of hospitality.

So maybe our national food conversation is simply evolving, moving past that contrast between high and low cuisine. Rather than a face-off, perhaps we can see it as a dance. We all eat differently on various days of the week, after all; we each love different foods, for different reasons. Sharing the hospitality of the common table is what's important, even if we order different dishes. With that in mind, I value the wide range of voices in this year's book, piping up not only from hefty cookbooks and photo-rich magazines, but from scrappy websites and blogs, from local papers and regional magazines. More and people are finding their voices at the table—let's welcome them all.

The Way We Eat Now

The Benefits of Eating Without a Map

By Keith Pandolfi

From SeriousEats.com

Through various senior editor stints at *Saveur* and Serious Eats, NYC-based food writer Keith Pandolfi has plenty of "insider" knowledge of elite dining scenes and hyper-connected gourmet trends. But sometimes, as he muses here, it can be liberating to go off the grid.

A few weeks ago, an old friend who was traveling to New Orleans for the first time emailed to ask me for restaurant and bar recommendations. I sent him my usual list—some personal favorites from the time I lived in the city, pre-Katrina, from 1998 to 2003: Willie Mae's Scotch House, Restaurant August, Molly's at the Market, and Dante's Kitchen—as well as newer places that have opened since I left for New York, like Cochon, La Petite Grocery, and MoPho. I told him to go to Shaya and Domenica, because everyone tells everyone to go to Shaya and Domenica these days, though I haven't been to either. I strongly advised him to grab a Grasshopper at Tujague's, and a Sazerac at The Roosevelt, then I reluctantly hit send.

The reason I say "reluctantly" is because I really didn't want to send him any recommendations at all. Instead, I wanted to send an email back that read something like this: "Go anywhere that looks good to you. Then let me know what you find." In other words, discover your own places to eat. *Eat without a map.*

It's something people just don't do anymore.

Thanks to social media platforms like Twitter, Instagram, Facebook, and Yelp—as well as the countless magazines, TV shows, and websites dedicated to food (this one included)—we are constantly being told where to eat. We can find out what the hottest restaurant in San Francisco is by simply Googling "What's the hottest restaurant in San Francisco?" There are hundreds if not thousands of city guides, top-10 lists, best-restaurants-in-America lists, and best-restaurants-in-Dayton-Ohio lists to abide by, whether we're traveling to a city for the first time or going out to dinner in our own hometowns. It takes just a click or two to find someone's take on the best hot chicken joints in Nashville, the best chowder houses in New England, or the best deep-dish pizza in Chicago. It's all so easy, so convenient. But are we missing out on something?

I've spent a good part of my career working as a writer and editor for various food magazines and websites. Part of my job is to tell people where to eat, and where to eat well. That's not a bad thing. I take a certain pride in letting people know, for example, that one of the best dishes in Manhattan is the *estrella* pasta coated with sautéed chicken livers at Justin Smillie's Upland; that any visitor to New Orleans would be a fool not to tuck into a meat-bomb pho of tripe, pork shoulder, chicken thighs, and smoked greens at MoPho; that one of the best fish dishes in the Boston area is the swordfish pastrami at Puritan & Company.

But, while I'd like to think all the virtual ink we food writers spill on great restaurants, talented chefs, and go-to food destinations benefits everyone, practically guaranteeing you'll never have to endure a bad meal again, I also worry that it takes some of the fun and the adventure away from traveling and eating. That it detracts from your own sense of discovery; your ability to throw caution to the wind. To make the best out of an ordinary meal at an ordinary restaurant. To screw up. Or to find something truly special—completely on your own.

If I'd been honest with that friend of mine, I would have told him that the best meal I ever had in New Orleans was at a restaurant that I would never in my life recommend to him, or anyone else for that matter. It was eaten in 1998 at a tourist trap just off Bourbon Street (I'd give you the name, but it never occurred to me to write it down). It was only my second time in the city, my first visit as an adult, and all I remember about the place is that it was mostly empty, that a kind old man in an old polyester tuxedo led me to my table. And, while the food was nothing more than passable, I'm still thinking about it 18 years later.

Part of the reason I remember that place so fondly is that it's the first place where I ever ordered red beans and rice, a dish, I would later learn, that's a staple of the city's traditional cuisine. A dish that, years later, would make me weep when I tasted it at a Katrina fundraiser in New York just weeks after the storm had passed. The beans at that restaurant were undercooked, and the rice was overcooked, and there were specks of spicy andouille sausage that I will never forget because they were the first specks of spicy andouille sausage I ever tasted. Yes, the restaurant was a solid C+ at best. One star. Maybe one and a half. I remember looking out the window at a crumbling French Quarter building across the street. I remember that it rained. I fell in love with New Orleans over that crap-ass meal. And I wanted my friend to fall in love with New Orleans over a crap-ass meal, too. I just wanted him to discover that meal on his own.

These days, whether I'm traveling for work or for pleasure, I try to make a point of spending at least a day or two doing cold visits to places I know absolutely nothing about. Sometimes it's a bust. Other times, it's just fine. But sometimes, I get my mind blown. Take, for instance, the gumbo fries I wolfed down late one night in Memphis a few years back. I had just arrived with a fellow food-writing friend of mine, and we were dashing around the city, frantically looking for good places to eat. We were Googling and texting people. We were searching the websites of the very publications we worked for, hoping for guidance. At some point, we gave up and settled on what looked like a touristy nightmare on Beale Street, called Blues City Cafe. Sitting in the booth, I glanced at the menu, smirking at one of the items. "They have gumbo cheese fries," I said, laughing. "And yes, I'm getting them."

Who the hell would ever think to pour seafood gumbo over cheese fries? Well, the folks at Blues City Cafe (which I later found out was once a branch of the famous Doe's Eat Place in Greenville, Mississippi), that's who. And, holy shit, were they good. The steak fries were golden brown and slightly crunchy, just thick-skinned enough not to disintegrate beneath the heavy weight of the gumbo ladled over them. There was ranch dressing on the side! Digging into the dish, I lifted up what I now consider the Holy Trinity of late-night dining—a forkful of French fries, gumbo, and gobs of stretchy melted cheese. My friend snapped a photo of me, looking perplexed as I dug in, a picture that remains on my Twitter profile to this day, because that dish signified everything I love about being a food writer. It signified the discovery of absolute perfection in the places where you least expect it.

Those gumbo fries reminded me that it pays to take a chance now and then. If not, we'll all just end up writing about the same dishes everyone else does—the same places. The same chefs. Sometimes I fear that's already happened.

Traveling without a map has also made me realize that there is really nothing wrong with a mediocre meal every once in a while. In fact, once the expectations of a great meal are lifted, it's possible to enjoy that meal even more. Recently I visited Los Angeles for a culinary awards ceremony, along with some of my favorite writers in the business. All of them had strict itineraries to visit every buzzy, of-the-moment restaurant they could. On a shared cab ride from LAX to our hotels, I listened as two of those writers ran through a laundry list of restaurants they needed to visit.

"Are you going to Gjelina? You definitely need to go to Gjelina."

"I'm meeting so-and-so at Petit Trois for breakfast tomorrow. Are you in?"

"Are you coming to Osteria Mozza tonight?"

"What about Night + Market Song Saturday? Will you be there?"

I was overwhelmed. Still, I went to almost all of these places, and while they were spectacular, I will save my praise and superlatives for another time. (Note: A solo breakfast over a crusty baguette and a café au lait at Petit Trois is among the most subtly beautiful experiences on earth.) What I want to talk about right now, though, is what was no doubt my favorite meal in Los Angeles. Yes, it was at a place I'd never heard of before; a place that didn't look the least bit promising, a place where the food was, like the children of Lake Wobegon, simply "above average." The most surprising part? It was at a Best Western.

After two days of palate-pleasing, gut-busting meals at God knows how many of the city's finest eateries, I decided to have a quiet supper at the diner located on the first floor of the Best Western where I was staying. Socially anxious by nature, I was in the mood to be alone. And I wanted to eat at a place where I wouldn't feel the pressure to be wowed by a plate of wilted water spinach or sour fermented pork sausage. I didn't have the mental energy to tweet about my croque monsieur, or Instagram a plate of oysters. I know what you're thinking. Tough life, right? I get it. Still, travel can be tough for the medicated.

While I expected little more than a hotel lobby–style restaurant, with bad carpeting and equally bad food, the diner was surprisingly cool-looking for a hotel chain. It had stone walls; schoolhouse lights; a long, Edward Hopper–style counter; and plush, 1960s-era leather booths. Sitting down in one of those booths with a pile of magazines, I ordered a chicken po' boy with trepidation, since, to me, a po' boy isn't a po' boy unless it's made with Leidenheimer's French bread from New Orleans. Probably more of a chicken sandwich, I thought to myself. But I was wrong.

When it arrived at my table, the po' boy was piled high with blackened chicken, crisp lettuce, and some damn fine-looking tomatoes. Biting into it, I recognized something familiar. Really familiar. That crunch. That pull. It was Leidenheimer's bread! It turns out that the chef had grown up in New Orleans. It turns out that the restaurant was pretty well known, too, having been featured in the final scene of the movie *Swingers*. So good was the po' boy that I almost—*almost*—Instagrammed it. But, while scrolling through filters, trying to decide between Juno and Amaro, I decided against it.

Instead, I chatted up the waiter. We talked about po' boys and New Orleans, why Los Angeles is a wonderful city, and why I should pack up my wife and kid and move there lickety-split. She said she thought she knew me, even though I was sure we'd never met before. Once I was finished, I stayed for a while, reading some magazines and drinking some coffee. I kept getting texts from my friends. They were headed to Venice for dinner at Gjelina, and asked if I wanted to join, but I told them I'd already eaten. If I'd told them I'd already had dinner at the Best Western, I'm sure they would have laughed, wondering why I'd wasted a meal. But nothing was wasted at all. I was content eating at a place no one had told me about. I was happy to be discovering something on my own. Because, when it comes to dining experiences these days, that's a pretty rare thing.

The Curious Appeal of "Bad" Food

By Irina Dumitrescu

From *The Atlantic*

In today's Instagrammed, Yelped, blogged-to-exhaustion foodie world, perfection seems to rule. Or does it? Canadian essayist Irina Dumitrescu (a professor of medieval literature at the University of Bonn) homes in on the defiant online rise of junk food and ugly food photos.

We live in a time of food perfectionism. Experts shout culinary commandments from every direction: Daily meals, they say, must be ethically sourced, organic, raw, gluten-free, meat-free, dairy-free, protein-rich, low-fat, low in sodium, carbon neutral, dirt-encrusted, pre-soaked, and fair trade. It can be hard to keep track of all these contradictory gastronomic rules. On the one hand, cooking should be simple and traditional, something our great-grandparents could recognize. On the other, food should be chef-inspired, executed with masterful knife skills in a professional-grade kitchen. One should eat with family, clinking wine glasses over a long table in a Tuscan garden. One should eat alone, undistracted, carefully controlling for portion size. We ought to eat like cavemen: nuts, roots, and seeds. We ought to eat like spacemen: foams and sous-vide. And by no means should anyone eat sugar, because sugar is poison and grandma is trying to kill us with those cookies.

At the same time, there appears to be growing interest in food that breaks rules. On blogs, in Facebook groups, in listicles and Tumblrs, people are celebrating "bad" food—dishes that are disastrous, unattractive, or just unhealthy. Some poke fun at the mishaps of chefs, bakers, and cookbook authors, like the website Cake Wrecks, with its pictures of tragically ambitious professional cakes. Other online collections, like the Gallery of Regrettable Food and Vintage Food Disasters, are filled with scans of disgusting-looking concoctions from old cookbooks. Websites like Someone Ate This celebrate the failures of home cooking in triumphantly unappetizing photos. Even Martha Stewart, who made a generation of homemakers feel inadequate, has been tweeting revolting photos of her meals, to general delight and horror.

Why has bad food become so popular? Didn't Julia and Alice and Jim and Marcella teach modern home cooks to draw on the best that continental cuisine had to offer, to buy fresh, local ingredients and treat them with respect? Which part of the culinary revolution was it that led to deep fried lasagna rolls or Mac n' Cheetos? At a time when blogs, YouTube videos, and specialized cookbooks can help even a novice produce respectable results in the kitchen, why are folks turning to 1960s recipes to make jellied chicken and Busy Lady Beef Bake? Often, the more stomach-turning the dish, the more gleeful the prose about it, as if making terrible food somehow maintained the noble tradition of human ingenuity and experimentation. Once, humanity asked if it could walk on the moon. Now, it aims to re-create the nightmare of Tuna and Jell-O Pie.

The current Rabelaisian relish for outrageous food is, at least partly, a playful rebellion against the excesses of gastronomic prescriptivism. After decades of being warned against butter, salt, coffee, chocolate, wine, and anything else that makes life on this miserable planet worth enduring, food lovers learn that they are healthful after all. (In fact, it was the foods people replaced them with—margarine, energy drinks, artificially sweetened desserts—that were deadly. Oops.) In the face of rapidly changing scientific recommendations, it feels liberating to throw caution to the wind and deep fry a Big Mac—or to at least fantasize about doing it.

Then there are aesthetic standards. It's one thing for magazines and cookbooks to have polished photography and food styling. They are professional productions, and most reasonable people do not expect what they cook in their home kitchen to turn out looking exactly like it did in *Bon Appetit*. But food blogs, Instagram, and Pinterest are also filled with glossy, sunlit photos of organic mason-jar meals and caramel-drizzled cupcakes. Theirs is a dark beauty. They suggest that home-cooked food could look that luscious, that perfect, given a little care and knowledge.

In most cases this is impossible. The majority of people who cook do so under limiting conditions: tired after a day's work, in haste, on a budget, to please a child's picky palate, using leftovers, with processed ingredients, without the special oil or herb that would have required a trip to a distant supermarket. They serve their meals on actual plates, not on slate slabs or rustic chopping boards. Their food is tinged yellow or blue depending on the light bulb they eat it under. Real homemade food often looks like failure, but it's not. Feeding yourself or others is a success, an act of love, even when the meal resembles unappetizing brown mush. This is why it's sometimes necessary to celebrate culinary disasters. They reveal the reality of cooking: tedious but necessary chore, creative outlet, daily ritual.

There's also something deeper to the current fascination with bad food, whether it's unhealthy, inelegant, unpopular, or just plain ugly. Food serves a variety of purposes, only one of which is nutrition. Shared meals strengthen communities, while food restrictions serve to keep groups of people apart. Culinary preferences signal one's class, ethical stance, or outlook on the world. The foods we eat, and especially the ones we talk about eating, tell others how we understand our bodies: sensitive or resilient, hardworking or overflowing, rebellious or disciplined. In short, food offers ways of telling stories about who we are and where we come from. And bad food does this better than good.

Jay Rayner, the *Observer*'s restaurant critic, recognized that terrible food makes for good narrative when he collected his harshest reviews into a slim volume titled *My Dining Hell*. Excellent restaurants are all alike, he points out in his book, a curse for the critic forced to find fresh ways of describing a yawningly pleasant experience. It is indeed easy for descriptions of good food and happy culinary memories to become cloying, as so many food blogs prove. How many more scrumptious, luscious desserts, or meltingly tender meats can readers stand to hear about? How many more inspirational grandmas, tending to the stove? Badness, on the other hand, is specific and endlessly varied. There are so many culinary catastrophes, each one with its own individual meaning.

In the kitchen, it's easy to founder in telling ways, with ingrained habits leading to strange fusions and awkward flavors. When I was growing up in Toronto, my mother would occasionally try her hand at a Chinese stir fry. Despite the Food Network's best efforts at instruction of the masses, her stir fries always tasted suspiciously like the Romanian food we usually cooked. No amount of soy sauce could take them out of the Balkans. One day I visited a friend whose Indian-born mother announced she would make us—what else?—a stir fry. I laughed when I tried the result, a sauté that ever so slightly resembled a curry. In their enthusiasm for the new, our mothers drew on the old: the familiar spices and techniques that gave their cooking an accent.

Even more revealing are the intentional monstrosities: those dishes eaten alone, late at night, generally in front of a screen. Or perhaps with a relative or friend who shares the same predilection. I recently asked my friends about the meals they eat when nobody's looking, their secret gastronomic loves. The answers came fast and thick—people like to confess to odd proclivities—and I began to notice a few patterns.

Many of my friends' guilty cravings are for wallops of predictably intense flavor: Nutella or peanut butter eaten straight from the jar, ketchup on everything, endless applications of Vegemite. They admit to loving processed food: Cheez Balls, Fun Dip, Froot Loops, Little Debbie Tree Cakes, instant mashed potatoes with bacon and cheese eaten dry from the packet. They like the intensity of burnt toast, popcorn, even chocolate, and the kick of weird combinations, like Doritos dipped in soft-boiled eggs. These are foods that speak of abandon, of a sensibility beyond diets and refined taste. One woman wrote that she loved drunk food—cheap, greasy pizzas, street meat—because it reminded her of eating what she wanted without guilt.

The vast majority of responses were also connected to childhood memories, usually carb-rich: macaroni and cheese (processed, not home-made), ramen (preferably the cheap kind), Wonder bread sandwiches filled with potato chips, sugar, or nonpareils. Men, in particular, seemed to have a talent for pleasing kids and grandkids with strange improvisations when women are out of the house. Respondents told me about the toast with cinnamon and sugar dad made for breakfast, or the mashed potato sandwiches with mint sauce that were a grandfather's specialty.

Most interesting, and most varied, were foods that people associated with the places they came from. I do not know if fried bologna and ketchup sandwiches are really "a Buffalo NY thing," as one woman insisted, or if Hormel Vienna Sausages on white bread with mustard are typical to Mississippi. What struck me was that people held on to the memory of these simple sandwiches as a marker of home. A German friend recalled pressing a Mars bar into a hot bread roll bought from the local bakery, and inhaling the gooey treat in seconds. A friend from Russia thought back to the raw onion salad, dressed only with mayonnaise, she made for herself when there was nothing else to snack on.

By now it should be clear that there is, in fact, no such thing as "bad" food. There's only food someone else considers bad. People craft identities and relationships through such differences in taste: In college, two friends and I took advantage of a local store's six-topping special to develop a pizza we considered divine. It featured chicken, roasted red pepper, hot peppers, feta, pineapple, and extra cheese, and when other students came to our dorm room to bum a slice, they left after one look at the pie. Naturally, "The Pizza" became a great source of bonding, a meal only we three could love.

What's more, so-called bad food is often intensely good. Martha Stewart defended her hideous food tweets by saying the meals were delicious, and she was right: Ugly pictures are a reminder that food can taste wonderful and be deeply nourishing even when it's not styled for a photo shoot. How a dish looks tells us little about how it tastes, especially since the long cooking that produces complex flavors often also results in uncomely brown mush. On the other hand, food that's bad because it breaks rules can offer an unexpected thrill. In *The Language of Food*, the linguist Dan Jurafsky explains the fad for bacon ice cream as a pleasurable violation of American food conventions—pork should be in the main course, and dessert ought to be sweet, so combining them feels rebellious and fun. This kind of playful fusion is trendy, but it's also, as Jurafsky points out, how culinary innovation happens.

It's a cliché by now that food is culture. But it needs to be added that much of what is important about culture lies in marginal cooking. People so often look to the highs to understand their relationship with food, but they also need to look to the lows—this, I propose, is what lies behind the fascination with food that breaks rules. Weird food is so often personal, the result of home cooking and experimentation in the kitchen. Bad food speaks to individual tastes, to the awful combinations people invent and eat when they're on their own. Junky, sweet, and processed treats recall the freedom enjoyed as children. And unorthodox food can reflect our identities and histories: from the pig parts that our ancestors set in jelly to the meatloaf only mom could burn right.

Let It Bleed (Humanely)

By J. Kenji López-Alt

From SeriousEats.com

Author of the indispensable kitchen bible *The Food Lab: Better Home Cooking Through Science*, Kenji López-Alt—Serious Eats' chief culinary adviser—is known for his meticulous deconstructions of classic recipes. Today's challenge: deconstructing a recipe of the future, for a meatless hamburger.

I'm not vegetarian or vegan, but I'm a big fan of veggie burgers, particularly those that taste like, well, vegetables. I've even written a couple of recipes of my own. But veggie burgers that try to imitate the taste and texture of meat? No thanks, I'll pass.

At least, that's what I used to say. The last few years have been exciting times for veggie burgers, with two extraordinarily well-funded companies—Beyond Meat and Impossible Foods—releasing plant-based burgers that they claim not only smell and taste like meat but look, handle, and cook like meat as well.

If you shop in the vegan section of your supermarket, Beyond Meat is a familiar brand name. They seem to be leading the industry in currently available faux-meat products, with a line of chicken strips, crumbles, burger patties, and frozen meals. Though not widely available across the country just yet, their Beyond Burger, a pea protein–based patty, was the first consumer-market-ready vegan burger patty to "bleed" like real meat,* thanks to the magic color of beet juice.

---

*Okay, smarty-pants, we all know that real ground beef doesn't technically bleed, and that what you're really looking at is myoglobin, the red muscle pigment, as opposed to hemoglobin, the blood pigment. Got that out of your system? Let's move on.

Back in June, Eater posted a summary of the reactions from various other food websites that had gotten their hands on a box of patties and tasted them. From their report, it sounded almost too good to be true. "Nobody could believe how good it was." "It was tasty and juicy, unlike most veggie burgers which can often taste closer to cardboard than beef." "Undeniably fresh." The Impossible Burger has been getting similarly positive reviews.

I'm always skeptical of these kinds of early reviews; it's easy to be wowed by a first-of-its-kind product, and, to be frank, I tend to want to taste something for myself before I believe the hype. Over the last couple of weeks, I've managed to have both of them multiple times.

Let me say this right off the bat: These things are a big step up from previous faux-meat burgers, though they still have a way to go before they're going to fool anyone who eats meat critically on a regular basis. Tasted on their own, they have their problems, but served the right way—cooked and topped—they become more successful.

Why Plant-Based Meat?

The question comes up frequently in vegan message boards and conversations: Why plant-based "fake" meat? If you like vegetables, shouldn't you just eat vegetables? Five years ago, when I first started exploring and writing about vegan food, I even said the same thing, in my article "Say No to Faux." But over the years I've changed my mind, and have come to realize that there are plenty of convincing arguments in favor of plant-based products mimicking meat.

Many vegans, for instance, are vegan for ethical or environmental reasons: They believe that killing animals for food is wrong or bad for the environment, therefore they choose to eat plants. But many ethical vegans still enjoy the taste of meat and crave it. Plant-based alternatives are a good way to satisfy those desires while still staying true to basic principles.

The world population is also expanding, and as the economies and middle classes of mega-populated countries, like China and India, continue to grow, so does their taste for meat. Livestock farming is an inherently inefficient form of production, using massive amounts of energy and land and producing waste (cattle are one of the largest producers of greenhouse gases*). Feeding that hunger for meat is going to be impossible without some major technological or logistical breakthrough. Many, including Bill Gates (who has invested in both companies) and food writer Harold McGee (who advises for Impossible Foods), believe that plant-based meat substitutes are going to cover at least part of the growing meat gap.

The math is convincing. According to Impossible Foods, an Impossible Burger uses 95% less land and 74% less water, and creates 87% less in greenhouse gas emissions, than a beef burger of equal size. And, of course, most important for vegans, it uses 100% fewer cows.

The Tasting

My sister happens to live in Boulder, Colorado, one of the test markets for the Beyond Burger patties, so I had her send me a few boxes of them on dry ice—they cost $5.99 for two patties, with an insane amount of cardboard and plastic packaging. I defrosted them and cooked them in a number of different ways, including as thick patties, smashed on a griddle, and grilled outdoors.

Until recently, you could find the Impossible Burger at only a single location: Momofuku Nishi, in New York City. Recently, its availability was expanded to three new West Coast locations: Jardinière and Cockscomb in San Francisco, and Crossroads Kitchen in Los Angeles. I was invited to attend an opening-night tasting event with all three West Coast chefs present, which included a multicourse Impossible Burger meal consisting of sliders, tostadas made with crumbled Impossible Burger, meatballs, and an Impossible Burger tartare made by Chris Cosentino. Company-sponsored events are not the best way to get a fair taste of a new product, so I also ordered a couple of burgers at the bar at Jardinière the following night.

Here's what I thought.

Aroma and Flavor: With both burgers, it's important to note that doneness seems to have a major effect on flavor, even more so than with real beef. I initially made the mistake of following the package instructions and cooking a Beyond Burger all the way to 165°F. The flavor and

---

* Note: This article previously stated that cattle are the largest producers. Among livestock, they are the largest producers, but this is not true when other industries are factored in.

fat got cooked out of it, and I ended up with a veggie burger patty that tasted not much different from the dry, insipid vegetable protein–based patties that have been on the market for ages. Cooking to medium-rare, though, produced much better results. The same was true of the Impossible Burger.

My theory is that when you cook one of these burgers rare, the flavorful juices stay inside, covering up the flavor of the wheat or pea protein the patty is based on. Cook it too long and those juices run out, leaving you with only the textured proteins, the flavor wrung out of them like water out of a dish sponge.

There are no two ways about it: In its raw state, the Beyond Burger does not smell good. The phrase "smells like dog/cat food" is often thrown around as a dysphemism, but in this case, it is literally true. Raw, the Beyond Burger smells like cat food. Thankfully, most of the more offensive aromas dissipate as it cooks, leaving behind only a faint meatiness, with the underlying pea protein peeking through. The Beyond Burger is similar to Beyond Meat's previous pea protein–based burger, the Beast Burger, which makes sense: Aside from a bit of extra fat in the Beyond Burger (in the form of coconut oil—an important addition, on which more later), the ingredients are quite similar. The flavor of pea protein is a little tough to describe if you've never had it. Not unpleasant, but not particularly beef-like. The burger packs an umami punch from yeast extract, and also has that faint, inescapable aroma of coconut.

The Impossible Burger does a much better job of imitating the aroma of beef, thanks in part to heme, an iron-based cofactor that's found in all sorts of living organisms but is particularly common in animals. It's abundant in myoglobin, the pigment found in red meat. Researchers at Impossible Foods discovered that by adding heme to their plant-based burgers, they could capture a lot of the aromas we associate with meat. They call it their "magic ingredient," and, combined with yeast extract, it does seem to do a pretty good job. Sniff an Impossible Burger patty and you'll find it smells remarkably like beef. (Or, at least, it smells like beef raised on a steady diet of coconut.)

When cooked, it fares better, too, with a mineral, meaty flavor—so long as you keep it medium-rare, as it was served at the launch event. The second time I tried it, at Jardinière, the burgers came cooked gray through and through, and tasted unmistakably and overwhelmingly like wheat, with barely any beefiness.

In both cases, adding flavorful toppings, like cheese, pickles, and condiments, helps a great deal, distracting from the subtle background flavors that whisper "This isn't real beef" to you as you chew.

Fattiness: One other factor affected both burgers. There's a critical difference between beef fat and the refined vegetable fats used in these patties. Both burgers are packed with fat—20% for the Beyond, 15% for the Impossible. That's about the same amount as what you'd find in a good beef patty. But not all fat is created equal. Beef fat is highly saturated, which means that it tends to be solid at room temperature, melting only as you cook or chew it. Most vegetable fats—including the canola oil used in the Beyond Burger—are liquid at room temperature. The coconut fat used in both burgers melts at a much higher temperature, though not quite as high as the fat in beef.

And it gets more complicated. Real beef fat is actually a blend of many different fats that melt at different points, which means that as you chew a real burger, some of the fat is completely liquefied, some is soft and tender, and some is still firm and waxy. This is an important feature, and critical to the way we perceive juiciness and meatiness. Refined vegetable fats have a single melting point. They go from solid to liquid pretty much all at once. Rather than the true juiciness of beef, you get more of a greasy feel.

Again, proper cooking is key to keeping that fat semisolid and the burger feeling juicy. The fat in the Impossible Burger is better distributed than the fat in the Beyond Burger. It's incorporated in discrete chunks that melt into pockets of juice as the burger cooks, very much like in a real beef hamburger. It still has the same problem of single-melting-temperature fat, but the distribution (and a higher proportion of solid coconut oil) makes this much less noticeable.

Texture: The Beyond Burger is made of a pea protein isolate, canola oil, and coconut fat, bound with starch, gum arabic, cellulose, and methylcellulose. In its raw form, it has the texture of lean, very finely ground beef, though it's a little greasier and slicker-feeling. When it's cooked, the exterior crisps and browns in a way that isn't particularly beef-like, but is pretty tasty nonetheless. The pea protein has a chewy, meaty texture that's a little bouncy and elastic compared to real beef.

Thankfully, the patties hold together very much like real beef, avoiding the mushiness that plagues many veggie burgers.

While the Beyond Burger errs on the side of being too elastic, the Impossible Burger's wheat protein–based patties go in the opposite direction. They bind together better than most veggie patties, but are a little bit looser than true ground beef. Like loosely packed beef burgers, Impossible Burger patties run the risk of falling apart and out of the bun as you eat. I'd recommend ordering them with cheese (or vegan cheese) as a mortar to hold them together. That said, the wheat protein pieces have a more realistically beef-like texture than the pea protein. In the context of a medium-rare slider, if I pinched my nose to avoid any slightly off aromas, I could convince myself that I'm chewing ground beef. That's more than can be said of the Beyond Burger.

How They Cook: The Beyond Burger cooks pretty much like any ground meat. You can form it into patties of any shape and size, you can fry it, you can grill it, you can smash it, you could probably even cook it sous vide (though I didn't try). It doesn't brown in quite the same way that real beef does—the patties come out much crisper and crunchier on the exterior—but if you have your favorite burger technique down, the Beyond Burger should work for it. (I did not try crumbling it.)

Impossible Burger meat is not available to the public, and I didn't have the forethought to try pocketing some of the raw tartare that was served at the dinner I attended, so unfortunately, I haven't had a chance to work with it. But by chefs' accounts, it behaves just like beef.....

Nutrition

Nutrition-wise, both burgers are comparable to a beef patty. The Beyond Burger has 22 grams of total fat and five grams of saturated fat per quarter pound, while the Impossible Burger has 17 grams of total fat but a whopping 15 grams of saturated fat! That's a full 72% of your daily allowance. No wonder it tastes so juicy. The Beyond Burger also has 20 grams of protein, while the Impossible Burger has 28 grams.

This high fat content translates to a familiar feeling of burger bloat after you've finished eating. I wanted to do nothing more than sit on the couch and faux-meat veg out after eating them, though that feeling was stronger with the Beyond Burger. These kinds of effects are very hard to measure in an objective way, so take all that with a grain of salt.

Ingredients

B eef has one ingredient: beef. To achieve similar texture and flavor, these veg-based patties need quite a few more. But bear in mind that while the labeling system here in the US is designed to be very informative, one consequence of it is that ingredient lists can also be frightening. There are a lot of words on the faux-meat-burger labels, and many of them are probably unfamiliar to you, but it's not particularly useful to ponder them too much. For what it's worth, they are all found in nature.

The Beyond Burger: pea protein isolate, expeller-pressed canola oil, refined coconut oil, water, yeast extract, maltodextrin, natural flavors, gum arabic, sunflower oil, salt, succinic acid, acetic acid, non-GMO modified food starch, cellulose from bamboo, methylcellulose, potato starch, beet juice extract (for color), ascorbic acid (to maintain color), annatto extract (for color), citrus fruit extract (to maintain quality), vegetable glycerin.

The Impossible Burger: water, textured wheat protein, coconut oil, potato protein, natural flavors, 2% or less of: leghemoglobin (heme protein), yeast extract, salt, soy protein isolate, konjac gum, xanthan gum, thiamin (vitamin B1), zinc, niacin, vitamin B6, riboflavin (vitamin B2), vitamin B12.

Beyond the Impossible

I 'm incredibly impressed with both of these burgers. They're marvels of modern science that make me optimistic about the future of our food system and our ability to sustain our growing demand for meat. But given the shortcomings of current technology, they both fall, to a greater or lesser degree, within the uncanny valley. That is, they are similar enough to real beef to make you think, "Oh, I'm eating beef!," but *just* far enough away from it to make you think, "Hmm, something is not quite right here, but darned if that isn't delicious."

If you're a vegan or vegetarian who hasn't eaten meat in years but misses it, your cravings will be easily satisfied. If you're an omnivore who has been considering cutting down on your meat intake (yay!), then either one will help get you there. And even if you're a hard-core meathead who simply can't live without the taste of real meat, well, these might just fool you from time to time.

Seaweed Dreaming

By Rowan Jacobsen

From *Yankee Magazine*

Journalist Rowan Jacobsen has a clear and present focus—
the intersection between environmental science and food
sustainability. In a world of dwindling resources, what are our
best options? Here, he takes us on a thrilling marine foraging
adventure, asking: Is kelp the new kale?

On a gray dawn in October, a half mile off a small Maine island far
from shore, Micah Woodcock and I found ourselves bobbing in a
rowboat precisely where they tell you not to go in boats.

That, in fact, was how Micah had described his foraging strategy to
me: "Look at a chart, look for trouble, go there." All around us, the teeth
of ledges rose in and out of the water with the swell. The water was the
color of slate. The sky was spitting a 50-degree rain into a 50-degree sea.
Micah expertly sidled the rowboat up to a ridge that breached the sea
for a few hundred yards and said, "Get out."

I stared at him in disbelief, teeth chattering. Here? Now?

"Get out fast," he said. "I can't get any closer."

And so I and my wet suit flipped ourselves out of the boat and into
the churning, neck-deep water. Micah tossed me an inner tube with a
laundry basket jammed into the middle and handed me a fillet knife.
"You should find lots of kelp along this ridge," he told me. "Try to cut
it cleanly. I'm going to work a little farther out." As he rowed away, he
glanced back at me. "Don't drop the knife."

Right. Iron grip on the knife, I scooched along the underwater shelf, the inner tube tethered to my wrist by a rope, hopping with each wave to keep from going under. Long, leathery things wrapped themselves around my ankles. They felt like eels, but I hoped they were kelp. Timing the trough between waves, I leaned down and grabbed one. Yep, kelp. I slashed at it with my knife, narrowly missing my leg, and tossed the slippery fettuccine into my basket. Then a wave picked up the basket and tossed it into my face. *Don't drop the knife.*

I spotted Micah, who is very tall, very thin, and very 27, way out on a submerged ledge, wearing snorkel gear and cutting kelp. He has the beard and wide eyes of a Byzantine saint, and he seemed to be walking on water. He brought up lovely, wide, 6-foot strands and quickly filled his basket. I, meanwhile, was fighting to wrestle my 4-foot kelp into the basket without spilling the basket, losing the knife, or getting smashed into the rocks. I was working so hard to stay on my feet that I barely noticed the rain and the icy sea. The boulders behind me were draped in slippery brown seaweed and glowing pink lichen, the waves burst with white foam, and the spruce trees on Micah's distant island were backlit by the dawn, and it occurred to me that of all the ways I'd ever imagined to make a living, this might be the hardest and the most beautiful. And I began to understand Micah Woodcock.

Micah is one of Maine's handful of harvesters of wild seaweeds—or sea greens, as I'd taken to calling them, to differentiate from the piles of sea compost I'd always avoided on the beach. It's an extraordinary lifestyle. During the eight-month harvest season (even Micah won't go out in winter), he lives in a simple cabin on a tiny island off Maine's midcoast. It's one of the ledgiest sections of shoreline, which is doom for boats but heaven for seaweed, which needs to attach to rock near the surface, where the light is. Most days, he visits the surrounding ledges and islets at low tide, fills his boat with seaweed, returns to the island, and hangs his harvest on clotheslines to dry (wet seaweed quickly spoils). There, blowing in the wind like a load of dark stockings, it loses all its slime and 90 percent of its weight in a few hours and becomes as stiff as shoe leather. Once a week, he packages it, hauls it to the mainland in his lobster boat, and delivers it to customers by hand or by mail. "It's an unbelievable amount of work," he admitted. "I had no idea what I was getting into."

While there are no slackers in the seaweed guild, some harvesters prefer the species that can be picked on land at low tide. But Micah likes to live his life in the crashing interface of land and sea. "A lot of edible seaweeds only grow in places that are turbulent," he said. "If sugar kelp is growing in a harbor or another place without much flow, you get much wider, weaker plants. But in a place like a reversing falls, where there's a lot more current, you get stronger, longer, skinnier plants. I like them better. They're more vital." Digitata and alaria, two kelp species, grow at the lowest point of the low-tide line on ledges; to harvest them, Micah sometimes has to ride big breakers over the ledges to get his boat into the more protected spots.

Why do such a thing? I wondered that more than once as the waves swept me and my basket off the ledge. I wondered it some more as we filled Micah's rowboat with hundreds of pounds of kelp and alaria and returned to the island in the rain. I wondered it again as we hauled baskets of seaweed from the landing up to a little barn and hung it inside to dry. And I was still wondering as we peeled off our wet suits and stoked the fire in the cabin and set the coffeepot to perk and my shivers slowly subsided, until I realized I was having a really good time. What could be better than a morning of hard work in a world primeval? Micah agreed: "I love how ancient these species are. How resilient they are. How they grow in places where nothing else can survive. It's such a beautiful, rarely seen world."

At the moment, the modern world's attention is fully on sea greens. Kelp is the new kale. Dulse is the new bacon. Which makes Maine the new California, because the great sea greens flourish on the Atlantic coast north of Cape Cod. "All the commercial seaweeds are cold water–loving seaweeds," Shep Erhart, founder of the country's largest sea greens company, Maine Coast Sea Vegetables, told me. "We've got a lock on it." Indeed, as we toured his brand-new plant in Hancock, about 20 miles northeast of Micah's island, we were in the Fort Knox of American seaweed. Women with band saws were cutting 10-foot-long pieces of dried kelp into bag-sized strips as a fine salt mist filled the air. Pallets of applewood-smoked dulse and Kelp Krunch energy bars sat on loading docks. There were bags, capsules, and shakers of nori, alaria, dulse, Irish moss, bladderwrack, and sea lettuce, all from the Gulf of

Maine and the Bay of Fundy. Shep kept letting me smell things, coaching me through the differences. "Nori's mild but nutty. Digitata tastes the sweetest. Alaria has an almost Soave quality to it."

The plant was so new you could smell the paint. You could also smell the skunky funk of dried seaweed infiltrating every corner. For decades, Shep ran everything out of an ever-expanding "rabbit warren" of lofts, barns, and temporary buildings. Now a balding and bushy-browed gnome nearing retirement and slowly handing over the reins to his daughter Seraphina, he finally has his dream facility.

With 20 full-time employees, Maine Coast Sea Vegetables is the primary buyer of American sea greens. In 1971 Shep and his wife, Linnette, began harvesting alaria, which they'd realized was a local version of the expensive Japanese wakame they were buying for their macrobiotic cooking, and started selling it to their friends, then to a few stores, then to national distributors. Pretty quickly they learned it made far more sense to process and distribute the stuff than to plunge into the waves after it, and today they buy from 50 wild harvesters and process 100,000 pounds of seaweed each year. Now that seaweed has broken out of the hippie aisle and gone mainstream, they hope to sell a lot more than that. Seaweed's rising popularity stems in part from its new "superfood" status—it is astoundingly rich in vitamins, minerals, fiber, and omega-3s—and in part from its having gourmet cachet in a culture obsessed with exotic, wild, and regional ingredients.

If there's an "it" seaweed, it's dulse. "It's getting very, very popular," Shep said, popping open a bag so that the rich applewood smoke smell filled the room. "You can eat it right out of the bag." We did. It resembled wrinkled red cabbage leaves and chewed like salty salmon skin—definitely not bacon—but after a few seconds it dissolved like taffy, leaving me craving another mouthwatering hit. "It's a great snack. It's not for sissies, but once you get into it, you get hooked."

Most of the world's dulse comes from Grand Manan Island, a 21-mile-long island in the Bay of Fundy seemingly designed for dulse. Its 300-foot cliffs shade the intertidal plant, which can bleach and toughen in the sun, and the Bay of Fundy's famed 30-foot tides create a vast amount of intertidal real estate where it can grow. Locals on Grand Manan eat dulse like popcorn. For decades it's been sold in small paper bags on the ferry, in gas stations, at roadside stands, and even as bar snacks.

Now that the rest of us have discovered dulse (or "Columbused" it, as Micah puts it), not even Grand Manan can produce enough to keep up with demand. "Supply is a big issue right now," Shep admitted. "We're not going to get enough dulse for the fourth year in a row. And I'm going to have a hard time getting enough kelp this year." Even in Maine, there are only so many places with the right combination of rock, current, and accessibility, and everyone involved is worried about overharvesting seaweeds that serve as prime habitat for many other species.

"Sustainability is a key issue," said Shep. "This is one of the few fisheries that still has a chance at sustainability. All the other ones have pretty much shot themselves in the foot."

Up to now, the grassroots nature of the seaweed industry in Maine has kept it in check, according to Micah: "With seaweed, the harvesters have a big stake in the long-term sustainability of it. It's all very obvious. We all know who's harvesting where, and we give each other area to work. It's culture and tradition, like with lobstering. And that's a huge part of sustainability. You need to have strong communities and people who are invested in the long-term health of the places where they live."

Yet no amount of rules or community self-monitoring can solve the new imbalance between supply and demand. If Maine sea greens are to feed the nutrient-starved children of America, we need a lot more than the wild can provide. That's why virtually all fingers in the industry point toward aquaculture as the future of sea greens. And in Maine, if you follow those fingers, they lead to Sarah Redmond.

On a January morning that made my fall dip with Micah feel like a day at Club Med, I hopped into a skiff with Sarah and sped out to a square of sea in Frenchman Bay marked by four orange buoys. Nothing else was moving on the bay. We were just a few miles up U.S. 1 from Maine Coast Sea Vegetables, which was not entirely coincidental: Shep was once Sarah's partner in this farm. The snowy bulk of Cadillac Mountain loomed above Bar Harbor and the breeze froze our cheeks until we could barely speak, but it felt clean and bracing on the water. I could see lines running between the buoys about 5 feet beneath the surface. Sarah hooked one and pulled it up. A curtain of footlong baby kelp plants hung from it, dripping diamonds in the winter light.

"Aren't they beautiful!" said Sarah, who when I met her was the seaweed aquaculture extension agent for the University of Maine; today she's a full-time seaweed farmer. A brown-eyed bundle of seaweed fervor, Sarah could make a sea greens fan out of a polar bear, but she was right: They *were* beautiful. And they were beautiful because they were supple, and shiny, and alive. The winter landscape was barren, but this kelp was burgeoning. Sarah had planted it in the fall, and it was just getting started. As the daylight increased in February and March, it would take off, growing several centimeters a day. By the time it was harvested in spring, each strand would be about 10 to 15 feet long and weigh about 10 pounds per foot. Unburdened by gravity or root systems, seaweed grows at a rate no terrestrial crop can touch, even in winter, and that has a lot of people very, very excited about farming it.

To say that seaweed aquaculture is the greenest form of farming on earth does not do it justice. It is so much greener than anything else that it needs to have some new color invented for it. It makes something from nothing, pulling excess carbon, nitrogen, and phosphorus from the water and assembling it into nutrient-rich organic vegetables. That gives it a negative carbon footprint. More seaweed, healthier planet. A seaweed farm can produce twice the protein per acre of a soybean farm and 17 times that of a livestock farm. And it does it all without any inputs of energy, fertilizer, or water.

Many experts believe seaweed farms could feed the world using a fraction of the resources used by agriculture. The industry in the U.S. is growing, but it lags far behind that of other countries. Most of the seaweed consumed here comes from Asia, where seaweed aquaculture is a $5 billion industry.

At UMaine, it had been Sarah's job to change that. "Stuff is happening so fast it's hard to keep track," she said. "There are farms up and down the coast. Tons of people are excited about doing this in Maine." Surprisingly, she'd been deluged with requests from fishermen who had either given up on cod or were looking to do something in the off-season. "Fishermen already have boats, they already have knowledge of the water, and they're into it."

What they don't have, yet, is a system. No one is waiting on shore to buy, dry, or distribute the seaweed they grow. Shep is looking into it, but for now his customers are attached to the robust flavors and perceived mojo of wild product. And even if the system were in place to get it to market, farmed Maine seaweed would still have to compete with cheap Asian seaweed.

Sarah was quick to point out the mismatch: "We have some of the best seaweed in the world! Asian seaweed can't compete with ours. There's a huge flavor difference. I didn't like seaweed at first, because my only experience was with Asian seaweed, which tastes fishy. Ours always tastes fresh and clean."

The difference, Sarah said, is that a lot of Asian seaweed is being grown in some grim industrial waters. But the market has not learned to differentiate.

Perhaps Maine seaweed needs a makeover, I suggested. And then I proposed the term "sea greens," which was exactly the wrong thing to say to Sarah Redmond, seaweed evangelist. "I'm not on board with that," she said as she glared at me and chewed on fresh kelp, her nose and cheeks frosty pink. "It's seaweed! Be proud of it! It's amazing!"

Sarah might be the only person in the country who grew up wanting to be a seaweed farmer. "I'm a plant person," she shrugged. "I like growing things. I spent a lot of time at the shore as a kid. Seaweed attracted me." She enrolled as a graduate student under Charles Yarish, the University of Connecticut professor who is America's leading expert on seaweed aquaculture. At UConn, she designed the seaweed seeding system used by the entire New England industry. Its simplicity is hugely appealing: When a kelp plant is ready to produce spores, in summer, you put it in a tank of water with some thin line. The spores attach to that line; when they've matured into juvenile plants, you wind this "seed" line around a rope and suspend it from the ocean surface. The plants do the rest.

Sarah graduated from UConn in 2012 and was immediately hired by the University of Maine to develop seaweed aquaculture in the state. In her labs at UMaine's Center for Cooperative Aquaculture Research on Taunton Bay, she produced spools of seed line and gave them away to new kelp farmers.

Sarah dropped the kelp line back into the water and we moved on to a line draped in alaria, the fernlike cousin to wakame. We nibbled on it as I stuffed a mesh bag to take home, freezing my hand in the process. It was tender, slender, and spunky, the Audrey Hepburn of salad greens. It had an addictive crackle and a lively green-tea flavor.

If these were the wimpy plants Micah disdained, well, I guess that made me a wimp too. I realized that in my seaweed travels I had accidentally recapitulated the Fall of Man, from Micah's prelapsarian wild forests to Sarah's convenient kelp plots. And as profound as dreamtime with Micah had been, it was Sarah who would be feeding The Future.

If The Future was willing to eat it. Of that I still wasn't sure.

Two days later, The Future came stomping into our mudroom after school, ravenous, and regarded the bowl of seaweed I set before him with suspicion. The Future is 17, his name is Eric, and after school he's in no mood to be trifled with until copious carbohydrates have been consumed.

"Dulse," I said, before he could ask. Then I gave him the spiel about the Grand Manan islanders and popcorn.

He flicked a piece into his mouth, chewed, swallowed. "Good," he said. Then he polished off the bowl.

OK, I'd figured dulse might be easy. The real test would be dinner, a full-on seaweed smorgasbord. When I consulted my new seafriends about recipes, I heard a lot of the same suggestions.

"Kelp is really good in heavy, hearty, pot-roasty dishes," Micah said. "I cut it up dry with scissors and add the pieces to any savory liquid dish and cook it for 30 minutes or five hours. You want to have either nice tender pieces, or you want it to dissolve. In the middle you get seamonster gooeyness."

"We love seaweed!" said Andrew Taylor, the chef at Portland's wildly popular Eventide Oyster Co. "Kelp makes its way into almost all of our stocks, soups, and sauces. It provides a wonderful depth of flavor to everything you put it in."

A flavoring, in other words, which is the same thing Shep told me. "It's just a no-brainer. Anything you're cooking in water, you put some kelp in that broth. It has that umami taste, plus all this rich mineral content, plus polysaccharides that give a little body to your soup."

Honestly, if every hockey mom in America started making her soup broth out of Maine seaweed, it would use everything the farms can grow and we could all declare victory. But I wanted seaweed to be more than the bouillon cube of the 21st century. I wanted it to be . . . food.

So I fried some nori in oil until wicked crisp. If dried dulse was the popcorn of the future, this was clearly the potato chip.

I tossed the alaria in sesame oil and rice vinegar and made a superb, if not terribly creative, seaweed salad.

I concocted a soba noodle soup flecked with bright green bits of alaria and enriched with a kelp broth. Who would object to such a thing? Certainly not The Future, who cleaned two bowls.

And for my pièce de résistance, I boiled a tangle of kelp noodles, drenched them in olive oil and garlic . . . and quickly threw them out. I felt like Captain Nemo battling the giant squid. A lot of people would like kelp to be the new linguine, but for now it just isn't.

Still, I thought my success rate was pretty high, and I felt confident that seaweed was more than a trend. I asked Eric how he felt about it.

He shrugged. "Just like any other . . . land weed."

"Shouldn't we call it sea greens?" I tried, ever hopeful.

He grimaced as though I'd asked him if he wanted to go to a James Taylor concert with me. "It shouldn't have to masquerade as spinach."

Right. "So, to you, it's just food."

"Yup."

"And it's good?"

"Yup."

"Would you say really good?"

Another shrug. "Good enough." And then The Future grabbed the bag of dulse and went up to his room to check his Tumblr feed.

Japan's Food Cult Drama "The Lonely Gourmet" Is Essentially Pornography

By Matthew Amster-Burton

From The AVClub.com

Seattle-based writer/comedian Matthew Amster-Burton nurtures a healthy obsession with Japanese food, as chronicled in his books *Hungry Monkey* (2009) and *Pretty Good Number One* (2013). He's the best possible guide to the weird ins and outs of Japanese food TV.

Flipping TV channels in Japan offers a sensory overload unmatched by anything in the world. *Click.* A girl group with 75 members in matching costumes, singing lyrics about the boyfriend they're contractually prohibited from having in real life. *Click.* A comedian getting punched in the nuts on a variety show. *Click.* A 50-year-old businessman eating lunch. Alone. Slowly.

Believe it or not, that last show, *Kodoku No Gurume* (*The Lonely Gourmet*), has been one of the most popular things on Japanese TV since its debut in 2012. Based on a bestselling comic and recently finishing its fifth season, *The Lonely Gourmet* has spawned hour-long specials, an iPhone app, and a series of collectible toys, all featuring its unlikely hero, European furnishings importer Gorō Inogashira.

By Western standards, it's confounding television. Essentially—and without hyperbole—it is pornography, with food in place of sex. It's a drama held together with the loosest of narratives, one where our protagonist is grudgingly placed in some vaguely plotlike situation, and before the first act is even over . . . *bow chicka bow*—it's tempura time.

Here is a typical episode of *Kodoku*, specifically season five, episode six: Gorō arrives in the O-okayama neighborhood of Tokyo and walks from the train station to a business meeting. He's tall, slim, and wearing a conservative navy suit. "If I'm able to land the deal today, it'll likely be a big one," he says in voice-over. He sits at a conference table with the boss, who has hired Gorō to refurnish the company's office. Gorō presses him about the details: What kind of office environment are you looking for?

"We just need to spend the rest of our fiscal year budget," says the boss, typing on his laptop. "In the end, how much money you make is all that matters, right?"

"I must decline," says Gorō. He runs out of the office into the street, where he immediately gets hungry.

It's important to note that we are now only four minutes into a 30-minute show. Here we've come to the narrative pivot, as nonsensical as a hunky plumber appearing at the door. Gorō's eyes lock. The loins stir with anticipation. The camera reveals a neighborhood fish restaurant. This shall be Gorō's conquest. He steps in, takes a seat at the counter. He orders a set meal with sashimi and stewed fish, with side dishes of omelet, simmered tofu, mustard greens, and white rice. It is sultry in every way.

Tenderly, graphically, Gorō inserts food into his mouth. Gorō eats, slurps, and moans, all the while maintaining a stoic exterior. But his inside voice speaks in utter satisfaction: "Delicious sashimi, soy sauce, and white rice. I'm glad I'm Japanese." At one point the camera pans slowly over fish tartare while a song that sounds a lot like Yello's "Oh Yeah" plays.

And that's how it plays out for the remainder of the episode. The soundtrack gets manic. Gorō, as if he can hear the music, eats faster. Groaning, he finishes off the meal without spilling anything on his tie. Finally, he thanks the staff and walks out, stuffed, muttering something about how a good lunch has washed away the gloominess of walking away from that big job. Roll credits.

Here's the even weirder thing: As a title card at the end of every episode reminds us, *Kodoku* is a *fictional* drama. Everyone who appears on the show—Gorō, the chef, the hostess, the old guy who sits next to Gorō at the restaurant and puts some of his sashimi into a Tupperware for later—is an actor. But the restaurants featured on the show are real, as is the food.

Kodoku isn't unique in featuring real restaurants on a fictional drama. Another recent hit show, *Ramen Daisuki Koizumi-San,* follows an eccentric, ramen-obsessed high school student as she visits actual ramen shops around Tokyo. But Gorō hits bars and diners, noodle shops and tempura places, which makes it a great introduction to the awesome diversity of everyday Japanese food.

So what do people love about these shows, anyway? In part, Japanese viewers have an insatiable appetite for insatiable appetites, especially when the eater is improbably slim. A few years ago, the country fell in love with a competitive eater named Gal Sone, an adorable sub-100-pound woman who could put away 10 pounds of curry in a few minutes. Japan also has its own version of Korean Mukbang videos, the cultural sensation where a YouTuber calmly devours a massive meal while addressing their fans. (Mukbang stars, many of whom are women, can be paid as much as $10,000 a month to eat on camera.)

Still, *Kodoku No Gurume* isn't a celebration of gluttony. When Gorō orders four times as much food as an ordinary customer, it's so we can see more of the restaurant's menu come to life—not so we can get off on watching him pack more into his own slim frame. Unlike many of the more blasé Mukbang personalities, Yutaka Matsushige, the actor who plays Gorō, is so much fun to watch. If there were a show where he played an electronics repairman who mused about life over extreme close-ups of circuit boards and red-hot soldering irons, I'd probably watch that, too.

There's something so inexplicably, universally appealing about *Kodoku*, in fact, my daughter, Iris, and I have watched them all together; it's one of the only shows we can agree on. (Now, when I chide Iris for pouring soy sauce over her rice before eating, she'll say, "Dad, Gorō does that all the time." I can't argue.) So when my family decided to spend two weeks in Tokyo this past July, we realized, "Hey, we could actually go somewhere Gorō ate. How about season five, episode six?"

The fish restaurant from that episode is named Kue. It has a cute blue roof and sits on a quiet corner near O-okayama Station. My wife and daughter and I squeezed into a communal table along with a couple of old women and a lone businessman (younger than Gorō) who seemed to be on his lunch break. We ordered what Gorō ordered: the Kue set lunch, which is about $12 for an improbable amount of food.

The restaurant holds about two dozen people, and as far as we could tell, all of them ordered the Kue lunch set. For half an hour, nobody got any food, and then the set meals started coming out from the kitchen one after another, and you could witness the faces brightening across the restaurant in a wave. I peered at my fellow diners' trays and saw that the sashimi and simmered fish assortment was laid out according to the chef's whim.

The whole experience felt like some bizarre combination of Space Mountain, the Travel Channel, and sitting at the *When Harry Met Sally* orgasm table at Katz's Delicatessen. It was crossing the fourth wall into a make-believe world. It felt impossible, like *Pleasantville* with miso soup. It took me a long time to figure out why. What's the difference between following Guy Fieri and following Gorō Inogashira?

The makers of *Kodoku* understand that one of the best ways to get at the truth is to apply a thin veneer of fiction. Bring a camera crew into a restaurant and the place changes. What's more uncomfortable than a person waving a camera in your face and saying, "Just do what you normally do"? Paradoxically, you can re-create the experience of eating at a neighborhood restaurant more faithfully by giving the staff (and customers) the day off and bringing in actors who are used to working on camera and giving us multiple takes until they nail the banter with the hostess.

Want proof? Just keep watching *Kodoku No Gurume* after the credits roll, when Masayuki Qusumi (who also wrote the *Kodoku* comic) visits the same restaurant. It's everything you expect from a mediocre food show: bad audio, weirdly enthusiastic voice-over, a stilted conversation with the chef. "Make this go away," you want to yell at the screen. "Give me the real restaurant back! I mean . . . the fake one."

If the thrill of watching fake people eat real food has awakened anything in you, you can stream every episode of *Kodoku* for free, albeit illegally, with excellent unofficial English subtitles written by a group of fans.

In New York City, What's the Difference Between a $240 Sushi Roll and a $6.95 Sushi Roll?

By GREG ROSALSKY

From *Pacific Standard*

A producer at Freakonomics Radio, Greg Rosalsky understandably is focused on economic metrics when he examines the dining scene in New York City. His analysis, however, lays bare some telling points about the gap between the haves and the have-nots in America today.

Columbus Circle sits at the southwest corner of Central Park in New York City. At its center, a statue of Christopher Columbus peers over a sea of people, as though looking for land, while yellow taxis whirl around him. The tallest structure around the circle is the Time Warner Center. It's a modern glassy building with twin 80-story towers, housing the headquarters of the eponymous media conglomerate, a hotel, a jazz concert hall, and a luxury shopping mall. If you enter through the building's giant glass facade, you'll pass by a Hugo Boss, a Whole Foods, and a Williams Sonoma. Take a series of escalators up to the fourth floor, turn right and you'll reach Masa—the most expensive restaurant in the United States.

Masa was founded by the sushi wizard Masayoshi Takayama. Born and raised in Japan, Takayama, 62, built a cult following in Beverly Hills during the 1980s and '90s and was lured east to work his magic when the $2 billion Time Warner Center was finished in 2004. Masa is one of the crown jewels in the center's "Restaurant Collection," which is best thought of as the world's most extravagant food court.

With the exception of the H&M you pass to get there, everything about Masa screams luxury. The sushi bar, hewn from one solid 30-foot piece of blonde hinoki wood at a cost nearly twice that of a new Mercedes Benz, is sanded daily for cleanliness. Much of its fish, the restaurant says, is flown in fresh from the Sea of Japan. The restaurant is "omakase," meaning Takayama hand selects the menu each night. On one recent Saturday night, appetizers included toro tartare with caviar, steamed king crab, and Ohmi beef with Bianchetto truffle. That was followed by a long list of sushi, from toro (tuna) to shimaji (striped jack) to hotate (bay scallop). Finally came dessert: grapefruit granite and buckwheat tea.

Food critics go crazy for this place. Masa's long list of awards includes the coveted three-star rating from the Michelin guidebook, a distinction held by only six restaurants in the Big Apple. Anthony Bourdain wrote that his experience at Masa was "a completely over-the-top exercise in pure self-indulgence, like having sex with two five-thousand-dollar-a-night escorts at the same time—while driving an Aston Martin." It's a hedonistic food orgy that comes at a mind-boggling price: a minimum of $1,200 for a couple, not including tax or drinks.

Takayama co-owns another restaurant just across Central Park called Kappo Masa. The menu there is *a la carte* and slightly cheaper, but just barely. Options include a sushi roll that's $240, a steak that's $68, and a bottle of sake that's $2,650. This restaurant has not been as warmly received by critics. Pete Wells, a food critic for the *New York Times*, wrote in his review of the restaurant last year: "The cost of eating at Kappo Masa is so brutally, illogically, relentlessly high, and so out of proportion to any pleasure you may get, that large numbers start to seem like uninvited and poorly behaved guests at the table." Wells gave the restaurant zero stars.

Kappo Masa is located on Madison Ave. in the Lenox Hill neighborhood of the Upper East Side, sandwiched between Central Park and the luxury apartment buildings of Park Avenue. Across the street are multimillion-dollar art galleries, the Carlyle Hotel (with rooms ranging from $400 to $15,000-plus per night), and Vera Wang Bride, a store for the designer's wedding dresses (the starting price of one is $2,900).

Wang is a regular at Kappo Masa, and so are many other locals. They can, after all, afford it. With a median household income of an estimated $217,070 per year, the blocks around Kappo Masa are some of the richest in New York City.

Fifty blocks north of Kappo Masa and across the Harlem River we find a very different economic reality, and a very different market for fish. The South Bronx neighborhood of Mott Haven is the poorest neighborhood in the city. In fact, with a median household income of $19,536 a year and a poverty rate of near 50 percent, Mott Haven and its neighbor, Port Morris, represent the poorest zip code in the poorest congressional district of the entire U.S. In some areas of Mott Haven and Port Morris, a typical household could save for an entire month, without paying rent or any other expenses, and they still wouldn't have enough for a single dinner date at Masa.

When it comes to addressing poverty and inequality, making artisanal sushi accessible to the poor has got to be at the bottom of the list of priorities. But food disparities remain a real problem—one that is manifested in issues like higher rates of obesity, diabetes, and heart disease among South Bronxites—and it's an issue reflected in the lower rate of fish consumption among the poor. Fish, which is low in fat and rich in protein, vitamins, minerals, and omega-3 fatty acids, is considered by experts to be an integral part of a healthy diet (especially if it is not fried and if it contains low levels of mercury). One influential meta-analysis of 20 studies in this area concluded that regular consumption of fatty fish like salmon, mackerel, and herring "reduces risk of coronary death by 36 percent." The Food and Drug Administration and Environmental Protection Agency recommend that Americans, especially pregnant women and young children, eat "at least 8 ounces and up to 12 ounces (2–3 servings) per week of a variety of fish that are lower in mercury to support fetal growth and development"—a recommendation they're concerned that many Americans are not following.

Part of the reason scholars and activists have believed that low-income households choose junk food over fresh fish and vegetables is that a lot of poor neighborhoods lack access to anything fresh and wholesome. Mott Haven and Port Morris have long been labeled "food deserts," places where the glow of fast-food signs light up the night streets but healthier restaurants and grocery stores are hard, or impossible, for families to find. In recent years, there has been a coordinated city effort at the federal, state, and local levels to change this scenario.

Yet, in an uncomfortable irony, amid the effort to bring healthier food options to the area, the South Bronx is home to the world's largest wholesale food distributors, including none other than the Fulton Fish Market, the second biggest fish market on Earth. The Fulton market, which enjoyed a 180-year stint in lower Manhattan, moved to new facilities in the South Bronx in 2005. It distributes across the Eastern seaboard—and its clients include Masa.

Mott Haven and Port Morris have their local seafood restaurants, too, even if they're far outnumbered by McDonald's and Dunkin Donuts. At Jay's Fish Market, which distributes raw fish but also functions as an eat-in restaurant, you can get raw red snapper for $5.99 per pound and a (rather tasty but not healthy) fried bluefish sandwich and French fries for $5.50. There was also Sea Food Kingz, until it went out of business. But the most interesting of the bunch is a sushi joint.

When I found out about Ceetay Asian Fusion, I was first surprised that it even existed and then doubly so that it had 4.5 out of 5 stars (with 178 reviews) on Yelp, so I called them up and scheduled an interview with the owner. Biking there from Brooklyn on a sweltering afternoon in late May, I passed Kappo Masa, scanned their menu (out of my price range), and continued pedaling up Madison Avenue into East Harlem.

The most recent Census data shows that median household income begins to plummet once you get north of the Upper East Side, starting at 96th street. It's a fact that becomes clear when you begin to see brick public-housing towers rising up into the sky and business-casual white people give way to working-class blacks and Latinos. The thought of what they could do with $2,650—the cost of a bottle of sake at Kappo Masa—popped into my head, and the world seemed crueler. I continued over the Harlem River.

Ceetay Asian Fusion was created by Amir Chayon in 2012. It's a small place that seats about 25. When I walked through the door, I asked for the owner; Chayon was standing nearby talking to two men and told me he would be a few minutes, so I sat down and glanced at the menu. Lunch specials started at $9.45. This was my kind of place.

Chayon, 42, seemed to be on a first-name basis with many of his customers: hungry Bronxites of every race and ethnicity. The restaurateur himself is originally from Israel, with piercing blue eyes and an athletic build. On the day we met, he was wearing blue jeans, a purple shirt, a neck-chain, and black sneakers. His journey to the South Bronx began eight years ago when he first arrived in New York City. In Israel, Chayon had been an aspiring actor and paid his bills working in restaurants. Arriving in Manhattan, he scanned a newspaper for jobs and found one as a general manager of a bar and grill in Mott Haven, just a couple of blocks from where Ceetay now stands.

"I didn't think much about the neighborhood. I couldn't care less," he says. "Then I got an apartment here right away. And I started working here. All of a sudden my life is the South Bronx."

Ceetay sits in the amorphous space where Mott Haven and Port Morris collide. Across the street, amid stylish graffiti, sit a tattoo parlor, a run-down antique shop, and Fordham Gospel Mission, a church with a purple awning that inhabits what used to be a storefront. Two short blocks away from the restaurant on Alexander Avenue are the Mitchel Houses, a public-housing project of 10 imposing brick towers ranging from 17 to 20 stories tall. It's a complex with a long history of crime and gang-related violence.

Chayon says in his first years in the neighborhood, he was scared to let his wife walk alone at night. But he was happy living there, especially with his low-rent loft apartment. While managing a bar and befriending the locals, Chayon began to plan his own place. He knew the restaurant business and he knew his neighborhood and he knew creating a place that served strictly sushi would be an economic loser—so he decided on Asian fusion. It's a business strategy that combines the first sushi bar in the South Bronx with key staples of Americanized Asian cuisine: fried rice, pad thai, chicken tikka masala, and so on. Every morning, Chayon's supplier brings in fish fresh from the Fulton Fish Market.

Crime, Chayon says, is not as bad as it once was in the South Bronx. And the numbers back him up. The New York Police Department's 40th precinct, the two square miles at the southern tip of the Bronx that includes Mott Haven, Port Morris, and the Fulton Fish Market, has seen an estimated 70 percent decline in crime since 1990, including an 87 percent decline in murder, a 50 percent decline in assaults, and a 92 percent decline in car thefts. That said, it remains one of the most troubled areas of the city, and, while it is undoubtedly much safer than it was, some of the NYPD's more optimistic data has, on occasion, come into question.

Chayon admits that people are still afraid at night. But he sees the seeds of economic revitalization. "It's the next Williamsburg," he says.

Williamsburg, Brooklyn, was once one of the poorest neighborhoods in New York City. In the 1990s, artists and writers, attracted by cheap rents, created a small colony of first-wave bohemian gentrifiers. Soon after came the trendy businesses and then the young professionals. Before long, it was crowned a hipster capital. Williamsburg is now seeing multi-billion-dollar development, with a new Whole Foods, an Apple Store, and luxury apartment buildings sprouting like giant beanstalks along the East River waterfront.

Chayon sees a similar process beginning on the South Bronx waterfront. "Already the gay community and a lot of artists are moving up here," he says. I began to think the restaurant was less a symbol of sushi egalitarianism and more a symbol of a neighborhood in the midst of demographic change. Williamsburg got its first sushi restaurant in 1998, once it was already well into the process of gentrification.

While Chayon and I sat chatting, my food arrived. The restaurant has a long list of healthy and affordable food options, including Lentil Soup for $5.95, seaweed salad for $5.50, and a salmon avocado roll for $6.95. After the long bike ride, I decided to splurge on a lunch special that came with two sushi rolls. First came spring rolls served with a shot glass of sweet-and-sour sauce. Their flaky texture was crisp and paired well with the gooey sauce. Next came a surprise—tuna bruschetta, made of crispy rice and potato, guacamole, and spicy tuna. It's Chayon's best-selling appetizer, and small wonder. Last came the sushi rolls, salmon avocado, and spicy tuna, which hit the spot on one of the first hot days of an approaching New York summer. At $12.45, this lunch special has to be one of the best sushi deals in town.

Ceetay Asian Fusion is an oasis for South Bronxites who want healthier food options at prices only slightly higher than neighboring fast-food restaurants. But recent studies suggest that the solution to bad eating habits in poor neighborhoods must go deeper than simply bringing healthy options to the area. In 2010, the New York City government experimented with a tax subsidy program to bring super-markets to poor areas, but a 2015 study deemed it mostly a failure; a new supermarket in the South Bronx neighborhood of Morrisania, just north of Mott Haven, had failed to change local eating habits in any substantial way relative to those in statistically similar neighborhoods. The researchers concluded that simply introducing wholesome food options is not enough to spur behavioral change and that a more con-certed effort is needed to make it affordable and enticing. Perhaps that's where efforts like Ceetay come in: restaurants that can make healthy fish dishes appealing in communities resigned to subpar options.

Chayon, the sushi pioneer of Mott Haven, is now the father of a 10-month-old baby. He and his wife have since moved to Washington Heights, northwest of Ceetay at the top of Manhattan, but his life re-mains firmly rooted in the South Bronx. Every May 2, his wife's birth-day, they throw a block party for the community with free food and a DJ. Judging by his many stellar Yelp reviews, it's a community that is growing to love Chayon's food.

"I *never* expected to find a place like this here in the S. Bronx . . . and I live here," says Steven "IntrepidBronx" B.; "still, the food here is top notch, and merits the attention of the snobbiest foodies." Steven gave the restaurant five out of five stars. Leslie L., after ordering Ceetay de-livery, was beyond happy: "They delivered to the door!!! Not to the lobby . . . but to the apartment door! To many people that's normal. But if you live in the South Bronx . . . that's effing amazing." Aida O. simply gushes, "OMG!!! This sushi is great! Nice to know that I can get quality food in my neck of the woods :)."

Ceetay Asian Fusion may or may not change local eating habits—but the city is certainly better with it there.

Noma Co-Founder Claus Meyer's Next Big Project Is in One of Brooklyn's Poorest Neighborhoods

By Jane Black

From GrubStreet.com

Food policy and sustainability are recurrent themes in Brooklyn-based journalist Jane Black's deep portfolio. Here, she focuses on an inspiring trend: socially conscious chefs developing restaurants for underserved neighborhoods. Here's how Danish culinary star Claus Meyer did it.

Claus Meyer sees me as soon as he walks into the 3 Black Cats Café, a new coffeehouse on Belmont Avenue in Brownsville, Brooklyn. I'm easy to spot because I'm the only patron in the cavernous space. Still, he stops to talk to Ionna Jimenez, one of the three sisters who own the café, then persuades her to pose for a picture with him and his lieutenant Lucas Denton. He quizzes her about what kind of cakes she has today and how late the café is open. He wants to take some carrot cake home to his family.

Meyer is the last person who needs to take dessert home. The Noma co-founder, who has called New York home for more than a year now, could easily pick up a few sea-buckthorn tarts at his bakery in Williamsburg or at the Great Northern Food Hall, which he opened this summer in Grand Central's Vanderbilt Hall. Or he could have the pastry chef at Agern (which recently won three stars from the *New York Times* and praise from Adam Platt) whip up an extra goat's milk cheesecake and sweet pepper sorbet. But Meyer wants to make an impression in Brownsville, and maybe even a few friends in the neighborhood. This winter, he will open what may be his most ambitious project in New York: a restaurant, housed in a former dollar store, run by and for the people of Brownsville, one of New York's poorest and most troubled neighborhoods: "I had a dream how I would explain myself to my grandkids in 20 years," he says when he joins me in a bright-orange booth. "I didn't want to be only a businessman. I wanted to be a social philanthropist and also mentor people in the same way other people had mentored me."

Meyer, 52, is a culinary legend in his native Denmark. For years he had his own TV cooking show, and he co-founded Noma, which is consistently rated one of the best restaurants in the world. When he moved to New York last August, he was invariably described as "tall" or even "towering," perhaps because we expect our Viking invaders, even culinary ones, to be giants. Meyer is, for the record, six-foot-two, and he is earnest—very earnest. He tells me that as he has gotten older he has realized that "what really counts are the number of people who have looked at you with tears in their eyes for what you have done for them." Over the course of several hours, Meyer starts so many sentences with "the dream is" that I ask him if that is a direct translation from Danish. He pauses to think about it, then admits, slightly abashed: "No, I think it's just me."

The chef has been idealistic for his whole career. He was the driver behind the New Nordic Food Manifesto, which in the mid-'00s shifted the culinary center of gravity from Barcelona to Copenhagen, from the modernist (hot potato foams) to locally rooted and environmentally sustainable (snails and moss). Eight years later, Meyer tried to do the same thing for Bolivia, working with NGOs to establish a national gastronomic vision and Gustu, a fine-dining restaurant in La Paz, to embody those principles.

In Bolivia, though, Meyer decreed that his restaurant also would train and employ disadvantaged youth. And when that proved tricky—poor kids with no restaurant experience lacked the grace required for fine dining—he tacked, launching a network of affordable cafeterias to train students. The graduates are eligible to continue their studies at Gustu, which is now rated one of the top 50 restaurants in Latin America.

Meyer's big ideas aren't limited to the food realm. Along with two friends, he recently invested in a second-division Danish soccer club, his home team as a child. Already, Nykøbing FC has graduated to the top division. "The dream is to take it to the champion's league for 2025," he says. "It's as improbable as making a great restaurant in La Paz."

Compared to La Paz, New York might seem like it would be easy. But the city has frustrated Meyer, who would, if he could, be doing more than he already is—and faster. (Two more restaurants, still under wraps, are in development.) Locating at Grand Central Terminal has proved a particular headache, as the city's notoriously onerous building regulations are even more so in a historic landmark. Among his complaints: The food hall has reached its limits on electricity ("so if you want to use a food processor or put another lamp in so you can see your bread in the darkness, it's impossible") and bandwidth ("I have to fucking finance infrastructure just to take payments on credit cards.") "I have been in the restaurant business for 30 years," he says. "I've never experienced anything like it."

The Brownsville project, officially known as the Brownsville Community Culinary Center & Neighborhood Eatery, also has taken longer to get off the ground than Meyer had hoped. In part, it's because Meyer and Denton are determined to consult community leaders at every step, building a restaurant that appeals to current residents, rather than the gentrifying hordes. But just negotiating a lease took a maddening six months, and Melting Pot, Meyer's nonprofit that is backing the project, has struggled to raise funds. Brownsville may have the highest concentration of public housing in North America, but it's still New York, and real estate, and everything else, is expensive. Meyer has assembled $1.1 million—more than the total to build and open Gustu—and he imagined (or perhaps dreamed) that when rich New Yorkers heard about the Brownsville project and his track record, the rest of the money would materialize.

After coffee, Denton, clad all in black, gives Meyer and me a quick tour of the still-empty, dusty space a few doors down from 3 Black Cats Café. He points out where the 45-seat restaurant will be; when it opens it will be the only sit-down restaurant in Brownsville, and will include production and teaching kitchens and a café to serve fresh breads and coffee.

Next, Denton whisks us off to a nearby church, where the first co-hort of culinary students is training until the new space is ready. After greeting the students with a series of hugs and high fives, Meyer huddles with Mette Strarup, the Danish chef overseeing the culinary training. He wants an update on whether the kids have been paid: It had been a contentious issue, with Melting Pot proposing that trainees receive a small stipend and community leaders adamant that the kids have "skin in the game." It wasn't what Meyer's people expected. "We have our ideas of how we want it to work," Denton says, "but for it to actually work, we have to be flexible." The trainees worked 30 hours a week for three months, but it was tough for the students: One is a single mom, another suddenly found herself with no place to live. When the first checks arrived that week, Strarup reports, 22-year-old Tameel Marshall did a victory lap around the kitchen.

The students cook lunch every day, and in honor of Meyer's visit, they lay a long table with wildflowers and sprigs of leaves, interspersed with green Post-it Notes stating "the plants are not edible." On the menu: jambalaya, salad with a creamy lemon dressing, and a salted jalapeño hot sauce (Meyer is crazy about hot sauce). It's the kind of food—what Meyer dubs "modern soul food"—that the new restaurant hopes to serve. As for what they'll charge, that's still up in the air.

This was always the plan because, Meyer says, to appeal to residents, the food has to be of the neighborhood: familiar and delicious, but healthier than the fast food that dominates. His students agree. Once everyone has served themselves, Meyer asks each student to take a turn talking about—yep—his or her dreams for the program. Nkenge Wiggins, 33, the single mom, says that after working in a hospital, she hopes Melting Pot can help change the culture of Brownsville, its sedentary ways, and the reliance on fried chicken. "Well, not really fried chicken," she adds with a laugh. "You gotta keep the fried chicken."

"I agree," Meyer chimes in. However great his enthusiasm for social change, it's good food that gets Meyer most fired up. Whether it's the students' hot sauce, which would be "goddamn amazing on a piece of cooked pork or chicken that is kind of bland, a little to the fatty side" or a modern version of oxtail he cooked at a Brownsville senior center that was "very intense, clean, very bright. Not muddy with all the fat in it, and packed with fresh ginger"—his years as a TV chef have given him the gift of letting an audience taste without ever taking a bite. "It's not that I'm tired of winning Michelin stars," he says with a laugh. "I do want to have three stars in the *New York Times*. But . . . " He stumbles, starting several sentences as he reaches for the right words. "It is correct to say this feels right. And it would feel very wrong not to try to do this."

The Last European Christmas

By Marina O'Loughlin

From *Bon Appetit*

Holidays brings out the traditionalists in all of us. But what if your traditions are boldly, proudly polyglot, as British travel and food writer Marina O'Loughlin's are? And is there room in today's super-charged political climate for such an inclusive approach?

Brought up in Scotland, with an Irish father and Italian mother, I've never felt British—"Heinz 57 Varieties" was the family joke. And despite living in England for years, it's painfully clear I'm not English. The UK's recent Brexit has left me feeling more out on a limb. Who even am I? For those of us who came up along with the EU these past two decades, and who have long been grateful for England's vibrant melting-pot heritage, the vote is little short of jaw-dropping.

I always believed that my country rejoiced in diversity, especially when it came to eating. Even the traditional British Christmas dinner is a mongrel thing. There's turkey, of course, originally from the Americas. Its trimmings: cranberry sauce, also American; brussels sprouts—well, the clue's in the name; bread sauce, a carryover from medieval times and none more English, but spiked with exotic cloves. Christmas pudding, shimmering with Sri Lankan cinnamon and reeling from its thorough soaking in French brandy. And roast spuds, obviously; each year the mission to perfect them intensified. How much rosemary? Olive oil or goose fat? Eventually a mixture of the two was declared potato perfection.

My family put its own spin on this menu, and it was at Christmas that our "foreign" roots came together in a joyful collision. The meal kicked off with brodo, homemade chicken broth that my mother beefed up like a true Italian with stock cubes. In its limpid depths bobbed croutons, basically cubes of eggy French toast, known forever as "cretins." Nothing came from supermarkets. All roasts were ordered in advance from Vincent's, the local "family butchers," a phrase I've always found a little sinister.

The least popular item was Dad's Irish spiced beef—its meat crusted outside from a coating of weapons-grade spicing: clove, nutmeg, mace, black pepper. The roast was lurid pink inside from the virtually tasteless preserving ingredient, saltpeter—a potentially poisonous element used, among other things, for gunpowder. This dish was eventually christened Ralgex beef after the wintergreen-whiffy muscle-relief spray.

We'd pass 'round the after-dinner torrone (Italian almond nougat, the most tenaciously sticky item known to man) and—as a Scottish touch—the addictive sugary fudge known as tablet. Occasionally, Mum would make a torta Montenegrina, a cake from her native La Spezia. This was a complex construction of architectural intricacy: layers of alcohol-soaked sponge interleaved with crema pasticcera, confectioner's custard in chocolate and vanilla, finished with Italian buttercream meringue. The idea of attacking such a project still fills me with anxiety to this day, but my mother carried it off with unshowy aplomb. It was exquisite, sultry, even better on subsequent days when the custard stiffened and the sponge collapsed under the weight of the booze.

My parents would serve all this to various waifs and strays—unlike today's England, our doors were always open. There were singers for the Scottish Opera from Australia and Russia, thousands of miles from home, and religious-maniac maiden godmothers who imagined ecclesiastical skulduggery from anyone wearing purple socks. We were frequently up to 20 people at the lion-footed oak table.

One year we decamped to a dilapidated farm in the Tuscan countryside; we could very easily, of course—there was no requirement for visas, something that's now being threatened by a Europe that's understandably provoked. These days, with my father gone and my mother in no way up to the labor required, we congregate on the Isle of Bute in Scotland, where one brother has an old farmhouse.

Many of our Pan-European traditions remain: the clove-studded bread sauce, the ancient recipe of stale loaves seethed in milk flavored with bay and more cloves. (This was something I found repugnant, with its creamy, pasty consistency, until one year I fell in love with it.) The brodo with "cretins," the vat of Nonna's pasta sauce—a reductive description for something that takes all day to cook—ever-bubbling for the children. But we've never been tempted into replicating the Ralgex beef, nor has anyone felt up to the work required to make the Montenegrina. Some things die; some things live on.

Brexit—ugly word, ugly situation—shines a light onto these family holidays that helps me see them with new eyes. As our current unelected government is making some hugely alarming noises, striking fear that we should "name and shame" foreign workers and regulate the number of students from overseas, it makes me wonder: At what point during genealogy does foreignness kick in? Would my parents, in today's climate, have even been allowed to stay? At the time of writing, the insanely convoluted mechanism to activate the actual severance hasn't been triggered, and nobody, not least of which our government, is clear on when, or how, it will. It hangs over our heads like a noose.

I don't know what a Brexit-flavored Christmas would consist of, stripped of its elements from elsewhere. Ashes, I suspect. But the whole thing has had at least one positive side effect, a personal one. After years of not knowing where I belong, not understanding whether I'm Guinness or Prosecco, turkey and trimmings or torrone, I finally know who I am. Whatever happens to the rest of the UK, I am—and will always be—a European.

Whose Food Is It Anyway?

Who Owns Southern Food?

By John T. Edge and Tunde Wey

From *The Oxford American*

As the food world struggles with the issue of cultural
appropriation, an open dialogue is a great way to begin the
conversation. John T. Edge, director of the Southern Foodways
Alliance, shared his pulpit with Nigerian-born cook Tunde Wey
for a frank—and by no means conclusive—airing of the issues.

In late March, *Eater* published a Hillary Dixler essay, "How Gullah
Cuisine Has Transformed Charleston Dining." The title was clickbait.
The real provocation came with the subtitle: "Exploring the line between shared history and appropriation." The real conversation began
when the white Charleston cognoscenti responded in a voice that was
often insular and offended and unflattering, challenging Dixler's command of the subject.

If the Charleston social media response played out like a get-off-
my-lawn rant, Dixler's article, on third perusal, read like an honest
essay—which is to say it read like an honest accounting of the debts
owed to the Gullah and Geechee people who have farmed and cooked
on the peninsula for more than three centuries. She dared to ground
the white-dominated restaurant cooking of modern Charleston in the
"enslavement and forced diaspora of West African people, and the con-
tinuation of the long-held traditions they brought with them to South
Carolina."

Her original sin was asking questions from a perch in New York City.
(What her critics failed to recognize is that this conversation is not

provincial. It is, instead, resolutely and broadly and importantly American.) Dixler's greater sin, in the eyes of some Charleston critics, was giving the mic to Michael Twitty, a Gullah descendant who is also from, as they say, off.

An autodidact historian of African-American foodways, Twitty made his bones a couple years back with an open letter provoked by Paula Deen's use of the word "nigger." He served as Dixler's primary source. He said things to her like, food "is a part of our culture that couldn't be beaten out of us." And, Gullah-Geechee culture is "not the community property of Charleston and Savannah, because it's not 1864 or any year before that." Twitty criticized Charleston chefs who are "projecting ownership and making it about them, not even considering the people who have been marginalized and exploited." I nodded at the first two statements and wished the third had showed more nuance.

By the time you read this, the vitriolic Tweetstorm that followed will be mercifully buried in a timeline of baseball box scores and celebrity dalliances. Among the worst moments: A white writer and farmer suggested that Twitty return to where he came from. "Charleston knows its past," Jeff Allen wrote, "we don't need help understanding it." (When I called Allen for clarification, he defended his position but admitted that he had spoken harshly, saying, "If my grandmamma was still living, she probably would have told me I needed to apologize.") Among the best: On his blog *Afroculinaria,* Twitty wrote a 3,000-word letter of invitation to Sean Brock, the white Charleston chef at the low-country citadel restaurant Husk. Brock quickly accepted the opportunity to talk. A jointly cooked meal is planned.

At a moment when conversations about food have become central to the American dialogue about identity, the issues Dixler and Twitty raised about authenticity and ownership and appropriation will fester if they're not further explored. That notion was top of mind the day after the article was published, when I sat down to eat in New Orleans with Tunde Wey, a Nigerian-born chef and provocateur whom I got to know when he opened Lagos, a food stall in that city's renovated St. Roch Market.

Our first meeting, six months prior, had gone something like this: I ordered the okra stew at Lagos. Tunde questioned whether a white boy would enjoy a bowl of that ropy stuff. I took small offense, declaring myself a citizen of the world who revels in okra slime, just as I recognize the West African roots of Southern food. Since then, Tunde has begun staging New Orleans dinner salons focused on the possibilities and burdens of blackness. At our second meeting, over dinner at Compère Lapin, a new Caribbean-inspired Creole restaurant, I learned that Tunde had read deep into recent Charleston conversations, and had some tough questions to ask me.

Inquiries about power were primary. If I bought the argument embedded in the *Eater* article—if I acknowledged the inequities and subjugations on which much of Southern cuisine was built, Tunde asked—was I willing to cede what whites have gained at the expense of blacks? Am I willing, now, to cede what I have gained? We settled on a scheme in which I cede half of my column for this issue. Tunde addresses the controversy and concludes with a question for me. I respond. And we split the pay.

Call me (or us) naive, but I think this is an honest beginning.

—JOHN T. EDGE

Since John T. is a familiar son, allow me, at the outset, to introduce myself. I am African—Nigerian to be specific, a Yoruba boy from Lagos who lived in Ikeja, on Alhaja Kofoworola crescent, about a mile from Airport Hotel, to be obscure.

I am not a chef, at least not in the uncomplicated sense. I never trained professionally in accredited schools, never studied under a brand-name chef or staged in a celebrated kitchen. Right before my first professional gig, a little under three years ago (a panicked production, to say the least), I called my mother in Nigeria for recipe refreshers even as a hundred hungry and impatient diners revolted politely just outside my kitchen, where an assortment of newfangled stainless-steel utensils hung, staring accusingly at me.

I am not a Southerner. I have lived in the South for only about a year—in New Orleans, "the most African city in America," as I have heard some folks describe it. And I nod sagely in agreement.

I am African, neither a Southerner nor a chef. But in the matters we're about to discuss, neither provenance, place, nor title matters. Like humidity, the truth thickens all air.

At age sixteen, I arrived in the United States, landing in Detroit. Sixteen years later, I moved to New Orleans. I remember sitting in the long airplane for the short flight, leaving Detroit for my new home, characteristically unsentimental: pursed lips and large headphones, listening to loud rap music from a glowing phone. Inevitably the boom bap faded into white noise, and my mind's voice floated from silence to remind me of Detroit's outsized influence in my life. It was in Detroit, within the city's actual boundaries—not its romanticized and imaginary borders—where I understood I was an African. There, by kind force, I learned to drop my christened name, which I had used throughout my abortive college career in the U.S., and returned to my first name, Tunde—the contracted form of Akintunde, which means "the warrior has returned."

After living in New Orleans for a year, I reflect now on how this city, still very new to me, has insisted I confront my identity in a new way. "Here you are *black,*" she says. And I nod sagely in agreement.

My cooking has always been political. It began as an oppositional response to foodie culture, nauseatingly self-referential and boastful. My politics were stated without vocal rancor, inherent in the sloppily plated colorful and strange dishes I served. This was my cooking before I moved to New Orleans.

When one realizes one is black in America—and subject to the political implications of that reality—then it is almost impossible for the immanent not to become conspicuous. It was in New Orleans that I moved from implicit to explicit politics. And because there is probably nothing more politically explicit than the assertion of (black) identity in the face of systemic censure, I launched a new dinner series, Exploring Blackness in America. Through these dinners I purposefully contrive dining spaces that prioritize black experiences—spaces where spicy Nigerian food is background music to lively conversations about black excellence, the erasure of the black woman, colorism, double consciousness . . . and on . . . and more.

Since I started the dinner series, a strange thing has started happening. From white perches, my opinions are being sought. Older, affluent, and privileged white folks want to know what I think about blackness and race and entrepreneurship and food. There was the early morning breakfast with a white New Orleanian power player—an understated and kind woman with more local connections than God and maybe just a little less money. Then there was the afternoon meeting with a local culinary institution. After we cut through her stadium kitchen and meandered the grounds of her restaurant to eventually find her office, she kindly gave me an hour of her time. It wasn't even a slow day. (Her establishment doesn't know a slow day.)

In these conversations, I felt a tipping toward me of some odd power. A tentative deference was offered in exchange for my "black" experience. My words were being elicited as a means to contextualize these folks' white privilege and power—and maybe subconsciously to defend it. In these people, I saw scales falling away; they were struggling to understand a responsible place for their privilege vis-à-vis blackness. When their frustration finally metastasized into wisdom, they slowly corrected their postures, straightening up after formerly leaning toward me: things are changing, the obviousness was heavy.

Enter John T. Edge—an honest man, to the extent that anyone can control deeply embedded attitudes. Genuinely thoughtful and exceptionally easy to talk to. Maybe it's because he snorts when he laughs, a single snort to contain all the amusement found in the prior jolly moment.

It was late March and, on invitation from John T., I bicycled over to the new and trendy Compère Lapin. I was still smarting from my recent tax filing. My restaurant stall at the St. Roch Market food hall, very much a "New South" business—trendy, hip, and white, with a problematic relationship to its gentrifying, middle-income neighborhood—had posted a loss of thirteen thousand dollars. (I have since left the market to work toward my own independent location.) I was hoping John T. would pick up the tab. After he texted that he was running fifteen minutes late, I sat myself at the bar and ordered a shot of Bulleit Rye. With tip, my tab came to $10.15. I was $13,010.15 in the negative and counting.

John T. arrived and we sat, caught up, and laughed—or rather, I laughed and he snorted. Soon after the servers deferentially collected our orders, the co-owner/manager came by and made sure to introduce himself to John T., who politely introduced me to the manager. The result of that obeisance was an off-the-menu item and comped cocktails. With embarrassed acknowledgment, John T. left a tip big enough to cover the comped food and drink, then we headed to another restaurant to resume our conversation about appropriation, race, and white grace in the face of a changing reality. It was a recently opened restaurant—wonderfully tattooed with expensive details and preciousness all around. The owner and John T. were friends. After we arrived, there was a momentary commotion at the host stand: the hostess informed us that we couldn't be seated immediately, despite a few unoccupied tables; I could only assume they were already reserved. She seemed vaguely unimpressed by our party.

As prerequisite to eventually finding us seating, the hostess asked John T. to provide his name for her waiting list. As soon as he uttered his name, a young white female waiter materialized.

"John T. Edge?" she said. "Oh my God—we have a burger named after you!"

We were whisked to a table—literally whisked, in a froth of compliments and speedy seating—and delivered cocktails and two off-menu dishes. I felt like I was eating with Michael Corleone—John T. was squirming, positively embarrassed at being feted, but I was enjoying it all. As our evening progressed, aided by honest talk and perfectly equilibrated cocktails, I felt what it must feel like to be him, capable and recognized for it. It left me giddy with privilege. And as I write this, distanced from our dinner by a few days, with the taste of that evening's sugary drinks still on my lips, I feel this privilege again as I reply to John T.'s prompt to contribute to his column. My preference is to wield this privilege wantonly, unforgivingly, and honestly.

Bear witness to my preference.

White privilege is an obscene thing. It takes everything, quietly, until there is only silence left. Then it takes that too and fills it with noise. Southern food culture—which to its corrupted credit is more honest than "Northern" food culture, where "modern" is mostly a euphemism for appropriation—is the perfect lens through which to observe this phenomenon. Southern food culture has openly appropriated black food culture and then prescribed the proper feelings the appropriated should possess regarding their hurt. Through kind concern, dispassionate reportage, and open quarrel, this privilege invalidates black folks by suggesting their experiences of prejudice are nothing more than overactive and hypersensitive imaginations at work.

That Hillary Dixler, whose essay for *Eater* flattened the most complex of issues into a standard and conclusive three-thousand-word piece, would purport to tell the story of the appropriation of black Southern culinary legacy and its contemporary exploitation by present-day practitioners, is an example of this particular sort of privilege—a privilege that has black actors as bit players in their own story. The sort that centralizes the discomfort of white people while pushing blackness to the outskirts. The story should have been written in a Gullah voice, full stop—as my mother would say in verbalized punctuation.

That Sean Brock or Jeff Allen would openly quarrel with Michael Twitty—and question his perspective on white folks who unabashedly cook black food—is the epitome and a caricature of this prerogative.

That John T. would broker peace between two necessarily Manichean poles, and then offer to share his byline with me, the "safer" nonthreatening African, instead of any of the many more qualified Southern African-American commentators, is the final statement on white privilege. Even its best intentions have been scrubbed with a dirty washcloth.

White privilege permits a humble, folksy, and honest white boy to diligently study the canon of appropriated black food, then receive extensive celebration in magazines, newspapers, and television programming for reviving the fortunes of Southern cuisine.

Yet because *his* (read: faceless white privileged person) hands were calloused and burned in the act of appropriation; because he labored hard to "refine" or "recast" this black food by using the language and techniques of his dominant culture; because his back is crooked from doing the devil's work in a hot kitchen; because his wrists rattle with discomfort from protracted writing; and because he, without question, deserves everything he has struggled enormously for, being conscious to always "celebrate the provenance of the food"—except that it was never his in the first place to celebrate—*they* (read: an accretion of faceless white privileged persons) now contrive in themselves the indignation at being confronted by a black man's question.

But things are changing.

There's discomfort in the house of the pilgrims. In conscious circles, Thanksgiving is now being discussed around the dining table as "Hell-Day," just as Nas would have it. A day when "The Chinamen built the railroad / The Indians saved the Pilgrim / And in return the Pilgrim killed 'em."

Yes, things are changing—albeit not fast enough for my "taste." Instead of a complete relinquishing, there's an offering of compromise, of "sharing." John T. has decided to *share* this column with me—why the fuck would I not accept half his column wage when I have these debts to pay? Brock has decided to accept Twitty's invitation to share a kitchen and cook together—shit, get some money out that pot, Michael, Sean seems good for it. But each of course will eventually retreat after this gesture to the safety of his own privilege: John T. to his writing and non-profiteering, Sean to his celebrated kitchen.

Unless we keep them honest and desperately uncomfortable.

Because now is the time for John T. and Sean (and Hillary Dixler, too)—these avatars of white privilege—to give up something, completely and honestly and permanently. In fact, let's accelerate this already. I'm impatient for a Tunde Wey Burger at some fancy restaurant. Matter of fact, I want to own the restaurant and be the one handing out branded burger names.

In the meantime—before I take over Husk and turn it into a proper Nigerian restaurant—I'll settle for both John T.'s and Hillary Dixler's jobs. And I'll craft my question for this contrived exercise.

John T., you have endorsed and celebrated the appropriation of black Southern food without consequence, and the consequences have compounded with interest. You have to return what you took to the place where it was, to the people to whom it belongs. And, after this principal has been repaid, the interest is due. You have to strip yourself of the marginal benefits of this appropriation willingly, with grace, or unwillingly by force and with shame. You're a graceful man, John T. So what will you willingly give up to ensure the Southern food narrative services properly and fully the contributions of black Southerners?

—TUNDE WEY

At a table in New Orleans, as we conceived this exercise, and I spooned into a bowl of pepperpot bobbing with coconut broth and shrimp crescents, Tunde told me, "This will be painful." Via text, he later asked, "Are you uncomfortable yet?" In both cases, he sounded like a sadist. But was I willing to be a masochist? Certainly, there was no pleasure in the exercise. But there might be lessons to learn.

The implication was that, if I am game to face down the realities that blacks suffer, not just historically, but today, then I must open myself to discomfort. Indeed, if I aim to understand the food and culture of the place I call home, I have to welcome discomfort. As I sat down to write this, discomfort settled in to roost alongside me, like a gator with a chicken in her sights.

It would be too easy to blame Donald Trump. Though it would not be inaccurate.

A couple months back, I gave a dinner talk to a meeting of SEC conference academic provosts. I opened by declaring that this was a hopeful moment. I told them that the South was in renaissance. I said that, just as economists customarily declare a recession or boom six months or more after it occurs, we will not recognize this renaissance until it has passed. But it is here.

To sketch what is different this time out, I talked about how all Southerners may now claim the region. And I cited Brittany Howard, lead singer of the Alabama Shakes. To mark her love of the place over which George Wallace once lorded, Howard wears a tattoo of the state of Alabama on her right bicep. This time, I said, "Southerner" is not code for "white Southerner." When we speak of the South and of Southerners, the reference is no longer monochromatic.

When I took a seat at table, after delivering a talk that focused on how food now serves as a unifying symbol for Southerners of all colors, one of my tablemates leaned in to question my vision. Faced with the Trump carnival of bigotry and intolerance, she asked kindly, how could I see the region (or the nation) with such optimism? Was I not paying attention? Or was I willfully ignorant? Identity, it seems, is an especially thorny subject at a moment when Trump supporters adopt Nazi salutes and Trump himself incites racial violence.

Tunde posed a complementary question, flipped to reveal an obverse that I hadn't glimpsed before. How could I claim the moral pulpit in the Southern food dialogue when I take my stances from the levee? If you live on the same street as me you know I'm a liberal. If you follow my Twitter feed, you recognize that I reserve a circle in hell for the neo-Confederates and country club privilege jockeys who knead and twist and shape the history of this region until they render themselves victims.

When attacks on my beliefs and stances occur, they come from the right. Or from someone who has a score to settle. But here came Tunde, without personal malice, and with great charm, saying things that made me supremely uncomfortable, making it clear that he saw me as a kind of colonial force, appropriating black cultural processes and products.

As a columnist for this magazine, I've observed that the true promise of writing about food lies in the opportunity to pay down debts of pleasure and sustenance to the cooks who came before us. I've acknowledged that, for much of our region's history, blacks and women did much of the conceptual and physical labor in the region's kitchens but received niggling credit.

I think of myself as a progressive. I'm proud of the subjects I've written about, from the race-baiting politics of Lester Maddox, the Atlanta restaurateur turned Georgia governor, to the booty-call white patronage of an Arkansas Delta barbecue joint. I suspect that if I had said any of this to Tunde, he might describe that as comparatively easy and riskless work. He might say that it's guilt-assuaging work. And he would be right.

After the *Eater* article came out, I exercised my power in what seemed a becalming way. I wrote Hillary Dixler to thank her for asking good questions. I called Michael Twitty to talk about the power I believe he now possesses. I spoke with Sean Brock about the reconciling possibilities I see in the meal they plan to cook together. And, as I barreled toward New Orleans, I suggested to Tunde that the article and its fallout might serve as a text for our dinner conversation. As you have now read, I got what I asked for. What I deserved.

I've been on this path for a while now. From Ta-Nehisi Coates, I learned to talk about racism instead of race. From Osayi Endolyn, I learned that Africa is not a country and West Africa is a more complex region than I could comprehend. From the fallout after the *Eater* article, I learned that a wide range of folks, both black and white, burn for these conversations. Now I brace for what comes next. Demographers tell us that 56 percent of Americans will be people of color by 2060. That doesn't mean that people of color will control the power. When blacks were the antebellum majority in states like Mississippi and

South Carolina, they didn't wield monetary power or control politics. Tunde suggests that, unless power is ceded this time, there will be hell to pay. I fear that he's right.

Over dinner in New Orleans, I told Tunde a couple stories about the late Will Campbell, the white Baptist preacher who was born in rural Mississippi, educated at Yale, and who practiced a radical Christianity during the civil rights movement. One story involved Campbell's decision, on a prompt from civil rights leader John Lewis, to work with his own people. Brother Will, I told Tunde, took that message to heart and began ministering to Klansmen, who needed God's grace, too. Instead of fighting on the front lines of the civil rights movement, as he had done in 1957 when he escorted black children to a Little Rock high school, Brother Will moved to the rear, where the wounded were white.

Tunde liked the message embedded there. And he interpreted it this way: Leave black culture alone. Let it find its own way beyond your white gaze. Stand down, and, in your absence, black voices might be heard, black thought might find purchase, black enterprise might flourish.

I heard Tunde as loud and clear as I was able. So loud and clear that, when I called Jeff Allen to talk through his incendiary comments, I heard myself voicing Tunde's power dynamic critiques.

Still, I know this about myself: I'm not willing to step away. I'm not able.

In the South, black and white culture are enmeshed and codependent. To walk away from writing about black life would be to divorce myself from writing about the South. To parse by color would be to render a syncretic culture a racial or geographical one. To step away, at the moment when Brittany Howard is climbing the charts and inking her troth, would be a rejection of the possibilities that she sees clearly and I squint to apprehend.

What I can offer rings meager, even to me. I aim to listen more and speak less. I pledge to cede what is not mine and try to understand the difference. And I aim to do this, not out of noble obligation, but owing to the thoughtful path Tunde charts. He may see that promise as inherently false. As much as I'm open to and appreciative of Tunde's reality, I can only act on mine. What I offer is as true and graceful as I can manage.

Despite my best efforts, and his, and despite my pledge, I didn't really get Tunde's point until I returned home to Oxford and opened my mail. A month prior, when I submitted the manuscript for my next book, a history of Southern food that begins with the Montgomery Bus Boycott of 1955–56, I treated myself to a gift. To commemorate a chapter focused on the black power movement of the 1970s, I bought a sweatshirt from a company called Philadelphia Printworks. The design was bold and elegant. At center on a field of dove gray, the legend people's free food program surrounded a leaping black panther, rendered in midair strike.

I knew the history behind the legend. I admired the actors in that historical moment. But I recognized, as I slipped the hoodie over my head: This shirt is not mine to wear. Removed from the context of Southern history, that story is not mine to tell. As I took stock of what Tunde said, I recognized that, by refashioning a symbol of black power and resistance into a white fashion statement, I had unwittingly made Tunde's argument. That next Monday morning, I repackaged my own gift and dispatched it as a present to Tunde. When the mail carrier arrived to pick up the package, I saw, out of the corner of my eye, a gator retreat. And then I saw her retrench.

—JOHN T. EDGE

Who Has the Right to Capitalize on a Culture's Cuisine?

By Laura Shunk

From Food52.com

Putting cultural appropriation issues into thoughtful context, journalist Laura Shunk—former dining critic at NYC's *The Village Voice* and Denver's *Westword*—adds the perspective of a college degree in global food politics, plus her most recent experiences as a Henry Luce Scholar in Beijing.

Six years ago, I published a story about a live octopus hot pot I ate in Queens that hinged on a video of the cephalopod writhing across a hot stew of vegetables. Predictably, animal rights activists skewered me for my insensitivity, and as someone who wrestles constantly with questions of ethical eating, I can't say that I blame them.

But I'm more uncomfortable with that piece today because it was sloppy journalism: it was a story built solely for page views, and to accomplish that goal, it removed an aspect of Korean food culture from its broader context and exploited its oddness for the American audience. Worse, I, a white woman who grew up on the Wonderbread cuisine of middle America (and had eaten Korean food about 10 times before writing that piece), potentially shamed Korean readers for their food habits while elevating myself for being "brave" and trying such a "bizarre" food.

This type of journalism—and dining—has been a major component of American food culture over the last several years. A few years ago, New York had an annual balut-eating contest, daring diners to house fertilized duck embryos popular in many Southeast Asian nations as fast as they could. The Travel Channel airs a show called "Bizarre Foods," and bills it as an exploration of other cultures via the weirdest regional specialties host and creator Andrew Zimmern can find. Outlets as diverse as *National Geographic, USA Today,* and *Buzzfeed* have run columns asking travel journalists, "What's the weirdest thing you've ever eaten?" Eating clubs fetishize dining on odd animal parts or racy chilies or fermented vegetables; restaurateurs and chefs scour the globe for inspiration that hasn't yet hit mainstream eating consciousness; and writers rush to collect street cred by "discovering" "new" cuisines and ethnic enclaves.

But over the last year, we—diners, chefs, journalists—have begun to discuss whether this is okay. Who has the right to capitalize on a particular culture's cuisine? Who has the right to cook it, and who can write about it?

I've spent the last year pondering this from afar. Last June, I touched down in Beijing, where I planned to spend a year studying Chinese food and agriculture so that I could eventually write a book, and so that I could immediately apply what I was learning to stories I'd pen for a variety of publications. I hadn't been here long when campus protests erupted across the States, bringing to the forefront, among other issues, a roiling conversation about cultural appropriation, which, as transgender writer and activist Julia Serrano masterfully articulates, takes issue with white Americans profiting off of cultural contributions made by minorities and outside groups, while erasing those groups from the cultural historical record in the process, or worse, denigrating those groups by perpetuating negative stereotypes.

I watched the discussion hit the food world soon after, when Rick Bayless caught flak for building an empire off of Mexican food, and Sean Brock and Mike Lata were chided for carrying the mantle of Southern food without properly acknowledging the slaves who'd originally brought to the region the dishes they were now using to form the foundation of their menus. In the journalism world, Eater's Hillary Dixler found herself in the middle of her own appropriation controversy when she asked a black DC-based food historian whether Charleston's food culture was appropriative (thereby launching that Brock/Lata controversy), after which John T. Edge and Tunde Wey discussed whether white writers should be commenting on black food at all.

It's been an odd conversation to observe from China, partially because I'm living in a culture where the power dynamics are reversed: I am the outsider. Moreover, unlike an immigrant in America, who can eventually become a naturalized citizen, I will never be Chinese, no matter how long I live here, how well I speak the language, or how much I fold myself into society. Even if I married a Chinese person and had half-Chinese children, I would still be a *wai guo ren*—a foreigner.

Therefore, it is totally non-threatening for me to write about, learn about, or cook Chinese food here—Chinese culture reigns supreme as the superior culture of the land, and China doesn't much care what a non-Chinese person has to say about it. Of course they should want to participate in this culture, the thinking goes. It's the best. The cultural appropriation debate is not a conversation China is interested in having, at least not in the way we're having it.

But this is not really a conversation about China—it's a conversation about America, and what it means to be American, and it's about to get personally relevant for me: I'm getting ready to come back to America, and when I start to write about Chinese food there, I'm going to be forced out of the observational perch into which I've comfortably nested abroad. I'm going to have to confront this conversation head-on, and, as Edge said, I'm going to have to prepare to be uncomfortable with other Americans who disagree with me or take issue with my context.

And context is not easy. Living and researching here has made me realize how much Chinese food—hell, Chinese culture—has been flattened in mainstream American conversation. Despite how it's presented, China is not a monolith. It's a country with incredible regional diversity, and it's more accurate to talk about Hunan cuisine or Xinjiang cuisine or Yunnan cuisine than it is to talk about Chinese cuisine. These are all Chinese cuisines—but they're about as different from each other as German food is from southern Italian, or Tex-Mex is from mid-Atlantic seafood.

Moreover, Chinese food, as with any part of a living culture, is not static. Sichuan food is world-famous for its spice, but the region boasts a 5,000-year-old history of civilization, and it didn't fully integrate chile peppers until the 1800s. The most common preparation of Beijing duck, an iconic dish here, evolved over at least 600 years, and didn't take its current state until the 1850s (and Da Dong, a celebrity restaurateur here, is famous because he tweaked that duck further in the 1990s). One of this country's most ubiquitous dishes, a spicy chicken number called *la zi ji*, was invented in the 1920s, and it didn't become a menu staple until the 1990s.

As I think about who should tell that story, it's weird to me that we'd necessarily expect Chinese-Americans to speak on behalf of the entire culinary canon. Asking your Chinese-American friend to weigh in on whether something is "authentically Chinese" strikes me as just as problematic as debasing their childhood comfort foods as "weird" or referring to a Chinese restaurant as a "discovery": It totally misses that individual's own history, personal identity, and, frankly, their American-ness, in favor of referring to them only by their race. (In a similar vein, any attempt to qualify anything in America as "authentic" misses the point—it's been removed from its own complex cultural context and layered into the complex cultural context in America. To qualify a dish as such is to imagine it in some sort of cultural vacuum, and implies a kind of end of history—that dish can no longer evolve or adapt to circumstance, we're saying, or it will lose something essential.)

And to insist chefs adhere to recipes from their own cultural background or demand eaters not venture out to experience new cuisine seems to build the very walls we're trying to tear down. Experiencing positive aspects of other cultures is often the first bridge to breaking down the other-ness barrier, and food seems like an obvious way to do this.

But to dismiss this conversation out of hand is dangerous. Because the problem is, a lot of us haven't been asking *any* Chinese-Americans—or Chinese food experts—to weigh in on our "discoveries" or "oddities," which means we've no hope of bridging any sort of cultural gap or increasing diners' understanding of the cuisine. We're stripping out the context, and so not only might we be unintentionally perpetuating negative stereotypes or myths, we're likely missing out on incredible stories.

So where does that leave me? I've always seen my role as a journalist as an imperative to immerse myself in something so well that I can explain it, clearly and entertainingly, to my audience. To illuminate murky subjects. To find the story. China is now inescapably part of my own story, and that's going to come into play, in ways both subtle and pointed, as I encounter things that are overtly Chinese and things that are not. It's going to color my writing even if I try to separate it. But it's on me to continue to expand my own understanding so that I can more accurately illuminate a realm of food that is tasty, relevant, and vastly underexplored, and it's on me to listen to Chinese people and Chinese-Americans who might have a different perspective or interpretation, or who think I'm dead wrong.

It's on me to be a better journalist. It's on all of media to elevate voices of diverse backgrounds to add to our collective understanding of the complex cultural and racial history that we're a part of in America. And it's on all of us to consider the context of our actions, to seek perspective that might differ from our own, to engage in breaking down walls, to listen to each other, and to understand that America is really a patchwork of contributions from a multitude of backgrounds, and culture is always a work in progress.

It's on us all to continue this conversation. And there's no better place than over a meal.

Writing About Food at the Intersection of Gayness, Blackness & Faith

By Michael Twitty

From Food52.com

The title really says it all. Culinary historian Michael Twitty—
who blogs at Afroculinaria.com—wields a multifaceted
perspective on the food scene. His 2017 book *The Cooking Gene:
A Journey Through African-American Culinary History in the Old
South* touches on all this and more.

My Daddy was not very happy with Mama's choice of holiday gifts for three-year-old me. Seeing my penchant for all things culinary, she bought me a Fisher-Price toy kitchen set. This particular toy lasted me a good five years of my childhood. Its fake ranges were where I enacted the kitchen rituals I'd witnessed since my first cup of potlikker and cornbread (my first food after milk and formula). I played at making greens, frying chicken, and stirring morning pots of grits. I hoped for a toy oven, too, so that I could make hot rolls and biscuits like my grandmothers did—one born and raised in Virginia, the other in Alabama.

It wasn't that the men in my families didn't cook—they certainly did. But my Daddy was old school, and to him, despite my action figures and love of toy guns, the play kitchen was a sure sign of my coming homosexuality and thus an unsuitable toy for his only son. For once, he was half-right: Although I wouldn't really fully know it for about seven more years, I was to be a gay male. I knew then and I know now that the play kitchen was nowhere near the culprit. I think the first dead giveaway was the fact that I gave my toy records the identities of Donna Summer and Blondie, but nobody really seemed to pick up on that.

I can't really blame my Dad—he was from "a different time"—but being gay has nothing to do with whether or not you will be a man drawn to cooking. Unfortunately, our American experience pretty much limited the black male cook to the sphere of professional/domestic servant unless it was something that had to do with poultry, meat, fish, or shellfish—in which case the idea of a "master cook" of an animal protein or a pot of stew was not uncommon. Go further back into our West and Central African homelands and men do just that—roast, fry, barbecue, boil en masse—but they did not by and large practice domestic cookery; this was the work of women. To be fair, I did inherit my barbecuing skills from my father, who got them from his father—something did come down the Southern masculinity pipeline after all. A love of barbecue, horse-racing, and making homemade liquor—that's about all I got from the ones who came before.

Fast-forward to now and I've made the cooking of enslaved people my niche, bringing to life the experiences, skill sets, and knowledge bases of enslaved cooks who prepared food for themselves and their slaveholders on rural farms, plantations, and in urban residences. At first glance, embracing my own gay identity seemed to be at odds with that niche: I often get asked how exactly queerness fits into my brand and the story I'm trying to tell about both the past and the present. There is a dialogue in the world of food about homophobia in the industry kitchen and little whispers about queerness and food—but what happens when you sit at the crossroads of gayness, Blackness, and faith and do this sort of work?

A little history lesson: The kitchen has always been a great place for gay men, a place for them to use the things that made them unique to their advantage. Across cultures, it's a place where we've often hidden ourselves in plain sight. We crossed the borders of genders determined by sexual identity; even in West Africa, there were men like the *gor-digen* (men-women) in Senegal who pre-dated Islamic culture and were known for their dancing, culinary skills, and aesthetic sense (sound familiar?). On the plantations of America—where

Western European culture associated masculinity with superior mastery in the kitchen and femininity with domestic cookery—many enslaved cooks in gentry households were male. Most were likely heterosexual as we would understand it, and many proudly used this position of authority in the defense and protection of their wives and children. But even when we look back, there is evidence that people we might think of as gay were present.

Combing through records left behind from slavery days, we see at least two Black male domestics from the Chesapeake region who sought their freedom by running away disguised in women's clothes, and both were noted for their effeminate nature and excellent cooking. There are journal entries about "saucy and impudent" Black male cooks who would have been sold off had their cooking not been so superior. The voice of free Black caterers of color comes across in old books with a mixture of Little Richard, the disco icon Sylvester, and Anthony from "Designing Women." The history of homosexuality in the enslaved community is complicated stuff, and I'm just scratching the surface— but I've found that a person like me, without a question, existed in multiple places across the long life of American chattel slavery.

Bringing that visibility to life has always made me consider the clothes I wear for my cooking demonstrations—waistcoat to tights to brass-buckled shoes—as a sort of historic "drag." Sometimes I'm scruffy and look the part of the beleaguered enslaved cook, but I prefer to be fierce in a historic kitchen and give that livery life. Most enslaved Black cooks commanded high prices as human chattel and they took this dehumanizing fact and turned it into a "read" of the society they lived in. Their attire alone inspired in them a feeling that they were a culinary aristocracy that was worthy of respect. I prance that energy every time I go into a kitchen—it's the start of reversing the narratives of both historic gay invisibility and of unchallenged victimization.

The contemporary push-pull of LGBT life in the United States, between greater acceptance and the backlash and recent hate crimes against the increasing of legal protections and social tolerance, has amplified what I'm doing in the kitchen. Over 150 years ago, more than one Black man wasn't afraid to be himself; to use that power within him, a certain strength that comes from embracing your difference and uniqueness; to do the unthinkable; to challenge the wealthiest institution in the American democracy; and to turn everything on its head by leaving it with the sort of ferocity that would make Ru Paul blush? To quote the Diva, "Ms. Roj" from George C. Wolfe's play *The Colored Museum*, "that's power baby!" That's my heritage staring me in the face, challenging me to stand up and represent—because I can.

But it's not just the social justice activism that comes into the kitchen with me: It's a pride in how the food should taste, look, feel, and what it communicates. Gay men have been culturally written out of history because we are often branded as individuals who will not contribute to the reproductive flow of the generations and therefore have little or no investment in normative tradition. And yet, so many of my colleagues in living history, historic preservation, and food history are very dedicated gay men with a mission to honor our collective heritage. In the same spirit, I want to honor the food past and ensure it is part of the cultural inheritance of everyone who loves the food of the African Diaspora and the American South. I embrace the idea that honing certain gay sensibilities helps me to appreciate the aesthetics of the Southern meal. I take a special pride in golden shimmering custard pies and chicken fried to perfection, in okra soup that will restore your faith in okra. Our food is spicy, saucy, sensual, *and* gendered and I'm standing on the seesaw in the middle trying to play on those themes and keep things in balance.

The African in both "Southern" and "Soul" is not just the colorful splash of the food but also its musical notes and spiritual force, hidden moral lessons and the commitment to making the food communal. I love that I was born into two very potent ways of experiencing and appreciating food. Intersectionality may be the buzzword of 21st-century identity-speak, but it's nothing new. In my kitchen, from the toy stove to the wood-fired hearth, it has really always been my signature ingredient.

Cooking Other People's Food

By Luke Tsai

From *East Bay Express*

Now writing for *San Francisco Magazine*, Bay Area food
writer Luke Tsai skillfully navigates the multiethnic landscape
of this foodie metropolis, where who cooks what carries a loaded
message. So when does "authentic" trump "tastes amazing"—
and vice versa?

The small, unassuming building on the corner of Market and 42nd
streets—a mostly residential, working-class stretch of North
Oakland—is an unlikely location for one of the most highly anticipated dining establishments in the East Bay.

Years ago, the building was home to a hair salon, and more recently
a restaurant serving high-end "New Baja"–style small plates. Now, Russell Moore and Allison Hopelain, the husband-and-wife owners of
Camino and two of the more prominent restaurateurs in the East Bay,
have taken over the space and plan to reinvent it as The Kebabery. Yes,
it's a restaurant specializing in grilled-meats-on-a-stick, but prepared in
the quintessential California style, with lots of organic vegetables and
other locally sourced, seasonal ingredients.

This is great news for fans of Moore's wood-fire-driven California cuisine—and also for those who don't have the budget to dine at
Camino on the regular. But it's also the latest example of a rather curious phenomenon in the food world: Seemingly overnight, and even
though the restaurant is still months away from opening, The Kebabery

might already be the most talked about kebab restaurant in the entire East Bay.

That's despite the fact that the region is home to a wealth of more traditional Middle Eastern restaurants: Kamdesh, with its deliciously savory rice; Aria Grill, with its assortment of excellent grilled meats; and both Oasis Food Market and its sister restaurant, Oasis Kitchen, with their spit-roasted *shawarma* and habit-forming garlicky red-pepper sauce.

All around the country, many of the most famous purveyors of global and immigrant cuisines—the so-called "ethnic" foods—are actually chefs without family ties to those particular cultures. As food writer Francis Lam documented in a 2012 *New York Times* article entitled "Cuisines Mastered as Acquired Tastes," many of these prominent "ethnic" restaurants are helmed by white fine-dining chefs, who later in their careers decide to dedicate themselves to a particular cuisine for which they've developed a passion.

In New York City, a white former high-end pastry chef named Alex Stupak runs what is probably the city's most highly acclaimed Mexican taqueria, Empellon. In Portland, Oregon—and, arguably in the whole country—Andy Ricker, another white male chef, is the king of regional Thai cuisine.

Here in the East Bay, often it's chefs with Chez Panisse pedigrees who own and operate some of the most-heralded restaurants, from Japanese ramen spots to upscale Mexican eateries. And when food reporters write about these places, there's a tendency to talk about how the chefs have "elevated" the traditional versions of the cuisine, whether it be through farm-to-table sourcing or fine-dining cooking techniques.

No one is making a serious argument that chefs should only ever cook foods to which they have a direct ancestral connection. But why is it that these mostly white, "pedigreed" chefs attain such incredible fame and success when equally talented immigrant cooks might labor in obscurity for years? And what does it mean that food pundits are so quick to hail these chefs as authorities on their adopted cuisines?

We need to have a talk, then, about this matter of cooking other people's foods and whether it's possible for chefs to do so in a respectful manner. Otherwise, the restaurant industry will always be rigged in favor of what Preeti Mistry, the chef-owner of Temescal's Juhu

Beach Club, calls the "Iggy Azaleas" of the ethnic-dining scene: over-hyped, culturally appropriative restaurants whose stories dominate the blogosphere and prominent food magazines, even as their white owners and chefs wonder why everyone always has to make a big deal about race.

Non-Denominational Kebabs

Moore, for his part, seems keenly aware of the tricky cultural terrain that he's navigating as he prepares to open The Kebabery. The chef, who is half-Korean—though he said that he looks mostly white, so many people don't realize that he's bi-racial—said he's sensitive to the typical narrative of a successful chef picking up a new cuisine and trying to improve on it.

"I'm not saying, 'I'm going to be like Oasis but better,'" he said. "That's never been my goal."

On the one hand, Moore feels good about the type of business he plans to run—one that will support small farmers, provide jobs for people who live in the neighborhood, and offer high wages and health insurance to everyone on staff. Although he hasn't set exact prices yet, he said he's committed to making the restaurant affordable enough that people who live in that part of North Oakland will actually be able to eat there regularly. And Moore stressed that, of all the things he hopes The Kebabery will be, a traditional kebab restaurant isn't one of them.

"This is going to be non-denominational," Moore said, explaining that he and Hopelain wouldn't have even put the word "kebab" in the name of the restaurant if there was an easier way to encapsulate the type of food they plan to cook—i.e., a small, rotating selection of grilled meats, served with flatbread and a variety of little salads. It was an affinity for that style of cooking and eating that drew Moore to making kebabs in the first place, more so than any particular transformational experience eating at some traditional kebab shop in Israel or Iran.

So, according to Moore, even though The Kebabery will prominently feature Middle Eastern flavors and spices when it opens later this year, the idea isn't to duplicate or improve upon someone's Persian grandmother's recipes. Lead chef Traci Matsumoto-Esteban is of Japanese descent and cooked mostly Asian food prior to working at Camino.

Her carrot salad might taste just like something you'd find at a Moroccan or Tunisian restaurant, but the strictly non-traditional sauerkraut salad that might accompany another kebab plate certainly would not. And over the past few years, Moore has developed a flatbread recipe—inspired by the one at Oasis—that uses whole-wheat flour and a slow leavening process, so that in the end it resembles a Chad Robertson (of Tartine Bakery fame) bread as much as it does a traditional flatbread.

But Moore also acknowledges that, because of Camino's great success, and because he too is a Chez Panisse alumnus, the fact of the matter is that The Kebabery is going to garner a ton of local and national press, much of it before he's even served a single kebab.

"That's privilege that a chef that came from Afghanistan isn't going to get automatically," he said.

And even if Moore is consciously trying to avoid being, as he put it, "the white guy who says [he's] going to make the best kebabs in the world," it's easy to imagine that some of the publications that write about The Kebabery will come at it with that angle—maybe not the part about the white guy, but they'll praise the restaurant's elevated versions of Middle Eastern–inspired dishes. They'll perhaps talk about how much nicer the setting is compared to your typical kebab shop.

"I'm aware of the cultural privilege that we have going into it. We're going to try to not make that into a marketing thing," Moore said.

Whitewashed Media

If you're a chef in Oakland or Berkeley, where even fine dining tends to be fairly casual, a stint at Chez Panisse—the mother ship of California cuisine—might be the best way to raise your stature in the public eye. So, when Ramen Shop opened in Rockridge in 2012, with its uniquely Californian interpretation of ramen, almost every article about the restaurant led with some discussion of the Chez Panisse pedigree of the three non-Japanese owners: Jerry Jaksich and Sam White, who are white, and Rayneil De Guzman, who is of Filipino descent. Peruse any roundup of best Bay Area ramen joints, and you'll find Ramen Shop at or near the top of the list.

Meanwhile, until recently, Berkeley's Comal was practically the only game in town when it came to high-end, regional Mexican cuisine. The chef, Matt Gandin, is a self-described fourth-generation Jewish American who has loved Mexican food since he was a kid.

Ramen Shop and Comal are both very good restaurants in their own right, and it's important to note that their chefs have been nothing if not respectful when discussing their passion for Japanese and Mexican cooking.

But this fact remains: You'd be hard-pressed to find a Japanese or Mexican eatery in the East Bay that got even a fraction of the pre-opening media hype both restaurants received, and both are often included when national publications do roundups of where to eat in Oakland or Berkeley—often to the exclusion of equally worthy immigrant-run spots.

Much has been written in recent months about the unbearable whiteness of the food-writing community. (I take no satisfaction in being, to my knowledge, the only food writer of color who has a full-time gig with a major Bay Area publication.)

One of the most egregious examples of the kind of tunnel vision this can cause was a recent article about a Chinese restaurant in Brooklyn, on the food blog TheInfatuation.com. Blog co-founder Andrew Steinthal opened his review of Kings County Imperial, a restaurant helmed by "a pair of non-Chinese Chinese food enthusiasts," by invoking just about every existing stereotype that Americans have about Chinese food: that it's "gross," that it leaves diners with "meat sweats," and that it primarily exists in the form of cheap, dive-y takeout joints. Kings County Imperial co-owners Josh Grinker and Tracy Jane Young might not explicitly be hailed as the white saviors of dirty, gross Chinese cuisine. But when the review opens as it does, and then Kings County Imperial gets praised as effusively for its artisanal soy sauce and "modern, clean" approach to Chinese cooking—well, it's not too hard to infer the subtext.

Here in the Bay Area, the dynamic tends to play out in more subtle ways, both in terms of what restaurants even get press coverage and what the chefs themselves say. You'll hear a lot of talk about how chefs were inspired by the flavors that they encountered in a certain village that they visited, and how they wanted to apply certain fine-dining techniques or sourcing principles in order to create their own version.

This being Alice Waters country, what you'll hear about more than anything is a restaurant's farm-to-table credentials: its use of local and sustainable ingredients, i.e., the amazing pasture-raised pork that the mom-and-pop takeout joint around the corner most certainly isn't using, or the locally sourced cabbage that's going to add a whole new dimension to a fancified Burmese tea leaf salad.

There is, of course, nothing wrong with any of this on its face. It's great to support local farmers who are doing things the right way. And no one expects a restaurateur to say, "We're serving a slightly less awesome version of this dish that we just learned how to make, but we're going to charge 30 percent more. Cool?"

But, as Taiwanese-American chef Eddie Huang pointed out in an interview with the *Express* this past June, a lot of times this business about a chef putting his or her own creative twist on a dish—or, in this case, using "higher-quality ingredients"—is code: "This is a better, safer version of this immigrant food."

And make no mistake: There are real financial implications to this, as well. It's why Ramen Shop can charge customers $18 or $19 for a bowl of ramen—compared to, say, $10 or $11 a bowl at one of the comparably esteemed Japanese-run ramen shops in the South Bay. It's why the Oakland restaurateur Charlie Hallowell can charge $20 for a plate of *kefta*-style meatballs at his North African-inspired restaurant, Penrose, whereas Aria Grill, a traditional Afghan kebab shop in downtown Oakland, charges $12 for a similar, more heartily portioned dish.

There are valid reasons for restaurants like Ramen Shop and Penrose to charge what they do—reasons having to do with paying fair wages, supporting sustainable agricultural practices, and so forth. So, perhaps the better question to ask is whether similarly ambitious, immigrant-run, farm-to-table restaurants are able to command similar prices.

Juhu Beach Club's Mistry, who is of Indian descent, argues that this often isn't the case: She said she gets a ton of pushback on her prices, which some customers feel are too high for Indian food.

"People are willing to pay more when the kitchen is full of straight white guys because they look like they should be paid more," she said. "If you see a bunch of brown people in the kitchen, the food should be cheap."

Beyond Delicious

O f course, there are chefs and diners who will read this article (or even just the headline) and have a visceral response against it—who will, perhaps, feel that Moore and others are being needlessly apologetic for something that shouldn't even be an issue.

"Delicious is delicious," the argument goes.

And if Moore's kebabs turn out to be tastier than any of the ones served at the Bay Area's more traditional Middle Eastern restaurants, why shouldn't he embrace that title proudly? Isn't this all just a case of political correctness gone haywire?

Jay Porter is the chef-owner of The Half Orange, a sausage and burger restaurant in Oakland's Fruitvale District, whose menu dabbles in Korean and Mexican flavors—the latter, in particular, a tribute to the years he spent living in San Diego and his frequent travels to Baja California. (Coincidently, Porter was also the proprietor of Salsipuedes, the restaurant that preceded The Kebabery at 4201 Market Street.)

According to Porter, intentions are what matter. In his view, every chef ought to have a good reason to be cooking whatever cuisine or dish he or she is cooking—perhaps all the more so if it's a cuisine they didn't grow up eating themselves.

"If the answer is, 'I learned these cool techniques and no one is applying it to this cuisine,' that's probably not about creating an experience or a bond with the diners," Porter said. "If the reason is this genuine love and community with your people, that shows—and that's a kind of authenticity."

Porter said that, if he were to open a restaurant that served a cuisine that he had no cultural context with, it would likely ring false with his guests.

Indeed, he acknowledged that this was true to a certain extent with Salsipuedes, which closed after less than a year: The small plates menu might have successfully captured the essence of upscale New Baja cuisine, but the restaurant wasn't able to re-create culture in which that particular food thrives—and, so, diners couldn't connect with it.

"I think that serving people food that doesn't have some kind of emotional component is really cynical. Deliciousness cannot be measured on a scientific meter," Porter said.

What's more, in extreme cases, immigrant cuisines in particular face the threat of having their stories erased, or taken away, from their native practitioners altogether. Take Mongolian food, for instance: In the United States, most diners associate it with the type of buffet-style grill restaurant that's commonly found in suburban strip malls, but those actually have nothing to do with Mongolia whatsoever. "Mongolian barbecue" was invented by Taiwanese restaurateurs and has been widely perpetuated in the United States by a fair number of non-Asian entrepreneurs, as well.

Meanwhile, real Mongolian food is mostly left to languish in obscurity, its banner taken up by just a handful of small, immigrant-run restaurants—including Togi's Mongolian Cuisine in downtown Oakland—that tend not to get much press.

Calavera, the upscale Oaxacan-focused Mexican restaurant in Uptown Oakland, also provides an interesting case study. The restaurant currently faces a lawsuit involving former employees, who accuse the owners of a number of different labor violations. At least one former cook claims that she was fired after the restaurant exploited her for her deeply rooted knowledge of tortilla-making, and other recipes she had learned as a native of Oaxaca.

The lawsuit is still pending, and the owners of Calavera—one of whom is Latino—have vigorously denied the allegations. But this narrative—of an immigrant cook having her cultural knowledge co-opted so that someone else can profit—resonated with many people.

Calavera's current chef, Sophina Uong, began working at the restaurant subsequent to the allegations and is herself a relative newcomer to Mexican cuisine, as a Cambodian-American who has cooked at restaurants specializing in everything from Southern food to California cuisine. She says she's spending a lot of her time tweaking Calavera's menu, but also learning techniques and recipes from the Mexican cooks who have been on staff since the restaurant opened.

When asked why she has always worked in cuisines that are fairly far removed from her own personal background, Uong said she's simply always looked to challenge herself by learning something new.

"There are no borders in cooking, I think," Uong said. "You cook from the heart."

Perhaps, as Porter argues, it does come down to intentions. For some customers, the chefs who aren't cooking from the heart are the ones who get in trouble when they cook a non-native cuisine—especially when it's a cuisine of people who have been historically oppressed, to whom the food has deeper significance than just playing with a new set of flavors.

Noah Cho, a multiracial Oakland resident whose father was Korean and whose mother is a white American, has commented extensively on this issue via social media, particularly as it pertains to Korean dishes, many of which were created as survival foods and thus have deep roots in hardship endured by the Korean people. To Cho, it becomes offensive, then, when non-Korean chefs tinker with a dish like *bibimbap*— the classic rice bowl with meat, vegetables, and hot sauce—to the point that it's unrecognizable: "You can make a quinoa bowl with veggies in it, and just not call it '*bibimbap*.'"

Cho explained that the reason he takes food so seriously is because it was the only way he was able to communicate with his paternal grandmother, who didn't speak English. He recalls sitting with her for hours folding *mandu*, a kind of Korean dumpling.

"If you serve me bad *mandu* casually, that's very offensive to me," Cho said. "Maybe if you understand that, you can even make it better."

The Iggy Azaleas of Food

Ultimately, this isn't about who is allowed to cook what food. Like so many different narratives that are playing out in America right now, this is just another story about privilege: who has it, and how those who have it should use it.

At the end of the day, chefs should cook whatever kind of food they love to cook, and they should do it with all of the passion, skill, and technique they can muster. But, as Juhu Beach Club's Mistry pointed out, white chefs in particular should also be willing to engage their critics and speak to why they've chosen to focus on a certain cuisine or why they've decided to prepare a dish a certain way.

"Since when did 'white' become a pejorative term? You are. You get a lot of privilege from it. In this instance, you'll have to talk about it— plain and simple," she said.

Mistry acknowledged that, even as a queer chef and an immigrant kid, she too benefits from privilege: "Embody that in how you run your business—how you hire, what neighborhood you're in, what your price point is."

In the meantime, those of us who write about food for a living should perhaps think a little bit harder before we declare some fine-dining chef's passion project to be the best Mexican (or Japanese or Chinese) restaurant we've ever been to. And everyone should make sure that there is a certain amount of respect paid to those who have come before us—to the generations of cooks who made a cuisine what it is before today's chefs started riffing on it.

In Mistry's view, at least, the chefs at Ramen Shop really do embody that kind of respectful attitude toward their adopted cuisine—a reverence for the techniques and sensibilities of Japanese culinary culture, even if some of the dishes the restaurant serves can only very loosely be described as Japanese. But she said other chefs take a more "Columbus-y" approach and then bristle when they're called out on it.

"It's very Iggy Azalea," Mistry said, alluding to the Australian rapper who has been accused of co-opting Black hip-hop culture and not having a particularly nuanced understanding of American race relations. "Have respect for the history and heritage—especially when you're a privileged person cooking a cuisine of a historically oppressed people."

Then there is the matter of how successful chefs use the platform that they've been given. Or, as Mistry put it: "When you come up, you bring others with you. That's a tenet of being."

One thing that stands out about The Half Orange's Porter is that, at least on social media and his personal blog, he very rarely talks up his knowledge of Mexican food culture as a way to drive business to his own restaurant. Instead, he constantly shines a light on the immigrant-run mom-and-pop businesses in the Fruitvale, who are ostensibly his competitors. It was through one of Porter's tweets that this critic first learned about Taqueria El Paisa@.com, which Porter asserted serves the most delicious tacos he's eaten in California. He also collaborated with one of his neighbors in Fruitvale, the Mexican ice cream shop Nieves Cinco de Mayo, whose owner, Luis Abundis, created all of the desserts for Salsipuedes. And he said nothing makes him happier than when he sees customers at his restaurant wander over after their meal to buy a *churro* from the cart parked outside.

"Whatever kind of food we're doing or whatever our background is, everything is going to be a better experience for everybody if we include our influences and our neighbors," Porter said.

When asked about Comal's success, Gandin stressed that the restaurant has never made any claims that it's serving "cleaned up" or more "refined" Mexican food. Then, he started talking about how not enough is said about the collaborative aspect of a restaurant—how one of his cooks in particular, a hardworking Jalisco native named Martín Blas, had contributed to the development of certain recipes.

Given how crucial Blas' role has been, and all of the articles that have been written about Comal, why hadn't we heard about him before?

In an email, Uong explained that executive chefs tend to be the ones who get all the credit in the restaurant industry as a whole. "The fact that kitchen staff don't get a lot of visibility in the front of house isn't unusual, nor does it indicate that they aren't valued," she wrote.

This is a fair point. But it seems like it might behoove restaurants that have non-native chefs, and that lean heavily on the deep-rooted, traditional knowledge of the immigrant cooks on staff, to find ways to shine more of a spotlight on those cooks—whether it be through pop-ups or other kinds of opportunities.

Dominica Rice-Cisneros, the Mexican-American chef-owner of Cosecha (and yet another Chez Panisse alum), said she understands that, for magazines such as *Sunset* and *Food & Wine*, there's real appeal to running a big photo spread of some blond surfer dude who cooks Mexican food. But she said what she looks for when she visits a white-owned Mexican restaurant is whether there are Latinos in high-profile, upper-management positions—"not just the part-time prep cooks," Rice-Cisneros said.

Moore, on the other hand, said he only hopes that The Kebabery might act as a kind of gateway for the type of customer who will drive out of their way to dine at a Russell Moore restaurant, but might never set foot in any of the Bay Area's many excellent traditional kebab restaurants.

"You're crazy if you live in Oakland and you don't try the Middle Eastern restaurants, Asian restaurants, or Mexican and Latin-American restaurants," he said.

"That's most of the good food in the area."

A "Pan-Asian" Restaurant May Seem Dated. In Fact the Trend Is Hotter Than Ever

By TIM CARMAN

From the *Washington Post*

WashPo staff food writer Tim Carman normally trains his sights on the D.C. market's affordable end, with his $20 Diner for the Weekend column. So when ethnic dining drifts into the chic/trendy market, Carman's got the goods, expertly delineating the fine lines that restaurateurs skate.

Standing in the Jade Room, a retro-chic lounge with a glass-walled wine cellar and the air of Japanese minimalism, chef Jeff Tunks instructs his staff on the proper way to serve dolsot bibimbap, one of several Korean-style hot-stone dishes available at the recently resurrected TenPenh in Tysons Corner.

"A lot of people don't really know how to eat it," says Tunks, a partner with Passion Food Hospitality, the group behind TenPenh.

The chef stresses the importance of the spicy gochujang sauce—"which is not super spicy," he quickly adds—and how diners need to squeeze at least half the bottle of the house-made sauce into their stone bowl before mixing the ingredients together. "If they don't know how to eat it, then they're going to be picking at the spinach with chopsticks," he says. "That, on its own, is not that flavorful."

The dolsot bibimbap is one of many new elements at TenPenh, a restaurant that once held down the corner of 10th Street and

Pennsylvania Avenue NW in downtown Washington. The address, in fact, provided the inspiration for the restaurant's vaguely Asian moniker, a mash-up of street names that mirrored TenPenh's approach to food, a fusion of Asian flavors and familiar Western ingredients, like its miso-glazed sea bass or its Wagyu beef tartare with wasabi guacamole. In its prime in the 2000s—it closed in 2011—TenPenh was a trailblazer in its ability to synthesize East and West for a (then) generally conservative D.C. dining public.

The new TenPenh is less a revival than a makeover. Tunks and his partners—David Wizenberg and Gus DiMillo—have salvaged precious little from the first incarnation save for the logo, a few dishes and some statuary they acquired in Asia. This time around, TenPenh is placing bets on its chef-driven (and playful) interpretations of Japanese, Chinese, Taiwanese, Thai and Korean dishes that have entered the American mainstream, no matter how tentatively. Think ramen, sushi, dim sum and those Korean hot stone bowls.

In that way, the revamped TenPenh has essentially shifted from Asian fusion to pan-Asian, a distinction perhaps lost on many diners. Yet both approaches seem to swim against the current of contemporary Asian dining. In recent years, chefs and restaurateurs have rejected the mantra of their predecessors who believed that Chinese, Thai, Vietnamese and other Asian eateries in America needed to pander to the widest possible audience, even if that meant dumbing down the cuisine or asking cooks to have a passing knowledge of an insane number of dishes.

These 21st-century Asian restaurants are hyper-focused on a single regional cuisine or a long-neglected cuisine or even the street foods of a particular country. You see these places popping up across the country, their reservation lists booked solid or a line of hopeful diners snaking down the block. This singled-minded charge into the U.S. dining scene has sometimes been led by white chefs, such as Andy Ricker (whose study of authentic Thai food led to his small Pok Pok chain, first launched in Portland) or Ivan Orkin (whose obsession with Japanese noodle soup led to his iconoclastic Ivan Ramen shops in New York).

But just as often, the modern Asian dining movement has been led by those who grew up with the cuisine and knew (or hoped) the time was right to present it to Americans with authority.

Master chef Peter Chang, the son of a poor farming family in Hubei province, has introduced real Sichuan cooking to the Mid-Atlantic via his eponymous restaurants. The family members behind Xi'an Famous Foods gambled that their Shaanxi cuisine could find an attentive audience in New York City. And the Filipino-American owners behind Bad Saint have created one of the best new restaurants in the country, based on a cuisine previously thought unmarketable in America.

This new wave of Asian eateries has had a ripple effect on those earlier restaurants, such as TenPenh, which adopted a pan-cultural approach to Asian cookery. Jennifer 8. Lee, a former *New York Times* reporter who has written extensively about the assimilation of Chinese food in America, put it bluntly via text: "I never trust a pan-Asian restaurant. If I see pad thai and sushi on [the] same menu, I cringe," she writes. "Pan-Asian is almost by definition not authentic."

This apparent conflict between old- and new-school Asian restaurants can raise some uncomfortable questions, such as: Who's qualified to present a region's cuisine to American diners? And is it okay for outsiders to alter a region's food because they think it's too funky for the stereotypical American palate?

"I always look at pan-Asian as sort of being racist," says David Chang, the Northern Virginia native responsible for the Momofuku empire. "Think about it this way," he says. "If I open a barbecue restaurant and I said, 'This is pan-barbecue, and we're going to serve barbecue from around the world,' I would get laughed out of town. No one would take me seriously. But if someone was doing it as Asian food, no one would laugh. No one would think it's weird."

Yet Chang is not calling Tunks and his ilk racists. It would be hypocritical: Chang, after all, operates his own pan-Asian restaurants, featuring Japanese, Vietnamese and Chinese dishes that are not part of the chef's Korean heritage. He just doesn't call them "pan-Asian" or "Asian fusion."

Both Chang and the Passion Food team know that those terms have become toxic, the victims of chains such as P.F. Chang's or even your favorite neighborhood Chinese restaurant, which have blurred the lines between regional cuisines or between the dishes of vastly different countries without losing sleep over who might be offended.

No, pan-Asian restaurants aren't dead, despite the rise of such places as Bad Saint, Pok Pok, Ivan Ramen and others. They're just hiding in plain sight, disguised as noodle houses or new American restaurants, where the chefs may bury their pan-Asian inspirations among a wider variety of culinary influences. Have you noticed how often Asian ingredients and flavors crop up at Rose's Luxury, that darling of the D.C. dining community?

In this context, TenPenh can come across as the middle-aged dude trying too hard to fit in with the cool kids, who see through this transparent attempt at relevance. They see the Nashville hot chicken steam buns, the bibimbap "arancini" fritters, the pork crackling chips with Thai chili and cucumber chimichurri. But what the kids don't see—maybe refuse to see—is that TenPenh has much in common with those restaurants that may be better at concealing their pan-Asian inspirations.

They share an emotional connection to Asian cooking. Their chefs have often spent time in the countries that inspired their food, and they frequently have been tutored by older cooks who had to patiently explain the importance of foreign ingredients like gochujang sauce.

Asia by way of California

Scott Drewno has been tutored by such a chef. After dropping out of college in New York, Drewno moved west and found a job at Chinois, the Las Vegas outpost of celebrity chef Wolfgang Puck's groundbreaking Santa Monica restaurant, which used French techniques to fuse Asian flavors and California ingredients. The inspiration for Chinois was little more than Puck's surroundings, the Asian markets and strip-mall eateries that make Los Angeles such an intoxicating food town.

The Asian flavors certainly went to Drewno's head. In 1996, when he was just 21 years old, this former meat-and-potatoes man fell for Puck's Shanghai lobster with curry sauce, an elaborate preparation that looked like an expressionist painter's cry for help.

"So many different ingredients go into making that sauce," Drewno remembers. "That was certainly a dish that started my love affair with Asian food."

Two decades and several trips to China later, Drewno leads the kitchen at the Source, Puck's restaurant in Washington, where diners can sample his refined takes on dishes from Taiwan, Shanghai, Sichuan, Thailand and other locales. It's pan-Asian fine-dining, though you'd be hard-pressed to find those words in the Source's marketing materials.

Puck wasn't the only chef looking East for inspiration. Jean-Georges Vongerichten made a strong first impression on diners and critics in 1992 when he opened Vong, his Frenchified take on Thai cooking in Midtown Manhattan. The late Barbara Tropp, a Chinese scholar at Princeton, would spend two years in Taiwan before moving to San Francisco and opening China Moon Cafe in 1986 in a space that conjured up old-time diners, not Chinese temples. The place became a magnet for celebrities and young cooks; one of Tropp's apprentices was Lee Hefter, who would become executive corporate chef for Wolfgang Puck—and have a formative influence on a young Drewno.

When David Chang was growing up in Vienna, Va., his father frequently would take him to Pho 75, a beloved Vietnamese chain in the D.C. area. The pho parlor imprinted itself on Chang's palate: In 2004, when the chef opened his first Momofuku Noodle Bar in Manhattan, he didn't provide togarashi, the Japanese spice blend often sprinkled into ramen. Instead, he offered Sriracha, the hot sauce found at pho shops everywhere. (Momofuku would later create its own chicken pho, too.)

A groundbreaking bun

Momofuku's opening menu also featured gua bao. They were a last-minute addition based, in part, on Chang's frequent stops at Oriental Garden in New York's Chinatown, where the spongy bao were stuffed with duck, scallions, cucumber and hoisin: a Taiwanese variation on Peking duck pancakes. Chang wanted to tuck pork belly into his steamed buns, since he would be producing the fatty meats for his ramen.

"If there's a claim to fame that I know that I can [make]," Chang says, "there wasn't a ramen shop in the world that served pork buns with ramen. Anywhere. It was only gyoza or fried rice. So the whole phenomenon of the pork bun really started when we served it with ramen."

Erik Bruner-Yang knows all about the pork bun phenomenon. The chef behind Maketto (a restaurant that mixes Bruner-Yang's takes on Taiwanese and Cambodian dishes) remembers when he was still creating the menus at Toki Underground, the popular ramen shop located on the same H Street NE strip in Washington. Toki didn't offer steamed buns on its opening menu.

"Literally, like, every other customer wanted bao buns, and that's because David Chang served bao buns at Momofuku," Bruner-Yang says.

Add up all those stories, and what do you have? A lot of pan-Asian restaurants that draw inspiration from a great many sources, some more random than others. For every dish inspired by research trips to Vietnam or Shanghai, two more were probably inspired by trips to a local strip-center Sichuan joint.

Tunks of Passion Food knows the value of travel in understanding another culture's food. He has traveled widely throughout Asia. But he and Miles Vaden, the executive chef at TenPenh, also understand the value of calling other chefs, watching YouTube videos and good, old-fashioned recipe testing. They've spent countless hours developing a recipe for Peking duck, landing on a painstaking, multiday process that involves shellacking, stuffing, skewering, drying and roasting the birds.

Still, despite the work they've invested, Tunks is not certain TenPenh 2.0 will connect with modern D.C. diners. It's not about the food, which Tunks will put up against the trendiest of pan-Asian haunts. It's the intangibles: The new TenPenh is suburban, family-friendly, eager to cater to many palates and, with more than 200 seats, very large. Plus, TenPenh doesn't make customers stand in line.

"That's what people like," Tunks says. "They want to wait in line for it a little bit. They want to … Snapchat about it, as opposed to making a reservation and coming in."

If modern diners are attracted to the smaller, more targeted and, well, more difficult-to-attain restaurant, Tunks says he's not about to reverse course and cater to that market, no matter how trendy it may be. "With two other partners and being at my age," says the 55-year-old chef, "it's hard for us to go back to a 35-seat restaurant and do that with a real, more finite focus."

In Defense of Mexican-American Chefs

By Gustavo Arellano

From *OC Weekly*

Here's the underbelly of the cultural appropriation debate: What happens when ethnic chefs turn on each other in the quest for authenticity? Gustavo Arellano, son of Mexican immigrants and author of *OC Weekly*'s "Ask a Mexican" column, has a ringside seat on this contest over culinary tradition.

Last week, our own Sarah Bennett wrote a cover story for our former sister paper, *LA Weekly*, about the ascendance of Mexican-American chefs in Southern California. It was a good piece that obviously focused on chefs in Los Angeles, hence leaving out OC's Carlos Salgado of Taco María, he of the James Beard nomination this year, Jonathan Gold's silver medal last year as the second-best place to eat in Southern California—but I digress.

Sarah's article got good traction online, but also brought on the haters. These weren't Trumpbros or jealous restauranteurs, however, but the most persistent threat to successful Mexicans: Mexicans. And these aren't the self-hating, George P. Bush–style *pendejos* but rather self-proclaimed *real* Mexicans, the kind who have a checklist of what makes a "real" Mexican that they obtained from Cuauhtémoc (with an assist by Zapata) himself. They started whining on Twitter and Facebook (including, alas, my own ¡Ask a Mexican! fan page) immediately: What Mexican-American chefs cook isn't authentic. It's overpriced, and therefore for *gabachos* instead of Mexicans. They're gentrifiers. They're trying too hard to appeal to non-Mexicans and hence selling

out Mexican culture. No taco is worth $3 even if the masa is from heir-
loom corn and doesn't use Maseca. They're not down with *la causa*. The
food sucks and can't possibly compare to even the worst *lonchera* taco.
Vendidos. Pochos. CHAVALAS.

Typical of this train of thought was one commenter on *LA Weekly*'s
Facebook page who saw a video and wrote, "Excuse me but traditional
pozole is not made with lamb, it's made with pork neckbones, lamb?
that's getting a little too gourmet." (Actually, *baboso*, "traditional" pozole had no pork, because pork isn't indigenous to the Americas. But
you knew that, right?)

I've covered food of all kinds in Orange County and Southern
California for 15 years now. And seeing the negative reaction to the
Mexican-Americans Sarah hailed reminded me of an ugly reality in the
food world: no ethnic group is less supportive of innovation in their cuisine than Mexicans in the United States. And that's a *pinche desgracia*—
a fucking shame.

It's true! The luxe lonchera revolution has seen the children of immigrants push their mother cuisines to all sorts of levels, picking and
choosing from other cultures to create dishes of dizzying heights,
whether Roy Choi's Kogi sorcery or Ed Lee's Southern-fried pan-Asian
grub. Regional American food keeps seeing homegrown chefs refine
the stuff they grew up on. African-American chefs play with soul food;
Native American chefs are doing the same with their long-suppressed
traditions, putting dishes that get praise from the rez to the Ritz. It has
led to soul-searching essays about cultural appropriation by brainy
types, sure—meanwhile, customers largely don't give a damn as they
weather hours-longs waits for everything from Halal Guys to hipster
Asian churros, and proudly cheer on their peers on social media and
beyond.

The same applauding has happened in the past with Cuban-
American and pan-Latino chefs. But there hasn't been that same level
of support by Mexicans in the U.S. for Mexican-American chefs like
Salgado, Soho Taco, Wes Avila of Guerrilla Tacos, Thomas Ortega of
Playa Amor and Amor y Tacos, and so many more. They do get Latino
customers—but at nowhere near the level that they deserve. And their
biggest fans? Not Mexican.

And that pisses me off. It's one thing to not patronize shitty food—we should never support a Mexican chef just because they're Mexican. But Mexican-American restauranteurs are cooking some of the most delicious, forward-thinking meals in Southern California right now—yet *raza* would rather hail Chalino and Chicharito as bigger heroes than them. Why? I get that some folks can't afford to regularly eat at the higher-end establishments these Mexican-American chefs inevitably run. I'd remind consumers, though, that cheap food is literally that—exploitative of some part, if not all, of the food chain, from the people tasked with picking or slaughtering the food to the dishwasher in the back—and that most of the acclaimed Mexican-American chefs believe in elevating our food system with higher wages and better-quality products that result in a higher bill.

No, the real sin here for yaktivists is the very act of Mexican-American chefs daring to reimagine Mexican food—nay, daring to reimagine Mexicans as deserving more than one-buck tacos. It's as if such chefs are expected to not aspire to be anything higher than a *paletero*, to hawk a humble, prepackaged product even if they have the opportunity and resources to do new things for a bigger audience and advance what we eat and who we are. Because Mexican food—like Mexicans—is sacrosanct and not expected to evolve, period.

This is an atavistic, ahistorical atrocity. Such a philosophy forgets what Mexican food fundamentally is—a mestizo, ever-progressing mishmash in which German and Czech beers (Bohemia, Negra Modela, et al.), liquors distilled via European techniques (tequila and mezcal), Lebanese meat on a spit (al pastor), French pastries (most pan dulces), Peruvian seafood (ceviche) and American-style sodas (Mexican Coke, Jarritos) combine to create one of the most thrilling foodways on Earth. Wanting to encase Mexican food in amber ignores the current scene in Mexico proper: young chefs from Baja to Mexico City and beyond are taking Mexican food to levels never before seen. And those chefs respect the hell out of their pocho cousins: earlier this summer, Salgado cooked alongside Enrique Olvera, who just happens to be the one of the most important chefs in the Americas right now.

But none of this is good enough for the Mexican haters, who fulfill with every snide Facebook comment or Yelp review that legendary Chicano Studies prophecy of crabs pulling down any crabs who try to climb out of the bucket. Shit, such anti-progress bullshit even extends to actual Mexican chefs in Southern California trying new things with classics. Take Danny Godinez of Anepalco's, whose cylinder-esque chilaquiles is one of the greatest dishes in Southern California but, when explained to pochos who haven't visited Mexico outside of their parent's ranchos for a week of *puro pinche pari*, are dismissed as fancy *paisa* bullshit. Shit, I've even heard such grumbling about birria de res masters Burritos La Palma: I've seen Mexicans walk away from their food truck, pissed off that the acclaimed *lonchera* doesn't sell carne asada tacos even though owner Albert Bañuelos is selling food straight from his family's restaurant in Jerez, Zacatecas. Somehow, birria de res burritos aren't "real" Mexican, while greasy-ass tacos are.

Fuck that.

Many Mexican-American chefs privately grouse about and even get stung by the lack of support by their own kind, but would never dare say publicly for fear of getting labeled a sellout or uppity. I have no such qualms, so lemme say it for them here: Mexicans in the U.S.: There is nothing wrong with our food being "gourmet"—shit, it was gourmet before gourmet was a thing. There is nothing wrong with our youngsters pushing and prodding our culture forward while simultaneously respecting it. Support your fellow *raza* doing new, delicious things and pushing us to reimagine what "Mexican" is.

Otherwise? You're no better than Donald Trump. Oh, and #fuckthehaters.

Foodways

Salt of the Earth

By Ronni Lundy

From *Victuals*

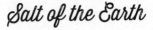

James Beard Book of the Year *Victuals* (officially pronounced, yes, "vittles") is a master work, documenting in essays, recipes, and stunning photographs the food culture of the Appalachian region. Scholar and native daughter Ronni Lundy not only knows whereof she speaks, she makes us love it, too.

Rich Valley Road, the asphalt two-lane into Saltville, Virginia, runs through a wide valley along the base of Clinch Mountain. I slow down as much to savor the glide as for safety, and in slowing, I note what is happening roadside. The closer I get to town, the closer it seems that the small frame and brick houses sit to the road, their porches facing it.

I come from porch-sitting people, so it pleases me to see most of these are occupied. Wearing clothes that still speak of work—jeans and overalls, apron and housedress—the older folk on them have earned the right to sit idle at noonday. Even in the yard of a single-wide—flower-bordered, well kept, yet porchless—three iron-haired men have arranged their lawn chairs out front in proper porch order: not clumped conversationally to face one another, but turned in a single line to the road, the better to see who is passing by. Raised in the vernacular, I don't wave but lift two fingers from the 11 o'clock position on the steering wheel and give a short nod as I pass, receiving same in return.

While porches in this valley would have been availed of an evening, or after church on a Sunday, such midday midweek idleness would not have been common in the past. In its peak years, the salt mining industry in Saltville required three shifts of workers daily and provided livelihood for both town and country dwellers. And well before salt was discovered here by colonial entrepreneurs in the 1700s, this was a lively, active place. The salt licks made a rich hunting ground for the Native Americans who came to seek the diverse game that flocked in abundance to satisfy their salt need. And before the deer, elk, bear, and buffalo, the salt drew huge prehistoric beasts: mammoths, mastodons, musk ox, the giant ground sloth whose bones have been found in local archaeological excavations.

And before those enormous creatures? These mountains were the site of activity of seismic proportions. What we call the Appalachian Mountains was once part of a larger chain on the ancient supercontinent of Pangea. When that continent split apart, the mountains came asunder, too, leaving sister peaks in what is now Morocco, while this section drifted on to slam and shift and shape into North America with these peaks, then steep as the Andes, running up its eastern side. Those shifts were not gentle when tectonic plates crashed and collided, creating sharp peaks and high plateaus. At one point a whole oceanic plate crashed in and under, storing in spots a secret wealth of saltwater beneath the ground, the Iapetus Ocean.

I see the record of all of this at the Museum of the Middle Appalachians in the quiet, almost deserted downtown of Saltville. In a large, softly lit room the huge skeleton of a woolly mammoth shares space with a tabletop diorama of the town and surrounding valley. The table lights up salient points in the town's historical geography when buttons are pressed.

The museum has a smaller space for rotating exhibits. When I am there, that room is full of quilts handmade by women from the town, a different sort of history told in scraps and imagination and impossibly small stitches. And in a large, sunny third room, the story of the first people who lived here—shown with flints and arrows, beads and feathered apparel—shares space with that of the latest. The early history of a 20th-century company town is told in photographs and artifacts, presented with fond nostalgia by those who lived here and their descendants.

Salt sparked the first extractive industry in the southern Appala-chians. Its processing required the harvesting of timber, then the exca-vation of coal, to keep the evaporative furnaces burning. In time, those resources were exported out as well, and that became a defining mo-ment in the history of the region.

Salt is also a defining ingredient in the foodways of the southern mountains. At some point in the ancient processing of carcasses in the salt/hunting regions, the flesh came in contact with the mineral and magic was born. Not exactly the immortality of the Fountain of Youth that the early Spanish explorers came here seeking in the 1500s, but an alchemical extension of viability. Salt curing was the way that early hunter/gatherers prolonged the edibility of meat to get through the winter. Salt curing is what fueled the industry created by the colonists who came later to make their fortunes by shipping salt downriver to the meat-packers in Cincinnati, Louisville, Knoxville, Nashville, and as far away as New Orleans.

Is it any wonder that salt came to define many of the core foods of the region? Lip-puckering country ham and salt-cured pork. Sour corn and pickle beans. Melon served always with a sprinkle of salt. The ubiq-uitous Cheese Nabs in the glove box that no mountain trucker leaves home without. Salty slow-simmered kale and pinto beans. Jerky, kraut, and pickles of all kinds. Salt is the element that enabled life and nour-ishment through the harsh, stark winters of the mountains, winters that helped create a cuisine that was in one sense distinctly Southern and at the same time distinctly its own.

Much to chew on as I make my way to the museum gift shop, so no wonder that what I gravitate toward is a spiral-bound volume with a soft yellow paper cover amid the many "official" histories. It's the *Saltville Centennial Cookbook*. I am most intrigued by the evocative names of the more savory, salt-laced dishes, and the stories they conjure up: Dead Man's Soup, Bert's (Big Mama's) Cat Head Biscuits, Brain Croquettes, Parsnip Skillet, Dr. Finne's Baked Doves, Hungarian Soup (Hunky Soup), Paprika's (*sic*) Csirke (Chicken), Hunter's Goulash, Chicken and Dumplings (two versions), Heirloom Scalded Lettuce, Old Fash-ioned Hash. Clearly there is history here as well. Delightfully, the chil-dren, grandchildren, and friends tell a good bit of that history as this cookbook is studded with old black-and-white photographs and laced with memories of the women, and a few men, who turned these dishes out, day after day.

"*There are few people in the Town of Saltville who have never eaten any of Granny Blackwell's cooking,*" I read.

"*After retiring from Olin with 42 years of service, Ralph enjoyed fishing as often as possible.*"

"*She was a generous person and worried over people who were in need. She liked to travel and ride the bus.*"

Such fragments remind me of summer evenings as a child. Lying on the grass down in Corbin with my cousins, lightning bugs flashing in the dark around us, we caught such pieces of the conversation my parents, aunts, and uncles were having on the porch above. From them we formed imagined pictures and stories of the past, our people.

We were all—my father, mother, sister, me—born in Corbin, Kentucky. But when I was about a year old and my sister twelve, my father got word of work in the distilleries in Louisville and we moved. My parents lived in the city the rest of their lives, but they never fully left the mountains. Like most members of the various hillbilly diasporas of the 20th century, we went "up home" whenever we could. My father worked in the boiler rooms, a fireman and oiler, hard labor but it suited his athlete's need for a physical challenge. (He'd been a boxer as a young man. The folks in Corbin said he'd been a good one.)

He worked swing shift, and "on call," and picked up overtime when he could to compensate for the layoffs that were a part of the distillery process then. Whenever a stretch of more than two days off came up, we'd make the four-hour winding drive to "see the folks." We spent every summer vacation of my growing up in those hills. The steeper and more winding the road became, the easier my father seemed to sit in his skin, to smile from someplace deep.

Summers up home were not lazy. There was always a little time on the lake for reading and cards, swimming and fishing, but there were also things to do and my parents were always willing to do them. My mother cooked with her aunts for the passels of cousins who showed up every night to visit and remember. She helped with the canning, strung beans and then threaded them up for shuck beans, cleaned and mopped and hung out wet clothes just as she did at home.

My dad loved any job that required muscle and took him outside. One summer he and my great-uncle Charlie built a garage from the foundation up, the sound of boards slapping and the two men talking and laughing riding like a melody over the rhythm of the locusts. They would come in the house still telling a story, riffing back and forth like jazz hipsters as they got tall iced tea tumblers from the cabinet, then filled them with spring water that came from the faucet. As they turned to go back out, my dad would grab the salt shaker from the table, pour some in his palm and some in Charlie's, licking it up on his way out the door. "A man needs to keep his minerals balanced," he told me when I asked why. "Work in the summer, you sweat 'em out, salt puts them back in." Salt and spring water: Hillbilly Gatorade.

We sweated, too, children playing hard or doing chores, women working in the steaming kitchen. Maybe that's why I remember salt so clearly as the taste of summer. We put it on our fresh cucumbers and onions, the tomatoes that accompanied every supper. We consumed it ravenously on crisp crackers topped with tangy baloney or Vienna sausages on the deck of the pontoon boat at the lake. My cousins and I poured tiny mountains in our palms and dipped tommy-toes, still warm from the garden, before dropping them into our mouths. My great-aunt Johnnie kept a saltshaker next to her as she sat on the porch slicing tart June apples to dry, for use that winter in stack cake and fried pies. The drying sweetened them, she told me, and I knew that to be true. So did salt, she said, as she sprinkled some on a crisp sour slice and popped it in her mouth, then made one for me. I wasn't so sure about that, but there was a mingling of flavor there that was both sharp and haunting.

Even dessert in the summer needed some salt. After supper I'd ride into town with Daddy and Charlie to a grocery store that stayed open late; it seemed just to sell the dark green melons they kept in the back in long tin tubs filled with ice water. We rushed home to slice the melon while it was still deep chilled, perfect half-moons of vermillion laid on yellowed plates with sweet flowers and tiny age veins around the edges. Nobody plunged in until the saltshaker made the rounds.

My cousin David ate cinnamon Red Hots on saltine crackers; we poured salted peanuts into our glass-bottled Cokes. Even ice cream, that pure sweet blend of milk and sugar, required salt. Not in it, but in the old crank freezer that Charlie and my dad would take turns turning.

The ice had to be crushed just right, then layered with a handful of rock salt. Inevitably in the process, one of the women would caution, "Don't let that salt get high enough to seep into the cream," and then someone would tell the story of the time that happened. And then another story, and another one, as we sat patiently on the screened back porch and waited for the cream to ripen, just a little anxious that the first bite should be a sweet, not salty, one.

When these visits ended—summer vacations, long weekends—there would be a sadness in the leaving. Tears—salt again—were shed by the women and children. The men cleared throats, mopped sweaty foreheads with handkerchiefs that just managed to slip by their eyes. Someone would say, "Going back to the salt mines, Pap?" My dad would laugh and we'd drive away.

I don't know where my child's image of "the salt mines" came from. A cartoon? A book I'd read? In my imagination, they were far, far away, part of an exotic desert world of swirling sand and spices. I did not know then that salt had been "mined" just one county over from Corbin.

Swing Shift Steak

Serves 2

My dad worked swing shift most of my life, and my mother, like many salt, railroad, coal, mill, and factory wives, adjusted our household schedule around his. When he worked 7 to 3, we gathered of an evening at the round oak table in the dining room, and platters of vegetables, hot cornbread, and meat would appear. On other shift days, supper and breakfast might merge into a meal that was a bit of both.

One of the fundamental building blocks in my mother's repertoire for such revolving mealtimes was the inexpensive and quick-cooking eye of round steak. She would pound the steaks with her heavy metal waffle-faced potato masher, then season and quick-fry them, keeping them surprisingly juicy even though well done. (Yes, they have a little chew to them, but we were a family of ruminators in more ways than one.) She would serve them with potatoes, biscuits, and vegetables for dinner, or with eggs in the morning.

My favorite of these meals was served to my dad and me late at night, before he picked up his lunch sack, kissed "his girls" goodbye, and went off in the dark to work. For those supper/breakfasts, my mother would fry the steaks and make a quick gravy that she served over soft rye bread laid to the side. She rarely joined us at the table in the kitchen where these meals were served, preferring to stand next to the stove, sipping coffee, smoking, and smiling.

(You may increase to serve four, though, you won't need to increase the flour for the gravy.)

> 2 eye of round steaks, each about ¾-inch thick
> Salt and freshly ground black pepper or lemon pepper
> 3 tablespoons all-purpose flour
> ¼ teaspoon sweet smoked Spanish paprika
> Vegetable oil or lard
> 2 pieces soft rye bread
> ½ cup whole milk

Lay the steaks on a cutting board. Using the tenderizing (pointed) face of a meat mallet, lightly pound each side. You do not want to pound the meat super-thin or to make holes through it. You want to thin it to about ½-inch thickness and make plenty of shallow ridges to hold the seasoning and flour. Flip the steaks over and do the same to the second side, then repeat for each side.

Lightly salt and liberally pepper each steak, and rub them lightly to help the seasoning sink in.

In a wide, shallow bowl or on a plate, blend the flour, paprika, and a generous pinch of salt well. Dredge each steak in the flour, coating both sides and using your fingertips to gently press the flour into the ridges, just to make sure the coating sticks. Reserve the remaining flour.

Set an amply sized, heavy, lidded skillet over high heat and add enough oil to slick the whole pan. (You can use lard, but an oil with a higher smoke point is easier to work with.) When the oil is hot but not smoking, add the steaks and brown them quickly on each side (this takes about 2 minutes per side). Turn the heat down to low, cover the skillet, and let the steaks cook for about 5 minutes, until just cooked through.

Lift each steak, allowing a little of the juices to run back into the skillet, and place it on a warmed plate. (If you would like to serve the steaks on rye toast, this would be the time to put the bread in the toaster.)

Sprinkle 1 tablespoon of the reserved seasoning flour into the skillet, and stir quickly to flavor it with the juices. Scrape the skillet to loosen the crust, and add 2 tablespoons of water to the juices to help scrape up the browned bits. Slowly stir in the milk, using the back of the meat spatula or a wide spoon to flatten any lumps as you do. When the flour is incorporated with no lumps (there will be solid flecks of the meat's breading, but no large lumps of flour), turn the heat up to medium and bring it to a boil, stirring steadily all the time. When the gravy just begins to thicken, remove it from the heat and add salt to taste.

Place the toast or piece of bread on the plate next to the steak, and cover with the gravy. Serve.

What's True About Pho

By Rachel Khong

From *Lucky Peach*

Former *Lucky Peach* executive editor Rachel Khong, whose
debut novel *Goodbye Vitamin* came out in July 2017, was making
a pilgrimage of sorts when she visited Vietnam to learn about
pho, the iconic noodle soup. The real surprise is what her trip also
revealed to her about America.

When I arrive at my hotel in Hanoi's Old Quarter, it's about eleven
at night. The day that I've lost crossing over the dateline is International Women's Day. "Just you?" asks the concierge, a my-size,
my-age woman—five four, about thirty. It's just haggard me. She has a
neat smile, neat ponytail in contrast. "Happy Women's Day," she says,
meaningfully.

What I'm leaving behind, in the United States, are the Republican
and Democratic primaries, newly under way. Marco Rubio still harbors some hope. Someone on the Internet has photoshopped Donald
Trump's lips where his eyes should be (he turns out to look exactly the
same: full of contempt). In my heavily Latino neighborhood in San
Francisco, the Trump piñatas are proliferating. This is before President
Obama visits Cuba, before the bombing in Belgium. It's right about
when the Supreme Court, minus Justice Scalia, has begun to hear the
Texas abortion case; Nancy Reagan has just passed away, at age ninety-
four; and in theaters, *Zootopia,* a movie starring animals and about racism, has just opened.

Here in Vietnam, the enormous turtle that used to live in Hanoi's

Hoan Kiem Lake—Great-Grandfather Turtle, he's called, an unknown number of years old—has recently died. The *New York Times* headline about it: "Vietnam's Sacred Turtle Dies at an Awkward, Some Say Ominous, Time." There's been an ongoing territorial dispute with China, which is laying claim to some islands in the South China Sea.

It's hard not to feel weird about stuff—why things are, and how they got to be the way they are. It's hard not to wonder what's relevant. Since the Vietnam War ended (in Vietnam, they call it the "American War") forty years ago, Americans don't trust their government the way numbers indicate we used to. In 1958, when the American National Election Study first polled Americans about their trust in the government, 73 percent said they could trust the government "just about always" or "most of the time." After the war, and after Watergate, that number fell to 36 percent. This past fall, that percentage fell to 19 percent—the lowest of all time. And there's a sizable contingent of the country that doesn't even care much about what's true.

"People eat before they learn," says restaurateur Steven Pham elsewhere in this magazine. It's a sentence I'm carrying around, reprising in my head. What I know about pho came first by way of my Southern California upbringing. My family's takeout food of choice was pho from a local shop called Saigon Noodle House. Eating pho as a teenager made me think I knew something about Vietnam. I also grew up with bubble tea and *niu rou mian* and soup dumplings, which made me think I knew something about Taiwan. Eating tacos made me think I knew something about Mexico. (I knew better than to think pizza taught me much about Italy, but hold that thought.) Say you're a person who knows Chinese food from Panda Express, or whatever form Panda Express takes in your vicinity. Hopefully at some point down the line, you learn that fortune cookies don't come from China. You learn that General Tso was a person, but Chinese people in China don't cherish his chicken.

At the time of this writing, "pho" is a term that, in the U.S., is almost as frequently Googled as "ramen"—they're neck and neck. In the D.C. metro area, the number of pho restaurants increased by almost a hundred in the past decade (from about 91 in 2003/2004 to about 195 in 2014/2015); Los Angeles shows a similar increase in roughly the same years. And Albuquerque, a city with zero pho restaurants in 2003/2004, had eight in 2014/2015.

In America, pho is at an interesting point: it's becoming a food that's familiar to us—that requires no explanation. Think about pizza, about ramen, about tacos—how these things that were once foreign no longer need to be defined. Pho is even becoming gourmandified. (Hand to God, while writing this, I received a PR e-mail about pastrami pho: "The flavorful pastrami provides a salty brininess to the pho that marries well with the other beef parts and flavorful broth. The end result is something that combines the best flavors of a crave-worthy deli pastrami sandwich and a warming Vietnamese pho.") But even when things get more coverage, we don't necessarily gain more knowledge.

I'd eaten pho in Los Angeles, in the San Gabriel Valley, in San Jose, in San Francisco. And now I would be eating pho in Vietnam—first in Hanoi, then Saigon. I would be learning about the pho that came before the pho I knew, and about the culture of pho in Vietnam: who eats it and who makes it. I wanted to encounter the real thing; I wanted to correct my ignorance.

I am not, by the way, Vietnamese. It seems relevant to mention that. But I don't *not* look Vietnamese. In Vietnam, people routinely speak to me in Vietnamese, and persist even when I stare stupidly back at them. At the airport in Hanoi, I notice that my last name, Khong, is everywhere. A sign says: khong duoc vao. Another one says: khong co gi de khai bao. *Khong* turns out to mean "no." *Do not enter. Nothing to declare.* I felt stealthy, though never for long.

The sky in Hanoi doesn't seem to exist: it's one color, like a sheet of off-white printer paper. My boyfriend texts me to say that there's a solar eclipse, but I can't really deduce where the sun is, or clouds, or normal sky things. The mugginess feels like steam from a shower. Women in conical rice-paddy hats carry jicama and kohlrabi on poles on their shoulders and wear wicker backpacks full of flowers or mini pineapples.

"The visitor to North Vietnam goes up and down on waves of emotion," wrote a *New York Times* correspondent in Hanoi in 1972, three years before the war officially ended. "He is gripped by the excitement of the unknown: the streets, the posters, most of all the extraordinary people of this most isolated place." (In that same article, he also writes, "Why were we doing these things? When historians looked back on this American war in the future, would it not seem as mad in its motivation as the religious wars of the 17th century seem to us now?")

Hanoi is on the western bank of the Red River, which flows from the Yunnan Province in southern China to the Gulf of Tonkin. During the French colonial period, which spanned from 1883 to 1945, the city and its surrounding region were referred to as Tonkin. It was an important city when the French were in charge, because Hanoi is in the top part of Vietnam's stretched-out S shape, and the French were interested in expanding their rule to China in the north.

My first pho in Vietnam is at Pho Gia Truyen, at 49 Bat Dan. It comes highly and multiply recommended. I arrive at seven in the morning and there's already a line into the street, which catches me off guard. Later I learn that the line is left over from *thoi bao cap,* Vietnam's subsidy period, which happened from 1954 to 1986. Everything from food to fabric was rationed then, and people used coupons out of a booklet to get their rice, their necessities, the little beef that was available. Even now, you don't just order and sit down to wait for your food. You watch as your meat is being weighed in order to make sure you aren't being cheated.

A woman slices the beef, and a man ladles the stock and showers each serving with green herbs. There are three pho options on offer: *tai,* rare beef; tai *nam,* rare beef and cooked flank; and *chin,* well-done beef; plus *trung ga,* egg yolk, for 5,000 dong per yolk, and *quay,* also known as *you tiao,* the Chinese doughnuts that are dipped into soymilk or congee. My tai nam costs 50,000 dong, about two dollars.

There are condiments on the table: vinegar with garlic slices; a thin, vinegary red chili sauce; little red bird's eye chilies that you aren't supposed to eat, really (later I'll learn that you're supposed to just drop them into your soup to infuse it with spice; Vietnamese food isn't about searing hotness). No basil, no jalapeños, no bean sprouts. In the bowl, smaller than what I'm used to, scallions float on the surface—the whites in longer ribbons, and the greens chopped—along with flecks of cilantro.

It's the noodles that are the main surprise: they're *soft.* Prior to this, I've only ever encountered dried or semifresh noodles in pho—noodles with more chew. As it turns out, these are the noodles I will have over and over again on this trip—silky, made-the-same-day noodles. At Chau Long Market, just outside of Hanoi's Old Quarter, noodles are brought in from the villages that specialize in them, wrapped in lotus leaves (or, less romantically, plastic-lined baskets). I learn that the banh pho noodles are at their most salable for only three hours, at which point they'll turn slightly sour, and vendors have to discount them.

The broth is more delicate than any I've ever encountered: gently spiced and onion-redolent, almost as clear as water. And though it's my first time ever having this food, it's as familiar and comforting as chicken noodle soup. I pick up the bowl to drink every last drop.

Over the next few days, I'll learn: how to cross the street (walk slowly into traffic without fear); where to put my purse while eating on the tiny plastic stools (folded between my lap and stomach); and that yogurt in coffee is unexpectedly addictive (try it!). I'll learn that roosters in Hanoi have abandoned circadian rhythms—they crow at all hours—and cats love to fight. I'll write in my notebook "People really love puffy jackets!"

And I'll find that pho is *everywhere*. It's on streets and it's in restaurants and it's in restaurants that spill onto the street. For 275,000 dong, you can get a bowl of "Hanoian pho: beef, chicken with garnishes" at the swanky Sofitel Legend Metropole hotel; outside, pho runs about 30,000 dong. Would-be vendors set up shop on the street: stools, tables, stools as tables, and a large, immovable-until-empty pot. I saw before my trip that my friend Dennis, who'd also recently visited Vietnam, had posted on Facebook: "After eating #pho non stop for 2 weeks I finally found my ideal bowl. At 4pm everyday on a street corner in the old quarter of #Hanoi, these ladies bring out a stock pot filled with clear, savory, delicate broth from an apartment across the street and ladle it over fresh rice noodles, adding a few slivers of brisket and tendon and some fresh herbs to create the cleanest and most elegant pho I ever tasted. It only lasts for one hour a day before they run out." Dutifully, I got the coordinates. But when I checked the intersection on multiple days, Dennis's pho vendors never materialized. Maybe it was just their side hustle. Maybe they got what they needed, and moved along.

Disappearing and reappearing is kind of the deal with pho. What you see on the streets when you visit Hanoi is only a couple decades old: street food was eliminated during the period of planned economy, and picked up where it left off when the government decided to return to a free market. In the late eighties, street pho stalls were some of the first small businesses to reemerge.

Today, again, street food is under some scrutiny. I asked Mark Lowerson, an Australian expat who hosts street-food tours for tourists visiting Hanoi, about it over e-mail: "The pavement police crack down on all kinds of activity related to the use of pavements and roadsides. They are trying to control (among other things) how businesses manage customer motorbike parking, the roving vendors who sell fresh produce and other goods and also the street-food eateries that commonly seat patrons on plastic stools on the pavements. It's very much like a game of cat and mouse. The police round the corner shouting through loudspeakers, everyone scatters—roving vendors disappear up alleyways, pavement furniture gets quickly shifted, people run to their motorbikes to move them—and then, five minutes later, everything goes back to 'normal' again." Some people have moved their operations partly inside, so as to avoid official gaze: they'll set up stools and tables in their low-ceilinged living spaces. (For lunch one day I ate fish noodle soup in what I think was a family's living room, hung with framed family photographs; there were fake flowers in vases on the mantel.)

That street pho ever disappeared is hard to wrap my mind around, because the street seems to be the place for innumerable activities. I watch people getting haircuts and manicures in the street. People crouched over little fires, burning paper money—counterfeit Ben Franklins—for their ancestors to use in the afterlife. In the afternoons, men washing their motorcycles using lots of soap. Men on their motorcycles asking do you want a ride. Men playing checkers. Women winnowing little bulbs of garlic, and the skins flying everywhere. Fringed pedicabs carrying older white people slowly being pedaled around. Old women in ricepaddy hats offering doughnuts, insistently, to tourists like me.

"The most important part of making the broth is balancing with the fish sauce and the sugar," Phan Thi Duyen tells me. She works as a chef at the Hanoi Cooking Centre, a cooking school that offers courses in traditional Vietnamese cooking. She's thirty-three, from a small village in Hai Duong Province, but left home in her teens to cook in Hanoi. Her first job was at a pho shop, which was also where she ate pho for the first time, in 1999.

It was a breakfast restaurant, as most pho restaurants were seventeen years ago. That's no longer the case—you can find pho around the clock now. And pho was expensive, Duyen says, for poor families. Pho was "only for the people who were really rich, or who worked in offices, important people. Not normal people." Pho was also food for the sick: "If children or old people are sick, it's easier for eating, easier than rice." She tells me that a family might buy one serving of pho and, to defray costs, split it among family members, mixed with rice.

Pho is something she never makes at home, because the ingredients are too expensive to cook in a small batch. Back in her hometown, they're almost unavailable. "When I come back to my country I cannot make it. I cannot get the beef bones, because one farmer makes one beef and sells it for the whole village," she says. "For example, my family has five daughters and two sons. Even sometimes my mom gets the beef, but she always gets 300 grams of meat or 400 grams of meat and stir-fries it with vegetables. But not every day, because the beef is very expensive. And in the countryside, the cow is an important animal for working. Now we're starting to learn how to eat beef. In the past we didn't know.

"Vietnamese don't have recipes. When you want to learn something traditional, you have to have good tongue, and to taste it, and you really love the food, and you can balance by yourself. You can get the experience for yourself," she says. "In Vietnam, you understand, we always make everything with the feeling, more than recipe."

Something else I should understand, Duyen insists, is that there are two types of pho in Hanoi. There is a traditional pho, with a darker, not clarified broth; and a less traditional, but very popular, broth that is lighter on spices—especially on the black cardamom, which Duyen particularly dislikes. The first pho I had, at 49 Bat Dan, was one of the dark ones, she explains.

To be honest, all the pho in Hanoi seem pretty light to me. All are lighter, at least, than anything I've ever had. Pho Cuong is another shop that serves a dark broth, according to Duyen. But when I inspect my pho there, the broth looks clear and light. "This bowl is heavy on the black cardamom," I write in my notebook. Then I add a question mark. "But maybe you are full of shit!" I amend.

I watch a little kid, maybe five, eating noodles in plain broth with a single egg in it, and wonder if that's the Vietnamese equivalent of pasta with butter—a plain food that picky kids will eat. Blowing my nose, I lock eyes with a guy who is also blowing his nose.

What I've read is that the pho here in Hanoi is the closest to the very first pho that ever existed (pho might have traveled to Hanoi from nearby Nam Dinh), but it doesn't strike me as particularly pho-like: its thorough softness and mildness. The pho I'm used to lingers in my clothes and hair, but pho in Hanoi doesn't do that. The spicing is reserved. The broth is gently sweet. It feels like convalescent food, in a good way. I realize this is like saying your grandpa has your nose—it was his nose first. At first I'm afraid to add things to my bowls, but I learn by example to add garlic and a splash of the vinegar it's been steeped in for spikiness.

What comes to mind is a piece published in 2014, in which an American writer, writing for an American food magazine, describing what he sees in American pho shops, declares the correct way to use sriracha in pho: "More times than I can count, I've watched people squirt that sriracha all over their beautiful pho. No! Wrong wrong wrong! No!" The comments are varied: there's bemusement ("I put sriracha in my pho. I love it. You mad?"; vehement agreement ("Yes yes yes a million times yes!"); and utter annoyance ("As a Vietnamese person, I'm surprised I could comprehend words with my eyes rolling as much as they were. The 'right' way, ugh.") In Vietnam, I'm not sure that it would even merit discussion.

One morning I notice a bustling street setup that looks so appealing I have to stop for my second bowl of breakfast pho. Almost all the stools are taken: women sitting with squeezed purses on their laps, men man-spreading to get low and close to their noodles. The only seat available is a purple-blue stool across from a young woman. We look like we could be friends meeting for a meal, except we can't actually communicate with each other. I watch as she puts a few spoonfuls of the vinegary red chili sauce directly into her bowl. It's enough to make her broth change color. It's a chilly morning; it's perfect.

In Saigon, there is blue sky—that's the first noticeable thing. The second thing is that it's a full twenty degrees warmer. Where temperatures in Hanoi hovered in the mid-50s and 60s, here in Saigon it's in the

70s through 90s. Out the window, in the cab navigating Saigon's wide, filled streets on the way to the hotel, I notice a lady in an orange jumpsuit and red lipstick with a cage of puppies on the back of her scooter. Something I will notice a lot of in Saigon—in contrast to Hanoi's puffer jackets—are matching patterned shirt-and-pant sets.

More differences between the cities become immediately apparent. First of all, the stools! It turns out those tiny plastic stools in Hanoi that have grown on (under) me are less ubiquitous—stools here come in a wider range of heights. And actually everything comes in a wider range—more establishments to choose from, more variation in pho from restaurant to restaurant, more options for sit-down restaurants—though there seems, actually, to be less in-the-street pop-up pho, and more partial-street situations: open restaurants with alfresco seating. Saigon's broths are brown and sweet and don't seem as virtuous or healthful, with the exception of bean sprouts (blanched) and herbs, which are abundant: not just basil, but sawtooth herb, rice paddy herb, and spicy mint, which are supposed to have various life-giving properties (the sawtooth is for stamina and the basil is good for your sinuses). There are hunks of beef fat floating in one pho, and stewed purple onions and a dense sprinkling of black pepper at Ut Nhung, one of those partial-street restaurants.

The meat in Saigon is more varied; here there is tendon and tripe in addition to the less colorful cuts found in the North. In one soup, I found a mysterious tubular thing, almost like a soft, white, miniature banana—it turned out to be spinal cord. (It didn't taste like much.) As on tables in Hanoi, there was fish sauce, pickled garlic, and limes (which appeared regularly in shops aside from 49 Bat Dan, and had a yellower flesh and tasted somehow more savory than California limes), but also hoisin, sriracha-esque hot sauce, and Vietnamese *sate* sauce. You mix the three together in a condiment dish, and dip your meat into that. In Hanoi there are little red bird's-eye chilies to steep in your soup; in Saigon there is a profusion of sliced peppers in neon hues of green and yellow and orange and red. I'm told those chili peppers first came from Africa, and appeared on pho tables about ten years ago.

More than anywhere else I've visited on this trip, Pho Phu Huong, on Saigon's eastern edge, looks a lot like the California pho restaurants I knew growing up: a spacious, newish-looking space with tables and chairs in many different configurations—tables for two, tables for eight. Phung Tran is the restaurant's proprietor and cook. She wears red lipstick and little glasses; she is stunning at sixty-two. When I ask about her soup, she says the focus of a good broth is its meat and bones— she used to be a beef butcher—not the soup's spices. She says shops use more spices in a broth if they use fewer bones, and the spices make you feel like the pho is good. She simmers her stock for ten hours. She still finishes her soup with *sa sung,* dried peanut worm, where a lot of other places no longer do. She also talks a lot about balance, about how various factors can affect your soup, like outside temperature and the quality of the meat, and how the quality of the broth is dependent on the experience of the maker.

She learned to make pho from the pho makers to whom she would sell her beef, and from her mother-in-law, who started a pho restaurant around 1975. Then came unification, the subsidy period extending to the South, and "pilotless pho." When I meet Trinh Quang Dung, author of an article titled "100 Years of Pho," he explains the phrase to me: "During wartime, the American bombers in Hanoi used automatic airplanes, airplanes with no pilots. And at that time in Hanoi, the pho had no pilot. The pho had no meat—some spices, but no meat. Because during the war the meat was very expensive." There was no incentive to do a good job, he explains, and there wasn't enough food for everyone.

Mrs. Tran's restaurant looked new because it *was* new. They moved on from their more basic previous rented space, because they were doing a brisk business.

As it turns out, pho is always a product of place and history, and of people. In America, pho is changing before our eyes, and it makes sense. Pho is a food that's been *defined* by adaptation, a food that has always been shifting, because it has *had* to—it's had to react to outside influences, to the Vietnamese government's various five-year plans.

There are purists, mostly outside of Vietnam, who will insist that pho has to be the way that they have always known it to be. I get it, and I don't. Not only because the products of change can be so much better than their forebears, but because that's not what pho has been about.

Mr. Dung, who's also a research scientist for the Vietnam Academy of Science and Technology, a solar-energy specialist, and a teapot collector, divides pho into two types: "handmade" and "industrial." Industrial pho is all pho made after 1990, with machine-made noodles and gas stoves and modern conveniences—but he described this without any particular animosity. He seemed partial to the traditional pho, but said, matter-of-factly, that it no longer existed; he spoke wistfully about the old Hanoi ("small and romantic"), but lives in Saigon now. What seemed to disappoint him was that people didn't really know the history of pho any longer—year after year, for Tet, he publishes his "100 Years of Pho" in the Vietnamese magazine *Khoa Hoc Pho Thong*. He updates it with details that he learns.

I think, for the most part, we understand—or are starting to understand—all the ways in which we have been wrong about things. We understand, now, that the Vietnam War, for Vietnam, had less to do with communism and more to do with independence—with Vietnam's getting out from under French rule and Chinese rule and finally being its own country.

We understand that there is such a thing as well-meaning, casually racist essentialism. We understand why it's kind of offensive that, as recently as 2010, Mimi Sheraton wrote, incorrectly, in the *Smithsonian* magazine, "Pho bo is an unintended legacy of the French, who occupied Vietnam from 1858 to 1954 and who indeed cooked pot au feu, a soup-based combination of vegetables and beef, a meat barely known in Vietnam in those days and, to this day, neither as abundant nor as good as the native pork . . . But just as North American slaves took the leavings of kitchens to create what we now celebrate as soul food, so the Vietnamese salvaged leftovers from French kitchens and discovered that slow cooking was the best way to extract the most flavor and nourishment from them. They adopted the French word *feu*, just as they took the name of the French sandwich loaf, *pain de mie*, for *banh mi*, a baguette they fill with various greens, spices, herbs, sauces, pork and meatballs." That pot au feu theory is still repeated, though it's untrue. The historian Erica J. Peters, in her paper "Defusing Pho," argues that the French have incorrectly gotten credit for pho: "Pho now stands for a particular colonial relationship between the French and the Vietnamese, an idea that the French brought modern ingenuity to a traditionalist Vietnam."

Most of us now know how pho is pronounced ("fuh?" with a question mark at the end). It's hard to pin down exactly when the correct pronunciation became widespread—people had already been saying it correctly in the seventies, of course, but plenty of others were also saying it incorrectly, in a variety of ways. The *New West*, in 1978, said it was pronounced "foo." The *New York Times* had it a bunch of different ways: in 1995, a *Times* article instructed readers to pronounce pho "FOE." And in 2002, Florence Fabricant wrote, "At open-air storefronts people perch on tiny plastic stools to down steaming, restorative bowls of the ubiquitous noodle soup, pho (pronounced feh)." Other magazines were across the board: A 2004 issue of *Orange Coast* magazine says, "pho (roughly pronounced 'fuh-uh')," though they got it right in a 2008 issue; a 2011 issue of *San Diego* says "pho (pronounced 'fun')." And cookbooks and books, like the *Complete Idiot's Guide to Cooking Chicken,* published in 1999, instructed complete idiots to pronounce pho "far."

Just as straitlaced Northern pho says something about the North, and Southern pho says something about the South, and pho says something about Vietnam, American pho says something about us. In the U.S., those once-foreign things—pizza, tacos, ramen—have become both fast food (think Pizza Hut, Taco Bell, instant ramen) and fetishized (think artisanal and upscale all of the above). The way whole cultures' foods turn into convenience foods and gourmet dishes in our country says something—for better, for worse—about *us*.

Pouring me a tiny cup of tea from a pig-decorated teapot, one of over two hundred in his collection, Mr. Dung tells me: "Pho is the only meal we call 'the meal for all seasons.' Spring, summer, autumn, all time you can eat pho, morning, lunch, dinner, and supper.

"Pho is also the only meal with no classes. It makes no difference: the poor people eat pho, the rich people eat pho. Intellectual people eat pho. Not-educated people eat pho, too. But some places are only for high class, some places are only for poor people. Third, pho is the only meal that artists are interested in. They have poetry for pho, they have songs for pho, pictures for pho. Now they have films for pho, and they also have some drama, too. No meal has this character!"

Can a S.C. Barbecue Family Rise Above Their Father's History of Racism?

By Kathleen Purvis

From the *Charlotte Observer*

After years as the *Observer* food editor, Kathleen Purvis knows a thing or two about the southern barbecue tradition. There's the meat on the plate, of course, but there's also the history behind each restaurant—and what happens when a complicated history gets in the way of the 'cue's success.

I did something recently that I haven't done in a quarter-century as a Carolinas food writer.

I drove to West Columbia and ate lunch at Maurice's Piggie Park, the classic barbecue restaurant.

I pulled up to the building made to look like a farmhouse and parked in the lot scattered with woodpiles. I walked in past American and S.C. flags at the door, grabbed a plate and hit a buffet packed with Southern country-cooking staples: Fried chicken, squash casserole, banana pudding studded with vanilla wafers. And barbecue, of course: shredded pork glistening with khaki-yellow mustard sauce and tangy barbecue hash, all true to South Carolina's Midlands tradition.

In some quarters, though, I didn't just eat lunch. I committed a political act.

Lloyd Bessinger, who runs the place now, wishes that weren't so: "We want to serve great barbecue and be known for that. Not for politics."

But that's difficult. Lloyd's father, the late Maurice Bessinger, once made politics a part of every plate of barbecue he sold.

The markers of Bessinger's segregationist thinking are gone now: The pro-slavery tracts he offered at the front door, some claiming African slaves "blessed the Lord" for slavery. The massive Confederate flag that once flapped over the parking lot. The smaller flags on bottles of his sauce.

Bessinger died in 2014. But the barbecue legacy he left behind is still stained. That raises a question: Do a man's actions forever taint the cooking of his descendants?

Astride a White Horse

The late Maurice Bessinger occupies an outsized spot in S.C. lore. A theatrical character who loved attention, he ran for governor in 1974 with campaign literature that showed him in a white suit astride a white horse.

It wasn't just that he posted signs at his restaurants saying black customers weren't welcome. It wasn't just that he fought and lost a case before the Supreme Court in 1964, Newman v. Piggie Park Enterprises, over his refusal to serve black customers. A lot of businesses in the 1960s tried to resist integration, in ways big and small. No, what made Bessinger so notorious was how far and how long he carried the fight.

When the Confederate flag was removed from the S.C. Capitol and placed elsewhere on the State House grounds in 2000, Bessinger raised Confederate flags over his restaurants, including one at the main location that was as big as a king-size bedsheet. He didn't just display white-supremacist literature and audiotapes by the front door. He'd offer discounts on your food if you bought any.

After expanding his business nationally in the 1990s, selling frozen barbecue and bottles of his mustard-based sauce, he had the largest commercial barbecue operation in the country. Then he began putting the Confederate flag on his labels.

That's when the world balked.

"I Was So Angry"

The State newspaper in Columbia, in a story in 2000, quoted the tracts he sold in the restaurant, including that slavery was a positive thing for Africans. National customers—including Walmart and the U.S. military—removed his products from their shelves. Bessinger later claimed it cost him $20 million.

The Rev. Calvin Griffin has been the rector of the historically black St. Luke's Episcopal Church for 22 years. When he first arrived in Columbia in 1994, he bought a Piggie Park sandwich. He didn't like it, because he's from North Carolina–he doesn't like mustard-based barbecue. But a short time later, he saw an article about Bessinger's policies. And he did something he calls unprecedented in his life as a priest: He asked his parishioners not to do business with the Piggie Park. "I'd never done anything like that," he says today. "But I was so angry about what I had read."

One of Griffin's parishioners is Kay Patterson. Now 85, Patterson served in the S.C. legislature for more than 30 years, first as a representative and then as a senator. Patterson is known as a fighter for civil rights, who sponsored the first bill to remove the Confederate flag from the State House in 1983. "A long, long time ago, everyone went to Maurice's for barbecue, back in the 1950s and '60s," he says. But while a lot of businesses had racist policies in those days, Bessinger's were worse– he made more of a point of it, Patterson says.

"Blacks just stopped participating, period," he says. "Even today, I still don't go there. The memory of the way Maurice was and that literature he had at the front, trying to justify slavery and say how good it was? Who the hell wants to hear that?"

The changes at the restaurant today aren't enough for him, he says. And he knows other black people in Columbia who feel the same. "They remember the battle of the flag, and they knew who was trying to keep it up. He was proud of that. He was proud. I said, 'the hell with him.' No reason I could go back. I don't care how good it gets. I don't go there."

"You'd Feel Weird Going in There"

Carolinas barbecue, with its focus on pork and low/slow cooking over wood, has captured the imagination of people all over the country. The names of well-known Carolinas restaurants have became part of the national roster for people who arrange their travel around barbecue pilgrimages. But Maurice's Piggie Park rarely turns up on the lists of important Southern barbecue experiences.

Several things should have made it interesting for serious barbecue fans: The mustard-based barbecue sauce that defines South Carolina is believed by some culinary historians to have been started by Maurice

Bessinger's father, Joe, who had a small diner in Holly Hill, S.C., in the 1940s. And even with 12 locations in and around Columbia, the restaurant still cooks completely over wood, with no electricity or gas. That has become so rare that it's usually enough to attract attention.

If you ask writers who cover the national barbecue scene, though, they say their policy on the Piggie Park has been simple: They didn't go. "There was definitely a split of people who did not go to Maurice's because they didn't want to be associated with his political views," says Robert Moss, a Charleston-based writer who covers barbecue history. "You'd feel weird going in there."

Daniel Vaughn, barbecue editor of *Texas Monthly* magazine, travels the country tracking barbecue. He's made repeated visits to the Carolinas, for places like the Skylight Inn, Lexington Barbecue and Bridge's Barbecue Lodge, but he's never gone to the Piggie Park. He hasn't heard many people recommend it, he says. And that could be less about the quality of the barbecue and more about the discomfort people have about the restaurant's history. "I cover a lot of places, I talk to a lot of pitmasters. I myself wonder, if I heap praise upon someone and it turns out they're this extreme racist or bigot, how does that affect the way I cover it in the future?"

What About Now?

There was a time when I was a fan of Maurice Bessinger's barbecue. When I came to Charlotte to work for *The Observer* in 1985, I discovered frozen packages of Bessinger's mustard-sauced pork at supermarkets. It wasn't the Parker's barbecue I had loved when I was a kid in Wilson, but it was handy for a quick dinner when I was working nights. The mustard sauce was a little different to my Eastern N.C.–formed palate, but it was good chopped 'cue.

Then, in the 1990s, I became a food writer and started to cover the Carolinas' barbecue culture. When I learned about Bessinger's history, I stopped buying his products. I followed a simple policy on the Piggie Park: I didn't go there. Ever. When readers asked my opinion on the restaurant's food, I would explain that my rule was the same as so many others': We all vote with our dollars, and I couldn't vote for that.

There are a lot of litmus tests in popular culture. After Woody Allen and Bill Cosby were accused of sexual abuse, it became more difficult for some of us to watch their work. The Piggie Park felt like that to me. I couldn't send readers to a restaurant where I wasn't comfortable myself.

But earlier this year, two years after Maurice Bessinger's death, I was at a gathering of Southern food writers when someone raised the question: The Piggie Park has changed. The racist symbolism has been removed. Does that mean it's OK to go?

So I made a trip to Columbia to see for myself. The Piggie Park I found was a different place than it used to be. The atmosphere was friendly and down-home, a little like a Cracker Barrel. The barbecue, lightly smoky and moist, was a good example of the South Carolina style.

Lloyd Bessinger now runs the business with his brother, Paul, and their sister, Debbie Bennett. The changes started when Maurice Bessinger retired in 2010, says Lloyd Bessinger. When his father turned the business over to his children, he let them run it as they saw fit. One of their first moves was to replace the Confederate flag with the American one. Eventually, other changes followed, including removing the flag from the label on the sauces and removing the white-supremacist literature.

Like his brother and sister, Lloyd has worked at the restaurants since he was a kid. When his father lost his national accounts over the flag, he says, it was a terrible time. They had to lay people off. The business will probably never return to the level of success it once enjoyed, he says. But the changes were something the whole family wanted. "Dad was passionate about politics. He was kind of overboard about it. We just want to serve good barbecue."

Debbie Bennett's daughter, Carolyn Shvetz, 27, is a graphic designer, and she has taken on the world of social media, adding Twitter and Facebook feeds and a blog that emphasizes their family-friendly, all-are-welcome message. "We're a local business, and people like to support local," she says.

The Bessingers still resist talking about the history, though. In an interview, Lloyd Bessinger spoke softly, smiling frequently. He made it clear that he's not interested in talking about his father, his politics, or the past. His only interest, he says, is in making great barbecue.

"We're not trying to hide anything," he says. "We're trying to move forward. We have children and grandchildren we want to work here."

He will say, though, that he was against the messages that his father's policies sent. He wanted those messages removed. "I disagreed with the message," he says today. "We want to get beyond that."

'Cue as "Unifying Thing"

Some people see the changes the Bessinger family has made and wonder: Is it only for profit? And does it matter if it is?

Rien Fertel wrote about the Bessingers' history, including the family's claim as the origin of mustard barbecue sauce, in his recent book, "The One True Barbecue: Fire, Smoke, and the Pitmasters Who Cook the Whole Hog." He thinks their story may be even more interesting now. "They're actually rehabilitating their history," he says. "They're humanizing the restaurant. They're making it a better place by putting a better face on it. That's a beautiful thing."

Others value the Bessinger story as a reminder of how complex barbecue history is, particularly in the Carolinas, where the origins are both white and black and many restaurants were once segregated. "It's such an interesting, historic place," says food writer Moss. "And if you just ignore it, you're ignoring the very complicated history barbecue has. The question becomes, do you sweep all that to the past and not talk about it?" Going to the restaurant while acknowledging the history may be a part of reconciling that history, he says.

Rodney Scott is an African-American barbecuer whose restaurant in Hemingway, S.C., has brought him national fame. He's building a new restaurant in Charleston that he hopes to open by the end of the year. He remembers going to the Piggie Park in the 1990s, before the Confederate flag flapped over the parking lot, but didn't pay attention after that. He doesn't dwell on segregation history, he says. "To each his own. Everybody has a right to be wrong."

Like the Bessingers, he'd like to see barbecue shake off that part of its past. "I like to use barbecue as a unifying thing. It all just brings us together."

If any of writer Daniel Vaughn's barbecue trips bring him close to Columbia, he says he would go. "I doubt any of us, even writers, would want anyone judging us based on comments our grandfather might have made."

The Art of Boucherie

By Jennifer Kornegay

From *The Local Palate*

Southern food writer Jennifer Kornegay (among other things she's a columnist for *Alabama Living* magazine and managing editor of the Montgomery, Alabama, visitors guide) geeks out over local food traditions—like this gathering of Nashville chefs to experience a classic Cajun hog butchering and feast.

A heavy wooden table stands in a field ringed by tree-covered hills. Pale green trails are visible in the dew-damp grass, tramped by a small crowd milling around and chatting in whispers. Rowdy chickens cluck and cackle, ignoring the hush, while chirping birds and humming bugs join the chorus of spring morning sounds at the century-old Wedge Oak Farm in Lebanon, Tennessee.

Most of the group is from nearby Nashville: chefs, cooks, and managers from lauded Music City restaurants like the Catbird Seat and Peg Leg Porker, along with other folks just into food, and farm owner Karen Overton. They are here to take part in a boucherie, a south Louisiana Acadian tradition of friends and neighbors coming together to slaughter, butcher, and process a hog.

Back at the table, a tall, lanky man in an apron and worn trucker hat methodically pulls blades from a holster on his hip, giving each a once-over and a wipe with a cloth before slipping it back in. Toby Rodriguez, chef, artist, and founder of Lâche Pas Boucherie et Cuisine—a Lafayette, Louisiana-based team that specializes in Cajun culinary heritage—is intent on the task at hand.

While Rodriguez works, Lâche Pas chef Chris McIntyre waves a wand of smoldering, smoking sage around him like an orchestra conductor, a rite both symbolic and sensible, meant to consecrate the occasion and cleanse the table surface of bacteria.

A little after 8 a.m., Lâche Pas members and a few men from the group of attendees and chefs lift the top of the table and carry it to a metal trailer in deep shade on the field's edge. Rodriguez walks slowly behind them, his steps weighted with purpose. He disappears inside, while Overton's mustached father says a short prayer, asking that all go well before offering thanks for the day's beauty and the coming sacrifice.

Rodriguez exits the trailer and places a bowl of food just outside its doors to draw the 300-pound Yorkshire hog inside into the open. In one fluid motion, he places the muzzle of a captive bolt gun against the animal's head, and a muffled "thwack" breaks the silence. The stunned hog drops to its knees. Rodriguez' quick, forceful thrust of a 16-inch scimitar blade slices the hog's jugular and pierces the heart, finishing in seconds what the bolt to the brain started.

A few reflex kicks bang the side of the trailer, but the hog is gone. Rivulets of blood stream down the trailer's lowered ramp; Lâche Pas chef Chanel Gaude catches as much of the still-hot liquid as she can in a large bowl and whisks it furiously with salt to halt coagulation. The hog is slid onto the tabletop, and the same men lift it and carefully carry the hog back to the table base, mute and respectful, like pallbearers at a funeral.

It's bloody work, but not brutal. The initial shot ensures the hog isn't aware of anything. Preventing fear and pain in the moments before and during its death is of the utmost importance to Rodriguez and his crew. It's why he chose to work with Overton, known for her ethical treatment of the animals—hogs, ducks, geese, and chickens—she raises. "This hog was happy up until the instant he died," she says. At Rodriguez' request, in the weeks leading up to the boucherie, she repeatedly placed an empty revolver on the hog's temple and pulled the trigger. "It helped him get used to the feel of cold steel and the sound," she says, "and I hope it meant he was not afraid in the seconds before it happened."

Some in the group are a bit shaken, and that's okay with Rodriguez.

The reverence he demands from boucherie attendees during the harvest—be on time, be quiet—makes it clear he'd be offended by anyone who took it lightly.

Cajun Crusader

Rodriguez has done boucheries in his hometown of Grand Coteau, Louisiana, for the last several years. He decided to take the show on the road and give folks far from Cajun country the opportunity to experience one. The two-year nationwide tour kicked off at Wedge Oak in May. Other stops have included St. Louis, Boulder, Santa Cruz, Seattle, and more with Atlanta and Birmingham still ahead and even Cuba on the calendar for 2017.

At each stop, local chefs and others in the food industry sign up to help butcher and cook the hog. The public is invited to buy tickets and attend as spectators and diners (although Rodriguez will put anybody who wants to help to work).

The two-day event starts solemnly with the harvest of the hog and ends with a festive, pork-centric feast paired with wines and other libations. In between, the hog is butchered and broken down, and 90 percent of the animal ends up on the multi-course menu guests enjoy at dinner the second night.

The mission behind these gatherings, fueled by bourbon, boudin, and beer, goes beyond good food and fellowship; it's Rodriguez' goal that folks leave with a greater respect for the farmers who raise what we eat, and the humble animals who are what we eat, as well as the knowledge that we can take control of our food systems. "Our species does not have to depend on industry to feed itself," Rodriguez says, his words quick, his accent, a mash-up of Cajun and Southern drawl, rounding his vowels and softening consonants. He spreads his arms wide. "This does not belong in a plant. We've lost our emotional connection to our food—that's why we're so wasteful. We need to get it back."

Like a Cajun crusader, he's committed to showing people how and why a return to roots is crucial, and he knows chefs can be influential ambassadors. "As the leaders in culinary communities, if they reconnect with food sources, then they'll spread the message farther," he says. He's passionate, but not preachy. Quick with a joke (often a dirty one), he puts people at ease with humor and talks common sense.

His idea that we should care about where our food comes from is not new. But getting close to your food when it has a heartbeat can be unsettling. Despite growing up on a farm where he saw and participated in boucheries routinely starting at age 10, Rodriguez still gets anxious. "I'm killing another creature; it's intense. It's not anything that I enjoy," he says. He's made a ritual of checking and cleaning his knives in the minutes before the harvest. "I put a lot of attention into getting my tools ready; it gets me out of my head a bit."

But he's never as tense as he was seven years ago, when someone asked him to do a boucherie after being away from the tradition for a time. After studying art at the University of Louisiana at Lafayette and a stint in the Army, he worked as a contractor, specializing in home renovations and carpentry. "I hadn't done one in years, and I was nervous," he says. "But as soon as the pig was on the table, it felt natural. I felt removed from everything around me. It's the same feeling I get when drawing or sculpting."

Beyond Boudin

The slaughter evokes powerful emotions that put a sharp point on Rodriguez' message, but the butchering provides a practical education that lures chefs eager to learn new skills. "Proper butchering is such an integral thing for a chef," says Jacob Wittenberg, a cook at Butcher & Bee in Nashville. "Plus, I think if you eat meat, you should be willing to see the death. It gives you increased appreciation for your food."

As the group at Wedge Oak gathers around the hog for the first step, hair removal, the mood moves from somber to celebratory. "Pass this around—and remember, the best way to keep any hog hair from getting in is to keep a pair of lips around it," Rodriguez says as he takes a swig from a bottle of whiskey and hands it off. Some use dull-edged metal rings to scrape off the coarse hairs already loosened by a spray of scalding water. Braver souls gingerly wield knives. "Don't cut the skin!" Rodriguez says, while expertly using a straight razor.

Once the hog is smooth, Rodriguez turns teacher, flipping the hog on its back and splitting it open with one long slit. He works with surgical precision and explains every slice. He instructs others where to cut, how, and why. He holds up a hunk off the backbone. "Look how pretty that is! Brought to you by Karen and God," he says. The meat, along with most of the organs, goes into coolers marked with names of the dishes they'll be used in.

When the butchering is done, the local chefs head to assigned stations and get to work chopping mounds of garlic, onions, and peppers in a makeshift outdoor kitchen where they learn the art of Acadian cuisine—head cheese, fraisseurs, cracklins, ponce, backbone fricassee, boudin—from the Lâche Pas team; most of the recipes and techniques are from Rodriguez' family. Lâche Pas chef Barrett Dupuis gets busy grinding shoulder and rib meat for boudin. Some of it is for boudin noir, a version of the staple sausage that owes its color and rich flavor to the addition of the blood that Gaude collected. "Boudin is definitely my favorite to make and to eat," Dupuis says. "It's such a major player in Cajun cuisine."

McIntyre gathers ropes of Dupuis' boudin links and hangs them in Wolfgang von Sausage, the cold smoker designed and built by the Lâche Pas team. He continually feeds Wolfgang coals from Big Sexy, a Lâche Pas–designed furnace surrounded by a quivering wall of vicious heat that renders oak into ash-white embers in less than thirty minutes.

Preserving Culture

Sausage-making is only one of the crafts the team is keeping alive. Boucheries were originally a necessary form of meat preservation, but Lâche Pas boucheries are about preserving culture. "Boucheries have never really been documented," Rodriguez says. "We're chronicling these old techniques; it may be the first time some of them have been written down."

The culmination of the group's labor, the "Lundi Soir" dinner the second night, imprints the flavors of Acadiana in the guests' memories. White-clothed tables are lined up in the field a few yards from the kitchen, under stars and strings of glowing bare bulbs. Rodriguez welcomes diners who are already digging into the first course—boudin boulette, an orb of boudin and rice stuffed with creamy, salty camembert, crusted in cornmeal and fried, then glazed with cayenne-laced honey. "Thanks for being here, y'all. We're here to show you why the origins of what you eat matter and to share our story," he says. "Lâche Pas means 'don't give up—never' and that relates to Acadian culture, the way it has held on and thrived all these years." Five more courses follow, including a sweet and savory dessert incorporating cracklins and figs steeped in cane vinegar.

Rodriguez' favorite marked the middle of the meal. "I love the fraisseurs, also called butcher's stew," he says. The thick brown medley of various parts—heart, tongue, kidney, and tenderloin—slow simmered to melt the ingredients together, yet let them retain a hint of their distinction, is a fitting metaphor for a boucherie: It's a history lesson, it's a cooking class, it's art, it's a party, all imbued with a higher purpose. It's just as applicable to Lâche Pas' goals and methods—to revive tradition, celebrate life by honoring death, and use the community and camaraderie that surrounds food to create something meaningful.

Who Really Invented the Reuben?

By Elizabeth Weil

From *Saveur*

Based in Berkeley, California, journalist Elizabeth Weil grew up
with a family claim to fame—her Nebraska grandfather's claim
to have invented the Reuben sandwich. But once she made that
claim in print, the food historians swooped in—and the battle
was on.

We all need stories in order to live. A cliché, yes, but true for writers, and a few years ago I decided to tell my family's best one: My
grandfather invented the Reuben sandwich.

To be honest, I'd been avoiding the inevitable throughout my young
adult life, more focused on defining my future than examining my past.
Plus, I had sauerkraut issues, having grown up in suburban New England in the 1970s, pre-fermentation boom. But just 500 words, not a
big deal, no definitive claim. On the back page of the *New York Times
Magazine*, I laid out the basics: My great-grandfather started a chain
of hotels along the railroad southwest from Chicago. He trained each
of his four sons in a hospitality skill, sending my grandfather to École
Hôtelière in Lausanne, Switzerland where he learned to cook. In the
1920s, my great-grandfather's friends in Omaha, Nebraska, began
gathering to play poker at the Blackstone Hotel. Inevitably the men
grew hungry and called down to my grandfather, who oversaw the
hotel's kitchen, for snacks. For Reuben Kulakofsky, one of the players,
my grandfather created a sandwich: corned beef, Swiss cheese, sauerkraut, and Russian dressing, pressed hot on rye bread. Reuben loved it!

Everyone loved it! The sandwich went on all the hotel menus. In 1956, a waitress entered the Reuben in the National Restaurant Association's National Sandwich Idea Contest. It won! Now you can buy Reuben-flavored potato chips. God bless America!

As expected, upon publication, I did receive a few e-mails from the Kulakofsky clan, laying out their family's claim. The Kulakofskys have long contended that my grandfather, whose name was Bernard Schimmel, just delivered a deli platter to the poker players and that Reuben made his sandwich himself. The movie *Quiz Show*, directed by Robert Redford, did include the question "Who invented the Reuben sandwich?" and the answer: "Reuben Kay." (I know.) But this is a well-established controversy and basically an in-house fight. What's more, the Reuben is pressed. Did the poker room include a panini maker? Make of that what you will.

Then Andrew Smith, a food historian and the author of 24 books—including *Pure Ketchup: A History of America's National Condiment* and what at the time was the forthcoming *New York City: A Food Biography*—sent a grenade of a letter to the *New York Times* that my editors were kind enough to share with me:

"Elizabeth Weil's 'My Grandfather Invented the Reuben Sandwich. Right?' tells a nice story about her grandfather inventing the Reuben sandwich in Omaha, Nebraska. It is a nice story, but the correct answer to the question is, 'Wrong.'"

He forwarded the theory that the sandwich was not invented at my family's hotel in Omaha but instead by Arnold Reuben at his eponymous sandwich shop on East 58th Street, in New York City. In the early 20th century, celebrities often ate at Reuben's deli after the theater. "Around 1914," Smith wrote, Arnold Reuben "came up with the 'Annette Seelos Special' for one of Charlie Chaplin's leading ladies. It consisted of 'ham, cheese, turkey, coleslaw, and dressing.'" Smith also cited a 1941 cookbook, *Menu Making for Professionals in Quantity Cookery*, which included a Reuben made of "Rye Bread, Switzerland Cheese, Sliced Corn Beef, Sauerkraut, Dressing." The author of that cookbook lived in New York. Ergo, Smith reasoned (if you can call it that), "The Reuben sandwich is a New York invention; it's time to put the Nebraska origin myth to bed."

What? Is ham, cheese, turkey, coleslaw, and dressing a Reuben? I don't think so. Was coq au vin invented in Cambridge, Massachusetts, where Julia Child lived when she wrote *Mastering the Art of French Cooking*? It was not. Still, I'm conflict-avoidant, so I wrote Smith back, soft-pedaling, "Thanks for your note...."

But he did not let it go. Within hours, Smith escalated, explaining (though he didn't need to) that he was "a pedantic culinary historian" who put his trust in primary sources, and if I had "primary sources, such as any menu with 'Reuben sandwich' that lists the ingredients before 1941," he'd love to see them and retract his letter. Without such documentation, he was calling it for New York.

I forwarded all this along to my husband, Dan. He's not from a food family. He's from an Irish storyteller family, but long ago my parents ordered him a foie gras torchon at Gary Danko, in San Francisco, and inducted him into the world of food. He now possesses the mania of the converted. Dan butchers whole lambs at home on our kitchen island. He makes his own veal demi-glace. Our kitchen table is our friends' favorite restaurant. He is so much more devoted to cooking than any of my cousins that my mother and her sisters decided that Dan, a goy-in-law, should inherit Grandfather's knife roll. It also bears mentioning that Dan has an unused Ph.D., and thus is happy to research arcana. He's also been known to enjoy a fight from time to time. He recognized Smith's type immediately—too wound up for his own good, the kind Dan delighted in tormenting when, say, such a man zoomed up and started tailgating his truck. His preferred method of combat, however, was not to drag race. It was to turn on his blinker—*flicka flicka flicka*—and linger in the lane, tapping the brakes.

Online, Dan found a reference to a 1937 Reuben and set about locating the menu.

Smith, meanwhile, wrote back to say he'd done some more research and while he did concede that the Annette Seelos Special was not a Reuben sandwich per se, Reuben's restaurant did use all the Reuben components (rye bread, Swiss cheese, corned beef, and sauerkraut) in its sandwich offerings. Thus Reuben's invented the Reuben.

Smith signed off that e-mail: "Sorry."

We had a stalemate for a few days. Or really, I should say, I tried to forget about Smith and what my neighbor began calling his Reuben-sanity, while Dan dug in. Dan called my aunt, who lived in Omaha, and impressed upon her how imperative it was that she dig through every box in her basement to find a pre-1941 menu. (She did not find one.) Then he called the Radisson in Lincoln, Nebraska. In the 1960s my family sold the hotels. Three out of four of the brothers' places were now shuttered. The Lincoln Radisson was the sole holdout. Sadly, there were no boxes of memorabilia in its basement. But a janitor did mention that a nice lady in town collected historical artifacts. Dan tracked her down and explained the cruel and heinous crime Smith was attempting to perpetrate on one of Nebraska's claims to fame. She scurried down to her basement and searched her boxes. She did not find a pre-1941 menu, also.

Life in my e-mail inbox became more pleasurable, at least for a time. Tom Brokaw wrote to say that his wife used to teach at an Omaha high school with Warren Buffett's wife, and while in Nebraska they considered dining on Reubens at the Blackstone Hotel, the height of haute cuisine. He even offered to ask Robert Redford, who according to Brokaw, had consumed a fair number of Reubens at Blackstone, where he got the *Quiz Show* "fact" that Reuben Kay invented the sandwich. What I mean to say is that beautifully, strangely, the Reuben turned into the Forrest Gump of sandwiches, a lunch-size window into American life. I learned that Michael Pollan married a Kulakofsky. A reader referred to my grandfather as "the original Oracle of Omaha." Another wrote to the *New York Times* that the last name of the poker player in question was spelled "Kulakofsky, not Kulakowsky." The *New York Times* ran a correction. Then yet another reader wrote the editor to say that the correction was wrong—"Kulakofsky" and "Kulakowsky" are both transliterations from either Polish or Russian, thus equally valid spellings. But by that point even the *New York Times*, which once corrected the names of My Little Pony characters, apologizing for confusing "Twilight Sparkle, the nerdy intellectual" with "Fluttershy, the kind animal lover," gave up. They let incorrect correction stand.

But Smith did not quit. After three days of silence, he wrote again: "Most humble apologies—but I do have some late breaking info." He'd discovered that Arnold Reuben's restaurant included on its menu a sandwich of corned beef, Swiss cheese, mustard, and coleslaw on toasted rye. With great chutzpah, he wrote, "It was called the 'Col. Jay Flippen' sandwich."

The Col. Jay Flippen! With coleslaw and mustard! Are you kidding me? (N.B.: Col. Jay Flippen was an actor whose first film, of his vaudeville act, was called *The Ham What Am.*) In what sense was this a Reuben? And how do you prove the intellectual property of a sandwich, anyway? Or any food? Among my grandfather's other creations were butter brickle ice cream and a concoction he called Schimmel Seasoning. Schimmel Seasoning is kosher salt, black pepper, and MSG. My mother still makes it, minus the MSG. She keeps it in a shaker and calls it Schimmel Seasoning. Did anybody invent that?

Origin stories may always require some emotional generosity. Did ice-cream shop owner E. R. Hazard invent the banana split in Wilmington, Ohio? Or was it David Strickler, a 23-year-old pharmacist in Latrobe, Pennsylvania? "We think the controversy is fun"—that's the wise, official position of the sweetshop owner in Wilmington. But Smith showed no such magnanimity. As he awaited primary documentation, he informed the *New York Times* that they were fools to publish my mendacious writing. *"Where's the evidence? If there is no evidence, it is time to put this nice myth to bed."*

But you've got to root for Omaha on this one, right? New York delis have adopted the Reuben because culturally the sandwich seems as if it should be theirs—it has a huge personality, it's loud, it man-spreads. But the Reuben is a deeply early-20th-century American Midwestern creation, a Jewish sandwich that isn't kosher, made by an assimilated Eastern European whose family left Russia, Poland, and Germany several generations before World War II. The Midwest was in its heyday then. The railroad was grand. So were my family's hotels. They had fancy dining rooms with white-gloved waiters rolling silver carts for haute French table service. The Blackstone's Cottonwood Dining Room featured a real cottonwood tree. The poker players, with a wink, called themselves the Committee. They were proud, prominent, going places—or some of them were. In the early 1950s, Reuben Kulakofsky moved to Los Angeles. My grandfather stayed in Omaha. The railroad magic faded. Nobody believes that anything inspired comes from Nebraska anymore.

Dan spent many hours on the phone with the Nebraska State Historical Society and the Douglas County Historical Society trying to uphold my family's name. He did find decent confirmation that my grandfather invented butter brickle ice cream, which nobody in my family really cares about—I'm not sure why. I spent many hours on the phone with my mother, assuring her that yes, of course, I believed the family story. No outsider could shake my concept of who we are.

In the end, Dan saved the day. His Irish heritage and storyteller pride led him to understand, far better than I did, how important it was not to let the Reuben go, how gutted and lost we'd all feel if we let our history get stolen. "New York has everything, and now they're coming for the sandwich!" Dan reminded every Nebraskan who would talk to him. The tactic worked. Within a week, the Nebraska State Historical Society unearthed a menu from the Blackstone coffee shop from 1937, offering a Reuben sandwich for 35 cents, 50 cents "with chicken." The Douglas County Historical Society found a 1934 menu from the Blackstone's main dining room offering a Reuben for 40 cents. Smith conceded—"Many, many thanks!" he wrote. "These are the earliest references for a specific 'Reuben sandwich,' and they do indeed support your grandfather's claim to naming a sandwich!"—though not without noting that he found the chicken option "worrisome." But that's his problem. We've all got only so many stories, and never any new ones about our pasts. I'm sticking to mine.

How My City Eats

The Slow and Sad Death of Seattle's Iconic Teriyaki Scene

By Naomi Tomky

From Thrillist.com

Seattle-based writer/editor/photographer Naomi Tomsky has eaten her fair share of teriyaki, the once-ubiquitous signature street food of Seattle. Is its decline a symptom of the city's exponential growth, or a sign of the food world's increasingly restless trend toward globalization?

Teriyaki, the dish that the *New York Times* called Seattle's version of the Chicago dog, is fading from the collective food brain of the city, as the residents who remember its heyday get priced out of their neighborhoods—along with the restaurants that served it. For the newly arrived inhabitants taking over, teriyaki holds none of the worldly authenticity of pho nor the trendy uber-local appeal of foraged mushrooms. As the city continues to grow at one of the fastest rates in the nation, its signature dish is getting left behind: there are a third fewer teriyaki restaurants in Seattle today than there were a decade ago. What happened?

Sweet and sticky with sauce, all Seattle-style teriyaki stems from the basic formula Toshihiro Kasahara developed when he opened his first shop, Toshi's Teriyaki, in 1976. The meat, traditionally chicken thighs slippery and brown from marinade, gets slapped on a hot grill. The high heat caramelizes the sugars, crisping the meat and leaving it with a crunch of barely burnt soy on the outside. Sliced into bite-size pieces, it's served fanned out across a molded mound of white-as-snow rice, the sauce seeping down between the grains. The salad, like the meat, is sweet and crunchy, the iceberg lettuce and slivers of carrot and cabbage reminiscent of coleslaw, with only the rice vinaigrette separating it from old-school American picnic fare.

Toshi's Teriyaki opened its doors on Roy St. in 1976 to almost no fanfare. Business started off slow for the transplant. After graduating from Portland State University, Kasahara had moved to Seattle from Portland, looking for better opportunities. He attended school as a competitive wrestler, but wanted to become an interpreter. However, that's not exactly how things turned out. "All of my friends had restaurants," says Kasahara, so he figured why not follow suit. While his pals ran traditional Japanese restaurants, Kasahara wanted to specialize. Specifically, he wanted to find something he could operate without depending on other people, "so when they quit, I could still manage it."

"I wish I could say it's from my ancestors," Kasahara remarks of the recipe he developed. He always liked cooking growing up, but the closest he can come to defining the origins is to say that what he makes is similar to the Japanese version of teriyaki—a light finishing of soy sauce, sake, and mirin (rice wine) brushed onto grilled or broiled proteins, often seafood.

Wherever it came from, teriyaki was a knockout. Kasahara owned—or franchised—as many as 17 stores, including one in Phoenix. Copycats and rogue former franchises sprung up, as the *Seattle Times* put it, "like mushrooms in a damp meadow." There was Toshio's, Toshi's Teriyaki the Original, Yoshi's, Yoshino, Yasuko's, and so on. Today, there are nationwide teriyaki chains: both Teriyaki Madness and Glaze Teriyaki operate around the country. Teriyaki Madness, which stemmed from a local shop partnering with two former customers, now operates an impressive 31 outlets in 14 states, with 18 more opening this year. CEO Michael Haith is bullish on the popularity, both with customers ("It's a flavor that everyone can relate to, it's healthier, and it's on the go"), and his franchisees, many of which are now opening a second or third location. But for Kasahara, after building up the franchise business, he had to admit he wasn't cut out for it. "I didn't really have the management skills. It was a hassle." For a while, he stepped out of the teriyaki business entirely, but he couldn't stay away. Now he cooks in a single three-table shop buried deep within the buildings of a Mill Creek strip mall called Toshi's Teriyaki Grill.

As quickly as the teriyaki tide rises around the country (part of the Asian fast-casual category that's the fastest growing restaurant segment in the country), it's ebbing in Seattle. The shops fall victim to the same problems as any other small, family-run business. Of the 15 teriyaki shops we rounded up as the best in town in 2014, two have closed (Yasuko's and Setsuna), one changed hands (Katsu Burger), and another is slated to close later this year (King Donuts, as the owners have decided to retire and have no one to take it over). It's a testament that even the best can't survive.

In 2015, Yasuko Conner closed her namesake teriyaki shop on Broadway after more than twenty years. Long a haven of affordable food alongside the now rapidly gentrifying tracks of the new streetcar, a combination of declining business and rising property taxes—the assessed value of the building increased 129% that year—sounded the death knell for the tiny Yasuko's. The bare walls (blank except for the haphazardly posted and amended menu) hid the vibrancy of the flavors served. The floors, tables, and chairs were all colorless save for mysterious stains, remnants left behind by the customers, homeless, working-class, and affluent alike, plus a good smattering of Seattle's high school students, coming together in a place serving simple food at eminently reasonable prices. Teriyaki was the ultimate everyman meal.

These days, Amazon workers living in new high-rises get whisked by the building's corner aboard the streetcar. For lunch, they'll choose between sushi delivered by Uber and pizza cooked by one of Seattle's star chefs. Teriyaki doesn't enter the equation. Its legacy in Seattle, the city where Kasahara created it, is fading.

In 2010, John T. Edge wrote an ode to Seattle teriyaki for the *New York Times*. He quotes Knute Berger, elder statesman of Seattle media, as saying the shops are "so ubiquitous as to have become invisible." And once invisible, they actually disappear; two of the four restaurants Edge focused on have since closed. For those who grew up in Seattle, teriyaki was a way of life. Eula Scott Bynoe of the podcast *Hella Black Hella Seattle* tells the story of bringing a dying relative teriyaki from a favorite spot: "I was there to say goodbye," but the relative, a Seattle native, she joked, "just wanted the teriyaki." For new transplants, the simple dish doesn't fit the narrative of the shiny, new city. Teriyaki shops—dirty and run-down—aren't listed on any hot lists of where to eat in Seattle. Not in *Seattle Metropolitan*'s 30 restaurant experiences you "must have," nor in alt-weekly *The Stranger*'s "Eat Like a Local." To Seattle's latest Amazon and Microsoft recruits—living here as Seattle earned (and is still earning) acclaim for its culinary scene—the city was built on Copper River salmon and Taylor Shellfish oysters. A place where neighborhood restaurants like Anchovies & Olives shuck bivalves fresh daily and serve pristine fish, even away from the waterfront tourist traps. To have arrived in Seattle in the last five years was to watch Zoi Antonitsas and Jason Stratton both win *Food & Wine* "Best New Chef" awards and appear on *Top Chef*, to see Ethan Stowell's combination of Northwest and Italian cuisines spread to more than a dozen outlets, to taste Blaine Wetzel's food at Willows Inn and Jamie Boudreau's drinks at Canon— as each were celebrated for being one of the world's best restaurants and bars, respectively.

But for all the seafood and all the awards, former *Seattle Times* food writer Nancy Leson admits of Seattle's iconic foods, "When people talk about ingredients, I would go with the salmon and oysters, and that's fine . . . but when it comes to definitive dishes, teriyaki is on top of the list." In the 2010 *New York Times* piece, Berger offers insight to why such a major dish isn't more prominent. "Seattle yuppies love the idea of going to some obscure Chinese place for dim sum, but they won't dare tell you that they eat chicken teriyaki."

And while new Seattleites might dismiss the dish, elsewhere people are just discovering its allure. Middle America, for one, doesn't care that teriyaki didn't descend from a centuries-old Japanese tradition or from Kasahara's grandmother. "We're in Jonesboro, Arkansas, for God's sake," laughs Teriyaki Madness's Haith. He confesses that the idea of authenticity never occurred to him. He'll even go so far as to compare it to Tex-Mex: "it's authentic Americanized-Japanese food. They [the customers] like the volume, they like the healthy aspect, and they like the customization abilities."

In the end, it comes back to a universal appeal: "There's a sincerity to it, from the owners, that really translates. It's comfort food," states Haith. And he's right. What Teriyaki Madness does is not only imitate the meals that have drawn in Seattleites for decades but also the environment that bred it. The corner store–style service, the friendly face behind the counter, the bare-bones atmosphere. The dish that Kasahara came up with to open his small Queen Anne shop, with its mangled roots . . . if it's authentic anything, it's authentically old Seattle.

But new Seattle—with the locals priced out of the area, those that remain forgetting teriyaki exists, and newcomers ignoring it—risks losing those real shops for good. Teriyaki could be heading the direction of deep-dish . . . just ask a Chicagoan about it and they'll say, "Oh, that's for tourists." Teriyaki is from a different era, and it's fading as fast as traffic-free days on I-5. Since teriyaki came to town, Seattle's waved goodbye to the Kingdome, Kurt Cobain, and the Sonics. A signature stadium, a signature musician, a signature team—and now, perhaps, a signature dish.

As cryptic as that may sound, it's still not too late. There are still shops that marinate their chicken and make that perfect teriyaki rice, that use fresh ingredients behind the closed doors of their sauce-stained kitchens. Sixty-six shops remain in Seattle with teriyaki in their name—plus one special one in Mill Creek. And Kasahara, like Seattle teriyaki itself, isn't ready to be counted out quite yet: "I'm not quitting. I'm waiting to see how things go here." Meanwhile, it's up to Seattle's umbrella-shunning stalwarts, incoming Amazon hordes, and everyone in between to know—and support—what's great about Seattle. To eat teriyaki. To support the small businesses, the independent shops, the unique and wonderful cuisines that define the town. By eating an affordable, delicious meal, you can save one more bit of old Seattle from going the way of grunge. And wouldn't that be something?

The Story of the Mission Burrito, Piled High and Rolled Tight

By John Birdsall

From *Bon Appetit*

Ah, the Mission District—a storied San Francisco
neighborhood, which even comes with its own iconic food:
the burrito. Award-winning Bay Area food writer John Birdsall is
an ideal guide to lead us on a pilgrimage in search of the perfect,
and true, Mission burrito.

The *carnitas*, frizzled a deep brown from braising in fat, have fibers
that splay open as I chew. The pinto beans are earthy and soft, the
pico de gallo a dense hash. The fresh avocado option, essential here at
La Taqueria in San Francisco's Mission District, unifies everything in a
buttery medium where the line between flavor and texture is indistinct,
irrelevant. I'm still sweaty after a four-block jog from the nearest parking spot on a Saturday night, but I don't care because the burrito my
friends have waiting is as good as it's always been, since my first time
here three decades ago. I can even look past the evil eye of the woman
peeved about my friends hogging a table. To find a seat at perennially
jammed La Taq you face the kind of public aggression that this historically chilled-out city isn't known for—except when it comes to scoring
one of the best burritos in America.

You see a mix of old and new Mission here, friends in their 20s loitering with coworkers over Tecates, and older couples in their black-
and-orange Giants caps, stopping on the way home from a day game.
There are plenty of out-of-towners, people who left the Bay Area and

still come back to Le Taq as soon as their flights land at SFO, and others checking items off their tourist to-do lists: In 2014 Nate Silver's ESPN-owned statistics website, FiveThirtyEight, chose this as the winner of its nationwide burrito bracket.

It's hard to believe in this age of the burrito emoji, but before the '90s, burritos existed mostly in Latino neighborhoods like the Mission. The ones that crossed over were visitors from other worlds, folksy Tex-Mex (BurritoVille in Manhattan) or California exotic (Tortillas in Atlanta). Then Chipotle happened. The chain's founder, Steve Ells, was a line cook in the 1980s at Stars, Jeremiah Tower's flashy San Francisco brasserie. Like most local 20-somethings, he faced down many, many burritos; Ells would sometimes grab one before his shift at the restaurant. "I had grown up in Boulder," he recalls. "A burrito looks totally different in Colorado—or did." Ells was mostly influenced by the form of the burrito, its self-containedness. So he opened his first Chipotle in Denver in 1993; within a month that shop was selling more than a thousand Mission-style burritos a day. A second outpost opened, then a third, then eventually 2,000 more stores, spreading Ells' generic version of this local specialty throughout the country.

Here in its native habitat, though, the Mission burrito is still lithe, still expressive, each one different from the other. There are burritos for drywall men and tech bros, skate punks and tourists, for luxury condo dwellers and drunks. Some raise a fist for Chicano pride, others are coded for bougie bohemians. Some are the batons for the city's current relay sprint toward gentrification; others live on as they have despite the pressures of a city in full-on boom. Most—and I say this as a man who has been eating burritos in San Francisco for more than 30 years—are delicious.

But in a city where the average monthly rent for a one-bedroom apartment in 2016 spiked above $3,600, these burritos face an existential challenge. San Francisco is shedding blue-collar workers and Latinos at a rate that has affordable housing advocates freaking out. Last year the city released a report showing that the Mission's Latino population fell from 60 percent in 2000 to about 48 percent. The same data projects Latinos could make up just 31 percent of the historically Latino district by 2025. Yet the Mission remains a place you cannot understand—or even enjoy—without the burrito, even as the streets where it was born become disturbingly high-end. So how does a cheap, working-class food endure in a place that's suddenly neither?

You take the BART train to 24th Street and make your way past the homeless and the loitering high school kids to get to El Farolito. There, you'll eat a burrito that shows you what the ones in other cities are not.

The *carnitas* in an El Farolito super burrito is savage and salty. It dominates the tubular form the way a 24-ounce T-bone commands a plate at Ruth's Chris: without equivocating, apologizing, or making excuses to vegans. The sheer volume of pork makes the orange grains of Mexican rice they're packed with recede. Avocado slices are necessary, just as *crema*, a cooling squiggle, seeps through the thick clump of ingredients. This is one of the defining burritos in the Mission style. This is one of the great burritos of San Francisco.

A Mission burrito starts with a large flour tortilla, typically steamed on a press like a laundromat's. Then it's filled egg roll–style with Mexican rice, beans (black, pinto, sometimes refried), salsa, and some chopped or shredded meat (*carnitas*, grilled or stewed chicken, carne asada, or offally things like tongue, chitterlings, or brains). It is universally known that "a super," which costs a buck or two more at each place, gets you a handful of cheese, sour cream or *crema*, either guacamole or sliced avocado, sometimes shredded iceberg.

The twang of these ingredients is what sets the Mission's burritos apart. *Carnitas* can be merely steamed pork in other places; beans can be canned or boiled lifeless; the guacamole scraped from a Sysco bucket. But there are hundreds of places selling burritos in the nearly 1.5 square miles of the Mission. To compete, owners must stand out, the way the roasted tomato salsa does at Papalote, or the *al pastor* does at Taqueria Cancún. Other places can have good burritos, but they don't have a culture of good burritos, a community of strivers.

The burrito maker—often a she—folds in the tortilla's ends and compresses the fillings into a fat, even cylinder as she rolls. That roll is everything. El Metate is known for its tight game. (But once, at a tiny Oakland burrito shop, Taqueria Las Comadres, I watched a woman roll the excess flap of tortilla into a crisp, chewy spine then embed it to run the length of the filling. It was a move of staggering artistry.) An optional turn on the griddle to crisp the tortilla's outer skin—what the menu calls dorado-style at La Taq—and then the burrito maker sheaths it in foil, pinches the ends, and drops it onto a plate or red plastic basket alongside a handful of chips.

The Mission burrito is a thing so fused to California's relationship with Mexico that its evolution is nearly impossible to chart. You can see the embryo of it in the *burrito de carne,* the rolled taco of Sonora in northern Mexico. It's plausible that some version of that spread to California through proximity. But the Mission burrito is specific to San Francisco, and a thousand miles of mutation separate these from the ones in Sonora.

San Diego has what it calls, with bombast, the California burrito. It matches in heft, except its bulk comes from fries, which kicks it closer to drunk food. The breakfast burrito, reportedly born in Santa Fe in the 1970s, is a hyperbolic blowup of Austin's breakfast tacos. And the Tex-Mex wet burrito, ladled with enchilada sauce, is a clunky scan of enchiladas *suizas.* Simply put, California's burritos are better than other states' burritos, but none are as good as San Francisco's. (I'm aware of the controversial nature of this truth.)

Los Angeles has spare, delicious burritos, sometimes only beans and meat, like the frozen ones you buy at 7-Eleven. San Francisco hardcores say they're weak; Los Angeles hardcores think Missions are vulgar. *Los Angeles Times* food critic Jonathan Gold once called San Francisco burritos "monstrous things wrapped in tinfoil, and filled with what would seem to be the contents of an entire margarita-mill dinner." It's hard to defend the aesthetics, except that a good Mission burrito requires talent. It's as dependent on proportion, balance, and ingredient quality as pastrami on rye or a bowl of ramen. It's just . . . big.

That girth has fueled their appeal since the beginning. Burritos are Chicano roots food, born as rations handed out to pickers at the huge produce farms in the central state. In the 1960s, restaurant consultant Peter Garin was working the lettuce fields. "I remember the texture of the shredded beef," he told *SF Weekly* in 1993, recalling field burritos, "the heat of the green peppers, and the proper proportion of rice and beans." You didn't need a fork, or even clean hands.

Taqueria La Cumbre is one of two places in San Francisco that says it invented the Mission burrito, down to the exact day: September 29, 1969 (the other, El Faro, claims an earlier date: September 26, 1961). La Cumbre's Number Six, a regular with carne asada, was my burrito initiation. It was back in the 1980s; I had moved to San Francisco from Berkeley with a few crates of English-lit paperbacks and some Hefty bags of clothes.

That carne asada burrito was one of the first things that sold me on the potential of cheap food. It demonstrated how a few basic ingredients can become perfected—unpolished, but perfected. You peeled back the foil and chewed at the compressed magma of grilled skirt steak with soft ranchero beans and rice rolled up in a flour tortilla with a slice of Jack cheese. It was large enough that you could feed like a ball python; after finishing, your body could forgo a few meals.

Today I'm a couple of bites into the loose roll of carne asada, shedding pale amber rice onto my plate, and La Cumbre feels like a place with its best burritos behind it. Same for El Faro, its historic rival. San Francisco's first generation of burrito creators is kind of like Madonna. The old fierceness is gone, but she'll always have your respect, even when she face-plants on stage. Don't worry, girl: In my heart, I'll always pick you up.

La Cumbre's sign juts out onto Valencia Street, its heavy black Mexican Gothic font looking defiant, like a collarbone tattoo with three-inch letters. It's at odds with the Valencia of 2016, a row of restaurants and boutiques with prim fronts and minimal signage, coding for the expensiveness within.

Of course, as with the rest of San Francisco, there's been a push to recast the burrito in upscale terms. In Hayes Valley, a central neighborhood that's in the throaty flush of trending up, I order a duck confit burrito at Papito Organic Mexican Cuisine. When I take a bite, it spills a pile of duck slicked with sugary mole, unloading so much confit that I worry about the number of birds compelled to sacrifice their legs. It's not bad, but it smears the original, dresses it up in a summer-weight linen blazer to accessorize the Mission right the hell out of it. I notice that the guys cooking are behaving just like the ones at El Farolito, though the confit they're heating up is a dubious update of crisp *carnitas.* Good for them, I think, working their way up. But I wonder what they think of this burrito.

Another, bleaker, version is a burrito I sample at ground zero of the tech capital that San Francisco has become: Twitter's headquarters. The Mission burrito is a pillar of that company's origin story. In 2006, lore goes, Jack Dorsey and a couple of buddies ordered burritos. It was then, while peeling back the foil, that Dorsey shared his vision for the social network. (Now Twitter's CEO, he declined to be interviewed for this story.)

The Market is a public food hall on the ground floor of the Twitter building. I order a chipotle chicken burrito from its taqueria, Taco Bar, and find a table outside. As millennial tech workers cruise by in their workout gear—guys wearing Vans with high socks, backpacks with logos for companies like Uber and Optimizely, vintage striped basketball shorts—I face the worst burrito of my life. The tortilla is stiff and cold. I get a mouthful of frigid sour cream in one bite and then slack white-meat chicken embalmed with cumin. I drop its heavy remains in the compost can, pick my way past young bearded guys wearing chambray shirts, and escape.

Bearded bros are nowhere in sight on the Mission Street sidewalk in front of El Castillito. There's only a mighty cliff of a man, sucking at the remaining inch of what must have been an epic blunt. Nearby, businesses sell car insurance and cheap bleached jeans—this is the kind of place where the Mission burrito was nurtured.

Since the 1950s, when the neighborhood started to change from Irish and Italian to Mexican, the Mission has been a place known for its texture. There's physical texture, in the crates of bruised plantains and shiny yuca fronting corner markets. But also cultural: the overlap of Latino and gay, wealthy and not, tagged-up and mural-covered. It's the San Francisco of cultural compression, which is the best San Francisco. You can't blame Facebook's Mark Zuckerberg and all those condo buyers for wanting to live here. It's nice, and it's got a real patina—despite changing demographics, classic places like El Castillito haven't been squeezed out.

Inside, a guy with a sparkly ear stud leaves the cash register, walks toward the ceiling-mounted TV, and flicks the remote at it. A telenovela flashes on. "*Ay güey!*" he says, clicking his tongue at the screen. He jabs the remote again and the Giants-Padres game stutters into focus. Half a dozen men slouching over burritos turn toward the screen, all speaking Spanish.

The cook reaches for a gob of *al pastor* from a bin on the line, spreads it down a tortilla piled with orangey Mexican rice and black beans ("You want espicy or mile?" he asks, salsa ladle poised), then twists it in foil.

El Castillito didn't make it into FiveThirtyEight's greatest-burrito bracket. But Gustavo Arellano, a member of the selection committee and author of *Taco USA: How Mexican Food Conquered America*, loves these burritos—so much, he says, that he felt they were too personal a choice to lobby for. Chef David Chang, another voter, stopped by after the bracket was set. "I don't know," he said at the time. "It might be the best burrito I've ever eaten." Anna Maria Barry-Jester, the bracket's author, called it the one that got away. I've been eating in San Francisco for decades, and I've never made it here.

I feel sort of ashamed.

I call Arellano to ask why a place that makes such good burritos has kept such a low profile. "Because it stayed resolutely working class," he says. "There's ones that become Instagram and Yelp sensations, and then ones that are better."

The *pastor* pork is crisp around its dark edges, chewy, animated by a charge of vinegar and heat that bucks like a gun in recoil. The rice has tooth, the beans a fine grain. There's a satisfying tightness to the roll, it feels good in my hand, and it cost less than ten bucks. This could be the best Mission burrito in San Francisco. This could be the best Mission burrito in the world. Damn, I'll go Chang one better: This is the best burrito I've ever eaten.

Maybe it's survived, with original Mission soul intact, by building enough of a wall to obscure it from the tourists, the techies, and the condo buyers. That's some irony: The most authentic Mission burrito is also the most obscure. Long may it roll.

I Want Crab. Pure Maryland Crab.

By Bill Addison

From Eater.com

As Eater's restaurant editor and national critic, Bill Addison constantly eats his way around the country; with previous dining critic stints in San Francisco, Dallas, and Atlanta on his resume, it's fair to say he's an expert on the latest American food trends. In Baltimore, however, only one food satisfies his craving.

The first steamed crab I pluck from the pile feels heavy in my hand, and I'm already content. The act of grabbing the shell smears my fingers with clumps of spices and coarse salt, but I don't mind. As a native Marylander, everything about being here at L.P. Steamers, a crab house in Baltimore's Locust Point neighborhood, feels familiar: its location in a tall, compact, red brick row house (Baltimore's signature architectural style); the butcher block paper spread across the tables; the shoreline scent of seafood in the air; the thwacking and crunching as diners dismantle the spindly red bodies to eat them for lunch.

I moved away from Maryland over 25 years ago, but if I don't make it back to the state at least once a year for steamed crabs, I'm like a bird whose migration pattern has been disrupted. I'm unsettled in the world.

But now I'm here, which is as it should be. I'm planted in front of a pile of swimmers, their raw blue shells turned brushfire-red in the steamer pot, a marvel of pigment and biochemistry. Ryan Detter, who covers restaurants for the *Baltimore City Paper* and writes the occasional Baltimore-themed Heatmap for Eater, sits across the table from me. This is our first meal together. We've met up to spend a few days gorging on classic Baltimore eats—especially crab, because it is high summer, and absolutely nothing tastes better on a sweltering day than buttery crabmeat zapped by sharp spices. Maryland's official crab season runs from April to December, but late summer and early fall is when crabs are at their heaviest, sweetest, and most plentiful.

Our server hustles by, and I call out the question that in my eagerness I forgot to ask when ordering. To me, it's a crucial query.

"Are these crabs from Maryland?"

"Yes," he says. "For now, our crabs are from Maryland."

For now. Meaning: When harvests of crabs fished from the Chesapeake Bay run low, or the prices become exorbitant, crabs may instead be overnighted from North Carolina, Louisiana, or Texas. This has become common practice in many Baltimore crab houses, and often the crabmeat used to make crab cakes and other local crab specialties comes from even farther afield. It's how restaurants accommodate the appetite for Maryland's most famous culinary tradition. Pollution and overfishing began taking its toll on the Bay's blue crab population as far back as the 1960s, and restaurants have adapted over the decades by looking beyond the state lines.

This year, according to the Maryland Department of Natural Resources, the blue crab populace in the Bay is more than 550 million, one of the highest tallies since the mid-1990s, due in part to a mild winter and recent crab harvesting restrictions. It seemed like an ideal excuse for me to spend some quality time in Baltimore, savoring the local catch at places like L.P. Steamers.

It was about more than that, though, if I'm honest. I've been on the road for most of the past two-and-a-half years, reporting on the meals I eat in restaurants of all kinds across America. It's the ideal life for a gluttonous wanderer like me, without question. But amid the heady dash toward constant, new-to-me experiences, I'd begun lately to feel a shimmer of loneliness, an ache to spend time in a place I know profoundly. That longing for connection ran deeper than me simply spending more time at my house in Atlanta, where I've lived off and on for two decades. I wanted to go *home*.

Baltimore is where I fell in love with food, where my parents took me to restaurants with names like Haussner's, Chez Fernand, and the Chesapeake—icons that no longer exist. Before weekend dinners my brother and I would often cruise around the city's Inner Harbor in a paddleboat, skimming along the urban coast while dusk settled and the lit-up skyline appeared as a glimmery reflection in the water. Our mother and father watched us from a cafe terrace, where they sipped white wine spritzers or scotch old-fashioneds. Then we'd head off to one of our favorite neighborhoods to eat, perhaps to Fells Point, with its cobblestone streets and cozy Waterfront Inn, or to cloistered Little Italy and its red-sauce stalwarts like Sabatino's and Chiaparrelli's.

But I hungered all year for family crab feasts, for their mess and their overexcited fellowship and the happy delirium that settled in afterward. As an adult, I've zipped in and out of my eccentric, complicated home-town enough to still grasp its essential character. But I was returning now to slow down, to reacquaint myself with the summer humidity, the occasional Patapsco River breeze, and the local treasures pulled from nearby waters. It would prove to be something of a hunt.

Baltimore is not a trendsetting food town. No national publication has proclaimed it America's surprise number-one dining destination. No Ace Hotel will be opening imminently to skyrocket the city's cool factor.

I'm not implying that my hometown is a culinary backwater. It keeps pace with your typical midsize American metropolis. Resident food lovers embrace new restaurants interpreting global cuisines: Indian, Peruvian, Basque, Vietnamese, Dominican. You can find solid examples of sushi and ramen. Upscale stunners in Harbor East, the buzzy neigh-borhood du jour, serve fancy pastas and flaming saganaki; they nod to the local love of Italian and Greek cooking, reflecting two of the city's most deeply rooted immigrant communities. (Every time the Greeks showed up on the second season of *The Wire*, I twitched with Pavlovian cravings for the spanakopita I scarfed in restaurants as a child.)

If you're celebrating a special occasion in town, I will readily send you to chef Cindy Wolf's beautiful restaurant Charleston. Mix-and-match options for her tasting menus might include sweet corn soup with summer truffles, heirloom tomato salad with lime and saffron vin-aigrette, and grilled Chesapeake rockfish with fresh artichokes and a carrot puree. I will urge you not to overlook the cheese cart stocked with rare finds shipped from Neal's Yard Dairy in London.

Really, though, what makes Baltimore a special place to eat is that the city itself transcends any notion of fashion. Maryland's love of *Callinectes sapidus*—the blue crab—may be a cliché, but it remains the defining food of our collective identity. Our devotion is primal. Crab cakes show up on higher-end menus around town; locals, however, tend to gravitate to versions served with saltines or on sandwich rolls in bars, cafes, diners, and at long-standing food halls. And crab houses— which first emerged post–World War II on Maryland's Eastern shore, often run by crabbers and fishermen or crab processing facilities—can be scruffy, chaotic affairs. The caked spices get under your nails. Your clothes reek of brine and beer. Filling your stomach crab by crab is a laborious process of demolition, though the effort makes the meal that much more satisfying. It's wonderful.

Of course, not everybody wants to work quite so hard for dinner. My dad, who has lived in the same Maryland county his whole life, relishes crab but refuses to dissect one. And the menus at crab houses have evolved over the years to accommodate all kinds of appetites and dispositions—including his.

Two classic soups appear nearly everywhere: Maryland crab (a tomato-based vegetable soup flecked with lattices of crabmeat) and cream of crab (roux-thickened, usually, and best consumed hot and quick before it congeals into a gluey mass). In this age of mash-ups, some customers ask for the two soups "half and half," and some kitchens comply; when I was growing up, to even conceive of mixing them in the same bowl would have been heresy.

I did, thirty-plus years ago, witness the emergence of "crab fluff"— a crab cake dunked in an excess of batter and deep-fried until it resembled a balloon-shaped funnel cake. The crab fluff at L.P. Steamers has actual merit: the meat inside tingles with sweet-hot spices, and the cooks toss extra wisps of crisp batter into the plastic serving basket for munching. Cream cheese–based crab dip shows up in myriad forms at crab houses: poured into a hollowed-out boule, spread across toast, as filling for potato skins, and, most notoriously, slaked across spongy pretzels, covered with cheese, and broiled. I doubt an exemplary version of the crab pretzel exists anywhere; it doesn't mean I've stopped searching for it.

These days most Maryland seafood restaurants oblige divergent tastes by, well, being *seafood* restaurants. Their menus may have crab at the center, but they also serve oysters (I prefer local varieties in the winter when they're generally more saline), clams, scallops, mussels, and fish, mostly from other waters. I have no interest in any of this. I am here to feed a rumbling homesickness. I want crab. Pure Maryland crab.

Picking apart a blue crab can be unnerving to first-timers. For me it is instinctual; performing the ritual lives in the lizard part of my brain. Watch my family tackle a heap of steamed crabs and you know who we are. My 90-year-old grandmother prefers her seasoning spare. My mother likes her spices bolder, and having grown up on a farm she is patient and steady with excavating every fleshy filigree. My father can't sit still long enough to really engage. My brother rips into his share like the cartoon Tasmanian Devil, scattering slivers of shells and debris in his frenzy.

I bring unrelenting perfectionism to the task. At L.P. Steamers I begin like I always do, by flipping the crab upside down to remove the limbs. The two rows of five legs twist off with the same effort it takes to unscrew the cap on a new tube of toothpaste. Sometimes tufts of pearly meat cling to their ends, prime for extracting with the teeth. I snap the crab's front claws in half at the joint and go to work on them with a wooden mallet, the ubiquitous tool that accompanies this sort of feast. The goal is to retrieve the frilly flesh inside intact—to extract it unblemished and still attached to the pincers, usually achieved by tapping the shell a few times with the brisk force of a doctor administering a reflex test. I pause a second to admire the shapes and the colors before devouring my prize.

Now for the body. I slide a knife into the crab's abdominal flap, called the "apron." Most crabs served in restaurants are males, or "jimmies," identified by the obelisk shape outlined on their aprons. I hold the knife steady and with my other hand lift off the hard, spiny shell to reveal the soft body within. There is no other sound on earth quite like that squishy crack. Once you tune in to its frequency, you'll hear it repeated over and over at every table in the restaurant. I use the knife to scrape away the gray, tapered gills that line both sides of its form; kids often nickname them "dead man's fingers." There is a film of yellow green gunk—the hepatopancreas, a filtering organ—which Marylanders call the "mustard." Some crab lovers find the stuff appetizing; I don't, but neither am I hypersensitive about scraping every last bit away.

Then, with both hands, I break the body in two. How a person un-earths the meat from the crab's labyrinths of cartilage is entirely individual. I approach the task by squeezing each half together to crack and loosen the cartilage. Then I get surgical, cradling each section in my palm and, using my thumb, carefully peeling away the outside chamber and the leg sockets until there's nothing left but a lush wad of alabaster meat. I use my fingers to dig out the remaining lacy threads of flesh.

Ryan eyes my handiwork from across the table and nods. I watch him break each half of his crab in two again, quartering the crustacean to more easily reach the choice clumps of meat. It's an efficient method. He knows what he's doing.

The steamed crabs are an unspoken test between us, a measure of our Maryland cred. Ryan, who hails from Ohio, has lived in Baltimore for 15 years. I am a prodigal son; I've been gone longer than Ryan's been around. This sizing up isn't a race or a competition. But noting how your tablemates eat steamed crabs—how efficiently and confidently they break them down, how cleanly they pick the shells for meat—is part of an innate Maryland dining code. Silently, without any acknowl-edgment, Ryan and I pass muster with one another. We plow through our dozen crabs. An ease, a trust, settles in between us. We sip from our bottles of National Bohemian beer, better known as Natty Boh, first brewed in Baltimore in 1885. Though it is is now made in North Caro-lina and Georgia, Natty Boh remains the city's liquid mascot.

The Maryland–not Maryland dualism follows us as we head off in search of righteous crab cakes.

Lexington Market—Baltimore's largest public market, established in 1782, more than a decade before the city was officially incorpo-rated—sprawls across two buildings and houses more than a hundred vendors in a rippling sweep of humanity. Shoppers are predominantly black, but the crowd includes faces of many colors. We shuffle between stalls that sell fried chicken, deli sandwiches, fudge-covered cookies, shrimp fried rice, shiny vegetables in meticulous rows, and pizza by the slice or pie. Faidley Seafood, in business since 1886, stands apart from the throng, with its own wing and its own entrance. It began as a fishmonger, but expanded into food service half a century ago selling fish sandwiches; in 1970, a raw bar was installed, and a decade later the operation assumed its most famous role: Baltimore's crab cake kingpins.

Nancy Faidley Devine, the granddaughter of founder John W. Faidley, stands behind a counter near the door. Her gloved hands are covered in a mix of mustard and mayo as she forms six-ounce globes of crabmeat and arranges them tidily on sheet pans. I watch her for a minute, and then ask my favorite question: "Are you using Maryland crab meat?"

She smiles, and answers by reaching for a small tub and handing it to me. It reads "Windmill Brand Crabmeat," packed in Hoopers Island on Maryland's Eastern Shore—a stretch of coast I know well. Most of my mother's relatives live within 20 miles of that arc of the Chesapeake Bay. I smile back at her and order two crab cakes, one lump and one backfin.

Devine, who runs Faidley Seafood with her husband and daughter, arguably sparked the mania for "jumbo lump" crab cakes. In the 1980s, as a bid to differentiate her product from the competition, she devised a recipe showcasing the large, feather-shaped muscles, or "lumps," that develop on the blue crab's back swimming legs. There are only two lumps per crab, so it's a costly extravagance. The idea had staying power, and by the 1990s "jumbo lump" became the gold-standard shorthand, not only in Maryland but nationwide in steakhouses and other restaurants peddling luxury.

Before Devine's jumbo lump revelation, the premium part of the crab was backfin meat, which comprises broken pieces of lump as well as stringier threads. This is the meat that made up the crab cake I grew up on, and as long as a backfin crab cake isn't padded out with too much breading (Marylanders are obsessed with crab cakes having as little "filler" as possible), it is a homely but eloquent expression of silky richness.

Ryan and I bulldoze through both of the crab cakes that Faidley's cooks broil for us. Preference between them, we resolve, is a matter of prioritizing texture versus taste. Undoubtedly, the lump-studded sphere shines in it golden beauty, each forkful weighty with plump morsels of flesh. The darker, squatter backfin cake isn't a looker, but I find its flavor more intense, more direct; it's the one that quiets my yearnings for home. It's the crab cake I'd return for, that brings me back to myself.

Every time I've stopped in Maryland, bought a crab cake, and posted a picture of it online, someone invariably comments with, "Go try the ones at Koco's Pub!" A neighborhood haunt in a residential stretch six miles from downtown Baltimore, Koco's canary-yellow exterior gives way to a long dining room swathed in sky blue, lime green, and a bright orange that brings to mind the Orioles logo. Customers fill every table, and no one seems to order anything but crab cakes.

Koco's specialty is a Frankenstein's monster of crab weighing in at eleven ounces—twice the mass of a regulation major league baseball. It's all lump, little filler, creamy, and with a spunky hit of Old Bay, the state's beloved crab seasoning. (Plenty of crab houses and seafood restaurants alternately use custom spice blends—perhaps oomphing sweet spices like mace, rearing back on the celery salt, or ratcheting up the paprika—often sourced from Old Bay's local competitor J.O. Spice Co.) The charm of this behemoth is obvious.

Is the crabmeat from Maryland? "It isn't," says a manager. "Sometimes it's from Maryland, but it's often from Indonesia and other places. We just do so much volume, we need a steady supply." Koco's is hardly alone in its approach, and I appreciate the staffer being straightforward. That isn't always the case in restaurants. A study published last year by the seafood watch group Oceana detailed some troubling results: The organization surveyed nearly 90 regional restaurants advertising Maryland crabmeat, and found that 46 percent of the places located in Baltimore were actually selling specimens from other parts of the world (most frequently Asia and Mexico). The researchers determined that this might not necessarily be the restaurants' fault: Mislabeling can easily happen in the distribution channel before the product enters the United States, and restaurants may believe they're buying locally when they're not.

(As one reaction to this type of fraud, two-dozen or so Baltimore restaurants—including Mid-Atlantic sensation Woodberry Kitchen, a perennial on Eater's list of America's essential restaurants—participate in the state's "True Blue" certification program, which verifies that a restaurant serves only authentic Maryland crab.)

From a dining perspective, here's what I'm learning on this trip:

Many customers may not care all that much about the origins of the crabs they're enjoying. Ryan and I walk into several packed crab houses during our days together—places that get raves in local publications, institutions recommended to Ryan by Baltimorean food lovers—and when we ask where the steamed crabs come from, the servers non-chalantly say "Louisiana" or "Texas." They tilt their heads, confused or amused, when we say thanks and wave goodbye without ordering.

I get that consistent supply is the bottom line for a business. We all have our own principles. Truthfully? At Christmastime, when I visit my family, I would gratefully wolf down Koco's enormous, deftly seasoned crab beast. But in the warm weather, in a year when the harvest is abundant, my native Maryland heart tells me not to eat blue crab from any other waters but the Chesapeake Bay.

Part of the ease with which Baltimoreans accept blue crabs from other shores, I think, is that a loyalty to their crab house is stronger than a loyalty to local foods. Everyone has the nearby haven that their family has patronized for years, where the steamed crabs have just the right amount of caked-on spices, where the seasoning isn't too hot or too sweet for their palate. And I can empathize, now that I have a new go-to crab house myself, though it's 20 miles from my parents' house. Schultz's Crab House is in Essex, a blue-collar community on the edge of Baltimore surrounded by the Back and Middle rivers.

When I look around the dining room at Schultz's for the first time, on my last day in Baltimore, it's as if someone tapped my childhood restaurant memories and reified them into this set piece: knotty wood paneling, a figurine of a fisherman in a yellow slicker, a mounted fiberglass marlin, faded pictures of boats and docks, white butcher paper on every table.

And yes, the crabs are from Maryland. Ryan and I ask for jumbos, six inches or more in length, typically the largest size available in restaurants, and the server tells us the kitchen steams them to order—at that size, it'll be 45 minutes. Fine. We fill the wait with speedier dishes: jumbo lump and backfin crab cakes (here, too, I find I'm partial to the lacey backfin version), thick cream of crab soup, and a crackly mound of crab fluff. I nearly burst into tears when the crab imperial—essentially a casserole of crab, mayonnaise, and spices—shows up in a foil crabshell, the way it did in restaurants when I was a kid obsessed with the dish. On the side are pickled beets, a cucumber salad, and a sight I haven't seen in probably 30 years: a bloodily crimson spiced apple ring, set atop a leaf of kale as garnish. It's alarming how far back in time I can travel at Schultz's.

The steamed crabs, when they arrive, are dense and full of such delicate, heavenly meat, and I swear I can taste cardamom zigzagging through the mud slick of spices. We chuck the shells into a blue bucket, but leave the papered tabletop littered with a carnage of claws and cartilage and murky stains. The server is cleaning up the crime scene, gathering the butcher paper at its edges, even before we reach the door.

Lunch at Schultz's is my final meal of the trip. Ryan and I hug goodbye ("It's like you were my best buddy at Crab Camp!") and I'm already thinking about the next flights, the next cities, the next meals. It's doubtful I'll have Maryland crab in Baltimore again this year.

It's doubtful I'll have much crab meat at all, frankly. I know it's silly, but eating my native delicacy in other places leaves me empty. In San Francisco, a bowl of taglierini twined with Dungeness crab (more gossamer in texture than its compact Chesapeake cousin) can certainly be a pleasure. In my travels, though, I find myself detouring around crab shacks on the coast of Georgia or Lake Pontchartrain, and in chophouses I'll always choose oysters or shrimp cocktail over a jumbo lump orb. Other people can rightly adore these things. To me they're only echoes of home, like the mirrored outline of downtown Baltimore rippling and blurring in the waves of the Inner Harbor.

The Burning Desire for Hot Chicken

By Danny Chau

From TheRinger.com

As associate editor of The Ringer, Danny Chau usually covers pro sports, which may explain his no-pain-no-gain approach to eating Nashville's famous local specialty, hot chicken. Traveling from his native L.A., he was a man on a mission—to put his rigorously honed spice tolerance to the ultimate test.

Years ago, when he was still the mayor of Nashville, Bill Purcell received a call from England. The son of Prince Charles's girlfriend wanted to meet him. *I don't know if that's something I need to do,* he thought to himself. The voice on the other line clarified the purpose of the meeting: He wanted to eat hot chicken. "Well, then I'm in," Purcell blurted out.

Purcell is a man who, while serving as majority leader in the Tennessee House of Representatives, declared Prince's Hot Chicken Shack to be the best restaurant in Tennessee. In 2005, the mayor and his royalty-adjacent guest met at Prince's and sat down to chat. Purcell's guest immediately said, "I will have the extra hot."

"Oh, don't do that," Purcell said. "You should have the hot chicken." He pointed to the window art that greets visitors on their way in. "See? Prince's *Hot* Chicken Shack. That's what they serve."

The men walked up to the counter to place their order through a little square opening in the wall that conceals the kitchen from civilians. The exchange feels like a negotiation at a box office.

"One quarter chicken, brown and white, extra hot," the guest said.

Prince's owner Andre Prince Jeffries attempted to talk him off the ledge, but extra hot is what he got. Purcell walked back to the table with a smile. He knew what was coming.

The Brit was Tom Parker Bowles, the son of Camilla, (now) duchess of Cornwall. Parker Bowles, a prominent food writer, was on a research trip for his book, *The Year of Eating Dangerously: A Global Adventure in Search of Culinary Extremes.* He got what he wanted, and he loved his first bite. Then it started to hurt. Then came the tears. Bowles would dedicate two pages in his book to describing the misery the Prince's extra-hot chicken put him through. "The only thing willing me on is pure, pig-headed pride," Bowles wrote. "Each mouthful becomes more and more painful and numbing until I'm uncertain as to whether I'm swallowing my saliva or just dribbling it out of my mouth."

"He thought he was going to die," Purcell told me.

Hot chicken was a dish created for the express purpose of bringing a man to his knees. Its origin myth wasn't the result of a mistake, like chocolate chip cookies, Coca-Cola, or the French dip sandwich. Hot chicken was premeditated; to this day, every bite of Nashville hot chicken is touched by the spectral presence of a betrayed lover.

The story remains such a foundational part of hot chicken's allure that it bears repeating (and, frankly, it never gets old): Back in the 1930s, there was a man named Thornton Prince, who had a reputation around town as a serial philanderer. His girlfriend at the time, sick of his shit and spending her nights alone, decided to do something about it. After a long night out, Prince came home to breakfast. His girlfriend made fried chicken, his favorite. But before serving it, she caked on the most volatile spices she had in the pantry—presumably cayenne pepper and mustard seed, among other things. If it didn't kill him, at least he would reevaluate his life choices. He didn't do either—Prince fell harder for the over-spiced piece of chicken than he did for any woman he'd ever courted. Prince implored her to make it for his family and friends—they all loved it, too.

An act of revenge became a neighborhood treasure, and Nashville's one true indigenous food. The identity of Prince's girlfriend (the real innovator here) has been lost to time, but the fearful flashes of mortality that hot chicken eaters have experienced for more than 80 years gives a particular angel in heaven her wings.

Technically, hot chicken is straightforward. The flavor profile has likely evolved since Thornton Prince took his first bite, and every restaurant claims to have a secret preparation. But in essence, it is fried chicken coated in a paste largely consisting of cayenne and other dried spices with a splash of hot oil from the fryer. Because the paste is oil-based and searingly hot, the skin stays crisp, unlike buffalo wings, which are prone to either drying out or getting gloppy in a hurry. (Hot chicken predates the first buffalo wing by three decades.) The finished product has a lurid, reddish hue that, depending on the spice level, ranges from California sunset to the bowels of hell. Hot chicken is served with two mandatory accompaniments: a slice of plain old white bread upon which the bird is perched and a few pickle chips skewered to the chicken with a toothpick.

That's it. It is, in my opinion, a damn-near perfect dish. The lines that separate love and hate, pleasure and pain, expectation and reality—they dissolve when you eat hot chicken. If you do it right, it will hurt. You might cry. And you will spend the next week thinking about when you might have it again.

Hot chicken has become one of the biggest national food trends of the last few years, but I didn't come to Nashville to Columbus a dish that has existed for nearly a century. I did come to see, from the source, why America's fascination with hot chicken is exploding at this particular moment. As recently as 10 years ago, hot chicken wasn't a universally acknowledged dish, even in its birthplace. For the majority of its existence, it was largely contained within the predominantly black East Nashville neighborhoods that created it, kept out of view under the shroud of lawful segregation.

Prince's old location was close to the Ryman Auditorium, where the Grand Ole Opry performed for more than three decades. Its late-night hours were perfect for performers, and early adopters like Country Music Hall of Famer George Morgan helped build a devout following. But in the segregation era, to get their fix, they had to walk through a side door. Prince's was operated like a white establishment in reverse: blacks order in front, whites out back.

Even after desegregation, hot chicken remained hidden in plain sight for much of Nashville, due to what Purcell described as "comfort" on both sides of the racial divide.

"I think in terms of the first 50 years or more, there was a satisfaction by the family and families that were making hot chicken that they were doing something special and worthwhile," Purcell said. "But they had no particular inclination or desire in those days to franchise it, or move it beyond their own capacity to ensure its quality. And it satisfied them to be that way, and that's how they proceeded. Not unlike in some ways, aspects of Nashville at that time."

Nashville appears to be growing into itself, and growing to accommodate strangers; you can tell from the afternoon congestion on the interstate, where the gridlock is beginning to resemble the kind you'd experience in Atlanta or Austin. "There are a lot of people moving here from California," Andrew, an Uber driver, told me. "And the traffic is as bad as Los Angeles." Nashville is different now.

There's 2,000 miles between us, but Nashville and I have mutual interests.

My favorite restaurants could double as a Medieval Times–esque show for misandrists, where the male tears flow like wine. In high school, a group of friends and I ventured to a traditional Sichuanese restaurant just up the street from my school in the city of San Gabriel, a suburb east of Los Angeles where more than 60 percent of residents were Asian as of the 2010 census. We ordered a traditional hot pot full of meats and vegetables covered in a bubbling broth, loaded with dried whole chili pods and anesthetic Sichuan peppercorns, and topped off with what looked like a tanker explosion of crimson chili oil. On a count of three, we all agreed to lean in and inhale deeply. Instantly, everyone at the table broke out into a fit of uncontrollable coughing. It was the most demanding meal any of us had ever eaten. It wasn't just a memorable lunch, it was one of the best I'll ever have. These are the kinds of restaurants I'm in constant search of, where what's being served challenges sensory norms and forces you to reckon with food's capacity to change you in the moment—not just emotionally, but physically.

My search brought me to Prince's, but it didn't stop there. In planning my journey, I found inspiration in Anthony Bourdain, who had tweeted earlier this year that eating hot chicken was a "three day commitment." And so that's what I did. I committed myself to eating at three hot chicken joints in three days, ordering the highest spice level available at each one.

I realize now that isn't what Bourdain meant.

Thursday, 9:28 p.m. // Prince's Hot Chicken Shack
Spice Level: XXXHot

"Boy, I want to see you eat this," the woman taking my order said.

Those who order the highest spice level at Prince's—usually tourists, as there seems to be an unwritten rule as a Nashvillian to never order the extra hot—are almost always discouraged by the staff. Maybe it was the crazed grin I had walking up the counter, but I was met with minimal resistance. "You must have been convincing," Purcell told me. "Because they will normally not just question the order, but attempt to talk you down." All I got was an offer of ranch dressing, free of charge. I politely declined.

Nothing could have surprised me upon first bite, except for what happened: nothing. No tears, no sweat, minimal pain. Maybe I should've seen that coming.

Before career aspirations, before standardized testing—hell, before first grade—I was fixated on increasing my spice tolerance, on fulfilling a family hallmark. As a 4-year-old, I cautiously began dipping my food into sriracha; as a 10-year-old, I was my brother's sous-chef and designated taste tester, helping him chop habaneros for a salsa at his first college house party; last year, I ate a Carolina Reaper, the hottest chili on the planet, in front of a camera. Two decades of pushing my boundaries had culminated in eating the XXXHot at Prince's, in front of a petrified couple visiting from Chicago, without a hitch.

Desensitizing oneself to the burn of chilies broadens the palate. When the sting is no longer a hindrance, it's easier to focus on actual flavor. Prince's spice blend is heavily weighted toward cayenne and paprika, among other spices; the earthiness almost reminiscent of nuclear Oaxacan *mole*. It's hard to overstate how beautiful this fried chicken is. It glows, with a sheen emanating from every crevice. The flesh itself is perfect; Prince's specifically is lauded for a clandestine marination technique that begins before the bird ever hits the fryer. Whatever they do in their preparation made that fried chicken the best I've ever had, hot or not.

Was I a little disappointed by the initial heat of Prince's? Sure. But Jeffries, the great-niece of Thornton Prince, calls her chicken a 24-hour chicken, and she tells no lies. My mouth may not have minded all the cayenne, but my stomach was under siege. The pain wasn't sharp, like a knife stabbing through you. It was round and blunt, but incessant, like blows from a hammer tenderizing you from the inside. It can do strange things to a person, as my hallucinatory dreams that night would attest. Even I hadn't escaped the wrath of Prince's mythic heat.

There are photos on Yelp of people passed out on Prince's tables trying to finish their food. Purcell once took a coworker to the restaurant for lunch. The woman behind the window shook her head. His coworker was visibly pregnant. "She can't have hot chicken," the employee said. "She'll have to come back after the baby is born." Of course, there are also tales of pregnant women who have asked their partners to fetch Prince's hot chicken for takeout in hopes of expediting the delivery process. Pain is pain, I suppose.

But the strange mysticism surrounding the business doesn't end with its alleged childbirth-inducing properties. Prince's calls a small, bumpy strip mall just off the Dickerson Pike in East Nashville its home, in an area known to be a hotbed for prostitution. And there are countless stories about the role hot chicken plays as an aphrodisiac for locals. Andre Prince Jeffries has seen firsthand the rabid sexual appetite hot chicken can cast upon diners.

"We do have a lady that comes and she's been coming for about as long as I've been in business, she and others," Jeffries told the Southern Foodways Alliance in 2006. "And she gets it hot. She brings her suitors down here, different suitors. She comes always on the weekend and she gets it hot. One night, she just couldn't wait to get out, so the finale was on the hood of a car parked in front of the chicken shack. She's not the only one. . . . We just shut our eyes and continue to do our work, what we're good at. Hey, different things turn different people on."

But why? And, more importantly, how? For those answers, we'll need a quick science lesson. Capsaicin, the compound in chilis that causes a burning sensation, activates a receptor in the body called TRPV1, the same receptor activated when the body comes in contact with anything hotter than 109 degrees Fahrenheit. Capsaicin is a fat-soluble compound, which is normally a tidbit used to tell you to drink milk, not water to quell the heat. But in hot chicken's case, it explains why the dish is so damn hot. All the capsaicin in the spice mix is drawn out in the oil-based application, so with every bite, the compound floods the receptors in your mouth, effectively signalling to your body that you've committed self-immolation.

The rest of the body responds accordingly. Your temperature increases. You start sweating profusely. The blood vessels in your face begin to dilate to rush blood in and out of the problem site, causing swelling and redness. Snot is dripping from your nose. But then you start to feel loopy. The body thinks it's on fire, so it unleashes a wave of endorphins to help quell the burning. You start to feel something akin to a runner's high. The sharp stinging pain will subside, but the rush—and subsequent sense of tranquility—lasts a bit longer.

But that's taking into account only one biological process that goes into eating hot chicken. As an imaginary fire envelops the senses, the body processes the fact that you're eating some of the best fried chicken in the country. "Palatable foods are working on similar reward centers in the brain [compared to drugs like cocaine, amphetamine, and heroin]," said Matthew Young, a neuroscientist who spent three years researching the effects of MDMA at Emory University. "That's what makes us like certain foods more than others." The pleasure and pain of hot chicken comes in layers—in waves. It is a simple dish, but what it inspires in the body is as multivalent as a designer drug.

All that science still doesn't explain impulsive sex on the hood of a car in front of an entire restaurant full of people.

"Based on what I know about the brain and what I know about people, first of all, there are obvious environmental factors involved," Young said. "I assume people are eating this stuff late at night. I'm assuming they're eating this stuff after being out and drinking. So if you're already kind of drunk and your inhibitions are down, and you're increasing your perceived body temperature by eating this very spicy chicken—all of these things, environmental as well as biological, probably work together to increase the likelihood of two people looking across the table at each other and wanting to get down."

Hot chicken's mythology has grown immensely in the past decade, but it's hard to divorce the dish's allure from the over-the-top experiences Prince's has fostered over its nearly 80 years.

"It's funny," Purcell, the former mayor, said. "It's a place where nothing seems particularly crazy. It doesn't matter, somehow, whatever people are saying or doing, it all seems just fine."

Friday, 10:20 p.m. // Bolton's Spicy Chicken & Fish
Spice level: Extra Hot

After chatting with people at Nashville bars and restaurants, it seemed that Bolton's Spicy Chicken & Fish was more often the site of out-of-body experiences. "Yeah, you have to try Prince's, but I died at Bolton's," a bartender told me. "And if you're going there, get the hot fish."

Nashville was recently rated the friendliest city in America, according to *Travel + Leisure,* so I wasn't going to ignore the kindness and wisdom of locals. Along with the extra-hot chicken leg, I ordered an extra-hot fried catfish sandwich.

Bolton's co-owner Dollye Ingram-Matthews included fish on the menu as a way of preserving one of her cherished childhood memories: the backyard fish fry in her neighborhood, which began to disappear as she grew older. What is placed before you at Bolton's might seem a bit unorthodox to an outsider: a whole filet breaded and deep-fried, with a healthy dousing of cayenne, raw onion slivers, pickle chips, and a squeeze of French's yellow mustard between two pieces of plain white sandwich bread, the filet overflowing the sides to a comical degree. It may be a humble dish of humble origin, but it weaves a web of interconnected flavors, textures, and sensations: the cayenne is boosted by the acidic components surrounding it, the delicate crisp of the fish is embraced by the pillowy nature of the bread. After a few beers, and the mile walk from Dino's in which Gallatin Avenue curves into Main Street, the fish sandwich at Bolton's feels like destiny.

The chicken is good, too, though less cosmically aligned. The spice application in Bolton's is dryer than what you'll find at Prince's, akin to a Memphis barbecue dry rub. The individual granules of the spice mixture are visible on a piece of Bolton's chicken; the residual shake glitters the piece of white bread beneath. The cayenne mixture itself has a brighter heat than Prince's, and, to my tongue, hotter, too.

Ingram-Matthews walked by to check on me. "Is that hot enough for you?"

It would've been nice to have a few tears fall out of my eyes, but, yes. I told her it's hotter than what I ate at Prince's. "Of course it is," she replied, with calm certitude. "It's what we put in it."

Bolton's is a celebration of Bolton Polk, the uncle of Ingram-Matthews's husband, Bolton Matthews, and his contributions to the proliferation of hot chicken. Polk was the owner of Columbo's, a hot chicken shack, that, for a time, was Prince's only worthy competition to the throne. The two businesses shared roots. Polk was the former fry cook at Prince's before a quarrel with the Prince family had him jumping ship and starting his own business. Grand Ole Opry singer George Morgan was a frequent customer and loved Polk's chicken so much he had a chemist analyze the spice blend so he'd be able to replicate it at home.

Purcell remembers Columbo's well. It was where he had his first bite of hot chicken.

"I can actually look out the window of my office and see where it was," he said. The former mayor generally speaks in measured, gentle tones, but is often consumed by his own emotions talking about the city and its food staple. "I remember at that moment thinking that I'd never had anything like this, I don't think there is anything like this—I think this might be the best thing I've ever had. And that's a memory you hopefully never lose. I haven't."

Purcell's devotion to the dish over the years led him to plan a Nashville hot chicken festival in 2006 while he was still mayor. It was Nashville's bicentennial year, and Purcell could think of no better way to celebrate the city than by paying a tribute to one of its great delicacies. Without a tinge of haughtiness in his voice, Purcell credits the hot chicken festival for the dish's propulsion into a Nashville mainstream cultural hallmark. "I think that the festival itself made it clear to people who haven't focused on it, or had it, or understood it before, just how unique and special it is—that it is ours," he said. "That it started here and it will always be ours, as long as we support it and keep it alive."

Music City Hot Chicken Festival celebrated its 10th year this summer. It's held on the Fourth of July every year, and while it may seem strange to want to share a day with the greatest celebration of America,

Purcell figured there was no better setting. "It's one of those times when people are celebrating the nature of their civic relationships," Purcell said. "[It is] the one day of the year where you could be sure that everybody would be thinking about what it meant to be a person in Nashville, in America."

Saturday, 11:40 a.m. // Hattie B's
Spice level: Shut the Cluck Up

It was strange, yet reassuring, to hear Purcell talk about hot chicken as an affirmation of the American spirit. Hot chicken reflects certain attitudes and values about food and culture that I didn't associate as American. It was certainly an America I'd longed for, but one I wasn't sure existed—an America that didn't always process extremes as pure gimmickry. The idea of a "challenging" food bringing people together in an immersive experience was always something I attributed more to my Southeast Asian upbringing.

It's not that America doesn't have a history of chili consumption: The Hatch chili is a staple of New Mexico, and we'll always have people experimenting with new weapons-grade sauces, but New Mexico chilies aren't cultivated specifically for heat, and toying with capsaicin extract is more of a sub-subcultural pastime. Hot chicken is an anomaly, a kind of extreme so rarely celebrated by Americans en masse. It's a dish that outlasted the Great Depression and segregation in America, and lived long enough to see itself become a modern American food trend and symbol of gentrification.

Just around the corner from Prince's and a short walk down Dickerson Pike is a KFC. Earlier this year, the chain took hot chicken and ran it through the Colonel's Transmutation Chamber, delivering KFC's Nashville Hot Chicken, a castrated product that, by mere mention of the word "Nashville," is meant to reinforce their modern branding: *vaguely Southern, vaguely something.*

Tuesday is hot chicken night at Zingerman's in Ann Arbor, Michigan. New hot chicken specialists have opened in the New York City, Seattle, and Chicago metropolitan areas this year alone. My first bite of hot chicken came courtesy of Howlin' Ray's in Los Angeles. Owner Johnny Ray Zone has worked for Gordon Ramsay, Joël Robuchon, and Nobu Matsuhisa, but found his calling during a brief stint with Sean

Brock's Southern bastion Husk in Nashville, where he was first exposed to hot chicken. Together with his wife, Amanda, he decided to bring a souvenir back to his hometown, initially as a food truck. Now, it's a limited-hours storefront in a shopping complex in L.A.'s rapidly gentrifying Chinatown.

Stylistically, the chicken at Howlin' Ray's is highly influenced by Bolton's dry application. It's a spiritually faithful re-creation: Howlin', the hottest option on their menu, is at least as hot as anything I've had from the source. I choked on my first bite of Howlin' Ray's hot chicken. My eyes geysered. I lost control of my body. I was in love.

Hot chicken's widespread popularity suggests a shift in the national palate. But it's a dish rooted in a strong sense of place; you'll always know how to go directly to the source. The most celebrated and emblematic dish of one of the 25 most populous cities in the country is something designed to hurt you. I'd never felt more American than when I was eating hot chicken in Nashville.

I wanted to make one last stop before boarding my flight back home. Hattie B's, established in 2012, is one of the newer hot chicken joints in the city; its location in midtown Nashville makes it a tourist-friendly alternative to many other iconic hot chicken shacks. I was skeptical. Hattie B's was a topic of discussion in nearly all of my Uber rides. On my way to Prince's, my driver, Hicham, wondered why I wasn't going to Hattie B's, which he heard was the best. (Hicham had never tried hot chicken before.)

On my way back from Prince's, my driver Eugene and I exchanged our versions of the Thornton Prince fable, and he, too, wondered why, as a tourist, I didn't try Hattie B's first. "Well, I'm glad you went to Prince's," Eugene said. "The guys at Hattie B's once sent their workers out to Prince's to try to steal their marination recipe, try to get that flavor. But they obviously couldn't."

Hattie B's had been open only 30 minutes, but the line—mostly white, mostly tourists—bent around the restaurant and ran down the street. While there are a few tables in the store itself, most ate from the trendy, raised patio deck. At Prince's and Bolton's, there was a sense of familial warmth, the product of years, maybe even generations, of patronage. Hugs were exchanged by members of the community who just happened to stop in for a bite at the same time. Considering that Hattie

B's hasn't even made to a half-decade of existence, it might be unfair to pit the restaurant against that standard, but in its four years, Hattie B's already has three locations in two states; Prince's, after nearly eight decades of serving hot chicken, only recently announced an upcoming second location. Same product, different ethos—though the enterprising spirit Hattie B's has demonstrated in its franchising is American, too.

I'll cop to being a little discriminatory. I'd assumed this third wave of hot chicken purveyors would dilute the product, at least a bit. When it was time to order, I asked the Hattie B's cashier how their hottest (regrettably named "Shut the Cluck Up") stacked up to Prince's and Bolton's. "Well, it's a different flavor profile entirely," she said. "We use ghost peppers. You'll enjoy it."

Fuck. It wasn't that I couldn't handle that—one of my favorite snacks is McDonald's fries with a sprinkle of pulverized ghost peppers—but I was well aware of the kind of havoc *bhut jolokia* can wreak on a stomach. My flight was in four hours.

The exterior of the chicken at Hattie B's is darker than what I had at either Prince's or Bolton's. Apparently at the Shut the Cluck Up level, the spice blend incorporates habanero, ghost pepper, and Trinidad Scorpion. The cashier was right; the flavor profile is markedly different from a cayenne-centric piece of hot chicken. The higher up you go on the Scoville unit scale, the more the pungency of a chili registers as acidic. Thai bird's eye chilies, habaneros, ghost peppers—they all release a fresh, floral essence that razors through other flavors as a trigger warning for the pain you're about to experience. That bracing sensation—not pain, but the liminal back and forth between the brain and the palate signaling that you're in for trouble—is, to me, one of the best feelings in the world. I ate on the back patio, overlooking the line to get through the door. Unlike the intimate scenes at Prince's and Bolton's, the Hattie B's experience is broadcast. I invited people to watch me and my trembling fingers, completely fine with the idea of people noticing my trembling fingers and heavy breathing. I asked strangers to take pictures of my busted face; my experience became theirs.

There have been fascinating studies in recent years linking body temperature and mood. While he was at the University of Arizona, Dr. Charles Raison began experimenting with whole-body hyperthermia (essentially toasting people from the neck down at high temperatures).

Raison's study was inspired by Tibetan monks up in the Himalayan mountains who used special breathing techniques in their meditation, which studies have shown were able to increase the temperature of their extremities by 15 degrees Fahrenheit. Coincidentally, the capsaicin that binds itself to receptors on the tongue and other parts of the mouth can trick the mind into thinking that something is 15 degrees hotter than it is.

"Capsaicin-containing foods have the potential, like heat, to activate sensory fibers and function of brain areas involved in affect and cognition," said Christopher A. Lowry, an associate professor of integrative physiology at the University of Colorado Boulder, who worked alongside Raison in the heat studies. "So, the infrastructure is there for hot chicken to affect mood and higher order brain function."

The hot chicken shack, then, becomes more than just a restaurant. It is a sweat lodge, a hot yoga studio, a sauna; it is a safe space to cry among strangers. There is no pretense; we all know the forces at work, beckoning those tears and beads of sweat. I once saw an old Chinese man at Chengdu Taste, my favorite Sichuan restaurant in Los Angeles, crying into his bowl of rice. I caught myself staring, and so did he. The man let out a nervous smile, and shrugged. My three days in Nashville were full of those moments. It struck me how the hot chicken trend has mirrored a recent boom in Sichuan restaurants in L.A.'s eastern suburbs over the last three years. The hot chicken shack in Nashville, not unlike the restaurants I frequent in the strange Asian bubble of the San Gabriel Valley, gathers a community, and, gimmick or not, everyone is there for the same reason: to feel the great relief of succumbing.

Last month, Jack White and his Nashville-based Third Man Records successfully launched the Icarus Craft, a space-proof vessel housing a turntable attached to a high-altitude balloon that floated out into the void. Sound, as perceived by humans, cannot be carried in the vast emptiness of deep space. Walking out of Hattie B's, my face and arms went numb, tingling as I glided in the cool, post-drizzle breeze. I stumbled down the road, hearing only the faint ringing of my own body fighting an imaginary fire as I floated along the sidewalk and into what might've been oncoming traffic. Hours later, encased in a high-altitude vessel myself, 25,000 feet in the air and climbing, the hammers began to descend. I was Icarus.

The City That Knows How to Eat

By Besha Rodell

From Eater.com

For *LA Weekly* restaurant critic Besha Rodell, revisiting the zesty, multiethnic dining scene of Melbourne, Australia—her childhood home—more than lived up to her memories. Which inevitably led her to wonder: Why can't Americans eat like this?

In 1976, Australia birthed three things: The AC/DC album *High Voltage*, the bratwurst stand at Melbourne's Queen Victoria Market, and me. When I was a kid, my AC/DC-loving stepfather and I would brave the throngs in front of the bratwurst stand to claim our breakfast: Two regular brats, please, with mild mustard on half white rolls, along with a flat white for my stepfather made on the old espresso machine that grunted and whirred a few feet from the smoking grill.

After breakfast, we would embark upon our Saturday food-shopping ritual, a serious undertaking that circled outward through the Vic Market's 17 sprawling acres of indoor and outdoor stalls. In the fruit sheds I could smell the edge of rot; in the chilly meat building whole carcasses hung, dead eyes staring. In the deli section, a vintage paradise of chrome and marble booths built in 1929, gold-painted lettering spelled out the businesses' names and specialties: French pastries, tea, confections, cheese, olives, butter, bratwurst. I marveled at stalls festooned with hanging kielbasa, and stalls where they scooped thick Greek yogurt from tubs, and stalls with delicate European chocolates displayed like jewels. Shopping was a skill and a joy and a competitive sport. My stepfather haggled with the meat guy and selected the best vegetables hawked by old Greek men who shouted: "Bananabanana-banana!!! Onedollaronedollarondollar!!!"

At the time, if you had asked me what I might miss most about my Melbourne life, the Markets wouldn't have even crossed my mind. Boys, friends, record stores—these were the things I considered most meaningful.

In 1990, my American mother decided it was time for her to return home, and for the rest of us—four kids, one husband—to go with her. I arrived in Denver, Colorado, as a pissed-off 14-year-old with purple hair and a funny accent, separated from my father and my friends. My new home seemed to lack any discernible street life, only cars and tidy neighborhoods and malls. The most visceral culture shock came in the aisles of American supermarkets, which were sterile and bright and exciting in a morally ambiguous kind of way. The yogurt was different (sweeter), the candy was different (better), the cookies were called cookies, not biscuits. Rather than the vibrant, stinky thrill of Vic Market's maze of stalls, in Denver, shopping for food was an act of sanitary consumerism. For my stepfather especially, the pleasure of shopping, and therefore of cooking and eating, was blunted. What had been a raucous joy became a cold chore.

My first true American friendship came once we left Denver and moved to Hartford, Connecticut. Toby was a crazy goth gay kid who wore black-and-white-striped tights with jean shorts and Doc Martens and only ate fluffernutter sandwiches. Like the rest of my new peers, he seemed to revel in his general dislike of food. The first time I went to his house, we stood in his gleaming, stark kitchen while he piled marshmallow fluff onto peanut butter toast and listed everything he wouldn't eat: "Meat, vegetables, rice, soup. I used to eat pizza but it's bad for my skin."

By the time I left Melbourne, my friends and I had already started throwing elaborate dinner parties together. We scoured the city for the best fish and chips, obsessed over new restaurants and declared our allegiance to old ones. Stuck in abstemious America, I poured most of my petulant, goth-kid energy into yearning for Melbourne like a lost love-of-my-life, a mythical home that no one in this myopic, poorly nourished country would understand.

"Australia," Toby said as we stood in his kitchen, his mouth sticky with peanut butter. "That's in Europe, right?"

Do we not know how to eat in America? I felt that way when I arrived and I feel that way now, though we're doing much better these days. (After all this time, I count myself as part of that "we." I hold dual U.S./Australian citizenship, and embrace all the tricky and proud self-examination that comes with identifying, even partially, as American.)

For the past decade, in my work as a food critic, I've witnessed America's food revolution firsthand, and seen how a combination of changing tastes and rising culinary ambition has reshaped entire cities. I lived in Atlanta as the New South's food identity blossomed, and I'm now in Los Angeles, right as the world has finally stopped turning up its collective nose at the city's culinary riches. I have massive amounts of admiration and respect for the chefs, farmers, writers, and cooks who have pushed America to this point. But something profound is still missing, something that feels like it's at the very root of my homesickness.

Why am I still not over Melbourne? I've lived in Colorado, Connecticut, New York, North Carolina, Georgia, and California, and all of them still, in some way, feel like home (except Colorado—sorry Denver). I spent 11 years in Melbourne (we moved there when I was three) and have now spent 26 in the U.S. And especially now, when avocado toast is taking America by storm (avocado toast is a 100 percent Australian invention, insofar as any one ingredient on a piece of bread can be), what is it exactly that I miss so deeply?

Traditionally, American chefs and food writers have looked to Europe to learn about cultivated eating. The story of the American ingenue taking her first bite of French baguette (with real butter!) or her first taste of a small, scarlet, perfect strawberry in a Provence marketplace—it's so ubiquitous that it's an utter cliche. America, we are told to believe, was settled too recently, was too influenced by industrialization, is made up of too many disparate cultures, and is burdened with too much shame to have a through-line of shared history that might allow a pure and pleasurable relationship with food. We fetishize Asia; we romanticize Europe. We reserve our most rapturous food epiphanies for travel.

But there is another young nation colonized by Anglos and defined by waves of immigrants that has incredible bread and strawberries and joie de vivre—America has just been too distracted by the kangaroos to see it. Beyond the cultural commonalities (including different brands of the same kind of shame), some of contemporary America's biggest food trends are right out of my hometown's playbook. Being from Melbourne and working in the American food world is like constantly being told—with great gusto—that the sky is blue. In the quarter-century I've lived here, I've seen America discover the joys of decent coffee, farmers markets become ubiquitous, and avocado toast spread like a plague. Food halls! Super creative breakfast using fresh ingredients and international flavors! Next-gen delis! All of these things have been happening in Melbourne since the 1980s, or in some cases, the 1890s. And not just as passing trends; they infuse the entire culture. The frumpily dressed grannies of Melbourne drink cappuccino and roast their legs of lamb with lemon and white wine and rosemary.

This isn't just teenaged nostalgia talking: I returned to Melbourne this summer and discovered that the magic very much persists.

Melbourne is a port city, built around the seashell-shaped curve of Port Phillip Bay. For 40,000 years or so, it was inhabited by tribes of the Kulin Nation, hunter-gatherers who took advantage of its lush, temperate climate. French and British explorers began showing up around 200 years ago, and the area was colonized by the British in 1835. The Victorian gold rush in the mid-nineteenth century sparked an explosion of both population and wealth. The city's grand, Victorian architecture is the kind of extravagance only gold could buy.

If the gold rush gave the city refined taste—during those years Melbourne consumed more Champagne than any other city on Earth—successive waves of immigration expanded its palate. The city's famous cafe culture springs from a well-timed Italian influx: After World War I, the U.S. put policies in place that effectively halted the flow of Italians to America, and Australia became the favored alternative. Through a trick of timing and history, that switch from America to Australia coincided with the invention of the espresso machine. The Italian coffee culture that never quite made it to America blossomed in Melbourne. I know, I know—New York had an espresso machine in 1904 or whatever, but I'm not talking about one or two or ten cafes. I'm talking about hundreds of thousands of people who brought their taste for espresso with them.

Even before the rise of Italian cultural influence, the dominant Anglo culture built much of Australia's social life around old, hulking pubs on practically every corner. Pubs have always been much more welcoming (and family-friendly) than any bars I can think of in America. That familiarity with a communal space primed Melbourne for the European-style cafe, another place in which to lead life publicly and socially.

Though the boom of Italian immigration to Melbourne began in the 1920s, it wasn't until 1954 that the first real Italian cafe opened. Pellegrini's, located on Bourke Street in the middle of Melbourne's Central Business District, brought to fruition 30 years of espresso-loving immigrants making Melbourne their home. My father, who was 20 at the time, remembers that opening distinctly. "There was nothing like it, there had been nothing like it before," he says. "It was the beginning of Melbourne becoming what it is."

Pellegrini's is still open, with its red mid-century signage, checkered floor, and a menu and atmosphere that have remained unchanged for more than 60 years. If it established Melbourne's cafe culture, its longevity reflects another key facet of the city's dining persona: The persistence of old-school family-run places that cater to the same people decade after decade. These restaurants used to be everywhere in the U.S., but we've lost many of them over the past half-century. It's not just a loss of history; these restaurants are surrogate family who know your tastes and the names of your kids.

I've always been a sucker for the kinds of fantasy novels wherein a hidden world is revealed, just beneath the surface. Melbourne has a lot of that. Many of the most interesting places to eat and drink are down alleyways, which wind through the guts of the city's center and grow odd little businesses like weeds.

Down a lane in the central business district, there's an unassuming door with a stairway leading up off the street. Up the stairs is a '70s-era room with faded posters of Europe on the wall and a blackboard menu listing the day's specials: pasta, grilled fish, stewed rabbit with rosemary and olives. This is the Waiter's Club, an Italian restaurant that has served as a hangout for journalists, gangsters, and—yes—waiters, for 70 or so years. It's also one of the restaurants that raised me. There are a few.

A mile or so away in Collingwood, Jim's Greek Tavern is easier to find, but in its own way it feels even more like an insider's club. On the way to your table, the host will walk you by a large glass refrigerator case filled with meat and fish: tiny pink lamb chops, coils of octopus, glistening whole snapper, carefully arranged translucent pinkish brains. That trip past the meat case is the closest Jim's comes to a menu. After you're seated, a brusque waiter, usually of the older Greek variety, will come by the table. "What do you want?" he'll bark at you. "You want some dips? Some meat? Fish? Eh?" At that point the negotiation starts. You try to remember things you saw in the refrigerated case, and he decides what you're worthy of eating. Everything is grilled simply, with olive oil, herbs, and maybe some lemon. You get pretty much whatever they decide you get.

"Do you have wine?" you might ask.

"Nah. Not really." But then later, once you've earned your waiter's approval, he'll ask if you prefer white or red and then plunk down a half-full carafe. "You drink this. You like it? I'll bring you another."

This is very Greek, but it's also very Australian, like you're being served by a gruff but loving family member. A few years back while eating at Jim's, our waiter was scolding us and feeding us so parentally that my stepfather said to him, "I might just start calling you Mum."

The Waiter's Club, Jim's, and other places like them are the foundation of Melbourne's eating life, one in which hospitality means something far more personal than the transactional nature of business. The city's dining history is also its present, not for nostalgia's sake but because there's continuity. Traditions aren't easily discarded; they're a source of pride. I feel looked-after in these restaurants in a way I've only experienced in the most service-oriented fine dining establishments in the U.S.

Over the 60 years since Pellegrini's opened, its influence—and the influence of the many immigrant restaurants that opened after 1954—has meant great coffee, and it's meant something much more. From early morning until late night, Melbourne's sidewalks are clogged with tables and chairs and people eating and drinking and sipping lattes as trams clang down the streets. Out in front of the Vic Markets, people carry their bratwursts and croissants and share happy conversation before they do the week's shopping. The cafes of Melbourne are not just places where great coffee happens. They're places where breakfast happens, where lunch happens, where mid-afternoon drinks and people-watching happen. Woven into the fabric of the city as surely as the tram tracks that crisscross its streets and the wrought iron that spindles across the facades of its Victorian row houses, the cafes of Melbourne are where life happens.

If Pellegrini's is Melbourne's original cafe, Mario's, located on Fitzroy's main drag, was the next great leap forward. Opened in 1986, Mario's was (and is) an Italian cafe with the bearing of a classy restaurant. They had all-day breakfast and really good coffee and carefully made bowls of pasta. Owner Mario Maccarone told *Gourmet Traveller* earlier this year: "We elevated the idea of what a cafe could be . . . We looked a bit like a restaurant, but you could still come in and get Vegemite on toast." Take away the Vegemite and Maccarone sounds like a lot of American restaurateurs circa 2012, but he's talking about 1986. Mario's turned Melbourne cafes into places where serious food happened, and where breakfast was as important as dinner.

It also primed Fitzroy's Brunswick Street to become the cafe capital of the universe. There are a few neighborhoods in Australia that might try to claim that title, but my money's on Fitzroy, which also puts Williamsburg and Silver Lake to shame on the hipster scale. You can't walk two feet in Fitzroy without stumbling over another cafe serving pumpkin, pomegranate, crispy kale, and goat cheese on toast, another craft cocktail bar with a more exclusive cocktail bar upstairs that you have to buzz into, another shop selling gorgeous clothes you can't afford. My brother lives above a disgustingly trendy barber shop that might as well be called "Bespoke," and a women's clothing store called "Who Invited Her," which simultaneously makes me want to applaud and claw my own eyes out.

Mario's and its neon cursive sign are still an iconic part of the neighborhood, 30 years after its opening. And all around it are evolutions, cafe menus that reflect an ever-broader array of cultures. There are more Greeks in Melbourne than any city in the world outside of Greece. Refugees from the Lebanese civil war flowed into the city during the '70s and '80s. In the 45 years since the repeal of the "White Australia" policy (yes, it was really called that), the city's Thai, Vietnamese, Chinese, and Indian populations have swelled. Somehow, despite the very real racism faced by each of these groups as they arrived, their food has become integrated into the life of Melbourne in a way I'm only just beginning to see in big American cities.

Those Greek and Middle Eastern and Asian influences have been folded into Melbourne's cultural identity, and they reverberate through the kaleidoscopic flavors found on its best cafe and restaurant menus. From Thai-style omelettes and creative congees to chicken and kaffir lime scotch eggs, breakfast alone in this city could kick the asses of America's best seasonal small plates.

Nostalgia often dictates that I spend much of my Melbourne time eating in those restaurants that raised me, but this time around I ventured farther, and found whole new reasons for prodigious hometown pride. Down one of those magical back laneways in the city, Tipo 00 embodies the rich inheritance that all those Italian immigrants gave to modern Australian cooking. Its small room was packed with diners at 3 p.m. on a Saturday, drinking wine and eating delicate handmade pappardelle with braised rabbit, hazelnuts, and marjoram; light but foresty, hauntingly delicious.

At Epocha in Carlton, owner and maitre d' Angie Giannakodakis greets guests with hugs, her slick black suit and spiky hair as timelessly stylish as the antique fireplace in the dining room. Located in a Victorian terrace house overlooking one of the city's stately parks, the restaurant's friendly formality mixes with a purposeful celebration of Melbourne's immigrant roots: The UK might show up in a black pudding that comes alongside the rabbit loin; a green sauce-bedecked lamb shoulder—basically a heap of fat and juices—channels the love of the thousands of Greek grandmothers who live in the city. I didn't find newness in Melbourne so much as progression, a careful amplification of what came before, which seemed oddly revolutionary. The American hunger for tossing out the old and worshipping the new is thrilling, but so much is lost in the process.

While eating and drinking at Gerald's, a cluttered storefront wine bar in Carlton North, the owner Gerald Diffey plonked down beside me and my brother and shared his fiercely held, basically proletariat beliefs about wine. "I don't really care how preciously you fondled the grapes, or where it was aged—who gives a fuck?" Diffey said amicably. "People forget that a lot of the pleasure and magic of wine is that it tastes good and gets you pissed." Sitting with a rowdy, foul-mouthed wine evangelist while drinking a casually poured, mind-bending Riesling, I felt as though I had slipped into the life I might have led, had it not been taken from me (or me from it).

It would be foolish to suggest that I've never had a meal in America that felt spiritually similar to what Melbourne offers so effortlessly. Portland sometimes comes close to finding that groove. Grand Central Market here in L.A. has some commonality with the Vic Markets, though the Vic Markets aren't burdened with the same strains of gentrification that plague GCM. Bacchanal in New Orleans, the wine shop with a sprawling, cluttered backyard where you can sit for hours drinking wine, eating cheese, and listening to music, feels more like home to me than almost anywhere else in the country, even though I have no personal connection to New Orleans.

Most of the literal interpretations of Melbourne I've come across here—the meat pie shops, the Australian cafes—are a little sad, though one or two in Brooklyn come close to the real thing. Sqirl in Los Angeles, a relaxed cafe celebrated for its creative rice bowls and lovely baked goods, is basically a very good Melbourne cafe on a corner in East Hollywood. Unsurprisingly, chef and owner Jessica Koslow spent time working at a bakery in Melbourne.

I'm sure that a food-obsessed American reading this might be able to come up with a plethora of other examples, places, and things that sound similar to the things I'm claiming as unique to my hometown. It's true that the differences are subtle—food as a way of life, a birthright, a source of pleasure, and a shared culture rather than a means of constructing identity or differentiating status. But to me they feel profound.

Don't get me wrong: Melbourne has plenty of crap, artifice, and hyped-up places that may or may not deserve the hype. There's a casino full of restaurants with international superstar chef names above the doors. Ben Shrewy forages his way through every big-name food magazine, and his restaurant, Attica, is currently at number 33 on the World's 50 Best list, serving dishes made with wallaby blood, as well as a fine-dining take on . . . avocado toast. I'm sure Attica is great; I'd love to eat there one day. But my hometown's greatest culinary gift, the thing I miss the most, the thing I've been looking for ever since I left, is the city's underlying attitude: That food is just a part of everyday life and, damn, isn't everyday life wonderful?

Am I overthinking this? Maybe I should write an essay instead about how sick I am of tasting menus. About all the things servers do that mildly annoy me. Maybe I should just move back.

My brother has moved back to Melbourne, as has my sister, and my stepfather. My stepfather tells a story about something someone said to him in the leadup to our move to America. He was 30 at the time, and our move would be his first trip outside of Australia. This friend of his, who had spent some time in the U.S., said: You'll go there and everything will seem familiar. You'll understand the language. The food will taste somewhat similar. The way people deliver the news on TV, the way people sing at rock shows, the way people drink at bars: It will all feel comfortably recognizable. And then after you've been there for a while, you'll begin to understand the real difference between America and Australia, and that difference is vastly more profound than anything you might point to on the surface. And then you'll realize you are as alien to that place as you might be on Mars.

I'm not sure on which planet I belong. Otherness is such a part of my identity that if I were to return to Australia now, I don't know who I'd be. The dominant narrative when it comes to immigrant stories is the struggles faced upon arriving in a new land, and the confusion of trying to survive while looking and speaking and thinking differently. In those regards my experience can't begin to compare to people leaving their homes in China or South America or Africa or even Europe. I'm white. I speak the language; I look the part. But the thing I share with immigrants and expats of all stripes is the intense feeling of otherness that comes with missing home, the belonging to different earth, different air, a different ocean. Leaving is the key event of your life—you spend all the time after trying to reconcile the person you were when you belonged somewhere with the displaced person you've become. It's this very condition that pushes people to re-create a taste of home in their new lives. It's the exact dynamic that created so much of the food culture I've spent my life longing for.

I've continued to displace myself, over and over again, moving away from cities once they become comfortable and familiar. My last move, from Atlanta to L.A., was the most wrenching since leaving Melbourne. I came to a city I'd never visited, where I knew no one, to take a high-profile job as a complete unknown. "I'm not from here" is at the core of who I am.

When I got back to L.A. after my summer trip to Melbourne, I had a conversation with my mother, another installment in the long line of conversations we've been having for 25 years, the one that goes: Why did we leave? Should we go back? What is it that we're missing so very much? What is the difference?

And my mother told me something I'd never heard her say before: "America was settled mainly before the Industrial Revolution, and it was all about pioneering, all about rugged individualism. Australia has this reputation of being settled by convicts, but the truth is that most of the country is built on immigration that came later, after the Industrial Revolution. These were working people, and they were familiar with the mind-set that came along with that. Unions! Solidarity! America was built on going out and conquering the West, all by your fucking self. Australia was built on the idea that you look out for your mates."

That's what I miss. The comfort of living in a place where the underlying principle is that we look out for one another. If that ethos leads to good coffee and grilled lamb chops, all the better.

In America we read the blogs, we obsess about which chef is leaving what job and what storefront will become the next hot restaurant. We stand in line for rainbow-glazed ramen burger bagels. But in the end, our newfound food obsessions founder on that with which America has always been concerned: commerce and status. I see—especially in the food world—an urge to connect, to put more stock in pleasure, to find some sort of fellowship in our dining rituals. Our seating is increasingly communal. Practically all of our semi-upscale eating is now done off of shared plates, in an attempt to force togetherness. These gestures are genuine, and yet they're received as fashion.

Culture is so interconnected. Maybe Australians can have their carefree, joyful attitude around food and life because they get so much paid vacation, because childcare is affordable, because there's no gun violence, because there's not so much pressure, because the great Australian dream is to have a house and some kids and a few good friends. Because ambition is undervalued. Because life isn't as scary.

In Melbourne, the look-after-your-mates ethos, the pubs, and cafes have created a food culture as charming as Europe's, as exciting as America's, as varied as Asia's. A place where the past and the future are often friends, where community feels tangible, where it's okay to relax. No wonder it haunts me.

And yet—I love living in L.A. I love my work, and the people and places I write about. One of my greatest joys and achievements has been conquering the West, all by my fucking self. So maybe I am American after all. And maybe it's too much to ask America to learn how to blend its rugged individualism with a sense of community. In the wake of the most divisive presidential election in modern history (and its pro-consumerist, anti-multiculturalist results), this seems like a particularly ludicrous thing to hope for. Maybe I'll just have to make do with avocado toast.

On this trip, as with every Melbourne trip, I went and stood in the throng at the Vic Markets and bought myself a bratwurst and a flat white. I ate standing at the counter that runs along the inside wall of the grand stone entrance. I felt embraced by those walls, by the spirit of the immigrants who have passed through over the last century, by the otherness and longing for home that has inspired so much good food and good living. I gave thanks for that longing, for the German guy in 1976 whose desire for a taste of home made the bratwurst in my hand possible. I gave thanks to Melbourne and also to America, for making me who I am.

Eat Your Way Through Melbourne

Queen Victoria Market: Corner of Elizabeth & Victoria Streets, qvm.com.au
Pellegrini's: 66 Bourke Street, +61 3 9662 1885, no website
The Waiter's Club: 20 Meyers Place, +61 3 9650 1508, no website
Jim's Greek Tavern: 32 Johnston Street, +61 3 9419 3827, no website
Mario's Cafe: 303 Brunswick Street, +61 3 9417 3343, marioscafe.com.au
Tipo 00: 361 Little Bourke Street, +61 3 9942 3946, tipo00.com.au
Epocha: 49 Rathdowne Street, +61 3 9036 4949, epocha.com.au
Gerald's Bar: 386 Rathdowne Street, +61 3 9349 4748, geraldsbar.com.au

Ballad of a Small-Town Bakery

By Scott Mowbray

From *5280 Magazine*

Okay, so it's not a city, it's the antidote to a city: Louisville, Colorado, close enough to Denver and Boulder to be cosmopolitan, but proudly wearing its small-town mantle. For former *Cooking Light* editor Scott Mowbray, the story of Moxie Bread Company proves the perfect mix of local vibe and urban hip.

On the floor in a tiny back room of a converted 1880s Victorian house in Louisville sits a hulking 1940s-era Hobart mixer, its single-phase motor turning a cake-batter paddle in a huge steel bowl while Andy Clark, owner of Moxie Bread Company, "juices" his ciabatta dough by drizzling in water. A dough hook, he explains, couldn't handle a mix this goopy. The stuff *fwap-fwap-fwap*s around while a stooping Clark coaxes it toward an even wetter state. It's tricky work that varies with the heat of the room and the weather outside. For Clark, it's also a daily obsession, one that takes place long before the sun rises.

Clark is devoted to producing crust with a fine crackle and crumb with a perfect spring and sheen. "As bakers," he says, "making the dough really wet and baking it dark are two things we can do to be cool." Anyone who has the good fortune to eat Clark's bread will appreciate that his definition of cool stretches to include things like finicky hydration rituals at 4:30 in the morning.

A few steps away, at a long marble-topped table in Moxie's other back room, Jeff Leddy, Clark's chief baker, works dough that will become the bakery's specialty treat: kouign-amann. Leddy is known for his ability to incorporate staggering amounts of butter into flour, the "bourraging" that renders kouign-amann even richer than croissants. "Jeff's the pastry whisperer," says assistant Nikki Albrecht. "He's the Bob Ross of the pastry world."

A couple of hours later, a conveyor apparatus slips hand-formed loaves into the heart of Moxie's four-deck oven, while just a few feet away, Keely Von Bank arranges pastries on the service counter. To her right, chief barista Sullivan Cohen dials up the espresso machine for the arrival of the first customer, who will poke her head in at 7:01 and expect a happy hello. Some of Clark's crew will be here until the joint, which makes a midday transition to sandwiches and pizza, closes at four.

A town wants to rise and feel warmly about itself each day. This is the purpose of the diners and shopworn cafes and bakeries that nurture regulars in small communities from Alabama to Alaska. These patrons expect the staffs to know their names, and they like to see other regulars with whom short chats string together, over months and years, into long necklaces of specific, local conversations about kids and family and town bylaws and the weather. It's not that such places don't exist in cities, but in small towns, they have a special savor that usually doesn't have much to do with food or coffee, often untouched by the trends that obsess urbanites.

Communities like Louisville, in orbit of Boulder and Denver, exist on fault lines between city and small-town life. Residents treasure the quaint, local vibe, but many have acquired commuter palates. They hanker for a spot that serves the cortados of RiNo or Old South Pearl Street and sandwiches that remind them of that trip to Italy or Provence, France. Yet serious chefs and bakers are often reluctant to open a business that's even 10 miles from reliable city crowds. Which is what makes Louisville's 17-month-old Moxie especially notable. It's a young place with an old soul where the owner has found a way to combine urban culinary exactitude with small-town ease and purpose.

During his first 22 years in Colorado, Clark, 41, ran big bread operations for Whole Foods and Udi's. Corporate work had him baking around the country: He knew what it took to keep a baguette from drooping in Houston humidity or turning into a cracker javelin in desert air and exactly how big the problem was if you made a proofing error with 700 pounds of dough.

But as a member of the Bread Baker's Guild of America (he eventually served on its board of directors), Clark had tasted what artisans such as Chad Roberston at Tartine and Jim Lahey at Sullivan St. Bakery were up to in San Francisco and New York City, respectively. Clark was a soft-spoken fermentation nerd, a quiet doctor of pH. Wanting to scale down, he hankered for a hometown corner bakery where he'd know the customers and the daily turbulence would be "more like landing a Cessna on a little strip in Baja, California." Bread, at its best, is small and slow.

Clark was scouting potential locations when he met Louis Karp, father of the proprietor of Louisville's Waterloo bar and restaurant. Several years earlier, in 2007, Karp's son had opened what quickly became the most congenial evening hangout in the historic downtown area, and he told Clark the place had the sort of small-town charm he was looking for. That, and there just happened to be a 19th-century house available on a prominent corner along Main Street.

Rumors that something special might be percolating spread weeks before Moxie opened. "When Andy came to town," says Randy Evans, 65, who can be found at Moxie almost every day around 8 a.m., yakking with the staff and sipping a cortado, "I tasted his bread and I said, 'This is what I've been waiting for. Nobody's doing this.'" Evans, now a freelance copy writer, previously ran food operations for Four Seasons Hotels and Resorts in California and raced Formula Ford cars in the '70s. For years, otherwise happy with life in Louisville, he'd been mourning the quality of local food.

The town quickly realized it had a new morning hearth serving pastries and bread that were something special. From the start, Clark showed a knack for hiring staff adept at the chatty-cafe greeting, essential when lines are long and the wait for a proper latte stretches to several minutes. Customers, even the shy ones, started to talk back. A few formed a spontaneous, informal board of advisers. These are the super-users for whom Moxie's success, not a sure thing in the food business, became important. Evans is a super-user. Matthew Coghill, 36, is another.

Coghill admits to three Moxie visits most days to catch up with staff and the regulars, yielding "serious overcaffeination." He's a bicycle nerd, CrossFit geek, and coffee connoisseur who's the president of a small, techy Boulder company. For him, the acuity of Clark's baking is matched by a mise-en-scène intuition and hiring acumen he compares to that of Noah Price, co-founder of Crema, the Populist, and Finn's Manor, three exemplars of neighborhood cheer in Denver. It wasn't just the food that turned Moxie into a hangout; it was the congenial way it was sold, finely tuned to the local temperament, which Coghill says gave him "a view into all the people that I live with in this town but I had no other mechanism to know prior to this."

Guys like Coghill are the ones with commuter palates. If something is lacking in an establishment, they tend to either stay away or stick their noses in. Early on, in Coghill's opinion, the quality of Moxie's coffee lagged woefully behind that of the bread. Longing for a local fix to match all the coffee action in Denver and Boulder, Coghill asked Clark to do something "meaningful" at the espresso station. Clark, remarkably, listened, another key to his canny nature.

"I gave him a list of a lot of equipment to buy," Coghill says, "and then I scouted Sullivan [formerly of Boxcar Coffee Roasters] and introduced him to Andy. He just slowly implemented what is standard best practice from there. I'd say the coffee is now in the top tier of what's available in Colorado."

Coghill also proved a fount of food insight. This summer, when Clark went on a reconnaissance trip to LA, Coghill suggested coffeehouses to visit. Clark was wowed by "fizzy hopped teas" and turmeric-infused nut milks, returning eager to try such things at Moxie. He also says he was a bit put off by the expensively curated aesthetic of many of those urban food temples. "It's a contradiction of mine that I love that and hate it at the same time," Clark says.

Which explains, presumably, why there isn't a damned thing even vaguely hip about Moxie's decor. There are two rooms for lingering, filled with tables, musical instruments, and bric-a-brac of such flea-market eclecticism that it's almost comic. Out front, a few chairs crowd a small porch overlooking Main Street. Out back, there's a shambolic space that on summer Wednesday nights hosts a bring-your-banjo, roots-music hootenanny with pizza. It adds up to what Clark describes as "a really homespun, pragmatic-farmer, middle-America, old-fashioned, your-grandmother's-house kind of vibe."

As regulars soon came to learn, Louisville was now home to a national-quality baker who had a knack for playing the local heart-strings: Not much more than a year after it opened, Moxie was named one of the five best new bakeries in America by *Bon Appétit*.

Moxie's succinct breakfast and lunch menu includes croissants and a few varieties of Leddy's now-famous kouign-amann (season-ally flavored with black plum or peach in summer, pear or apple in the fall, and dark chocolate and grapefruit in winter), along with something called the King Egg, a diabolically buttery turban-shaped creation with croissant pastry wrapped around a warm egg and cheese. There are a few well-made sandwiches and lunchtime pizza. There's a salad or two and some cookies and muffins (not all of which equal the quality of the best items, and the music-night pizza can be uneven).

The place runs all out, seven days a week, which is why Clark tends to limit his holiday-season offerings to wintry kouign-amann and crois-sant variations, though last year Leddy produced a persimmon pud-ding with a spiked hard sauce. A walnut bread will likely make another appearance, and Clark yearns to produce a complex, chewy European gingerbread whose formula has eluded him despite years of trying.

For a guy who is a bread man in his soul, however, there's pain in the truth that it's these treats—and not the beer-inspired malthouse loaf or the mighty-crusted Algerian—that keep his little ship afloat. "It's trag-ically, comically sorrowful how little bread we sell," he says. Maybe 80 or 90 loaves a day. Another baker had warned him: *You'll basically be a sandwich shop.*

Yet he persists in not selling the one thing that would up his tally: white baguettes. Clark does not disdain baguettes and may eventually cave, but for now he persists with sour starters, long rises, and mostly multigrain blends. These breads are his passion. He's like a musician who plays beautifully from an old songbook and waits for the audience to catch on. There is a cheerful spirit in Moxie's front room and the prep rooms, but it's in the bread that local converts find Clark's true gospel. Someday, he believes, his adopted town will fully understand.

Updating the Classics

Burritos, Remixed

By Anna Roth

From the *San Francisco Chronicle*

While John Birdsall (see page 140) celebrates the classic Mission burrito, Anna Roth—former *SF Weekly* restaurant critic and a contributor to everything from *Lucky Peach* to *Civil Eats* to *Modern Farmer*—dissects how a new wave of cooks have put their own spin on that iconic San Francisco treat.

It certainly looks like a Mission burrito: a tight cylinder with heft encased in foil that would be folly to unpeel all the way. It tastes like a burrito, each bite a perfect medley of ingredients, with flecks of grilled meat mingling with pinto beans, rice and pico de gallo inside a stretchy flour tortilla. It's good at lunch; it would be better at 1 a.m. as a savory line of defense from the coming morning.

But the meat in question is *sisig,* a citrusy Filipino pork, and the rice is garlic, not Spanish. So here's a question: Can this creation from Filipino fusion truck Señor Sisig rightfully call itself a burrito? And for that matter, do the dozen other non-Mexican burritos in the city deserve the title, or should we be calling them wraps, or slabs or some other euphemism?

Is this the natural evolution of the Mission burrito, or is it an invasive species?

As far as burrito-related identity crises go, this one's not quite as trivial as it seems. The California-Mexican Mission burrito is still as essential to San Francisco identity as Karl the Fog, in spite of its co-option by chains like Chipotle and Qdoba. The taquerias that provide them are important democratic spaces in the Bay Area, and though they don't seem in any immediate danger of gentrification, many feel that if the taquerias go, so goes the city.

Fusion wraps had their moment in the '90s, but the recent non-Mexican burrito creep started in the late-aughts, when would-be food truck entrepreneurs took inspiration from the Korean tacos of Kogi in Los Angeles and began making their own Mexican-fusion creations. Bay Area trucks like Señor Sisig and Curry Up Now, with its chicken tikka masala version, both come from that school. A few years later, Sushirrito's sushi burrito, a concoction of raw fish, creamy sauce and other bits wrapped tightly in nori, was born; the poke burrito, lately washed up on our shores, is its sibling.

At Papalote in the Mission, brothers Victor and Miguel Escobedo were pushing the boundaries of the form as well, turning out everything from chicken adobo and soul food burritos to the Triple Threat, bursting with carne asada, chicken and shrimp.

The hybrid burrito movement fully reached the mainstream last fall, when Danny Bowien created a "Chinese burrito" made with mapo tofu and salt cod fried rice at his New York Mexican restaurant, Mission Cantina. Like everything Bowien and the Mission Chinese crew does, the Chinese burrito received plenty of media attention, even a segment with Jimmy Fallon on "The Tonight Show." It was soon on the menu at Mission Chinese Food in San Francisco, along with a brother made with the restaurant's signature kung pao pastrami.

Bowien isn't especially concerned about the Chinese burrito's implications. Authenticity, whatever that means, has never been a huge concern of the restaurants, and he sees this as just a novel way to eat Chinese food quickly.

"It's repackaging. You're just putting something in a piece of bread," Bowien says. "It's just a vessel to get the components inside into your mouth a little easier."

Thinking along these lines, all of the other items in the stuff-in-bread genre—the sandwich, the pizza, the bao—have been co-opted by multiple cultures. The real question may not be whether the burrito concept has spread throughout the world, but rather, why it's taken so long.

It's difficult to define the burrito for a number of reasons, not in the least because everyone has a different idea of the ideal one. People have "feelings" about rice, lettuce, salsa, vegetables and the inclusion of french fries (if you're from San Diego). And most have a complicated taqueria hierarchy in their head that shifts based on craving, hour and mood.

One thing all enthusiasts can agree on is that a great burrito has an intangibility about it, a magic that is greater than the sum of its parts. Charles Hodgkins, who spent nearly a decade sampling and rating a thousand San Francisco burritos for his now-defunct blog, Burrito Eater, likes to compare it to a musical ensemble.

"Everything has to play together well for the entire burrito to work," he says. "You have the rice playing with the meat, offsetting the cheese and vegetables, and the construction and the sauciness and the spiciness—all of it kind of comes together."

This is the beauty of the Mission burrito, which was born in 1960s San Francisco taquerias, probably at El Faro as a salve for hungry firefighters, although La Cumbre also claims ownership. But the burrito was not especially Mexican to begin with. The thing started in the borderlands, a food of laborers, just leftovers encased in a tortilla. (It has this in common with the Cornish pasty, both highly transportable delivery systems of protein and carbohydrates borne out of poverty and necessity.)

Does this Cal-Mex food deserve the same reverence that we place on more traditional forms of Mexican food? Probably, says Gustavo Arellano, author of "Taco USA: How Mexican Food Conquered America" and the man behind the OC Weekly's popular "Ask a Mexican" column. He points out that there is an entire generation of Mexican Americans who grew up with dishes like burritos and hard-shell tacos, but old-school Cal-Mex is becoming endangered as new waves of immigrants come and American interest in Mexican food moves on.

This doesn't necessarily mean we need to put a wall around Cal-Mex food to preserve it. "Mexican food is always evolving. Mexican food that was considered authentic in the 1960s is not the same thing we consider authentic to this day," Arellano says. "If people say, well a burrito of orange chicken is not authentic because orange chicken is not Mexican, my response is that flour tortillas aren't authentic, either. The only reason they exist is because Spaniards brought wheat into the New World.

"The authenticity debate is bull—."

Authentic or not, there is still the question of whether the Mission burrito, as a Cal-Mex entity, needs to be somehow preserved before it gets diluted any more. There is a school of people who believe in the Mission burrito as a stand-alone category. Hodgkins, the burrito blogger, is one of them ("all burritos are wraps, not all wraps are burritos" is his stance). Another such believer is the enigmatic, anonymous Burrito Justice, who told me via Twitter, his medium of choice, "Not all cylinders are burritos. Some of these fauxrritos may even be delicious, but not burritos. We've gotta hold the line."

In the abstract, I agree with them; the Mission burrito has been here for a half-century, long enough to inspire respect. But in practice, it's probably too late to stop the creep. These new burritos are popular. They are, by far, the most popular item on these trucks. ("In the end, it's the tikka masala burrito that pays my mortgage," Akash Kapoor from Curry Up Now told me.) Wes Rowe, of WesBurger 'N' More, says that customers order his Southern fried chicken burrito as much as the fried chicken plate.

Then there's the issue of finding alternative nomenclature when "burrito" is such an easy, well-recognized concept. "Wrap" is an imperfect term, polluted not only by memories of '90s Peking duck and Caesar salad concoctions but also by those horribly dry pinwheel sandwiches on lavash or flavored tortillas. Both "slab" and "cylinder" sound stupid ("I'll have the fried chicken cylinder, please"). It seems to me that if there's a qualifier—breakfast burrito, Indian burrito, mapo tofu burrito—no one is threatening the dominance of carnitas or carne asada.

Finally, there's the evolving nature of cuisine itself, which, like language, is always in flux as people migrate throughout the world and take their ingredients and dishes with them. There had to be some eye-rolling at the Oxford English Dictionary when "awesomesauce" and "bitch face" were added last year, but its editors' job is to record language, not judge it. Cuisine should have that same inclusiveness.

Anyway, we should be reserving our judgment for the real scourge: bad burritos. We should be banding together to fight against lame salsa, cold spots and poor ingredient dispersal, not quibbling over vocabulary. When the basic tenets of the burrito are treated with respect, such as the gloriously saucy and spicy mapo tofu burrito at Mission Chinese, or the sweet-hot jerk chicken burrito at Scotch Bonnet, or that bright, savory sisig burrito at Señor Sisig, it doesn't matter to me that it's not Mexican. It's more than that. It's San Franciscan.

"Gil (our chef) and I are both from San Francisco. We grew up eating burritos in San Francisco. It's really all I've ever known," says Señor Sisig's Evan Kidera. "I definitely would consider what we do as burritos and nothing else."

If that ineffable Mission burrito-ness is somehow in there, I agree that "burrito" is a term not only earned—it's deserved.

Pimento Cheese in a Parka

By John Kessler

From *Gravy*

/

Transplanted from Georgia, where he was for years the esteemed restaurant critic of the *Atlanta Journal-Constitution*, John Kessler was willing to adapt to his new home in Chicago. What he didn't reckon with was the new Chi-town vogue for Southern restaurants—authentic and otherwise.

For my first winter in Chicago, I bought a goose-down parka with a hood trimmed in coyote fur. Whenever I came home from walking the dog in the snow at night, the hall mirror reflected me as a dark lump topped by a pair of freezing, bulging eyeballs set in a ring of fur. I looked like Kenny from South Park, if not Death himself in a cowl.

A Chicago winter can feel like end-times to a Southern transplant. I arrived to join my wife, who had begun a job a year ago at the University of Chicago. Before that, I had worked for nearly two decades as a columnist for the *Atlanta Journal-Constitution*. In Atlanta, I ate my way Southern. During that time, I documented a sea change in the city's food culture, as the regional standard bearers turned from cafeterias and all-you-can-eat buffets to restaurants directed by studious chefs. When I speak of chefs who supported area farmers and researched foodways, it now sounds cliché, but goddamn if Scott Peacock's fried chicken and vegetable plate at Watershed circa 2005 didn't change my world. As the city came of age, so did I.

I expected to miss Southern food in my new hometown. I did not expect to spy a funhouse version of it around every corner. Chicago is in the throes of an energetic (and, honestly, slightly bananas) infatuation with the South. The word "Southern" has become a capacious vessel into which hungry people slop buckets of desire and nostalgia. It is, yes, fried things. And bourbon cocktails and hockey-puck biscuits (go Blackhawks!). It is also more. Random burgers here earn the sobriquet Southern. Chicken tenders are Southern. Pimento cheese Southernizes furls of cavatappi pasta.

"People here love that whole hillbilly chickenshit attitude," says Art Smith, the former personal chef to Oprah Winfrey whose Chicago restaurant, Table Fifty-Two, helped pave the way for this current cohort of Bubba Come Latelys. He's right. I have seen completely nonsensical "North Carolina pulled pork po-boys" and "Nashville hot wings" at restaurants. One menu boasted "Georgia lake prawns." Really? I'm going to have to look for those trawlers on Lake Lanier next time I go back.

My family and I settled in the Bucktown neighborhood, on the ground floor of the former Wojciechowski Funeral Home, which served as a major triage center during the 1918 flu pandemic. We liked the old bones and history. The day we toured the building and put in an offer, we ate brunch, on our realtor's suggestion, at a nearby restaurant called The Southern.

A dark retreat for the hungover, The Southern stocked bourbon behind the bar and featured a sign lettered in the same font as the *Gone with the Wind* movie credits. The menu was pure redonkulosity—an eggs Benedict variation made with biscuits and fried boneless chicken, a "Southern Reuben" of braised brisket and pimento remoulade. I dug into a pile of Breakfast Macaroni, tossed with curds of scrambled eggs and slivers of bacon. It didn't taste too bad for a dish that, posted to Instagram, would have recalled a medical textbook image. Despite its name, The Southern, with its day drinkers, hefty sandwiches, trendy avocado toast, and indifference to seasonal vegetables, seemed so very Chicago to me. Restaurants like these are Southern in the way that *The Mikado* serves as a meditation on Japanese culture.

A spot in nearby Lakeview, Wishbone, employs a flying-chicken decorative theme (think scores of soaring chickens painted on rafters and soffits overhead, like a comic vision of Hitchcock's *The Birds*) and serves what it calls "Southern cooking for thinking people." The implication is not that inchoate emotions typically rule diners from the former Confederacy. Instead, the motto is meant to convey that the kitchen prepares the food with supposedly healthy ingredients. The Wishbone menu throws around descriptors like "Asheville" to indicate blue cheese and honey-mustard dressing in a salad. And it takes liberties with established dishes. Hoppin' John translates as a bottomless bowl of black beans and brown rice under a thick cap of melted cheddar cheese. Bless their hearts.

At Buck's in Wicker Park, the tagline is "Southern fried funk" and the website promises "a taste of 'Down South, Up North.'" It is a place of lounge seating, grandma china, buckets of fried chicken, Cheerwine floats, ironic hospitality-pineapple wallpaper, and hot biscuits served with forlorn little plastic cups of pimento cheese. Look at the booze menu, though, and you couldn't be anywhere but Chicago. The signature "Bucknasty" brings a Schlitz tallboy and a shot of Malört, the locally beloved bitter liqueur that tastes like Fernet-Branca's evil twin. This is food and drink designed to help you endure the cold.

A restaurant called Dixie will soon open five blocks from my home. The name gives me pause, as does chef-owner Charlie McKenna's talk of taking design inspiration from "the antebellum South." McKenna, a South Carolinian who worked in high-end restaurants before opening a well-liked local barbecue spot, Lillie's Q, has strong ideas about the kind of South that Chicago wants. That vision includes cocktails and non-traditional small plates, such as Nashville hot sweetbreads with white bread sauce. (Itself a riff on hot chicken and the white bread that traditionally accompanies it, a version of the dish first appeared at The Catbird Seat in Nashville.)

I walked to Dixie in an early-April snowstorm that swirled to a near whiteout before blowing off. McKenna met me at the site on a hopping restaurant block. Tucked alongside a French bistro and a Japanese izakaya, built as a typical A-frame brick house, the Dixie space had once been the Michelin-starred restaurant Takashi. McKenna gutted the building and poured a raised concrete front porch for rocking chairs to face the busy street. Inspired by the piazzas of Charleston architecture, he tucked the entrance at the side of the building, halfway down a narrow alley. ("We're thinking of putting up a sign that reads, 'In the South we enter on the side,'" said Nick Bowers, head of the architecture and design firm overseeing the buildout.)

I tried to ask McKenna about the words "Dixie" and "antebellum." To my ears, both are charged with layers of complicated meanings. I had to push, perhaps a little too stridently, the question of slavery. I could tell this wasn't where McKenna expected the conversation to go.

"For me, the name Dixie kind of represents the South as a whole," he said, pausing to find the right tone. "You know, it's where I came from. I'm going to be taking a lot of the food and ingredients the slaves brought over and celebrating it in a better light. It's just a word. It's the people who make the South great."

I pursued the question later with Bowers, who had been researching antebellum color schemes ("greens, blues, reds: bold colors") and design accents ("brushed brass and gold"). Historical photos, purchased from a restaurant-prop supplier, would blanket the side walls. I asked if they planned to vet the pictures to find out if they depicted slave owners. I asked if any of the pictures would include black faces. Bowers grew uncomfortable, saying, "Obviously slavery is not a focus to the restaurant. If we know it's somebody who was negatively impacting the South, we wouldn't use that image."

I wonder if Dixie will be a place where no guest will know the tune to whistle it. I am looking forward to those sweetbreads, and when McKenna talks about serving country ham and cheese straws at the bar, the very words thrill me to my toes. But with its rocking chairs and brushed brass, Dixie promises to thematize the pre–Civil War South for a curious dining public, much as the lace curtains, art nouveau lettering and pressed tin ceiling of its neighbor evokes the idealized Paris of a hundred years ago. Southern food and Southern history belong to all of us, and after living in Atlanta, I can't separate them.

Paul Fehribach, the Indiana native who runs the city's best and most thoughtful Southern restaurant, Big Jones, thinks Southern cooking resonates because it is, at heart, American country cooking. He says that's why you see the word "Southern" on Chicago restaurants as often as (if not more than) you see "Midwestern." "Southern" translates, in the minds of diners, as a kind of idealized home cooking.

Fehribach, who builds historical research into his recipes, serves collard-green sandwiches on cornbread, house-cured tasso ham, Sally Lunn bread, Memphis-style barbecue, and Edna Lewis–inspired fried chicken that earns national praise. His menu surveys the subregions of the South in their fractured glory, but it all feels of a piece.

All of these restaurants are on the predominately white North Side of the city. Most black Chicagoans who can trace their roots to the South and to the Great Migration make their homes on the South Side. My own family began its Chicago adventure last summer in the South Side neighborhood of Hyde Park, a diverse community where we lived for a couple of months in University of Chicago housing. Our flat was in a dark, stately Renaissance-revival apartment complex that made me think of Rosemary's Baby. It has, through the years, apparently housed more Nobel laureates than any building in the country.

There were no "Southern" restaurants nearby, but the local market stocked produce I recognized from Georgia, including okra and scuppernongs. Once when I returned home laden with groceries and couldn't open the massive wrought-iron grille door, Belinda Clark, the African American woman working the front desk that day, leapt up to help me. "Now what are you going to do with those greens?" she laughed, looking into my shopping bag. I explained that I cooked a good, if non-traditional, pot of collards. To prove my bona fides, I let it slip that I had just moved from Georgia. Clark's face lit up. Her grandparents emigrated from Alabama and Mississippi. The South fueled her imagination. She and her husband hoped to take a long driving vacation once they could get the time.

Clark grew tomatoes, collard greens, beans, peas, and okra in her home garden. Some years she wouldn't plant until May for fear of a frost. Her husband hunted to stock the freezer. They loved fishing together. Her cooking was not that different from her grandmother's. For the next couple of months, we talked about food every time our paths crossed. She helped me deal with the dull ache of homesickness and the equally insistent ache for okra.

Home. That's surely what I miss when I miss Southern food. I get it. When I mutter that the grits at some trendy brunch place suck, I'm also saying that it shouldn't be 42 degrees outside in May, that I miss my backyard garden and my friends, and that I fret I will never experience in Chicago that sense of food and place, of season and cook, that was the soul of every meal at Cakes & Ale in Decatur.

Then again, sometimes I wonder if that's what everyone here looks for in Southern food, even if they've never been to the South. Maybe it's part of our shared cultural memory, our American identity. Or perhaps Southern is the new Thai—a crowd-pleaser with a whiff of the exotic.

I'm cooking more Southern food now. I keep Anson Mills grits in the freezer, and I cook a pot of greens whenever I find any that look half good. And now that I live on the North Side, I can walk a few blocks for a pimento cheese and fried green tomato biscuit sandwich. It's an unholy trinity, let me tell you. I sometimes want to stand on my bar stool and yell to all Chicago, "People! Cold pimento cheese and hot biscuits: not a thing!" Then again, on a chilly May night, it doesn't taste too bad.

Chicken Potpie for the Modern Cook

By Julia Moskin

From the *New York Times*

A reporter for the *New York Times'* Dining section since 2002, Julia Moskin*–who has also been a cookbook editor and co-writer (with chefs Bobby Flay and Patricia Yeo)–applies her recipe skills to a nagging question: Were the dishes we loved as kids really as good as we remember?

I never like to argue with the bible of American cookery, "Joy of Cooking." Much of its advice is timeless, like the best way to skin an eel and how to make fritters from day lilies.

But in search of advice on chicken potpie, this confident statement made me pause: "None of us has lost the taste for creamed foods served on toast or in bread or pastry containers."

"Joy of Cooking" was published in 1931 and now, 85 years later, I must admit that I have mostly lost the taste for creamed foods, contained or not. Apparently others have as well.

Apart from a few holdouts who insist on creamed onions at Thanksgiving, I don't know a modern home cook who regularly turns out creamed mushrooms, chicken à la king or the dreaded creamed chipped beef on toast.

But still lingering on American menus is chicken potpie, a dish based on creamed chicken that is so beloved that the taste of it doesn't seem to matter.

If it did, would we ignore that most versions have very little flavor? Without the crust and the mini pie dish, would we be made happy by a bowl of chicken in gummy sauce stirred with frozen peas and carrots?

Probably not.

What our "creamed" dishes have in common is not cream, but white sauce, a thrifty substitute with many uses in the kitchen. (It is called béchamel in French and besciamella in Italian.) It is made by lightly cooking flour in fat (this is also known as a roux), and then thinning it with milk.

In early American kitchens, white sauce stood in for cream, which was reserved for making butter. Later on, canned "cream of" soups supplanted white sauce in many creamed dishes, like the filling for a "Joy of Cooking" quick chicken potpie: a poached chicken, canned cream of chicken soup and milk. (No, thanks.)

I grew up believing that a frozen potpie was one of life's great rewards, signaled by the arrival of a babysitter. This meant relief from my usual monotonous diet: home-cooked dinners made from fresh ingredients by my parents, both excellent cooks. (This is the food version of unconscious privilege.)

At that age, I loved the frozen version's salty crust, the Day-Glo peas and carrots, and the soft bits of chicken. As an adult cook, I labored to reproduce it by making homemade chicken potpies: blanching tiny cubes of fresh peas and carrots, poaching organic chicken breasts and stirring all manner of herbs and spices into my white sauce in an attempt to wake up the taste.

They were O.K., but all of them had the telltale blandness of milk, which tends to muffle flavors instead of brightening them. Chicken breast generally has no taste to start with, and when bound in that sauce, even sweet, fresh carrots and peas give up.

Finally I realized the underlying problem. As an emulsion of flour and fat, white sauce itself is a kind of liquid piecrust.

White sauce has its place, on biscuits, heavily peppered and cooked with sausage meat or between the layers of a lasagna. But in a pie, it doubles the starch and blandness.

I first received inklings of an alternate potpie universe at the sleek

and modern NoMad Bar in New York. It is not the kind of place associated with American comfort food: The room (and everyone in it) is
chic and expensively accessorized. Similarly, the NoMad Bar's chicken
potpie, introduced in 2014, is decorated with a skewer of foie gras and
spiked with truffles.

But the big-ticket ingredients are not the real draw. Nor is it the pie's
burnished brown crust, lofty as a hot-air balloon. It's what lies underneath. When I cracked through that crust for the first time, I discovered brown gravy instead of viscous white fluid, and it was scented with
chicken juices and wine, like the best kind of stew. This has possibilities,
I thought.

I tried making a pie filling with stock instead of milk: an instant im-
provement. And then I began to question all the rules for the traditional
recipe. What purpose is served by the carrots and peas? Why cook the
ingredients separately if you're going to combine them anyway? Is a
bottom crust really necessary?

Here are the updated rules for a modern potpie:

- There is no need for a double crust. A single crust is enough, and
  pie crust, biscuit dough or puff pastry can all do an excellent job.
  But the flakiness of pie crust makes the ideal topping.
- Instead of milk, use stock, wine, vinegar or a tasty combination as
  the liquid in your binding sauce. Season the sauce aggressively.
- Boneless thigh meat has more taste and better texture than boneless breast.
- Vegetables should be served separately, not force-marched into
  the filling. (Roasted carrots, peas with mint and buttered steamed
  asparagus are all nice to serve with chicken potpie.)

After some messy experiments, I realized that the right filling for
my modern pie was at hand: a basic chicken sauté. Brown the chicken,
deglaze the pan and there it is: meat and sauce, fully cooked, in one
pan. Flouring the chicken parts before sautéing not only thickened the
sauce, but produced more of the stuck-on brown bits at the bottom of
the pan that make the best pan gravy.

On a mission to make a lively filling, I found that the components of a French poulet au vinaigre—sherry vinegar, parsley and

mushrooms—called to me. But it would be just as effective to swap in white wine, tarragon and shallots or another combination of aromatics and liquids. (If you miss the creaminess of the old-school filling, stir a little crème fraîche into it at the end.) Whether made in one large pie pan or several small ones, it makes an easy, impressive and reasonably quick main dish.

Most satisfyingly, it has the reassuring textures of the old-school recipes, with the deep flavor of chicken. There is nothing wrong with the traditional white sauce version, but it's not all that chicken potpie can be.

Modern Chicken Potpie

Time: 1 hour

Yield: 6 servings

1 tablespoon vegetable oil
1 garlic clove, peeled and smashed
6 ounces bacon or pancetta, preferably thick-cut, sliced into strips
1 medium onion, chopped
8 ounces mushrooms, such as button or cremini, thickly sliced
¼ cup all-purpose flour
1 teaspoon dried thyme
½ teaspoon paprika
Salt and ground black pepper
1 pound boneless chicken thighs, cut into bite-size pieces
2 tablespoons butter
2½ cups rich chicken stock
¼ cup Marsala, Madeira or sherry
1 tablespoon sherry vinegar
2 tablespoons finely chopped parsley, more for garnish
1 9-inch pie crust, chilled, or 1 sheet puff pastry
1 egg, beaten with 1 tablespoon water

Preparation

1. Heat oil and garlic together over low heat. When it sizzles, add bacon and onions and cook, stirring often, until fat is rendered and

bacon is golden brown. Adjust the heat so the bacon slowly gives up its fat. Remove garlic clove and add mushrooms. Cook, stirring, until mushrooms are browned and slightly softened.

2. In a sealable plastic bag, combine flour, thyme, paprika, 2 large pinches salt and 1 large pinch pepper. Add chicken and shake well to coat.

3. In the skillet with the bacon and mushrooms, add butter and melt over medium heat. Add chicken pieces and any flour that remains in the bag. Cook, stirring, until chicken pieces are golden and the flour on the bottom of the pan is browned. Pour in stock, Marsala and vinegar. Scrape bottom of pan, and let simmer about 5 minutes, until thickened. Taste for salt, pepper and vinegar and adjust the seasonings. Turn off heat and stir in parsley.

4. Heat oven to 400 degrees.

5. Transfer chicken and sauce to 9-inch round pie dish or 8-inch square baking dish. Roll out piecrust to desired shape and size. Drape crust over filling, making a few slits or decorative holes on top. Tuck edges down around filling and brush crust with egg wash. If the dish is piled high with filling, place on a baking sheet to catch any overflow before transferring to oven.

6. Bake until crust is browned and filling is bubbling, 20 to 30 minutes.

7. Let cool slightly, at least 10 minutes, before serving with a big spoon. If desired, garnish each serving with parsley.

A Mother's Lesson in Cooking for a Crowd

By Joe Yonan

From the *Washington Post*

Journalist and cookbook author Joe Yonan* has been the food
and dining editor of the *Washington Post* since 2006, with a
goodly stint at the *Boston Globe* before that. But as a native of
West Texas, he sometimes gets a hankering for the dishes he
grew up on—well, with a few tweaks here and there . . .

Of all the dishes my mother made for special occasions, the one I
remember most fondly was Texas Salad. The ingredients:

1 head of iceberg lettuce
1 large can of pinto beans
1 tomato
1 onion
1 large bag of Fritos
1 block of cheddar cheese
1 bottle of Kraft Catalina dressing.

Notice anything about those amounts? Texas Salad represented a
class of recipes that were easily passed around and replicated, and, most

important, remembered because they were built on single units. No measuring required.

For my mother, who spent about four decades cooking for her family, it was a godsend to have dishes she knew by heart and could make quickly. Another was something she simply called broccoli cream cheese casserole: 1 head of broccoli, 1 onion, 1 block of cream cheese, 1 stick of butter. The only break in the one-unit measure was with bread crumbs, which went on as a sprinkling.

My mother was a child of the Midwest, born in the late 1920s in an Indiana town a couple of hours' drive from Chicago. By the time she was cooking for me and my sister Julie, the last two kids left at home, we were in San Angelo, Texas, because my father had been stationed there as an Air Force pilot after a tour of bases throughout much of the South. And by that point, she had cooked for six other children and two husbands. In my memory, she approached cooking as a labor of love—but labor nonetheless. She didn't seem out-and-out tired of it—that would come later—but merely not too excited. Who could blame her?

So she returned to her favorites time and again, and we loved them. Ground beef and broccoli over rice. Meatloaf with cream-of-mushroom (as in the Campbell's soup concentrate) gravy. Stuffed peppers, stuffed cabbage, pecan tassies (little mini-pies with a cream-cheese crust). That Texas Salad was a soggy mess the day after, but freshly made it was always a hit, every Thanksgiving, every Christmas, every birthday. In hindsight, I know Mom was teaching me that variety and experimentation were all well and good, but especially with a crowd to feed, there was nothing wrong with a repertoire, even a small one, of dishes that worked.

I also learned the elements of a satisfying salad: fresh greens, something crunchy, something a little fatty, some protein, a pungent dressing. Mom hasn't cooked in many years because of physical and mental frailty, but I'm one of several of her children who have taken to it with gusto. These days, I make what I jokingly call Ex-Texas Salad, using romaine, fried corn tortillas, feta, slow-roasted tomatoes and a homemade cilantro vinaigrette. I may not be able to put the exact quantities to memory the way she did, because they don't divide up so neatly, but I do something else: improvise with what I have on hand, and taste and adjust as I go.

Maybe she did that, too, and I just never noticed. When I first started showing interest in cooking, she indulged me, but let's just say my interest was scattered. I was 8 or 9 and fascinated by her stand mixer (a machine!), so my preferred tasks used it. I remember pleading as soon as she started cooking a holiday meal: Don't forget to let me mash the potatoes! Please let me whip the cream! Then I would disappear for hours, probably riding my bike who knows where, while she kept working—crushing the Fritos in the bag, grating the cheese, chopping the onions, boiling the potatoes—and I would return to find the stand mixer warm and its bowl soaking in the sink.

I was infuriated: Why didn't she wait for me? She would apologize with a shrug and a smile and move on. Now, of course, I know why: She needed to keep the cooking on track, and when the moment was at hand—the potatoes boiled, the cream chilled—she looked up, probably looked around, perhaps even called for me, and I was nowhere.

I don't have kids, but I can imagine how the on-again, off-again presence of a little one who insists on doing *just this one thing and nothing else* would be less than helpful when 20 people were due in an hour. If I could do it over again, I'd stay put in that kitchen and ask, "What else can I do, Mom?"

I bet she would've appreciated that.

Ex-Texas Salad

This is a radically updated version of the 1970s-era salad popular at potlucks in Texas.

Make Ahead: The vinaigrette can be refrigerated for up to 1 week. The tortillas can be fried and stored in an airtight container at room temperature for up to 3 days.

Tested size: 6 servings

For the vinaigrette

¼ cup fresh cilantro leaves, coarsely chopped
¼ cup extra-virgin olive oil
¼ cup canola oil
¼ cup red wine vinegar
1 clove garlic, coarsely chopped

1 teaspoon sugar

½ teaspoon fine sea salt, plus more as needed

For the tomatoes

8 large tomatoes, stemmed (but not cored) and cut in half vertically

Salt

Freshly ground black pepper

¼ cup olive oil

8 teaspoons cumin seeds, toasted and ground

For the salad

½ cup peanut oil, for frying

Six 6-inch corn tortillas

12 cups lightly packed, torn romaine lettuce leaves

3 cups homemade or no-salt-added canned black beans, rinsed and drained

6 scallions, trimmed and thinly sliced on the diagonal (white and green parts)

12 ounces feta cheese, crumbled

12 large pieces 12-Hour Tomatoes, drained and chopped (may substitute 18 oil-packed sun-dried tomatoes)

Directions

For the vinaigrette: Combine the cilantro, extra-virgin olive and canola oils, vinegar, garlic, sugar and ½ teaspoon of salt in a blender; puree until smooth. Taste, and add salt as needed. The yield should be about ¾ cup.

For 12-Hour Tomatoes: Preheat the oven to 200 degrees. Line a large rimmed baking sheet with aluminum foil or parchment paper; do not overlap. Place the tomatoes, cut side up, on the baking sheet. Season on the cut side with salt and pepper to taste, then drizzle with olive oil. Sprinkle ½ teaspoon cumin on each tomato half. Bake for 8 to 12 hours, or until the tomatoes have collapsed and shriveled to about ¼ inch thick; they should still be moist inside. Cool completely, then refrigerate in an airtight container.

For the salad: Line a plate with paper towels.

Pour the peanut oil into a large skillet over medium heat. Once that oil starts to shimmer, add 2 or 3 tortillas (or as many as will comfortably fit); fry them on each side until crisp and golden brown, 1 to 2 minutes. Lift each tortilla with tongs and let the excess oil drip off, then transfer it to the paper towel–lined plate. Working in batches, repeat with the remaining tortillas. Let the tortillas cool, then break them into bite-size pieces.

Toss the tortilla pieces with the lettuce, black beans, scallions, feta, tomatoes and ½ cup of the vinaigrette in a large serving bowl. Add the remaining ¼ cup of the vinaigrette if desired, or reserve for another use. Serve right away.

Someone's in the Kitchen

The Genius of Guy Fieri

By Jason Diamond

From *Esquire*

Brooklyn-based, Chicago-born Jason Diamond takes pop culture seriously (just read his 2016 memoir, *Searching for John Hughes*). Among the many jobs he's had—magazine editor, website founder, freelance writer—he's also been a barista and a fry cook. Who better to really get TV chef Guy Fieri?

It's supposedly 97 degrees and I'm grossly sweating through my shirt on a rooftop in the middle of Manhattan. From where I'm standing, New York City is all floating buildings and blue skies; no sidewalks overcrowded with tourists bumbling past self-important men in suits rushing to wherever they have to get to. All around me are grand buildings like St. Patrick's Cathedral, 30 Rock, and the Scribner Building, and the roof I'm on has the greenest grass I've ever seen in the city, a little pool, and four huge steel letters that spell out M-E-A-T with unlit light bulbs that I'm guessing will be turned on once the sun sets. I'm on this rooftop with a beer in one hand and a plate in the other that's piled with Andouille sausage and chicken. That's when I realize: Holy shit, I'm in Flavortown.

I let that sink in as I take one last sip of the warm beer, and begin to follow a very tan woman who leads me to meet the ruler of this mythical land, Guy Fieri.

I know a fair amount about Fieri. He was born Guy Ferry, and he changed his last name to honor his immigrant great-grandfather. I know he hates eggs—not necessarily eggs in his food, but actual eggs:

scrambled, sunny side-up, omelets. I'm aware he's the subject of a fair amount of ridicule from some of our best restaurant critics and biggest celebrity chefs. Some people confuse him for a member of Smash Mouth or Insane Clown Posse. He's practically a meme walking among us. I get all that, I do. But I need to put all of that to the side of my overflowing plate for now.

As I start talking with Fieri, who is in town to promote his new BBQ venture with Carnival Cruise Line, I think about all of that stuff, but I try to be a good interviewer and strip away any preconceived ideas I might have about him. He greets me with an enthusiastic fist bump. (Later I notice a nick on my knuckle oozing blood from where I grazed my hand on one of his impressive signet rings.) We strike up a conversation about Sammy Hagar. ("I was even more of a Hagar fan when he was just Hagar and not Van Hagar," he says.) It's hard not to look up above the *Diners, Drive-ins and Dives* host's face and focus on his famous head of bleached blond hair. It sticks so straight up that you could imagine him lowering his head and charging toward a line.

I have a small rush of panic that shoots through me—like when I worry I left the house with the faucet running or forgot to feed the cats—when I can't find his famous pair of white sunglasses, usually perched on the back of his head. My eyes dart desperately and I see them resting atop a bag nearby. There they are. The fear subsides and we continue.

Here's where I admit I'm an unabashed fan of Fieri's television shows and that I definitely watch several hours of *Diners, Drive-Ins and Dives* each week. "Because you have good taste," Fieri says when I make my confession. Of course, I tend to agree with Fieri, but when I tell any of my friends how much time I spend watching Triple D, and I see the look they give me in response, I feel the need to also mention that I really enjoyed reading Dan Fox's *Pretentiousness*, that I love to work to William Basinski's minimalist masterpiece *The Disintegration Loops*, or that my wife and I put money away every few months because we're on a mission to eat at Blue Hill at Stone Barns at least one time for each month on the calendar.

I feel as if I have pretty decent taste by the standards of those strange enough to share them, yet when I mention that one of my favorite things to do is to sit on my couch with my dog and watch any of the Fieri shows that pretty much make up the bulk of the Food Network's programming, people tend to laugh—or worse, assume I'm hate-watching. "No," I tell them. I really enjoy watching Fieri drive around America in search of what he calls "real food for real people."

I love food television. I'll watch Julia Child reruns or anything with Andrew Zimmern, plus *Chef's Table* and, of course, *The Great British Bake Off*. I also love Anthony Bourdain's many shows and books, and I understand why he'd find a person like Fieri such a personal affront. But while Bourdain looks at the bigger picture on his shows, examining the political economy of every city he visits, Fieri visits the real unknown. He takes that bright red convertible to little spots that are uniquely unexciting, places that aren't owned by celebrity chefs, and parks firmly outside of the hype stream that steers the bastions of good taste. His episodes don't have unifying themes. They don't even focus on one geographic area, a strangely democratizing choice when it comes to place and space. Not one city is elevated among the rest, even by editing. Yet once Fieri shows up, all of his fans are in the know—and more often than not, they tend to remember.

There's this place called Sidecar on the southern end of Park Slope. It opened in 2006, and I'd have to imagine it's considered older by Brooklyn standards since good restaurants don't tend to last a decade around there thanks to rising rents, ticket-happy health department employees, and the finicky tastes of New Yorkers (not to mention a host of personal dramas that factor into a restaurant's longevity). I've been going there since around the time they started serving food and drinks, and from the fried chicken and club sandwiches to the "Hangover Soup" they serve at brunch (it has saved my life more than once), I've never been disappointed in a visit to Sidecar. It's a late-night place, the kind of spot chefs go to when they get off work and want to grab a few beers at two in the morning.

Yet there it was, resting prominently on the bar's chalkboard for at least a year: a hyper-realistic drawing of Guy Fieri. Having seen the episode where Fieri stands outside of Sidecar and says that brothers John and Bart DeCoursy are "rockin' the neighborhood" with the best Cuban sandwich (disclaimer: I've never had the Cuban at Sidecar, so I can't vouch for the validity of the statement), I finally had enough drinks at the bar one night to ask why the hell they've kept that thing up so long. The bartender looked at me and smiled. "A lot of us pay our rent because Guy Fieri tourists come here to eat."

Yes, *Guy Fieri tourists.* They're a thing. Even in New York City, a place with never ending things to do and places to eat, has benefitted by the constant loop of Fieri's shows driving foot traffic into restaurants. They get a leg up from the boost. All across the country, restauranteurs can attest to the "Fieri Effect" that starts when the Bleached One features a place on his show. "They told us, 'We can do a lot for your sales,'" Ann Kim, co-owner of Pizzeria Lola in Minneapolis, told MinnPost last year. "We had no idea." Another restaurant owner reported his sales were up 500 percent after Fieri rolled up in his red '68 Camaro.

As somebody who travels quite often, I'll admit to have taken a few of Fieri's suggestions and enjoyed the occasional thrice-fried monstrosity when out of town. I can't always follow the Eater Heatmap, so I take the leap.

Beyond all the jokes about his appearance and the fact that, no matter how much I wanted to think otherwise, the *New York Times*' Pete Wells was totally right about the place being truly terrible (even Fieri seems to know that), I know that Fieri is a smart chef. You watch reruns of the second season of *Food Network Star* that he won, which aired ten years ago starting this past April, and you realize he's got skills. A French-trained chef with a Michelin star would probably rather feed whatever Fieri makes to dogs, but that's never been who he was cooking for. The art of cooking was never what he was interested in.

"I was pretty driven with what I wanted to do," Fieri tells me. His dad, his hero, helped him lay out his plan at an early age. Fieri never wanted to be Thomas Keller or Daniel Boulud. "I wanted to work in corporate restaurants," he says, repeating something I've heard him say proudly a thousand times in various interviews. But it's a line that speaks volumes about Fieri's personality: He had a plan this entire time. Fieri's food is not an art, but a craft—practiced with care but not pretension. And yet he takes every plate piled high with burgers and fries as seriously as you might an entry in the Bocuse d'Or. Simple food—diverse American Food, in all styles, made by Americans—is Fieri's rallying cry and religion.

"Real food for real people," I think to myself as I listen to him talk. It's so damn simple, yet totally brilliant. It's the food version of bipartisanship in politics: You can't make fun of it because then you're a classist snob, but you also have to take it with a grain of salt because it's really perfectly pandering. And that's what Fieri intrinsically understands. He knows he's not Oprah or Ellen. He's not a good-looking late night talk show host like Jimmy Fallon. He'll never be America's sweetheart. His first job is to get viewers, and he does that by making everything super simple. He knows more viewers are going to tune in to see him talk about good pulled pork (for what it's worth, Fieri knows a good deal about BBQ—enough to get him inducted into the Barbecue Hall of Fame)—rather than some young hot shot chef in Los Angeles talk about his experimental cooking with compost.

You can watch his Food Network audition tape from a decade ago; it's clear that he's stuck to that plan all of this time—and it has made him incredibly wealthy. He's also helped out a number of small, independent businesses along the way; no matter what you want to say about him, it is hard to argue with his success.

As our interview winds down, I notice how many handlers Fieri has around him—including his publicist, his manager from William Morris, another publicist, and a few other folks with clipboards. I know the drill. I've done a few of these before. These people are here because I might ask some questions to trip up their client, to get some sort of funny quote out of him, or to press him into a mold that I walked in with in mind. The media wants him to be a clown, to perform the sort of comedy that comes at his expense. A journalist scheduled for an interview after mine told me, "I just want him to say something dumb."

Yet Fieri is articulate and engaging. He's got his spiel. He curses. He talks about business—not like a person with an M.B.A., but like a person who has learned what he knows by paying attention and doing the work himself. He's off the cuff and unscripted, but he's genuine, clever, and warm. You can call Guy Fieri a lot of things, and by the end of our brief time together I know that "smart" is definitely one of them. How many of us are as resolute in our self-knowledge, in our personal aesthetic, and in our plans for life and work? Fieri is more confident and assured than I am—and certainly more well liked. I shake his hand when I turn off the recorder.

I watch his shows, often claiming that they help me zone out after a long day at the office—comfort TV, if you will. Just about everybody has a *Diners, Drive-Ins and Dives*. But it dawns on me that even I've been taking Fieri for granted. I'm not yet giving him the credit he deserves. When I get up to leave, he gestures at my Chicago Cubs hat and asks if I'm really from Chicago. I know it's suddenly trendy to wear a Cubs hat now that they're finally good, but yes, I answer proudly. "I am." He stares me dead in the eyes and tells me that my hometown is his favorite food city. He's probably told people from Boston to Seattle the same thing for all I know, but the conviction with which he says it rings true. My heart leaps with the places he names off—a little Cuban spot, a random Greek joint, not somewhere cool like The Publican or Longman and Eagle.

Guy Fieri's on the ground, eating with locals *like* locals, never giving a thought to Yelp but rather turning to somebody's grandpa and asking about the counter stool they've occupied for 30 years. The shades he wears don't shield his eyes from the sun; they're there because his star shines fucking bright. The spikey hair, the flames on his collared shirts, the over-accessorizing? That's all part of his plan, but also part of a diversion from the reality of his empire: that despite everything, Guy Fieri might actually be a genius.

The Chef Loses It

By Brett Martin

From *GQ*

Award-winning writer Brett Martin (you'll find his work in
GQ, Vanity Fair, The New Yorker, Bon Appetit, and many other
publications) has a gift for going deep with his subjects, revealing
their character as well as their achievements. In this profile of
Charleston chef Sean Brock, that gift yields touching insights.

Every morning this week, Sean Brock has woken up and vomited.
This is not, in and of itself, that unusual. Brock inherited a tricky gag
reflex from his father, and the smallest thing can sometimes set him off:
picking up after his dog, for instance, or the toothbrush scraping too far
back on his tongue.

This week, though, the throwing up has been from nerves. In ten
days, he's scheduled to complete the re-invention of his flagship
Charleston restaurant, McCrady's. The first stage, which opened a few
weeks ago, was McCrady's Tavern, a bustling, meat-heavy canteen with
a menu inspired by Brock's collection of 19th-century cookbooks. The
second will be housed in this small, rectangular space: 18 seats, 12 of
them around a U-shaped counter, and a tasting menu that aspires to
compete with the imaginative culinary standards of the best restaurants in the world. Brock says it's everything he's ever wanted as a chef.
Which is enough to make him barf.

What the future looks like, at this moment, is four men staring silently at a white plate. Brock and three of his top chefs are gathered
in the gleaming open kitchen of the new McCrady's. Strewn about are

crates of crystal wineglasses, boxes of flatware, a small forest of bonsai trees to be used in the presentation of the restaurant's first course. "I've wanted these ever since I saw *The Karate Kid*," Brock says.

The men are regarding a dish that, on closer examination, contains an arrangement of food as white as the china it's plated on: an ivory rectangle of poached cobia, a tumble of brunoised matsutake mushrooms, and a pool of white sauce made from green, or uncooked, peanuts. It is the consistency of tahini but tastes loamy and raw.

"We peel each peanut by hand. It's a fairly fast process," deadpans John Sleasman, McCrady's chef de cuisine. Like the others, he's wearing a look best described as "pursued by werewolf."

"Nobody's been doing a lot of sleeping around here," Brock says.

He peers at the dish from beneath the flat brim of his black baseball hat. If there is a template for southern chef these days—burly, bearded, bespectacled, baseball-capped, and bedraped in tattoos—it is in large part a look based on Brock's. Tonight he's wearing sneakers, a chef's jacket over a Slayer T-shirt, and a cap reading Mc, for McCrady's. He can almost seem to have two faces: at times, boyishly mischievous, quick to break into a barking laugh. At others, blank as an Easter Island statue and older than his 38 years.

This is already the tenth iteration of the cobia-and-matsutake dish. At about the 12th or 13th, the chefs hit on the idea of mixing the peanut sauce with a shot of liquefied lovage; at the 16th, of pouring out the combined sauce in front of the diner, creating a spidery puddle of green and white.

Brock takes a bite and goes for a little walk away from the plate, as he often does while tasting. "That's really delicious," he says finally, smiling for the first time. The cooks imperceptibly relax, like the unwitting subjects of a Columbo interrogation, before Brock turns back with just one more thing: "Should it really be just one piece of fish?" And the whole process starts again.

Several more versions down the line, Brock removes his hat and runs his hands through his hair and across his face. "I'm about to boot this whole dish out onto East Bay Street," he mutters. Sensing a break, the other chefs depart. Brock sits down heavily on a stool, traces a finger along the line of solder that runs the length of the black-walnut counter. "This is the restaurant I've always wanted to have. This is the place

I've dreamed about and never thought I'd be able to open," he says. "Every person in this building and every person in the public is expecting something big, something important, something impressive," he says.

Part of the quiet mood tonight, he explains, has to do with the fact that he exploded at his team earlier. The specifics are already fading, but the effects haven't. "I feel sick. I feel like I got beat up," he says. He holds up a hand, swollen and weirdly crooked, to show the knuckle still bleeding from when he punched a wall.

"These dishes we're working on, I could taste them in my head as soon as I came up with them," he says. "It's just not coming out onto the plate."

And there's something else. Brock sighs and rubs his eyes: "I haven't been able to see a fucking thing all day."

There are approximately 16,000 photos on Brock's iPhone. By rough estimation, about 10 percent of those are of various iterations of matsutake and cobia. Another 20 percent are of Ruby, his French bulldog. And the rest are of eyes.

There are bruised eyes. Battered eyes. Eyes leaking actual tears of bright red blood. There are eyes with stitches and eyes with bandages. Eyes drooping as though dragged down by fishhooks and eyes goggling in a grotesque simulation of surprise. Eyes hidden behind patches, shielded by stained gauze, buried beneath great sockfuls of ice.

All of them are Brock's eyes.

For the past three years, Brock has been sick—most of that time mysteriously and secretly so. In March, after countless doctors, blind alleys, and medical red herrings, he finally received a diagnosis of what had been plaguing him: myasthenia gravis (MG), a rare neurological auto-immune disease that inhibits the body's ability to interact with its own muscles.

If, as Susan Sontag wrote, "everyone who is born holds dual citizenship, in the kingdom of the well and in the kingdom of the sick," Brock passed through customs to the wrong side in January 2014. It was a hard season: He had just completed the arduous opening of Husk Nashville, a version of the Charleston restaurant that had propelled him to new heights of acclaim. He was spending nearly all his time in

Nashville now, in the late stages of a difficult, guilt-ridden divorce from the woman who had been his high school sweetheart. Coming home from dinner one frigid night, he slipped on a patch of ice and went down hard on one knee. A driver pumping gas some 50 yards away nevertheless claimed he could hear the *crack* as Brock's kneecap smashed into the pavement. He was incapacitated, unable for several weeks to even make it to the bathroom alone. For a while, it seemed that this might be a backward blessing, an enforced vacation from the stress of the kitchen that Brock would never take on his own. "It was the first time I had not worked six or seven days a week since I was 19," he says. He and his girlfriend, Adi Noe, holed up in their apartment through that unusually cold winter, binge-watching *Breaking Bad.*

Then they both ended up with a bad case of food poisoning. Brock spent one night vomiting so violently that he was almost bemused to wake up the next day to find he had double vision. "Man, I must have pulled something throwing up," he thought. A few days later, though, the symptoms remained. The two consulted the chamber of horrors known as WebMD. "You do *not* want to Google double vision," Noe says.

After a few weeks, the parade of doctors began: ophthalmologists, neurologists, neuro-ophthalmologists, oculoplastics surgeons. And the tests: One consisted of repeatedly placing ice up against his eyes and gauging the response. That was a spa treatment compared with the next test, in which a recording needle was inserted into the junction between the muscles and nerves of his eye and left there for 45 minutes, gathering data.

MG is a sneaky sickness, often called the snowflake disease because it seems to manifest in as many unique ways as there are people who have it. Why it strikes is a mystery, but as with all auto-immune diseases, the body mistakenly attacks itself, in this case disabling receptors for a substance called acetylcholine, which acts as the crucial connection between one's nerves and one's muscles. This short-circuits both voluntary movements, like raising and lowering your eyelids, and involuntary ones, like breathing.

All of Brock's symptoms were in line with an MG diagnosis, but, perplexingly, he tested negative for the disease's telltale rogue antibodies. Meanwhile, his condition worsened. The double vision made it difficult to walk, much less drive. One morning, he stepped outside to walk Ruby and tried to squint in the bright sunlight. His eyes refused to obey. Back inside, he looked in a mirror to discover that one eye had drooped to nearly closed while the other was stuck wide open.

"You can't go out looking like that," he says. He took to wearing sunglasses at all times, both because the mildest light was blinding and because he was so keenly self-conscious. The glasses, though, had their own problems: He worried that he looked like the kind of asshole who wears sunglasses in restaurants at night.

And, still, a definitive diagnosis remained elusive. "Do you know what that's like?" he says. "The feeling you get when the best doctors in the country look at you and say, 'We don't know what's wrong with you'?"

Life began to shrink, a series of waiting rooms and doctors' appointments and torturous surgeries, five in all: Believing the problem was fourth cranial nerve palsy, a surgeon detached his eyeball to tighten its surrounding muscles; attempting to treat the ptosis, or drooping, doctors snipped through his eyelids, inserting stitches to raise and lower them like Levolor blinds while cutting tissue from the undersides.

"I wasn't a chef anymore. I was a patient," Brock says. "It was the most depressed I'd been in my whole life. I was thinking about suicide. I didn't want to leave my house."

He had always had a collecting streak, the acquisitive glee of someone who had grown up poor enough to worry about being able to afford school lunch. Among other things, he has amassed collections of Danelectro guitars, vinyl Mississippi-blues records, and southern folk art. Now he poured his energy into learning everything about bourbon, building a world-class collection of American whiskey. Amply documented on Instagram, the shelves filled with Pappy Van Winkle and Willett seemed like the happy outgrowth of a life well lived. But it was also a beachhead against a terrible possibility: that he would never be able to cook again.

After each procedure and recovery, the symptoms would abate for a week or two but then come back. Brock began strategically scheduling the procedures for when he needed brief periods of sight, like when he traveled to Modena, Italy, to take over the kitchen of Osteria

Francescana and cooked Italian culatello in southern redeye gravy and shrimp and grits in Parmigiano-Reggiano whey.

He began to privately confront what had begun to seem inevitable: "I may not ever be fixed," he said. "I may have to deal with this for the rest of my life."

It's tempting to see Brock's restaurant empire as a manifestation of his own body: The Tavern—where, he says, the menu is "a list of my favorite things to eat"—is his stomach. Husk, with its devotion to showcasing southern ingredients, is his heart. And the new McCrady's is his brain. (It would be too cynical to say that Minero, Brock's taqueria, with branches in Charleston and Atlanta, is his wallet, but nobody has ever gone broke selling Americans hot cheese and beans.)

McCrady's occupies a brick building that dates from the late 1700s, a block away from the marshy shallows of Charleston Harbor. It's a sprawling space of hallways, stairways, and kitchens, the kind of place a man could rattle around in forever, like the Phantom of the Opera, barely seeing daylight. Which is more or less how Brock has been operating in the weeks leading up to the McCrady's opening, emerging only late at night to hop in his beat-up pickup strewn with cassette tapes.

He navigates the building like . . . well, like he could do it blind: Out the door of the new McCrady's; past the brick archways and 18th-century hearths of the Tavern; up the wide staircase, past Minero's bustling kitchen and into the Long Room, where George Washington once dined and which is now used for private parties. On the roof is a small garden and a locked shed housing a wall of bubbling tubs producing homemade vinegar in flavors like Mountain Dew and Harvey Wallbanger. Great feathery clumps of bacterial mother pulsate inside them like alien jellyfish. There is also a wood barrel of pork fatback curing in salt, and rack after rack of meticulously labeled canned vegetables and fruit, all of it nestled amid $200,000 worth of wine. (Which would Brock save first in a fire? "Probably the wine. I can make more vinegar.")

The building has been his home base since 2006, when he first arrived as head chef, a 27-year-old wunderkind recruited from the Hermitage Hotel in Nashville, where he had been making improbable waves with 30-course modernist tasting menus inspired by the likes of

The French Laundry and WD-50. All but three members of the staff quit within his first week.

He won a James Beard Award making brainy, overtly modern food at the original McCrady's. But it was Husk, which opened down the street in 2010, that made him famous. Husk was the culmination of Brock's emergence from the kitchen as one of the action-intellectuals of the food revolution. Not content to just cook with southern ingredients, he decided to grow his own, persuading his investors to lease land for a farm on nearby Wadmalaw Island. He began breeding his own hogs. He became a seed evangelist, obsessed with the mission of reviving crops long lost to the rise of industrial agriculture. At Husk, the steadfast rule was that no ingredients could be used from north of the Mason-Dixon Line. Brock became both a local hero and an international one, the hard-drinking, Waffle House–loving Southern Delegate to the international conversation about where food was going.

"I'm getting pretty tired of looking around for salt."

Brock woke up this morning still vexed by the cobia and matsutake dish. Maybe a few drops of fish sauce would bring out the flavor? Just a few extra grains of salt? Within moments, dishes of the stuff bloom like mushrooms on nearly every surface of the kitchen in which the McCrady's R&D team is ensconced. One cook is at work at the arduous task of peeling the rubbery jackets from a bin of muscadine grapes and then digging seeds out of the squishy orbs that remain with a marrow fork, a process that, in context, is inescapably reminiscent of eye surgery. Nearby, two women are engaged in a shadow version of kitchen drudgery, rolling and pressing endless balls of masa into tortillas for Minero. They tolerantly roll their eyes when a wave of dry-ice fog Brock is using to chill some dishes comes billowing across their station.

Sam Jett hovers nearby. The 33-year-old cook's title is Culinary Coordinator, but his portfolio can be summed up as monitoring Brock's mental and physical status and taking anything off the chef's plate that he can be persuaded to relinquish. These days, he projects the air of managed panic you'd expect from Santa's head elf around December 23.

"He's gotten really good at hiding when his eyes are bothering him," he says, watching closely as Brock tastes a dab of peanut sauce.

Indeed, you'd need to pay close attention to note the slightly drunken lean Brock adopts as he moves downstairs, the way he needs to place things he's looking at closely in front of one eye instead of both. Brock pauses every four hours in response to an unheard alarm, reaches into his pocket, and discreetly swallows a pill, one of a seeming pharmacy he consumes daily.

In March, having hit a diagnostic dead end, Brock's doctors decided to start him on the treatment for myasthenia gravis—a combination of the steroid prednisone and a drug called Mestinon—in the hopes that he was among the sliver of MG patients who test negative but nevertheless respond to medication. The morning after he began treatment, Noe woke early to find him already downstairs in the kitchen, whistling and cooking breakfast. "It was like magic," Brock says. "One of the greatest days of my life. I was reborn."

On the one hand, this was the confirmation he and Noe had feared for nearly two years: There is no cure for MG, and at its worst it can be fatal. On the other, there was finally something to *do,* action to be taken. Brock quit drinking. He cut gluten out of his diet, and most sugar. "All of a sudden, I was springing out of bed at 6:30 in the morning. Everything started pouring out," he says. He was filling notebooks with ideas, dreaming of dishes and then waking up in the middle of the night to scribble them down. "I couldn't stop cooking. I couldn't stop creating. It was like I had superpowers."

Waiting to absorb this burst of creativity was McCrady's. As the tenth anniversary of Brock's arrival there approached, discussions about a revamp were already under way. McCrady's had always been a somewhat awkward chimera: part avant-garde modernist, part traditional restaurant, a mix that reflected its clientele. For every diner willing to commit to one of Brock's tasting menus, there were at least two or three who wanted a steak and a salad—often at the same table. It was impossible to serve both masters as well as Brock wanted.

Now the Tavern would handle Brockian versions of classic dishes— an aged New York strip steak goosed by a crust of shio koji; caviar service with tater tots—while at the new McCrady's, he would be free to create the kind of rarefied place he had seen and fallen in love with while traveling far beyond South Carolina's borders. It was, he felt, an overdue return. Husk had made him famous, but life as an Orthodox Southerner could also be a straitjacket.

"I'm tired of making burgers," he says. "I'm tired of making fried chicken, I'm tired of making corn bread. I've been doing that every day for six years and I'm sick of it. I love eating it, but I'm tired of making it. Because I know these other dishes are swimming around in my head, and they're being wasted."

The restaurant he envisioned was a chef's dream of total control: 36 prepaid covers per night, a set menu. It would move quickly, send diners out the door stimulated instead of staggering. "I want you to leave like you just went to a spa. I want you to feel like you just had a massage, like you just meditated, like you did yoga. I want you to feel like you're nude," he says.

For a model, Brock looked to Japan, both in the kitchen—where he adopted ingredients like miso, kombu, and koji—and spiritually. He's hardly the only chef for whom Japanese culture presents a seductive fantasy of simultaneous intense control and Zen serenity. Never mind that the evidence suggests such intensity has its own price: a Japanese suicide rate one and a half times that of the U.S., for starters.

Never mind that there's a price for everything.

In late August, still reeling from the grueling process of opening the Tavern and beginning work on the new McCrady's, Brock and Noe were driving on the Ravenel Bridge, between Charleston and Mount Pleasant. Brock was behind the wheel. Suddenly, the road split and lurched into two. For the first time since he started treatment, Brock's double vision was back.

"I just punched the steering wheel as hard as I could," he says. "I thought, 'I can't. I can't be back here again.'"

In the passenger seat, Noe felt her heart drop. It was true that as the novelty and relief of Brock's treatment had subsided, he had grown less careful about his health. They had both allowed themselves to believe that the sickness might be in the past. But in the coming weeks, as the symptoms started appearing at night, and then earlier and earlier each day, the cruel irony became clear: The very thing that the miracle treatment was allowing Brock to do was the thing that would inevitably bring the disease roaring back.

I s there another way?
That is the question that lurks in the margins of Brock's story. Chefs' health—mental and physical—has become much discussed lately. As cooking has made the transition from blue-collar work to professional, it's only natural that chefs would begin to challenge the often brutal conditions previous generations took for granted. On the face of it, the need for change is self-evident, but the knotty problem is that those same conditions mimic the kitchen culture's agreed-upon virtues: perfectionism, intensity, stamina, toughness, drive. And it is often these very things—not, say, love of food or cooking; those come later—that made the kitchen attractive in the first place.

He grew up in deep rural Virginia. His father, the owner of a fleet of coal trucks, was a generous and successful man who died when Brock was 11, plunging the family into poverty. Such is the stuff that chefs are made of: Dead fathers, cruel fathers, physically or emotionally absent fathers—all are so common behind the stove as to be axiomatic. One of the reasons professional kitchens have remained so stubbornly resistant to gender equality is that their bonds are so deeply patrilineal, so downright Freudian.

Brock's first kitchens were a twisted hybrid of boot camp and surrogate family, and he loved it. To be 16 years old, on the line for the first time, Metallica blaring from the boom box, surrounded by rough men bragging about their overnight binges and conquests . . . Who cared if half the steaks you sent out to the dining room got sent back? "It was the greatest feeling I'd ever had," he says.

Later, he thrived in the hotbox of kitchens run on screaming. Like many young chefs, when he took over his own kitchen, he assumed it was the only way: "I was just yelling and screaming all day. I was the most miserable, angry person you can imagine." After one early bad review at the Hermitage, he pledged to his staff that he wouldn't take a day off until they were reviewed again. It took ten months, during which Brock slept at the restaurant most nights.

"We're insane. We shouldn't be doing this to our bodies and to our brains. That's sick. That's an illness," he says, though not without a touch of pride. "But, look, *somebody's* gotta feed everybody."

So is there another way?

There's no way of knowing whether the chef's lifestyle caused Brock's myasthenia gravis. What is clear is that it does exacerbate it. It is a one-to-one equation: When Brock gets upset, his eyesight blurs. When he loses sleep or drinks a little bit, he pays in the days after. It falls to Noe to remind him of these things. "She's the only one who can keep me in line," he says.

Still, there are limits to what even love can do. "Look, this feeling in my chest is temporary," Brock says on the eve of the McCrady's opening. "In two or three weeks, I'll be standing at that counter enjoying myself eating, and then I'll go back to Nashville, get some nice furniture, build a fence for my dog, and chill out."

It is, of course, the Junkie's Creed: "Tomorrow everything's going to be different. Tomorrow I'm going to be fine. I'm just waiting for everything to line up perfectly and then it's all going to be smooth sailing...." Meanwhile, plans are moving forward for a Husk in Greenville, South Carolina, to open this coming spring, and Husk: Savannah after that. His dog, one starts to fear, may have to learn to live without a fence a little longer.

But is there another way?

Brock sighs, slightly lubricated now, at The Griffon, a dive bar nestled among the hotels and manicured facades of downtown Charleston. He's allowing himself a drink, or several, tonight, in part because Noe won't be back from Nashville until later; in part, one fears, guiltily, because he feels that doing so is part of the Official Sean Brock Experience for visitors; and in part because the McCrady's team has just completed its final dress rehearsal before its official opening tomorrow night. This, too, is a part of the chef's birthright that's hard to let go of: "You work your ass off, you take care of complete strangers, and at the end you give yourself a treat," he says.

The bartender brings over his usual order: a bottle of Budweiser and a shot of Jägermeister. Brock refuses to drink bourbon in most bars because he refuses to drink any bourbon made after 1992, this for arcane reasons that seem like a good warning about the perils of knowing too much.

Earlier in the day, in the midst of a meltdown over the Tavern's much Instagrammed béarnaise-filled burger (the problem being that a small but significant portion of those Instagrams showed hot béarnaise spurted onto diners' clothes), he had sat down in a quiet corner of the restaurant and wondered whether it was all worth it. Then came service.

"It happened to me tonight: The same thing that happens every time I'm doing something I worked really hard toward. I'm in the kitchen, and I just start getting waves of highs. I feel this amazing rush. My arms break out in goose bumps. I imagine it's what heroin is like. I'm so *happy*. This is me at my happiest: cooking this food in this place. I feel like I just won the football game. Like I won the heavyweight championship of the world. It's the greatest thing you can imagine."

But is there another way?

"Dammit, I don't know that I *want* to do it any other way."

If Brock's myasthenia gravis begins to progress, the first sign will likely be difficulty swallowing, as the disease moves into his throat. In a worst-case scenario, it could then move to the rest of his body, eventually to his lungs. Noe has found herself watching for signs, catching her breath every time Brock clears his throat. She knows that after the five-year mark of living with the disease with no progression the odds that it will develop into a full-body condition plummet dramatically. What's unclear is exactly how much of the outcome is predetermined and how much is the result of how you behave for those five years.

"I could live like a nun and the disease could still take off," Brock says.

One prominent neurologist who has not treated Brock but has studied MG for decades points out that there are more and more effective treatments available for the disease than ever before. And he adds, "Nobody has ever shown that the best course of action for this disease is to not do what you want in life."

Opening night, McCrady's is filled for the first time with 18 strangers. The front two-thirds of the rectangular space are bathed in a warm, amber glow that reflects off the black-walnut counter. The kitchen seems to be caught in the flash of a silver strobe light, framing Brock and his chefs as they bend over plates, tweezers at the ready, as though playing a game of Operation. Things move fast and light: There's an oyster secreted in a fog of seawater and dry ice; a square of uni-and-pawpaw ice cream that unfolds in the mouth like a perverse gobstopper; and, of course, the cobia and matsutake, which in its 24th or 25th iteration has emerged as a space-age diorama: equal-size chunks of fish and mushroom arranged, Stonehenge-like, around a green-and-white psychedelic pool. It looks like a Yes album cover, and it tastes of sea and forest and also somehow like an after-school snack of peanut butter spread on celery. Brock seems relaxed, loose. At one point, he peers at the dining room through the tree line of bonsai like a twinkle-eyed giant. Who knows? Maybe he's right. Maybe everything will soon go back to normal. When the last dessert, a tiny lozenge that explodes in the mouth with an invigorating menthol blast, is dropped, the kitchen lights snap off, as though a curtain has fallen, and the chefs silently march out the door. The guests applaud.

Upstairs, in the Long Room, watched over by an unblinking bust of George Washington, Brock and his team sit at a banquet table. Nobody talks. The room is silent except for the sounds of Sam Jett slowly packing away Brock's roll of knives, tweezers, and other tools. There is, strangely, an air of deflation. Everything was flawless, and yet . . . "It's so weird," Brock says. "There's a disconnect."

Perhaps this is just the crash that follows getting what you've always wanted. Or, Brock has another idea:

"Maybe it wasn't hard enough?"

Becoming Janos

By Debbie Weingarten

From *Edible Baja Arizona*

Debbie Weingarten doesn't just write about food, she's also an activist, working with farmers, chefs, and local leaders to advance food security and justice in Tucson. Her portrait of chef Janos Wilder celebrates his devotion to Arizona regional cuisine–no matter how winding the path that brought him there.

On a warm March morning, Downtown Kitchen + Cocktails is empty. Chef Janos Wilder sits in a booth facing the windows that look out onto Sixth Avenue, his phone lighting up with messages every few minutes.

The day will unfold in a series of meetings, interviews, and installations in The Carriage House, Wilder's new culinary teaching space and dim sum restaurant. The quiet of the morning is quickly broken—a UPS employee raps on the door to deliver a package; a produce truck shows up to unload the day's vegetables; an accountant brings Wilder a stack of checks to sign. From the kitchen comes the clinking of dishes, the clanging of pots, and the smell of a gas range.

Before he is Janos, a 4-year-old John Wilder watches his mother prepare a leg of lamb. The leg is whole, nearly down to the hoof, all of the small bones, gristle, and fat still attached. His mother, Joyce, rubs it in mustard, garlic, and soy sauce. She makes a flour paste and then studs the leg with rosemary. As always, she is without a recipe; intuition is her guide.

It is 1958 in East Palo Alto, California. John's oldest siblings are at school, and his father, Dave, is at work. The kitchen belongs to John and his mother. From the record player comes the smooth crooning of Frank Sinatra. For a moment, Joyce is lost in the music; Sinatra is her celebrity heartthrob. She smiles at John, her youngest son, and twirls him across the kitchen.

John equates the kitchen with love, with mother, with the savory-sweet smell of garlic browning in the oven. As he grows older, he sneaks pieces of meat off the bone when his mother isn't looking. These are memories that John will carry for the next 50 years—as he becomes Janos, moves to Colorado, falls in love and marries; as he works in kitchens in Santa Fe and France and finally lands in Tucson. Just the thought of a leg of lamb floods his senses with nostalgia—he remembers the gamey smell of the lamb, the rosemary, the layers of flavors that permeate the meat as it cooks. For Janos, it is the dish that most expresses the love that can filter through food.

In the 1960s, Berkeley is alive with the civil rights movement. People spill into the streets, carrying signs and chanting. Throughout elementary school, John goes with his parents to community meetings and rallies where they protest housing discrimination and racial segregation. When Martin Luther King Jr. is murdered in 1968, John and his family march through Stanford holding hands with strangers in the street.

In his junior year of college in Boulder, Colorado, where he studies political science, John gets a job as a cook at The Hungry Farmer. It is 1975, and there are so many Johns working at the restaurant that it becomes hard to keep them all straight. Nicknames are doled out by the chef, and he begins referring to John Wilder as Janos. When the chef quits six weeks later, the broiler cook, David Ruby, continues the nickname. David and Janos are two young chefs learning the dance of a busy kitchen. Together they cook fast and well. They are understaffed that summer, and the two must cover the entire line. They cook and plate shrimp, ribs, potatoes, steak, and Rocky Mountain oysters for 450 diners every night. For Janos, the choreography of the pace is exhilarating. Here in the busy kitchen at The Hungry Farmer, Janos lets his new name settle around him.

In the summer, the Colorado mountains smell like ponderosa pine. Gold Hill, population 125, sits 10 miles outside of Boulder. At an elevation of 8,300 feet, steep roads and winter snows keep Gold Hill largely inaccessible to visitors for much of the year. But in the summer, the town buzzes with tourists.

In 1978, Janos meets his future wife, Rebecca, while working at the Gold Hill Inn. Janos is the chef and Rebecca—an artist and weaver who works as the K-3 teacher in the town's two-room schoolhouse—waits tables at the Inn over the summer.

As a chef in a remote community, Janos faces a major sourcing problem: no one will deliver to Gold Hill. Early each morning, Janos walks down the dirt road to take stock of his ingredients at the Inn. Bleary-eyed from late nights spent in the kitchen and partying with friends, he takes his truck down the mountain to Boulder. In Boulder, he visits supermarkets, the butcher, the fish market. On his way back up to Gold Hill, he writes the day's menu in his mind. As he rounds the last mountain curve, the expanse of the Continental Divide opens up in front of him.

Finally, it occurs to him to begin sourcing his ingredients from neighbors in Gold Hill. He notices that someone is growing sorrel and rhubarb; another neighbor has a small garden. *Oh my God*, he thinks, *Maybe I could sleep in.* He begins buying vegetables, wild mushrooms, and trout from neighbors, avoiding the early morning trek to Boulder whenever possible. This is the beginning of Janos' interest in local food, and at first, it's just practical. It's sleep-motivated. But the concept sticks, becoming an anchor for his career.

Every summer for the next 30 years, Janos and Rebecca go back to Gold Hill. They hike through the woods, taking in the columbine flowers and the green of fiddleheads unrolling. Their walk is a meditation, a casual hunt for the red-orange of lobster mushrooms and the bright yellow of chanterelles, which they carry back to the old miner's cabin that they now own.

In 1981, newly married, Janos and Rebecca leave Gold Hill for Santa Fe. They are in their mid-20s, and the world seems to shimmer with possibility. Rebecca studies graphic design and Janos finds a job in a restaurant. They rent a 300-square-foot apartment, a converted stable that still resembles a barn. Too broke to afford furniture, they eat their meals on the surface of a yellow foot locker.

Janos becomes fascinated by French cooking and decides to apprentice under a French chef. He writes letters to the best restaurants in

France, offering to intern without pay. One after the other, the restaurant owners say no—except for one, Roland Flourens, who writes that he will be in the United States and asks if he can visit Janos and Rebecca in Santa Fe. In preparation for Flourens' visit, they buy a picnic table for the living room. When Flourens arrives, Janos serves an elaborate multicourse dinner on the couple's wedding china. Flourens, though not entirely sold on Janos' meal, admires his drive and potential, and invites him to France.

Janos is captivated by the smells and sounds of France. For four months, Janos apprentices under Chefs Jean-Pierre Bugat and Didier Pétreau, absorbing the flavors, the technique, the philosophy of French cooking. He goes with the chefs to the outdoor market, where farmers sell produce from the back of their trucks. On one visit, a farmer flags down Chef Bugat and hands him a paper bag filled with the season's first tarragon, saved especially for him. There is a spark to this exchange and Janos is mesmerized. The relationship between producer and chef, he realizes, is the heart and soul of French cooking.

When Janos returns from France, he and Rebecca leave Santa Fe for Tucson—Rebecca was raised on the border, and they want to stay in the Southwest. In 1983, Janos opens his first Tucson restaurant, Janos, in an old adobe home in Barrio Viejo. Soon, it's heralded as one of the top regional restaurants in the United States. The experience is like being pulled through a tunnel—on the periphery, the world is happening, the desert is blooming, but Janos is moving too fast to take it all in. He stops only for a month, in July of 1984, when Rebecca gives birth to their son, Ben. That summer, the monsoons come early and water fills the streets. For a month when Ben is born, there is no restaurant. He and Rebecca focus on the baby, exploring the strange new space of parenthood. In August, Janos goes back to work. Days begin at 6:30 in the morning, and end at 10 or 11 at night. He often has the sensation of never actually leaving the restaurant.

At the restaurant, they make everything from scratch. They bake bread, they can tomatoes, they make pasta. Janos changes the menu every day. Twice a day, before lunch and dinner, he takes a handwritten menu to the copy store, where he uses a typewriter to type the menu before making photocopies.

After five years in Tucson, Janos and Rebecca start taking Ben hiking in the Tucson Mountains, and Janos begins to fall in love with the desert. He is introduced to Native Seeds/SEARCH, still a new organization focused on saving seeds of desert-adapted plants. He is asked to cater a fundraiser dinner, which he does using only foods sourced from Native Seeds/SEARCH. He begins to connect with the stories of the foods that have grown in the Sonoran Desert for thousands of years— tepary beans, cholla buds, chiles. He describes this as "a window, a portal, a door opening."

By the age of 30, Janos has spent half his life in the kitchen. His palate is developed; his technique is honed. The flavor profiles of the desert Southwest begin to collide and intersect with his French technique. He studies regional dishes of the Southwest as though they are science projects—chilaquiles, tacos, enchiladas. He takes the chile relleno and reverse engineers it, questions how and why it is prepared the way it is—the batter, the type of chile, how it's roasted. And then he rebuilds it.

He stuffs Anaheim chiles with lobster and brie. He covers it in French sauce. He pairs it with jicama salad. He makes taco shells out of egg roll wrappers. He infuses it with place: his California childhood, a visit to Tokyo with his parents, the mountains of Colorado, the French countryside. "I'm a guy that has tremendous respect for what's come before me," he says, "but tremendous respect for what's possible."

In the spring of 2010, Janos is planning the menu for Downtown Kitchen + Cocktails, set to open in October. At the end of April, Governor Jan Brewer signs Senate Bill 1070 into law, which sets off widespread protests against the anti-immigrant legislation. At Armory Park, just one block from the new restaurant, thousands of people gather to protest the law. Janos feels compelled to make a statement against SB 1070, and the new menu is the perfect vehicle. Since his youth, he has experienced the power of protest and the power of food—how it defines home, and how it returns us there, despite time, borders, or miles traveled through the desert.

Let's do American food, he thinks, *But let's do* real *American food.* And so the menu is born, an eclectic mix of worldwide cuisines, full of the foods that follow people as they migrate, dishes that serve as "touchstones to home."

By now, Janos is conditioned to change. In 1995, he opened Wild

Johnny's Wagon, a food truck enterprise well before the era of food trucks. In 1998, Janos relocated to the scenic Westin La Paloma. J Bar was created in the same location in 1999. In 2002, Janos spearheaded Kai at the Sheraton Wild Horse Pass Resort & Spa in Phoenix. And in 2010, Janos returned to downtown Tucson to open Downtown Kitchen + Cocktails.

There is a fire in Janos that keeps him dreaming and creating. Perhaps it's this same fire that has made him a self-professed browbeater in the kitchen. Janos admits to having developed a chef's temperament that he is not entirely proud of. He wants his employees to be great, and cannot understand why anyone would give less than their best. Now, he says, he has softened, perhaps with age, and "would rather inspire people by appealing to their highest selves." Time has also decorated him with numerous awards and recognitions, including a James Beard Award for Best Chef of the Southwest, the MOCA Local Genius Award, and acceptance into the Arizona Culinary Hall of Fame. He is chairman of the board of Native Seeds/SEARCH.

The Carriage House is the latest of Janos' endeavors. A culinary teaching and event space, The Carriage House is the manifestation of a decades-long dream of integrating education and cooking. In October of 2014, Janos was walking back to his restaurant from a meeting when he noticed a 1917 brick building in the alleyway directly behind Downtown Kitchen + Cocktails. He contacted the building's owner immediately. The design process began in May of 2015; construction began in October. In order to function as a restaurant, the space required new plumbing, grease traps, sewer connections, new electrical, gas lines, hoods, and extra ventilation.

"After so many moves, you gain perspective that everything will be all right, but you don't take that for granted by any means," Janos says. "It's exciting, but there are times when the stress just mounts. It doesn't all go perfectly. Things come out of left field that you had no expectation of."

In February 2016, The Carriage House finally opens. On a Sunday afternoon, Janos hosts a Friends & Family Dim Sum event, which happens to fall on his mother's 87th birthday. As she sits with Rebecca, Ben, and other family members, Joyce Wilder watches her son move around the room, greeting the many friends and colleagues who have come to celebrate his latest endeavor. The dining room is expansive, with high ceilings and exposed beams. Bartenders pour mimosas and servers push rolling glass carts filled with plated food. At the end of the meal, Janos surprises his mother with a birthday cake. His voice wavers as he honors the woman who inspired his love of cooking. She stands, tears in her eyes, and embraces her son. Nearly 60 years after they danced to Frank Sinatra in their East Palo Alto kitchen, the cooking space belongs once again to this mother and her son.

Promised Land

By Tienlon Ho

From the *San Francisco Chronicle*

Bay-Area writer Tienlon Ho writes about food, culture, and the environment, a trifecta of interests that naturally pair with farm-to-table dining. But is farm-to-table a true movement, or just a fad? For a young couple opening a much-anticipated new Sonoma restaurant, the query is anything but academic.

For the last two years, the buzz has been streaming in from both sides of the Pacific about Single Thread, a farm, restaurant and inn in Sonoma County. Even when it was just an empty building off Healdsburg's downtown square and 5 acres of weeds a few miles north, it was already being talked up as "the most highly anticipated," "most important restaurant" headed by "the best chef you've never heard of." It has been regularly mentioned alongside veritable institutions such as the French Laundry, Manresa and Blue Hill in New York.

If all goes accordingly, Single Thread will finally serve its first guests, at a price of $294 each, at the end of November.

No fewer than 250 well-publicized restaurants opened in the past year in the Bay Area, each trying to distinguish itself with some form of farm-to-table fare, although for most that means simply sourcing from the California growers we are so lucky to live nearby. In comparison, Single Thread has all the trappings of a PR coup: the farm, a dedicated R & D kitchen, a full-time forager, cooks and servers fresh from stints at three-Michelin star restaurants in San Francisco, New

York, Copenhagen and Tokyo. There is a cement fermentation tank in the dining room for guest vintners, plus custom ceramics by obscure artisans, a rooftop garden and tasting menus of California cuisine with strong Japanese and French influences.

The setup is so perfect that it would be reasonable to deem Single Thread as just another play for the deep pockets of the food-obsessed—that is, until you meet Kyle and Katina Connaughton, the utterly unpretentious and earnest couple behind this most hyped of hyped openings.

"It certainly is a lot of pressure, isn't it?" Kyle admits when you bring all this up. "But the biggest pressure is knowing that people on our team have moved here from all over the world to help us do this."

And this is when you begin to understand, despite all the hype, how very personal this venture actually is. It is, in many ways, a culmination of their professional lives.

Its germ was planted in Kyle's childhood over tuna rolls in Los Angeles sushi bars with his dad, who sold gymnastics equipment in Japan. But the idea sprouted in 2000, when Kyle took Katina on her first trip there. The two met in their early teens at a Face to Face punk show in Southern California. Since then, they've never left each other's side, through Kyle's early stints in pastry at Spago Beverly Hills and the Ritz-Carlton, sushi at Hama Sushi in Venice, then working with Suzanne Goin at Lucques and AOC, and Michael Cimarusti at Water Grill. Katina cooked, too, in a bakery, at home for the couple's two daughters, and alongside Kyle when he needed.

In Kyoto, Japan, they stayed in old *ryokans*, roadside inns from the era of traveling merchants and samurai, where dinner and breakfast were cooked with ingredients plucked from surrounding fields. The most elaborate meals were in the form of *kaiseki*, a progression of courses that celebrate the seasons, where everything from the condensation on a bowl to the order of each dish's arrival symbolizes something in nature. In the 1970s, kaiseki so inspired great French chefs such as Paul Bocuse that they created modern degustation menus, the signature of Western fine dining we all recognize today.

"With kaiseki, the menu can never be the same as it was the day before," says Kyle. "It reflects that particular moment and place." Someday at his own restaurant, he decided, he would only cook with ingredients at their peak of flavor.

For Katina, dinner in the ryokans was theater, but breakfast was something else. "When you are just starting your day, you are in a vulnerable mind-set, not fully dressed or pulled together, needing to be nourished and cared for," she says. She wanted to find a way to introduce restaurant guests to *omotenashi*, the utmost of personal and dedicated hospitality that she and Kyle experienced every morning. She thought then that their restaurant should have guest rooms, and to do that right, they would need a farm.

But first, Kyle wanted to learn more. He accepted an invitation to cook for Michel Bras, the influential French chef and vegetable master, at Toya in Japan, up north on the Hokkaido tundra. For three years, Kyle's main task was to execute Bras' signature gargouillou dish, which required wandering the countryside, rooting for the 30 or so distinct greens, herbs, flowers and vegetables that compose the dish, then preparing each in its own way, and finally, setting them in delicate postures, like a salad plated by God. On off-days, he apprenticed in local kitchens learning more about sushi, soba and kaiseki.

Meanwhile, Katina was studying sustainable Japanese farming techniques, spending the girls' school hours on strawberry farms, picking up the techniques she might someday sow into her own land. In the winters, the Connaughtons gathered around *donabe*, clay pots that braise, stew, steam or smoke whole meals while warming everyone nearby. (Kyle co-authored a book on donabe last year.)

But they delayed their plans when celebrated conceptual chef Heston Blumenthal called with an offer to Kyle to head the Fat Duck's experimental kitchen in the village of Bray in the English moorlands. Starting in 2006, Kyle oversaw the development of some of the restaurant's most iconic dishes and techniques, including "granulated" beef, a method of neatly arranging the strands of ground meat for extra tender burgers; the Sound of the Sea, where ocean waves conveyed by an iPod in a conch shell were designed to enhance the flavors of seafood atop edible sand; and even a gilt "pocket watch" that the Mad Hatter might fancy—one that melted into a veal consommé, a recipe that took 18 months of iterations to realize.

In the summers, Kyle and Katina came home to California and found themselves regularly in Sonoma and Napa counties, where they met kindred spirits among the growers and winemakers. They scouted for the right plot for the project there, for years watching deals fall through, until finally in 2014, they heard the Seghesio family might make available their building on the site of Healdsburg's old post office and a sizeable corner of a fallow vineyard.

By then, the Connaughtons felt more than ready. Supporting Blumenthal at the height of his fame, Kyle says, taught him about the motivations that drive a chef in the long run. After topping out on Michelin stars and the World's 50 Best list, "Heston said it best—accolades like those are a pat on the back and punch in the stomach. There's nowhere to go but down," Kyle says. "So the only thing you can ever do is to cook authentically, take creative risks and hope the rest follows."

Kyle says his mentor also taught him how innovation depends on each member of the team feeling free to exercise their own expertise. In developing dishes for the Single Thread menu, for instance, he often calls upon each cook to prepare his or her own take.

Innovation can spring from anywhere this way, including the farm, which is Katina's domain. Katina plots the plantings for the year broken down into 72 seasons, which breaks down to five-day increments of peak freshness. There are perhaps only five days for a certain variety of negi (leek-like onions), longer for the squashes. Katina sits in bed most nights reading seed catalogs and tracking climate and growth in an almanac of sorts on Google Drive. ("She'll ask, as I'm falling asleep, whether I'd be interested in purple something-or-other," Kyle says.) By day, she moves earth in a wheelbarrow bigger than herself.

"I can't say that all the varieties are so different to me flavorwise," she acknowledges. "I grow them because they are each distinct to Kyle. I love that man so I grow him negi!" (Currently, six varieties.)

While it took more than a year of tilling and growing cover crops to get the farm back in shape, Katina's beds are so prolific that with the restaurant yet to open, colleagues at other restaurants have been benefiting from gift baskets. The cooks have been practicing dealing with overabundance, too, using whatever is ready in a regular series of test dinners for friends and investors. (Single Thread's backers include Tony Greenberg of UPVentures; Plan Do See, which owns Omotenashi Hotels in Japan; and numerous local private investors.) Pastry chef Matt Siciliano says resourcefulness is so important here that when Kyle interviewed him for the job, he asked, "How would you feel if a bunch of peas came off the farm right now?"

Though guests are welcome to visit, the farm isn't for show. It will supply the restaurant with about 70 percent of its produce needs, mostly Asian varieties of greens like mizuna, mitsuba, tatsoi and specialty herbs like *okahijiki* (saltwort) that are difficult to source—plus plenty of eggs for breakfast, Katina adds.

"We don't plan on growing everything ourselves when we live in such a rich agricultural community with generations of farmers who do what they do so well," she says. She cites Bernier Farms, a Geyserville allium specialist since the mid-1970s. Not only can Bernier grow masses of quality onions, the growers there were excited to respond to cooks' specifications, like blanching a crop under soil mounds as they grow so the leaves will be pale and superbly tender.

That leaves room for Katina to experiment with varieties uncommon in the Bay Area. Along a deep bend of the Russian River, which runs along the farm, she has a crop of *myoga* (ginger) adapting to the Sonoma heat. In the greenhouse, thick hedges of shiso varieties are thriving. They bolted up so fast, in fact, that the leaves are now too tough for the cooks to use. Rather than waste what was already grown, she took the problem to the research and development team.

The R & D team is officially Pilot, a food lab in a low-slung house just a 10-minute stroll from the restaurant and four blocks from Kyle and Katina's home. Kyle founded Pilot in 2014 with Ali Bouzari, a food biochemist; Dan Felder, the former head of the Momofuku Culinary Lab; and Dana Peck, a lawyer who specializes in startups. Besides supporting the restaurant, Pilot develops food products and hones the methods to make them for private clients. Among their early projects were cricket-flour energy bars and a specialized Dremel saw that slices through an eggshell in seconds.

For Katina's shiso leaves, Bouzari and Felder tested various methods of pickling and lacto-fermentation to see which countered the toughness while preserving its minty flavor, eventually settling on a straight salt brine.

The challenges the Single Thread cooks bring the Pilot team run the gamut. When Kyle came with an idea to serve the 11 opening canapes in a way reminiscent of the formal opening course in kaiseki, where little bites are arrayed on a wooden platter, Felder headed to the woodshop to carve insets in planks of raw-edged redwood, adding lichen and moss as cover to make the experience like a treasure hunt in a Sonoma forest. Another week, the cooks wanted a lower-fat ice cream that retained its smoothness.

"Other ideas come from living in a beautiful place where delicious things just fall off trees," Peck says. A couple months ago, loquats were ripening all along the neighborhood streets, so the team picked buckets full and cured them like olives, making "oliquats," sweet and briny explosions of flavor.

Between all this, the Pilot team has been consumed for the past six months with creating a bread course for the restaurant. In Western tasting menus, bread is a traditional transition from small bites to the heart of the meal, but for Single Thread, Kyle wanted a new approach.

The team liked the idea of *osembei*, thin rice crackers. Instead of mostly rice, Bouzari (whose doctoral thesis earned him the moniker Dr. Potato) proposed a blend with potato starch broken down to a creamy texture with diastatic malt powder. There were troubles with flavor (too much like Pringles) and fleeting crunchiness. They tried molding them in pastry chef Siciliano's old stove-top pizzelle iron. They played with ratios of starches; temperatures; and other molds, tracking more than 80 iterations until last week when everyone agreed they had a winner. With the recipe set, Kyle and chef de cuisine Aaron Koseba are working on service details, such as how to keep the crackers warm long enough to survive guests caught up in conversation (the current plan involves a bed of heated obsidian and loosely woven cloth).

All this was just for the interlude between the third and fourth courses, which probably strikes anyone outside fine dining as borderline obsessive. In explaining the motivation behind six months of work, Kyle distilled it to this: "We just didn't want to destroy appetites with an 'Oh my god, I ate too much bread' moment."

Kyle and the culinary team continue to work on finalizing the rest of the dishes, which will fall into three 11-course menus—vegetarian, pescatarian, and full-on omnivore—though what particular dishes each guest can expect will depend entirely on conversations when making their bookings, and with their servers over the welcome bites served in the rooftop garden.

"I've always thought tasting menus are so often presented as something locked in, really missed opportunities to serve guests what they want," Kyle says. "We wanted to use this format as a way to engage more, not just make things easier on ourselves."

Though the menus will follow the flow of kaiseki, with its transitions from refreshing to savory and moments of reprieve, they will otherwise be unbound by formalities. In kaiseki, for example, there is always a *futamono* course, a soup with a lid to capture the aromas wafting from the broth. Kyle's take will be abalone with white alba mushrooms in a silver leaf tea—no lid.

He is keenly aware of the dangers of adopting another culture's tradition without fully conveying its meaning. "The whole world is open to us. That's the freedom that we have being outside that tradition," Kyle says. "We can draw from tradition and pay respect with careful consideration of its nuances. But it would feel weird if we insisted that there were always a lid on this course. It would be replicating a form without its meaning."

"This is ultimately food about Sonoma," Siciliano says. In planning the capping sweet course, known as *wagashi*, traditionally involving rice flour sweets served with tea, Siciliano deliberately held back from direct references, playing instead with a beet dish with chicory and chervil and a bite of apple butter layered with a lemon coriander cream. "I'm never going to make wagashi the way they do in Japan, because those makers started doing so generations ago," he says, "so I'm trying to move the conversation forward and create something unexpected."

As they await the restaurant kitchen to be completed, the entire culinary team has been working out of Kyle and Katina's renovated farmhouse on a four-burner Viking range, a portable Cuisinart oven that is usually relegated to the garage for lack of counter space, and the family's donabe. On one afternoon, three sous chefs and the sommelier were touching shoulders as they used every available countertop and a makeshift plywood workbench to prepare a vegetable tureen, a black cod dish, a melon dessert and various cocktails. Katina squeezed by, dropping off some of the day's harvest and lugging buckets of flowers she was arranging for the next evening's test dinner.

"There's something about these moments in the very beginning, how you handle the challenges together, that reflect how things will be the future," Kyle says, surveying the scene. "It's a moment you can't have again."

In this era of Bay Area startups (culinary and otherwise), there can be a reflexive eye-rolling when you hear someone talk about farm-fresh anything, or R & D, or the romance of cramming a team into cramped quarters before the big launch. It doesn't help that to pay for all that, prices have to be high—out of reach to many, which is especially wincing as Healdsburg adjusts to hordes of wealthy weekenders while holding town meetings to find ways to keep rental prices down for everyone else.

But now Kyle attends those meetings and makes a point to be transparent about Single Thread's hiring and sourcing. Everything within Single Thread is interconnected, and so it is becoming with the community outside it, too. "We live here now, and we want to live here for the rest of our lives," he says.

Which is to say that when Kyle and Katina tell you Single Thread is an extension of their home, you can't help but understand. And when they say they want to give each guest a truly personal and memorable experience, you believe it. Not because of the breathless press or the hefty bill, but because every detail will come from a real piece of the Connaughtons' journey—from Katina's mornings in Kyoto, to Kyle tweaking the details of recipes for famous chefs for endless months, and their quiet evenings over donabe as a family. All of this will be distilled into each dish.

On an afternoon visit to check on the construction of the restaurant, the Connaughtons lingered outside, looking at a barren two-story trellis on which Katina will eventually nurse creeping vines to climb skyward. There was a riot of hammering coming from inside.

"Sometimes you can't plan everything, and then it all comes together anyway," Katina says with a shrug. Like all the parts of their past that have coalesced into this moment, it all feels inevitable.

A local man who has been admiring the changes peers in the window as he rolls by in his wheelchair. "You gonna buy this place?" he asks.

"Thinking about it," Kyle says.

Michel Richard, 1946–2016

By Todd Kliman

From ToddKliman.net

The immediacy of social media can be powerful. Todd Kliman, award-winning food critic and cultural essayist (the *Washingtonian*, *Lucky Peach*, *The Oxford American*, et cetera), brought that power home in this viral Twitter tweetstorm, eulogizing one of the world's great chefs in the hours after his death.

Michel Richard was a genius. That's not a word to be used indiscriminately, though it often is. But it's true. He was. One of the few.

It was easy to see the virtuosic brilliance in his dishes, the dazzling wit that made you smile before you'd even taken a bite.

What was not easy to see, in part because the brilliance was so blinding, was the world that gave rise to this invented world. A real world of pain and heartache. His food was an escape.

His father came to Brittany after WWII, to find work rebuilding the country. A drunkard, he beat his wife and abandoned the family when Richard was 6. His mother worked in a factory, and took the five children to live in a house with no running water. At 8, Richard had his first job—he was the family cook.

He learned how to use every part of the animals he killed, collecting the blood of rabbits to mix it with vinegar for making boudin. He thickened stews with the innards.

He later went to work in a bronze factory. His skin black with soot at the end of his shifts.

Somewhere around this time, he made a discovery: the Impressionists. He was enchanted by their renderings of reality. Renderings that improved upon the actual.

By 14, he was on his path, working 16 hours a day for a pastry chef in a town 100 miles away. This alone was brutal. But the fear of reprisal was just as harrowing. One slip-up, and he could be smacked around by the boss.

And so he learned not to slip up, to mind the tiniest, most insignificant detail. Three years later, he became a pastry chef.

After an army stint—he told me a story once about serving an inhumane higher-up his own cat in a stew, a story I have never verified, and never tried, believing it to be true in some form or fashion—he went to work for the great Gaston Lenotre, the granddaddy of pastry chefs.

Lenotre did not just make pastry; he worked confections up into arrangements that made people's jaws drop in awe and wonder.

It was here that Richard learned that food could be more than nourishment; it could dazzle; it could provoke; it could prompt contemplation and even study.

More than that: it could take you out of one world—our fallen world, brutal and unfair—and into one that was more beautiful and even magical.

When he was making the transition from sweet to savory, becoming a chef and not just a pastry chef, fine dining was a more solemn and restrained business than it is now. He played his own game. I'll never forget seeing him walk up to a diner at Citronelle who was gawking at Richard's version of a Napoleon. The diner was right to gawk. "Smash it!" Richard shouted, standing over him. The man was too paralyzed with fear and perhaps too awestruck. "Smash it!" And so Richard picked up the spoon and, like a little boy, demolished his own creation.

He smashed things. Rules. Conventions. Should-dos. Expectations. So many of Richard's greatest dishes were not just great-tasting. They were feasts for the eyes and the mind. His mushroom soup, which was made to look like a cappuccino, complete with a top layer of (potato) foam. (And let it be said that the soup itself was the most mushroomy I've ever tasted, as if the chef had produced not simply a broth but a liqueur.) A mosaic-like arrangement of eel and tuna set on a layer of

Saran wrap over a bowl so that it cast shadows below. "Breakfast," which was, in fact, an over-the-top display of dessert in the form of a grand room-service breakfast.

Very few chefs have a recognizable style. They have a genre, a way of plating, a philosophy, an approach. Richard had a style, in the same way that Van Gogh had a style, or that Woolf had a style. Distinct. Inimitable.

The razor-like line of his creations. The trompe l'oeil wit. The irrepressible need to overturn assumption and expectation.

He will be remembered for many things as a chef, but this has to be foremost among them—that no one did more to demonstrate that French cooking is not a period piece. That it need not be beholden to the past, to tradition. That it is possible both to honor the canon and revere the classics and also innovate. Swapping peak-of-season August tomatoes for beef in a steak tartare. Turning squid into capellini. Making caviar out of pasta.

Are these lessons that other chefs can be inspired by and follow? Yes. Will we see another like him? I somehow doubt it.

I've tasted the work of many great chefs—here in DC, around the country, and around the world. Great dishes, great experiences. But I have never left the table the way I left the table at Richard's restaurants when he was there.

With a sense of lightness and possibility.

With a belief that life was, or could be, beautiful.

And this was yet another trick that he performed at the table. The ability to make life look better than it was.

Yet for all his genius, I think what I will remember most in the weeks to come is his vulnerability and unappeasability.

He oozed vulnerability. Many chefs are deeply, deeply vulnerable and either hide it or run from it. He didn't. He used it as a spur to creativity.

He was up front about what he needed from people. Up front about what he felt he was denied. No amount of recognition or affirmation was enough for him. No amount of honors, accolades, commendations, or stars. There was a massive hurt there, a wound, and that wound was an open wound.

It was attractive in him, I thought, and not repellent.

It had its roots in the world that made him. The kitchen, the plate, his imagination at play in a new dish—these were escapes. But that world never left him.

There were hangers-on. People who wanted to be in his orbit, and share in the spoils. And he did not say no enough. He should have.

He was bad at business, and that was a terrible shame, too, because it deprived him, and us, of opportunities.

But I won't remember those things.

I will remember his vulnerability, his unappeasability, his genius, his sense of wonder, his refusal to live outside of his imagination.

I will remember going to the Phillips Collection with him some months ago, and just walking around, taking in the work of the masters.

And him with his keen and observant eye. His hungry, his devouring eye.

They Also Serve

The Chef, the Dishwasher and a Bond

By Peggy Grodinsky

From the *Portland Press-Herald*

As food editor at Maine's *Portland Press Herald*, Peggy Grodinsky chronicles one of the Northeast's most dynamic food scenes. Here, she pays tribute to an aspect of the restaurant world that's all too often overlooked: the vital dynamic between chefs and their kitchen staff.

Larry Matthews Jr., chef and owner of the elegant Back Bay Grill in Portland, and William "Franco" Tucker, dishwasher at the same, have worked together for about two decades. Longer than many marriages last. Longer, by decades, than dishwashers typically stay at restaurants. Longer than either ever expected, and longer than Matthews has worked with anyone else at his reliably first-rate restaurant.

Matthews, 43, grew up in Kennebunk, where he still lives. He was raised a strict Baptist, and today is married with two children. After getting a college degree in the culinary arts, he worked in a few restaurants—some quite distinguished—before arriving at Back Bay Grill when he was about 22.

At 24, he was the executive chef, and five years later, he owned the place. He left once, for two months, to cook at a restaurant in Ogunquit. But for most of his life, Matthews has had one home, both professionally and personally.

Tucker, 68, spent his childhood at the Waco State Home and in reformatory school in Texas; the state removed him from his family when he was a preschooler. He was raised "Southern fried Baptist," he said. He dropped out of school after eighth grade—he has since got his GED—and a few years later he spent time in jail for stealing cars. He has never been married, and he doesn't have a girlfriend now, though he smiles when he says he is "always in the hunt."

Before he came to Maine in the 1970s, Tucker was a rambling man, living in Alaska; New Mexico; Seattle; Denver; Buffalo, New York; and Tucson, Arizona. He wandered around Maine some, too, looking for work, he said, always looking for work. Over the years, he has held many odd jobs, in welding, construction, and mason tending; making sandwiches, harvesting potatoes and working at an auto parts plant. Home was wherever he hung his hat.

One packed New Year's Eve in the late 1990s, the dishwasher at Back Bay Grill walked. Tucker was hired at the eleventh hour to fill in, a trial by fire in more ways than one; that evening the dish-washing machine broke down.

Since then, he's left just once, for a year, to be reunited with his sister in Texas whom he'd last seen when he was 4 years old.

In this industry, two years employment is practically a lifetime. Dishwashers often cycle in for just six months. As for finding one who cares about his work? As likely as finding a fiddlehead in January.

"It was a long year," Matthews said of the time Tucker was away.

"I'd rather be up here," Tucker said.

"We Got It Done"

Tucker mostly works in a tight space directly behind Back Bay Grill's open kitchen. He's a scrawny man, which turns out to be handy, as a large man might not fit or be able to pivot with bus buckets stacked with dirty plates, racks loaded with clean glasses, and chinois and bain maries to fetch for the line cooks. Such specialized equipment, called in professional kitchens by their French names, hangs from the ceiling between the kitchen and the dish station, and Tucker can name every item.

Once, when Matthews was new and cooking on the line, something he does only occasionally these days, he asked Tucker to bring him lettuce.

"I wanted mixed baby lettuces. I didn't think he knew what it was," Matthews remembered. "I tried to describe what mesclun mix looks like." Tucker went downstairs and came back with the wrong stuff. He made a second trip. And a third. "Finally, by process of elimination he got it and he showed it to me and I was like 'yeah, that's it.' And he says (to me) . . . " Here Matthews speaks very slowly in imitation of Tucker's voice, telling the chef, as if explaining to a not very bright child, "Mes-cu-lun mix."

Tucker doesn't remember this, though he does remember the painfully slow evening years ago when Matthews sent everyone in the kitchen home but him. Suddenly, the place filled up, "and the next thing you know, Franco and I were flying around and figuring out how to get it done," Matthews said.

"We got it done," he added.

Common Core

In the beginning, their relationship wasn't all truffles and foie gras—two items that are, incidentally, sometimes featured on Back Bay Grill's menu. Tucker is set in his ways, Matthews said, and things could get tense. Matthews remembers bickering. A lot of it.

"I was a chef trying to make my bones, I suppose," Matthews said. "Everything was very important to me all the time. If I needed a particular pan, that was the only thing. He saw other priorities.

"Once we understood that we both had the restaurant's best interest in mind," Matthews continued, "that's when I think we (made) a more cohesive team."

When he isn't washing dishes, Tucker stands at the pass between the kitchen and dish room and watches the line cooks with fierce intensity. He hands them the correct clean pans they need when, say, an order for lavender-marinated duck breast comes in, and he grabs their hot, dirty pans with tongs or kitchen towels, disappearing to scrub them, reappearing a minute later to return them clean.

He's got a system. He's got systems. He knows just how to remove greasy, cooked-in rings from the top of stock pots. He separates the utensils before putting them through the machine—knives with knives (blades up), forks with forks (tongs down). He knows which scrubbies to use with which pans, so the pans don't get scratched.

When the waiters come in at 4 p.m., relaxed and sociable, they can annoy Tucker. He starts his day at 2 p.m., and before the dishes pile

up and depending on the day's menu, he peels fava beans and potatoes, cleans fiddleheads, de-beards mussels, shucks corn . . . He has
plenty to do, and it looks to him like the waiters don't. He can be gruff,
Matthews said. Tucker likes his routines, seconds Back Bay Grill General Manager Adrian Stratton, who at 12 years with the restaurant is
the next longest-serving person on the staff.

"Franco is at the bottom of the food chain—supposedly," Matthews
said. "In years past, I had a cook who didn't get along with Franco.
'Don't put me in a position where I have to choose between the two of
you,' he told the cook. 'It won't be a hard choice.'"

Who Would Do the Dishes?

Matthews understands the work of a restaurant dishwasher firsthand. He's done the job himself. Before he cooked at the Relais
& Châteaux White Barn Inn in Kennebunk, before he cooked at the
James Beard award-winning Inn at Little Washington in Virginia, before he helmed Portland's beloved Back Bay Grill, he washed dishes at
the Lobster Pot in Cape Porpoise.

"Every chef should spend some time doing the dishes," he said. "It's
a thankless job, but in a lot of ways, it is the most important job in the
restaurant."

He actually remembers the dishwasher at the Inn at Little Washington. We're talking 20 years ago. A guy named Roy, whom Matthews
called "a career dishwasher."

"He took it very seriously," he said. "He was very good at it. I felt very
lucky to find a similar partner."

On occasion, Matthews has substituted for Tucker at Back Bay Grill.
It's easier to do the job himself than try to find someone else to do it, he
said. Someone who will live up to Tucker's exacting standards, which
Tucker describes this way: "Do it right the first time, so you don't have
to go over it."

Once, Matthews tried to get Tucker help in the dish room, someone
to do the pots for a few hours each day. That didn't work out.

Not that Tucker needs a substitute much.

"If Franco doesn't show up, that means a train ran him over," Stratton
joked. Which got Stratton and Matthews to thinking about the traits of
a good dishwasher.

"Reliability," Matthews said. "Reliability," he repeated.

Until some five years ago, Tucker worked five to six days a week. He cut back to four days so he could get up early Sundays to take the bus to Boston—he doesn't own a car—to see the Patriots play. His Social Security checks make his new schedule possible.

"I've always been into sports," Tucker said. Others move to Maine for the beautiful coastline, the outdoors life, the reasonable pace. He said he stayed because he likes the Patriots and the Celtics.

Did you know Matthews wrestled on his high school team? he added admiringly.

Tucker substituted for Matthews, sort of, just once. Matthews had the bright idea that Tucker should get a promotion to cook. This was "double digit years ago," Matthews said. "I thought it would be a great story if I could turn him into a great chef."

The tryout lasted all of a day.

"He had no interest in doing it," Matthews said. "He didn't have the passion for it."

Tucker didn't dispute this. Does he cook at home? "Microwave," he said. About that possible promotion? First of all, cooking in a restaurant kitchen is too hot, Tucker said. Second, "like I told Larry," who would do the dishes?

"We could probably get a dishwasher," Matthews said.

"I'd probably be dissatisfied with what I see around," Tucker replied. "Very few (good dishwashers) right now. I can't recommend anybody."

He's the Metronome

Tucker has been at Back Bay Grill twice as long as he's held any other job.

"Everybody treats me with respect," he said when asked why. "Not every job they are gonna treat you with respect."

Then there are the occasional celebrity sightings. Like two weeks ago, when George Bush Sr. showed up to eat soft shell crabs.

Tucker has eaten in the comfortable, understated dining room himself. Once, when he had a date, the kitchen prepared a 14-course tasting menu for the couple. Only one problem: The date was a no-show.

"Actually it turned out good because she was a bad girl," Tucker said. "It brought me up to what she was all about."

He ate the meal by himself. "I usually don't eat that much."

Usually, he is very particular about when he eats. Tucker doesn't like to work on a full stomach. If he is busy, he may not stop to eat a slice of birthday cake for a co-worker. Sometimes, he eats staff meal with everybody else at the end of service. More often, he scrapes a portion into a container and brings it home to microwave.

"Everything goes to his time frame," Stratton said. "I'm pretty sure my day starts on his time frame."

"There are a lot of times I feel like Franco sets the rules, and we just follow them," Matthews agreed, laughing.

"He is the metronome of the kitchen," Back Bay Grill server Ian Bannon said of Tucker.

That respect Tucker feels, that any customer to Back Bay Grill has felt—it's no accident. It's in the DNA of the restaurant, the DNA of Matthews and Stratton.

"If you are respectful to all your employees, your employees will pass that respect on to the guests. It's trickle-down," Stratton said. "Your first guest is your employee."

Arriving Today

Eighteen years years ago, Tucker attended Matthews' wedding at the Danforth Inn in Portland. Do the pair consider themselves friends?

"Oh yeah. He's a boss and a friend," Tucker instantly answered the question.

"It's definitely, ah . . . not a traditional friendship," Matthews said carefully. "We don't hang out outside of work. But I try to make sure he's taken care of, he gets whatever he needs. He hurt his knee a few years back. He had appointments across town. I took him to all those. I don't know if that's a friendship, exactly what you'd call it."

Tucker interrupted, laughing: "He's not my enemy, anyhow."

Now that Tucker is 68, now that he's reliably held the same job for 20 years, now that he knows what he knows, what would he tell that 16-year-old boy who stole cars so he could run away from reform school?

"I never wished I didn't do it. I would do something else just to get away," Tucker said. "They don't give you a bus ticket, they don't. It could have been a lot worse."

Not surprisingly, Matthews sees things differently. He got his own big chance as a young man at the White Barn Inn. He'd already worked at other restaurants by then, but then-chef Gethin Thomas opened his eyes to what the culinary field could be. I could do that, he thought to himself. I want to do that.

"I think Franco just really needed some consistency and some stability, something he could count on," Matthews said. "He works very hard. He comes here and is appreciated and taken care of, so he comes back again the next day. And 20 years later, we are doing the same thing.

"I always wonder what would have become of Franco if he'd had some form of stability earlier in his life . . . what would happen in a different parallel reality.

"But this is where he is," Matthews said.

When Matthews was young he figured he'd move around from good restaurant to better restaurant cheffing and climbing the ladder. He didn't figure that then Back Bay Grill proprietor Joel Freund would get terminal cancer and want to sell the place to his star chef. But this is where Matthews is, too.

The Piano Man of Zuni Café

By Rachel Levin

From *Lucky Peach*

⚘

The San Francisco restaurant critic for Eater.com, Rachel Levin has also covered the Bay Area culinary scene for the *New York Times*, *San Francisco Magazine*, and *Lucky Peach*. Her focus isn't only on what's new and trendy, either—witness this fresh take on the classic SF restaurant Zuni Café.

The six o'clock sun streams through the floor-to-ceiling windows, illuminating the long copper-topped bar and an oddity for a Thursday evening or any evening, really, at Zuni Café: a room full of empty tables.

Bob Carrau doesn't seem to notice. He strolls in with his embroidered seat cushion under one arm and a tattered yellow Mexican market bag slung over the other, like he has twice a week, every week, for the last nine years. He nods hello to the hosts, whose names, he admits, he really should know by now, and heads downstairs, to Zuni's underworld—where dishes are washed and ties are ironed and the staff shares big bowls of pasta—and grabs a small ceramic Mexican plate from his cubby: his tip plate.

Bob's not hungry. He had a couple of carrots before he arrived, but otherwise, he never eats before he plays. He rarely sticks around to eat afterward either, unless friends come in. Doesn't matter what plates pass by: the thick slices of *levain* with sea salt–sprinkled butter; the Caesar of all Caesars. Not even Zuni's famed roasted chicken, nestled in warm bread salad, tempts. (As much as he likes it, he likes his partner Tony's roast chicken more.)

Somehow, unlike everyone else in the restaurant, his mind isn't on the food. It's on his music.

For the next three hours, beneath "a flower arrangement Liberace could die for," he'll play a polished K. Kawai grand piano that's stood there almost as long as the restaurant itself.

First, Bob opens his wallet. "Don't tell anyone I'm doing this," he says, and proceeds to do what everyone knows everyone with a tip jar—in Bob's case, a tip plate—does: and feeds himself a five dollar bill.

Bob never wanted to play for tips! He wasn't even sure he wanted to play for people. On an average night, he might pull in thirty bucks; fifty on a good night. Tonight—Game 1 of the NBA Finals for the Golden State Warriors—it's so far looking slow.

"I've learned, how I play has no bearing on how much people tip," he says laughing. "Depends on the night, their mood . . . " He could make a million mistakes, he says, and some big hitter might still slip him a twenty. Bob appreciates every penny, but he doesn't play for the money. He can barely believe Zuni pays him at all.

"I guess that means I'm a professional?" He half-balks/half-marvels at the thought as he pulls what looks like forty pounds of spiral-bound jazz fake books out of his bag, some dating back decades.

From fifth grade through age fifty, playing piano was just a hobby for Bob. Something he did on his own, rarely if ever singing along, and always without fanfare. If there happened to be a piano at a friend's house, he'd sneak off while everyone was making dinner. A performer, he was not, he promises. "I'd just see a piano and want to know what it would sound like."

But the thing is: his friends thought it sounded pretty good.

And his friends owned restaurants. Like Alice Waters (whose speeches and books he sometimes cowrites, including her latest, *Fanny in France,* which comes out this fall.) And Gilbert Pilgram of Zuni, which had a piano in need of a player. So one rainy Monday afternoon in 2007, he invited Bob to come in and play a few tunes while he and Judy Rodgers worked on the books.

He doesn't remember what he played, just how he *felt* playing. The acoustics were incredible. He gazes from the polished cement floors to the mile-high cathedral-like ceilings. "This room is just beautiful," he says. "Especially when no one is in it."

Tonight it's just a few fellow regulars: a gray-haired woman in a trench coat sitting by herself. Another who gives him what he calls "the Princess Di wave" as she passes the piano. A bearded man in a blazer stops to give him a hearty hug, marveling at having his pick of tables. "Who knew the Zuni crowd were such Warriors fans?"

Bob agrees. The Zuni crowd used to be "gayer," he says, chatting as his fingers flutter effortlessly over the keys to "The Caissons Go Rolling Along," a WWII tune he sneaks in every time. "The first night I ever played at Zuni, the U.S. had just sent more troops to Iraq, or some-where, and I was just sitting at the piano, looking around the room, real-izing how insulated we were from the world," he says. "It's my own silly little protest."

Bob was a regular back when Zuni was a sliver of an American-Mexican place. Before Judy Rogers took over in 1987, installed the brick oven, expanded, and turned Zuni Café into the iconic restaurant it is today.

There was always a piano, he recalls. "This one old guy from the Fill-more would play the blues and I'd just stare at his fingers, at how fast they could move." Like I now sit and stare at his.

"Zuni was the kind of place you'd come to cruise," Bob reminisced. In his thirties, he'd drop by around 11 p.m., hoping to maybe meet someone. "I never did," he says laughing. "But it *felt* like you could."

Now a graying fifty-eight year old in a twenty-year relationship, Bob's certainly not here to meet men. He's here to play. And people watch. "I'm a voyeur," he says. "This gig allows me to be out in public, with-out, you know, really going out." Originally a gofer-turned-screenwriter for Lucasfilm (he actually wrote his first script with George), he can't help but watch the well-coiffed gaggles slurping Fanny Bays and sipping fresh lime margaritas and wonder who they are, where they've been, why they're here.

He barely chats to anyone save the bartender, who pours him a single snifter of mezcal halfway through his set, or the server who always snaps as he strolls past. "That's how I can tell the music is getting through," says Bob. "Sometimes I think I sound great. Sometimes I think I sound like a guy on a cruise ship."

Hardly, says Gilbert, who appreciates the warmth and intimacy that live music adds to a restaurant, a rarity in this age of piped-in playlists. "What I love about Bob is he's *not* your typical lounge player. You'll never catch him playing 'New York, New York.' He has standards."

He's Zuni's "regular celebrity," according to Gilbert. To Bob's mind, he's pure background. "People don't pay attention to me," he says. "It's okay."

Once, though, Michael Tilson Thomas cruised through and gave him a thumbs-up. That felt good. A few years ago, Hillary Clinton came in, with a friend of his who asked her if she had any requests. She suggested "Moon River," then ordered a Manhattan. But her friend urged her to try Zuni's margarita. "'Oh, I'll just have both,' she said!" Bob recounts. "Wait, maybe don't print that. She's trying to get elected president of the United States!" (Oh c'mon, if Gerald Ford liked his lunchtime martinis and Teddy Roosevelt drank mint juleps and even President Obama puts back an occasional pint, there's no harm in Hillary Clinton double-fisting a couple of cocktails, is there?)

Bob flips the pages of his fake book. He has no premeditated lineup. "I let the room tell me what to play," he says, and launches into a riff of "Have You Met Miss Jones?"

Time for his break.

He rises and wanders out the side door, onto Market Street. "This stretch used to be scarier, all addicts and homeless," he says, strolling a few doors down to his "office," an entrance to a mattress shop and a respite from San Francisco's wintry summer wind. He points to a shiny tech bus and the sleek new sushi spot across the street. A woman jogs by, as does a man pushing a baby stroller, then two matching hoodies. "You never used to see any of these people here—or if you did, they were lost."

An almost forty-year-old restaurant with a wall of windows exposes more than just the waning evening light. Somehow, though, because this is Zuni, the changing city remains beyond the glass.

The clock strikes nine and a few Warriors' revelers start to trickle in. Bob packs up his music, closes the lid on his borrowed piano, and slips the sole fiver back into his wallet. Time to head home. Perhaps Tony's roasted a chicken.

My Dinners with Harold

By Daniel Duane

From the *California Sunday* Magazine, December 1, 2016

A contributing editor to *Men's Journal* and *Food & Wine*, Daniel Duane has written memoirs about surfing, rock climbing, and learning how to cook. It was cooking that first led him to Harold McGee's essential tomes on food science. Actually meeting his (and so many others') culinary mentor? Priceless.

The first time I had dinner with Harold McGee, he didn't touch the food. McGee is the bookish 65-year-old author of *On Food and Cooking: The Science and Lore of the Kitchen*, first published in 1984, last revised in 2004, and so dense with gripping material like the denaturing effect of heat on meat proteins that it cannot possibly have been read cover to cover by more than two or three people, McGee included. *On Food and Cooking* is also a perennial bestseller with hundreds of thousands of copies in print—a bible for home cooks and chefs all over the world and the primary reason that McGee has become the great secret celebrity of the contemporary food scene.

I knew for years that McGee lived in my San Francisco neighborhood, and I had been fantasizing about dinner with him ever since the night I tried to make mayonnaise by putting an egg yolk and a teaspoon of water in a bowl and whisking in half a cup of extra-virgin olive oil. This mixture deteriorated into such a disgusting pool of grease that I threw it out. I cracked a second egg, separated the yolk, added more water, and tried whisking in another half cup of olive oil. Heartbreak again, this time coupled with self-doubt.

I repeated this process five times, ever more certain that something was wrong with me, until I had gone through ten dollars' worth of oil and all but one of my eggs with only minutes before my dinner guests were due. I owned *On Food and Cooking*, having bought it long before in the hope of making myself into a superior cook, but I had given up on reading it after repeated runs at Chapter 1: "Milk and Dairy Products."

The mayo mess broke my *OFAC* impasse. Frantic, I scanned the index, found my subject between matzo and mead, and read McGee's primer on emulsified sauces, of which mayonnaise is one. I felt calmed by McGee's explanation that the essence of an emulsion is the dispersal of oil into a zillion tiny droplets suspended in water, aided by an emulsifier in egg yolks known as lecithin. I felt reassured by the news that fancy olive oil is notoriously temperamental in mayonnaise, and I nearly wept with relief at the sight of a section titled, "Rescuing a Separated Sauce." Following McGee's directions, I put a few tablespoons of water in a cup and then, whisking vigorously, slowly drizzled in my final batch of yolk-speckled oil. Moments later, I emerged as the man I am today, capable of making mayonnaise with confidence.

I promptly bought McGee's second and third books, *The Curious Cook: More Kitchen Science and Lore* (1990) and *Keys to Good Cooking: A Guide to Making the Best of Foods and Recipes* (2010). I soon experienced similar triumphs—like making french fries that did not fall limp within minutes of leaving my deep-fryer. I came to think of McGee as an imaginary friend who lived in my kitchen, knew everything, and was happy to share.

I offer this story because it is the quintessential McGee story: *OFAC* purchase with intent to self-educate; failure of will; years of ignoring book on shelf; culinary crisis leading to Hail Mary reference; success; love. The story is also quintessentially modern, speaking to the widespread belief that data and the scientific method can make us all happier, slimmer, fitter, and better in bed. Results are decidedly mixed—if not terrible—in most of these areas, but cooking's variables are more knowable and controllable. Cooking involves near-daily experimentation with chemistry (baking soda), physics (heat), and biology (kombucha). Its methods are mostly traditional, too, resulting from a thousand years of unscientific trial and error and therefore rife with easy targets of the kind identified and shot down by McGee in a 1985 article for *The New York Times* about the time-worn notion that searing meat seals in juices, which turns out to be nonsense.

The language of science, meanwhile, has replaced French classicism as the lingua franca of the culinary world. Major culinary schools offer a food-science major with *OFAC* on their reading lists, TV shows like Alton Brown's *Good Eats* have enshrined the scientific method as the secret to kitchen success, and bestselling books like J. Kenji López-Alt's *The Food Lab: Better Home Cooking Through Science* describe elaborate experiments proving that burger patties smashed flat on a griddle do not, in fact, turn into hockey pucks. We are living, in other words, through a period of what you might call Peak McGee.

Back to that first dinner. McGee is working on a new book that he describes somewhat cryptically as "a guide to the smells of the world," and he fiercely guards his writing time. So I didn't actually ask him to dinner. I asked if he might consider meeting me for conversation, maybe at a restaurant. The chefs of every fine-dining eatery in San Francisco would have recognized and welcomed him, but he insisted on a modest French bistro called Le Zinc near his home in the Noe Valley neighborhood. McGee apparently likes to take a walk after his writing day.

I arrived at 5:30 p.m. on a Tuesday and found Le Zinc empty except for the maitre d' and McGee: long-limbed and slender almost to the point of delicacy, with a neatly trimmed beard, gold wire-rimmed spectacles, and a social awkwardness obvious from ten paces. McGee sat at a little round table in back and was drinking white wine. I joined him and, hoping to lure him toward a meal, ordered steak tartare to share.

While we waited for the food, I asked how McGee came to write *OFAC*. Sitting up straight in his chair and speaking in a genteel and controlled manner, McGee began: "I grew up mainly in the Chicago area. My mother was a housewife, and my father worked at the Sears mother ship downtown." A chemical and electrical engineer, his father met McGee's mother during a postwar stint in India. The family lived in what were then newly built suburbs, where McGee spent nights in the backyard with a ham radio, communicating with people on the far side of the Earth.

Our waiter set down a white plate with a red cylinder of raw chopped beef surrounded by green salad and toast. McGee ignored it and said that he went to the California Institute of Technology to study astronomy but, after one year, "realized that I had friends who could look at a question on our homework, look at the sky for a minute, write an answer, and then go to the beach. And I would sit there and sweat even when things were explained to me." McGee also discovered a love of literature "to the point where I was like, 'Maybe I'm in the wrong place and should transfer to a liberal arts school.'"

An English professor convinced McGee to stick around and study the Big Bang and Romantic poetry side by side. McGee described this as a remarkably happy period followed by equally enjoyable years in the Ph.D. program in English literature at Yale, studying under Harold Bloom. McGee's college girlfriend, Sharon Long, joined him at Yale, first as an instructor in the biology department, where she gave a lecture on the thermodynamics of fudge making. Later she became a doctoral student in biochemistry and genetics.

McGee said that he finished his dissertation on John Keats in 1977 and began an unsuccessful three-year search for a tenure-track position. McGee was getting to the part of the story where he struck on the idea for *OFAC*, and I could feel his tone change to emphasize doubt and happenstance more than genius or vision. "We had friends in biology and literature, and we would get together on weekends for a potluck," McGee said. "Often, what we had in common to talk about was food. You spill wine and someone says, 'Put salt on it,' and someone else says, 'Why?' Then the chemists start to speculate."

McGee said that he finally gave up on his dream of becoming a professor—a painful passage—and looked around for a writing project, perhaps a book on some aspect of science. At one of those potlucks, a friend confessed that he loved beans but suffered terribly when he ate too many.

"He wanted to know if there was such a thing as a 'Fart Chart' of different kinds of beans," McGee said. "And if he used a different kind of beans, could he maybe eat a couple more servings? He also wondered if there was something he could do to the beans ahead of time."

The next day, McGee went looking for answers. At the Yale biology library, he discovered that plenty of food-science research had been published by and for the food manufacturing and packaging industries, but little of it had been shared with chefs or home cooks.

"I spent hours in that library because I had never seen anything like it," McGee told me. "Poultry science and agricultural and food chemistry. I would just flip through random volumes and see microscopic studies of things I eat every day. It seemed so cool and unexpected. It took more than a day to home in on the right sources about beans, but not only did I find out what's in them and what you can do about it, but there *is* a fart chart and there *are* things you can do to lessen your suffering. Most of the research in the field of flatulence was funded by NASA. If you think about it, it makes good sense—these were still the days of capsules."

McGee quit his last Yale teaching job to write a book proposal. "Fear, shame . . . I had a terrible time around then with panic attacks," he said. "They just set in. A colleague of mine who got a professorship at Wellesley, his wife was a clinical psychologist. So I was able to confide in them. You know, 'You're not about to die . . . '" McGee laughed. Richard Drake, a Yale friend who also failed to land a tenure-track job, described this period as "a very rough time for Hal. What is he going to do for a career?"

At about the same time, Long was out at dinner when she mentioned McGee's book idea to a man who happened to know a scout for Scribner's publishing house. Not long after, "I get a letter out of nowhere saying Mr. Scribner is coming through New England, and could I find time to have lunch with him?" The two met and, after they ate, Scribner said, "I want to publish your book. What do you need?" McGee asked for and received a $12,000 advance.

McGee had recently moved to Boston to live with Long, who had a postdoctoral fellowship at Harvard. He soon discovered Radcliffe's Schlesinger Library on the History of Women in America and its immense collection of food books. "I could walk into a room lined with books arranged chronologically, so when I was writing about meat, I could start with the Greeks and work my way forward." The longer McGee worked, the more certain he became that he was onto something special. "The excitement of pulling things together that I knew belonged together that no one had put together before," he said. "I was always looking over my shoulder, convinced that someone was going to scoop me by a year."

The second time I had dinner with Harold McGee, once again at

5:30 p.m. at an empty Le Zinc, I asked him if he would consider sharing some food.

McGee nodded, so I ordered steak tartare again, foie gras with brioche, and niçoise salad. This time, when the tartare arrived, McGee began to eat.

I said, "Is steak tartare really safe?"

"It isn't always," McGee replied. "You have to trust. You had it last time, and I did not."

"You were waiting to see if I died."

McGee smiled and told me that his father loved rare hamburgers. Near the end of his life, this predilection worried McGee enough that he developed a method of preparing safe rare hamburgers at home based on the insight that harmful bacteria live only on the surface of muscle tissue: He bought beef chuck in large intact pieces, immersed them briefly in boiling water, then ground them shortly before cooking.

Our foie gras arrived, and, while we ate, I asked to hear the life story of *OFAC*—how it transformed McGee from failed academic to his current role in the culinary world. It took a while to air out all the false starts, setbacks, and lucky breaks. McGee began by saying that, before he even finished *OFAC*, Long was offered a professorship at Stanford.

On their drive west in 1980, the couple stopped in New York so that McGee could hand-deliver his manuscript at the Scribner building on Fifth Avenue. The book languished for four years. A young editor took over the project and cut out everything that Charles Scribner Jr. asked McGee to include—history, anecdote. McGee threatened to return his advance and take the project elsewhere and was then invited back to New York, where he spent days in a windowless room restoring the book.

When *OFAC* came out, reviewers ignored it, and the book sold poorly. "You have to remember there was no Starbucks, no balsamic vinegar. Nobody cooked with olive oil except horrible cheap stuff," McGee said. "It was a completely different world." American professional chefs, furthermore, saw food science as the province of industrial food manufacturing. McGee got a break in 1985, when the food writer Mimi Sheraton reviewed *OFAC* for *Time* and called it "by all odds a minor masterpiece." Sales picked up, McGee signed with an agent, and he received a modest advance to write *The Curious Cook* around a series of home-kitchen experiments—but it was still not an easy period.

McGee was the primary parent of his and Long's two children, filling his free time by cooking for his family—he had a big pizza phase—and writing articles like "Matching Pots and Pans to Your Cooking Needs" for *Science Year 1987*, a supplement to the *World Book Encyclopedia*. "Colleagues of my wife's would try to make connections for me at Stanford, so that I could be an instructor or something," he told me, "and they all went uniformly nowhere. People had a 'Who do you think you are?' attitude, like I was just a hanger-on looking for a handout, which did nothing for my confidence in what I was doing with my life."

In 1992, the year Long won a MacArthur "genius" grant for molecular biology, McGee helped organize a small cooking-science conference in the Sicilian village of Erice. The venue liked events to have serious-sounding names, and The Science of Cooking didn't cut it. "Molecular biology was chic at the time," McGee told me, "so we settled on The First International Workshop on Molecular and Physical Gastronomy."

Throughout the late 1990s, as McGee prepared a second edition of *OFAC*, public interest in the topic began to grow. Robert Wolke launched a cooking-science column for *The Washington Post* at the same time that Alton Brown's *Good Eats* debuted on the Food Network. But the biggest change in McGee's fortunes came from his friendship with a young English chef named Heston Blumenthal.

Years earlier, before Blumenthal had a restaurant of his own, he systematically worked his way through the French classical tradition at home—"while all my friends were going out and having pints, a kebab, and a fight," as he put it. Reading McGee, Blumenthal said, transformed the way he looked at food. The revelation about searing meat not sealing in juices "was a life-changing moment, because it questioned one of the most biblical laws in cooking." Blumenthal eventually opened The Fat Duck outside London, which became by far the most famous restaurant in the U.K.

McGee, taking his last sip of wine, recalled receiving a note from Blumenthal asking if he would serve as a consultant. "I think he replied to me over email," Blumenthal said, "but I never read it as I was computer illiterate at the time." Blumenthal began to produce dishes like sardine-on-toast sorbet and edible spheres of vodka and green tea dropped into liquid nitrogen. He soon gained recognition as a leading practitioner of a wildly experimental—and science-driven—new cuisine that was also taking root in Spain, erroneously called molecular gastronomy out of the mistaken notion that it emerged from those Erice workshops.

Blumenthal and McGee finally met in the Milan airport en route to Erice, where they were both scheduled to attend the 2001 Workshop on Molecular Gastronomy. "I was completely thrown off by the chance encounter," Blumenthal said. "My mind was running through the endless experimentation with food that his book had inspired, so I blurted out the first thing that came to mind: 'It's all your fault!' I think he was a little taken back."

The two began having long phone conversations, like the one on Christmas Day 2004 when McGee, who had just published the second edition of *OFAC*, said something like, "I need to catch up on the world." Blumenthal invited him to Europe for an eating tour. The next August, after The Fat Duck claimed the top spot on *Restaurant* magazine's list of the World's 50 Best Restaurants, the two dined at El Bullí in Spain, where they met Ferran Adrià, who famously closed his dining room for six months a year to work with scientists on the development of new dishes.

The following summer, Blumenthal and McGee returned to Spain to stay on the yacht of Microsoft billionaire and cooking obsessive Nathan Myhrvold. They got to talking about the widespread misunderstanding of what they preferred to call "modernist cuisine." So few people could afford to eat in restaurants like The Fat Duck and El Bullí, and their more dramatic dishes were so easily sensationalized, that the entire movement was at risk of looking like a novelty act aided by laboratory equipment.

"We wanted to write a statement on the new cooking to give some clarity," said Blumenthal. Together with Myhrvold, he and McGee dined yet again at El Bullí, discussed the issue for hours with Adrià, and then returned to Myhrvold's yacht. "We'd spend a couple hours at a time, talking it over and writing drafts," McGee recalled. "Then we'd go have fun and come back and have arguments about how it should be released."

The result, published by *The Guardian* in December 2006, was titled "Statement on the 'New Cookery.'" Co-authored by Blumenthal, Adrià,

Thomas Keller of The French Laundry, and McGee, it rejected the term "molecular gastronomy" and, among other things, declared that "the disciplines of food chemistry and food technology are valuable sources of information and ideas for all cooks. Even the most straightforward traditional preparation can be strengthened by an understanding of its ingredients and methods." In effect, the three most famous chefs in the Western world officially joined the author of the definitive work on the subject to send every serious cook scrambling to learn a little kitchen science.

"That statement was important for a while," said McGee. In Blumenthal's view, it still is. Modernist cuisine was arguably the most significant transformation in global culinary culture in a century or more, and, he said, "My conversations with Harold were the seeds that led to the modernist movement."

The third time I had dinner with McGee, I wanted to know what it would be like to dine with so much wonderful information about food in your head. I knew that experimental cuisine was not where McGee's heart lay—his intellectual and gustatory compass points more toward the humanistic true north of simple pleasures. His own cooking has always been modest, and his home kitchen is not cluttered with fancy equipment. So I chose another classic French bistro, called Monsieur Benjamin, run by Corey Lee. I picked McGee up one evening at the Victorian home he shares with Elli Sekine, a food and travel writer (he and Long separated in 2003).

Chef Lee, I knew, had found *OFAC* early in his career and was one of the many chefs who emailed McGee for advice—in Lee's case, on a plan to air-cure foie gras. In 2007, *The New York Times* asked McGee to write a column titled "The Curious Cook," and he began receiving an endless stream of queries. Daniel Humm of New York's Eleven Madison Park sought insight on why the combination of quince and gelatin caused stock to become cloudy. Thomas Keller invited McGee to give a talk to the staff at The French Laundry and asked his help in identifying the best way to preserve the bright-green color of vegetables during cooking. He still spends time answering questions from culinary students, too, and cooking-school instructors, and home cooks ("Good Afternoon Harold, I am trying to lighten up my grandma's carrot cake recipe . . . ").

McGee is now a regular at culinary and food-science conferences, and he recently did a series of short videos for Anthony Bourdain's *Mind of a Chef*, floating over an animated background as the official nerdy professor of contemporary food television. Each fall, he travels east for Harvard's Science and Cooking course to give the keynote lecture. The class came about because of a collaboration among mathematician Michael Brenner, physicist David Weitz, and Ferran Adrià. As they developed the syllabus, Brenner said, "There was no question that *On Food and Cooking* was the best thing ever written on the subject. Harold is the leading food intellectual of our time." When the course debuted in 2010, more than 700 Harvard undergraduates signed up for 300 spots. It has now become the new "physics for poets," the standard gut-science course for nonmajors. The online edX version has drawn nearly 200,000 subscribers.

McGee is no longer the only player in the field. Myhrvold's six-volume opus, *Modernist Cuisine*, self-published in 2011 at a cost of more than a million dollars and currently retailing for $625, is an obsessively exhaustive encyclopedia of the science behind experimental cooking. Newer titles include *The Science of Good Cooking* by the editors of *America's Test Kitchen* and *Cooking for Geeks: Real Science, Great Cooks, and Good Food*. But all these writers acknowledge McGee. "He taught us that most of the stories we had been told about food were just that, clever stories," said Myhrvold.

The maitre d' at Monsieur Benjamin recognized McGee and led us through the well-heeled crowd to an excellent table in back, where I ordered oysters and sea urchin, aged serrano ham, melted Époisses cheese with toast, cold beef tongue, chicken consommé, blanquette de veau, and quail à la chasseur.

McGee seemed delighted to be there, and he gamely offered that urchin tastes the way it does because of the bromine and iodine in seawater. He tasted the ham and told me that pork legs can be thought of as machines for moving pigs, complete with small enzymatic machinery for dismantling worn-out old cells and building new ones. Beef tongue provoked a disquisition on the fact that its muscles have to move in complicated ways and are not supported by bone—like, for example, biceps. "The tongue is a really unusual free agent that has to do whatever it does independent of the rest of the body," McGee said.

Then our waiter set down a beautiful plate of charcuterie that I had not ordered. I suspected that it was a gift to McGee from Chef Lee, who had once told me that he owned *OFAC* for years without using it. Lee finally met McGee at The French Laundry, where Lee trained under Keller. "I remember expecting to talk to a scientist," Lee said, "and realizing I'm actually talking to someone who has great appreciation for cuisine and deliciousness."

Watching McGee now, I saw what Lee meant: Behind the erudition, those gentle eyes closed with every bite, savoring flavor and texture. I noticed something else, too—not just modesty but lack of ego. McGee was not like a great novelist or musician who set out to make his mark on the world. He was curious and listened to his authentic interests and never stopped trying to be useful. In an industry dominated by big personalities competing for attention, chefs can't help but love McGee's combined dedication to service and lack of interest in the spotlight.

"Very clean and fresh," he said suddenly, after swallowing an oyster. "Fresh like a cold ocean, not a lukewarm one." Perhaps thinking of his new book, McGee said, "When I taste that, I think of two different things, cucumbers and blue borage flowers. It turns out that among the aroma molecules we're tasting, several occur in both plants, and that's why you can use borage as a garnish to give the hint of the ocean when there's no seafood in a dish." McGee then picked up another half-shell, slipped the oyster into his mouth, and closed his eyes.

Down the Hatch

The Crown That Sits upon Heady Topper

By Michael Kiser

From GoodBeerHunting.com

Photographer/writer Michael Kiser finds endless ways to tell
the story of American beer (with food and travel chasers) as
founder/creative director of the website Good Beer Hunting. It's
all about the storytelling—as in this profile of one of Vermont's
most sought-after craft beers.

I am unfit to tell the story of Heady Topper. Every beer geek has heard
its name. Many have stuffed the 16 oz. silver cans into their luggage,
said a quiet prayer, and sent them packing. Still others drive up to Burlington, VT, with a timed list of stops for the delivery truck, hunting
them down like they're the last remaining perishables on a planet be-
sieged by tragedy. But really, it's the locals that deserve to tell the story
of this legendary beer—and if you give them a chance, they still do.
There's a quick eye roll from some, a darting glance from others. But
eventually they'll all slouch off their bar stools and say yes, yes it is
amazing, and yes, yes they have some here and there, and yes, let's go
get some.

"With that said," Alchemist co-founder and Heady Topper inventor
John Kimmich begins, "I still remain shocked at how many people walk
through these doors and have never heard of it before. Walk in and are
like, 'What do you guys do here?' I find that astounding at this point,
but not particularly shocking, because it's a big world. If you think everybody's found out about it, far from it. The reality is, even as big as
craft beer is, it's still a pretty small slice of the overall fabric of the world."

You can get Heady at the Burlington airport—casually, and just as easily as you can get Sam Adams Boston Lager in most other airports. Or a Magic Hat Number 9, for that matter, which is sold with a chipper introduction that's so jarring it's almost convincing—wait, what the hell are you talking about, the Heady please. The can pops, it thuds on the bar, she walks away, you drink it from the can.

There's more Heady Topper being made than ever before. And that's important to understand, because it's actually being pulled back off the streets a bit. The Alchemist just opened its long-awaited production brewery where they now sell mixed cases of Heady, Focal Banger, and, at the moment, another Double IPA called Crusher. All are monstrously hoppy beers, but it wasn't always this way.

There were always long lines and on-site sales, but between the fervor of its first and its most current iteration, the Alchemist beers flowed freely, if insufficiently, into town. But now, with a shiny new production brewery, the assumed promise of a Heady in every pot has taken a different turn. The bars, restaurants, and retailers who sold Focal on the regular—and Heady when they could get it—are now coming up short. Focal is exclusive to the brewery, and Heady has been cut by a significant percentage. The age of the full-margin brewery-retailer is in full swing.

Primordial Soup

It's easy to see The Alchemist's new production brewery as The House That Heady Built. I sure do. After the original location flooded, Kimmich and his partner Jennifer—together, a young married couple—had a bizarre decision to make. They could walk away, or transition from brewpub to a production brewery in one leap. They had just purchased the canning line to start packaging their beers and, in the literal wake of that flood, the tiny brewery stood like a singular choice—start canning Heady, or go home.

"We were a pub for nine years before anybody anywhere in the world was able to get Heady Topper in a package," Kimmich says. "For nine years, our reputation spread and grew through word of mouth, internet, strictly by people coming in and coming to our restaurant."

Whether that original brewpub and the approach to making beer lives on through Heady is hard to say. Some origins are instrumental, and some just get lopped off in the process. But it was supposed to organically grow from there.

"We kinda got pigeonholed into Heady Topper because, after the flood, we got wiped out—that's all we had," he says. "We were fully planning on running a restaurant, the two of us, and me going over there and brewing Heady—for the first time ever, to put it in a package and sell it. We thought that was going to be small, something we'd do in conjunction with the pub."

But even the production line was a reluctant opportunity for Kimmich. His business partner and wife, Jennifer, was the one who saw the upside, and at the time, there were no real examples to look to for a brewery going all-in on one beer. When asked who else has built a brewery off one beer, Kimmich tilts his head, smiles, and says, "Um, Rodenbach?"

"I couldn't even wrap my head around it," he explains. "When I was in that pub in the basement constantly making beer just trying to keep beer flowing at the pub, and Jen's talking about building a canning brewery. I thought she was insane. I fought her on that for at least a year or more, until she finally convinced me: 'Look, we need to do this. This is our next step.'"

That transition from brewpub brewer to single-brand production is a mighty step toward focus and reduction. Brewpubs are notoriously hard to keep up with, requiring a constant pipeline of new recipes and fast turnarounds. But brewing and canning Heady? To any brewer, that'd seem like an unreasonable constraint. For Kimmich, looking back, there's some rationale to it all.

"Nine years of proving my skills at making any other beer under the sun, I don't feel the need to constantly prove myself," he says. "The result is in the cans, and the beer people get from us. I don't feel I have anything to prove by showcasing a zillion different beers. We did it for nine years."

Down to one beer, the act of brewing became a different thing altogether. It became an exercise in repetition, perfection, focus. It calls to mind the sequences in *Karate Kid*—wax on, wax off. For a less mature brewer, the constraints would feel like torture. But Kimmich found his groove. And, ultimately, that muscle memory paid off.

"The art of brewing, the act of brewing, no matter what you're doing, it's a very repetitive, structured task at its most basic," he says. "It is this. You do this. And you do it every time, and you do it right every time. So regardless of the ingredients that are in that mash or in the kettle, it doesn't really matter. Whether it be a Golden Ale or an IPA or an Imperial Stout, if you're doing it and you're crushing it every time and it's great, and you're maintaining that—what else do you need to satisfy your ego? There's plenty of ego in the craft beer world. I don't think we need to add any more to it."

Evolutionary Tree

It's just an IPA. Really. It has unique characteristics. It's somewhere between cloudy and sparkling depending on the time it spends in the can. It will, in fact, flocculate some on its own after packaging. It has an immense aroma that leaps out of the can or the glass, depending on your chosen vessel. *The Alchemist, of course, votes can.*

But Heady Topper's real claim to fame is that it's the most well-known missing link between the English IPAs that populate the Eastern U.S. and the more recent evolutionary offspring of the hazy, juicy IPA vein of New England. Of course, by comparison, Heady's intensely bitter. In fact, many of today's hazy IPA brewers are trying to harvest the Heady yeast to propagate their own, hoping for similar results. What started as a hand-me-down culture from his mentor at Vermont Pub & Brewery, and, before that, an English brewer in the '90s, has become the progenitor of an entirely different strain of IPAs. And that's not necessarily a good thing.

"They're brewing with the runtiest of the runts that you might be able to culture out of the bottom of the can," Kimmich says. "When you get to the bottom of the can, there's a very fine layer on the bottom. Sure, there's yeast in there—it's unfiltered. But that yeast didn't drop out over 3.5 weeks of conditioning. That's what you do not want to brew with. That is far, far removed from the best, healthiest yeast. So when you culture that up to brew with it, of course, you're going to have even hazier beers."

If haziness were the goal (and some who are cashing in on the trend might argue that, in fact, it is), Kimmich has some experience with that too. But it wasn't pleasant.

"I've been using that yeast over 20 years, and I've fucked it up at times in the pub," he says. "It creates different flavors. I had a Cornelius can that I stored my yeast in. I hadn't vented it properly. We've got cleaners out, cleaning the toilets, washing dishes. We're juggling. We had a small child. Here it is, I gotta brew, I can't get a new culture in time. I gotta pitch this yeast. It smells fine, but it was pressurized, which I later found had mutated it. Brewed three batches of beer with it, all of a sudden Lightweight, our house light beer—a golden, gorgeous, crystal clear beer—looked like a goddamn milk shake and never, ever, ever cleared up in the entire time it was in the tank. Thank god when it was finally gone. How many times do I get Double IPAs and it looks and smells just like that? Hmm, wonder what yeast they're using in that beer?"

For his part, Kimmich was after something very different with this one. "Beer that tasted like great weed," he says matter of factly. "That was pretty much the goal with Heady Topper."

It's also a living, breathing thing for him. In some ways, it's the re-petitive, machinelike churn toward perfection that keeps Kimmich en-gaged. Other times, it's a battle against all odds for consistency. "I have a very specific idea of what I want Heady to be, and it is what it is," he says. "I've been making it since 2004, so it went through many, many changes and incarnations at the pub. By the time we got to the produc-tion brewery, it was pretty well refined, but even then you're still devel-oping techniques and different ways. How can we drive our dissolved oxygen even lower? How can we get even more flavor and aroma out of these hops? There's little tricks and tweaks, but at this point, it's like a well-oiled machine over there."

But it's also not all under his control. "Heady's different year to year," Kimmich admits. "Every beer is different year to year. You got a totally different crop of barley and hops. I've tried so many different barley combinations. The one we have now is my favorite. It's the mouthfeel and that little bit of malt flavor underneath. It doesn't come off as sugary and sweet, which I find quite often with a lot of American and Cana-dian barley. The clarity of the beer, stuff like that. That's all product- and process-driven."

These days, it takes a team to make Heady. And hiring for a produc-tion brewery that only recently started making more than one beer is a job description unlike any other in the U.S. It's a job more appropriate for a brewing engineer or a chemist from a place like Anheuser-Busch than an up-and-coming young brewer trying to spread their wings. And that reality isn't lost on Kimmich.

"We look for a very different type of brewer," he says. "I've had a young, ambitious brewer that told me what I wanted to hear but then did the opposite. I learned my lesson. Those are not the kind of brewers we're looking for. I'm not looking for somebody that thinks they know better than what we know. Because they don't. Maybe they're going to go on and do great things, but they're going to do it their way—not our way. We're not looking for some dude that wants to take all the knowledge and move on. They're a dime a dozen. I get emails all the time from guys like that. It's just not who we look for. If they want that, go get it. It's there for you. Just like it was there for us. The information, the opportunity, go get it yourself. But then I see someone that's just working some shitty-ass job that deserves to have a great job and wants to stay in Vermont, which is a difficult thing. We have several brewers that have never brewed beer in their lives, and they're fantastic. Their main focus is doing exactly what I need them to do. So you couldn't ask for a better situation, really."

Living Forever

For all the growth and sense of normalcy around Vermont these days, the hype hasn't died down. Other things have cropped up, spread the attention around a bit. All around New England, the hazy IPA style alone is building breweries, some of which have become stops on the way to The Alchemist and vice versa. And with the move back to exclusive brewery releases, even Kimmich may have learned a thing or two about the gravity his beers create, and how to maximize the business value of their reputation, despite all the peripheral nonsense.

"Anything that's regarded as 'worth it' and delicious or exceptional, of course, it's gonna create that [zealous culture] around it," he says. "We've been accused of doing that on purpose. 'They limit their production to create hype.' Fuck you! We went from 400 barrels a year and, a year and a half later, we're making 9,000 barrels a year. You're actually going to accuse us of limiting our production to create hype? The more popular you become or the more coveted you become, the more lovers and the more haters."

But for all that fervor, and a relatively long-standing fervor at that, it's not clear what it all adds up to in the lifetime of a brewer and beyond. Even for a guy that may have brewed one of the most iconic American craft beers in history, Kimmich finds some darkly funny perspective in it all.

"Whatever, I'll be fucking dead," he says of the legacy of Heady Topper. "What will I care? I'm going to be dead and gone. It doesn't mean a hill of beans the day I take my last breath. I can only hope at that point we have people involved that are ready to take it into the next generation. We have one son, maybe it's him. Maybe it's one of our nieces or nephews. Maybe it's someone not related to us at all. Maybe the aliens come down in 10 years and fucking eat us all. Then it doesn't matter."

And just like that, he heads toward the door, his water bottle swinging at his hip. He lets out a laugh and gestures back for a final word: "I'm going to go eat a big fucking salad, get real high, and watch the Olympics."

Strange Brews

By John Wray

From *Food & Wine*

Truth can be stranger than fiction, as novelist John Wray
(*The Lost Time Chronicles, Lowboy*) discovers in this somewhat
bemused foray through some of the weirdest craft beers on offer
at his local Brooklyn brew shop.

Lately I've been drinking some odd beers at bars. Some of them have been pleasant surprises; others have made my mouth feel possessed. I may be getting frumpy in my early middle age (actually, I've always been frumpy), but I've started to wonder whether the craft beer movement, which has explored so much fascinating territory over the past decade, has strayed off the map altogether. When I found out that Colorado's Wynkoop Brewing Co. was making its Rocky Mountain Oyster Stout with roasted bull testicles, I was forced to ask myself: Has craft brewing finally gone too far?

"One of the great things about making beer," Jeppe Jarnit-Bjergsø said to me on a recent visit to Tørst, the Greenpoint beer bar where he curates the list, "is that there are almost no rules." Jarnit-Bjergsø, a Dane who now lives in Brooklyn, is widely regarded as one of the superstars of the craft beer world; for his Evil Twin Brewing label he is as likely to create fairly classic IPAs or pilsners as he is concoctions like his Imperial Doughnut Break, a jet-black porter made with, apparently, 1,000 glazed doughnuts. "If I want to put olives in a beer, or strawberries, that's OK—as long as what I end up with tastes good," Jarnit-Bjergsø told me. "If you tried to put olives in a wine, on the other hand, no one on earth would drink it." I asked him for his opinion of the much-hyped Beard Beer from Oregon's Rogue, which is fermented with wild yeasts harvested from Rogue brewmaster John Maier's facial hair. "If you're going to put yeast from your beard into what you're brewing, it's fine," Jarnit-Bjergsø said, weighing his words carefully. "But you'd better have a really good reason."

So, do these experiments in extreme brewing still qualify as beer? At what point do they turn into something unrecognizable—and, more importantly, not worth the risk? Inspired in part by my conversation with Jarnit-Bjergsø, my good friend Alex and I decided to do a tasting (this might be the place to state, for the record, that I'm not a craft beer fetishist). I went to St. Gambrinus Beer Shoppe in downtown Brooklyn and spent just over $100 on what struck me as an interesting, albeit highly unscientific, sample of what's out there these days. Then we drank everything. The result? Suffice it to say our tongues are in stable condition, and we're told we'll be able to drink beer again one day.

It might be useful to examine the term *beer*. According to the Beer Academy, a UK-based group of fermentation enthusiasts, beer is "an alcoholic drink brewed mainly from malted barley, hops, yeast and water." From a historical viewpoint, it would seem, the beverage is relatively easy to define—but not so fast. The Beer Academy goes on to state that "other sources of fermentable carbohydrate (e.g., maize, wheat, rice) and other natural ingredients may be added to create different styles and flavours." This begs the question of where the boundary lies between beer and not-beer. Peanuts are a source of fermentable carbohydrate; so are plantains, yuca root and beans. Maybe the only reason we aren't drinking bean beer at our local football stadium is that beer drinkers, at least in the US, have traditionally been a pretty conservative bunch. Thanks to the craft beer craze, however, that attitude is changing quickly.

"I remember being at a brewer's convention in 1994," Garrett Oliver, the editor of *The Oxford Companion to Beer*, told me. "IPAs were considered an almost forgotten, historic British brew at that time—few breweries were making them. Now you can get an IPA in any decent bar in America. Change can happen rapidly, but you do want to be careful. As they say in one of my favorite movies, *This Is Spinal Tap*: 'It's such a fine line between stupid and clever.'"

Many craft beer devotees would claim, by way of rebuttal, that the array of styles and flavors now on offer is less a voyage into the unknown than it is a return to brewing's wild and storied past. Our understanding of what beer is, they argue, has been narrowed over the course of the modern age by a domestic brewing industry that's encouraged mass production and a drift toward monoculture. As anyone over the age of 30 can attest, in the recent past, *beer* essentially meant lager; even a Belgian wheat beer like Hoegaarden or St. Bernardus qualified as exotic.

To fortify our courage for our tasting, Alex and I started things off with a brew that probably wouldn't rate as strange, much less extreme, to most craft beer cognoscenti: Oude Quetsche, a lambic beer that's brewed with plums at Gueuzerie Tilquin in Belgium. Craft-brewing fanatics have been geeking out about sour beer in recent years, and in an era in which high-acid, unoaked white wines are all the rage, it's hard not to see a correlation: Sour brews tend to be tart and bright and wonderfully unsentimental, with a funkiness that calls to mind natural wine as much as it does lager.

Alex and I were expecting great things from Oude Quetsche, and we weren't disappointed. Far from introducing any sweetness to the experience, the plums create a particular spike of sourness in the middle, just at the moment the sip you've taken clears the back of your palate. Alex compared it to sneaking into a farmer's orchard and filling your mouth with not-quite-ripe-yet plums; I had to admit, there was something almost illicit in the pleasure this beer gave us.

The next beer we sampled, though, was unquestionably extreme. Higher Math, from Delaware's well-known Dogfish Head brewery, is a golden ale made with both cherry juice and chocolate, and described by the brewery as a "luscious chocolate-cherry birthday cake in liquid form." This should have been warning enough to proceed with caution—ditto the fact that it was 17 percent alcohol, right around the level of, say, Night Train Express—but we were still giddy from our happy experience with Oude Quetsche. Our judgment may have been clouded. "Smells like Russian black bread," Alex said cheerfully, taking a sizable gulp.

Before I could follow his lead, Alex gave a kind of grunt and set the glass down very carefully, like someone backing away from an angry gorilla. Ignoring his look, I took a small sip of my own. Something had gone dreadfully wrong in the making of Higher Math; that much was clear to us both. I recall the sensation of having my mouth stuffed with drugstore bonbons steeped in cherry-flavored schnapps. "Ah! That's so bad," I said, but it was Alex who summed it up best. "This is the worst bottled beverage I've ever tasted," he said. "And I'm including sour milk."

Still reeling, we opted for the relative safety of Bozo Beer, an Evil Twin imperial stout "with coffee and with natural flavors added." It became clear that Jarnit-Bjergsø is far from infallible. Because stouts tend to be so sweet and robust, brewers tend to regard them as particularly useful when experimenting with outlandish ingredients. That may be the case, but the one-two punch of Higher Math and Bozo nearly wrecked us. Bozo is the foie gras goose of beer, so packed with flavors that it seems a moral outrage. I managed to work my way through a small glass; Alex did not. "Molasses, chocolate, almond, hazelnut, oak spiral, chili, marshmallow," he read from the ingredient list, then added a few of his own: "air freshener, candle wax, Old Spice soap on a rope from 1976." In fairness, Bozo Beer describes itself, right on its own label, as "made for bozos." We found out later that Jarnit-Bjergsø had originally intended it as a parody of the excesses of the experimental brewing craze. Looking it up later that night on beeradvocate.com, we found that it has received a rating of 91—"outstanding." The world of craft beer is an eldritch one.

The final beer in our tasting was Rogue's Beard Beer. We approached it, as might be imagined by this point, with deep circumspection. I poured no more than a knuckle's width into two mason jars—mason jars seemed safer, somehow—and we stuck our noses in and sniffed like sommeliers. Unlike sommeliers, however, we weren't after subtleties in the bouquet; we were smelling for danger.

"No red flags yet," said Alex, and I had to agree. All we smelled was an agreeably sweet and wheaty aroma. We mustered our courage and drank. For all its hype, Beard Beer proved to be a mild-mannered ale with blessedly few quirks. Sweet at the beginning, very much like a Belgian blonde ale, it tapered to a subtly tangy finish. Wild though the yeasts may have been, there was virtually none of the potent funk

I'd come to expect from spontaneously fermented beers, which use whatever yeasts are present in the air. This was a beer brewed to please. Which made me think that those in the true vanguard of craft brewing are less interested in finding out what they can do with chocolate or habaneros or prairie oysters than they are dedicated to creating beers you'd want a second bottle of.

How Much Is Too Much for a Glass of Wine?

By Ray Isle

From *Food & Wine*

As *Food & Wine*'s executive wine editor, Ray Isle is well aware
of the world's top wines, and the prices they usually command.
Even he is bemused to see restaurants more and more frequently
offering those noble vintages on a per-glass basis. Is it a bargain,
or proof that the world has gone mad?

Not long ago I was with my wife at a restaurant that had a $190
glass of wine on its list. My wife, who is also known as the voice
of reason, observed that this was—if I can get her words right—"just
ridiculous." I pointed out that the wine in question, a 2004 Château
Rayas Châteauneuf-du-Pape, was one of the great wines of the world.
She replied that she didn't care if it was made by magical elves—paying
$190 for a glass of wine was still ridiculous.

Yet in the past few years, more and more restaurants have started offering surprisingly expensive wines by the glass. I'm not going to say my
wife was wrong—in fact, one of the fundamental rules of journalism
is, Don't say in print that your wife is wrong—because I feel that the
vast majority of people would agree with her: $190 seems like a crazy
amount to pay for a glass of wine. But at the same time, more and more
people are buying, spending anywhere from $25 to $400 a pop.

Michael Ploetz created the by-the-glass program at The Peninsula
Beverly Hills' restaurant The Belvedere. He recalls, "Immediately, we began selling a lot of high-end Chardonnay, like $40 to $50 a glass—Paul

Hobbs, Peter Michael, that sort of thing. And not really to wine-geeky people; more our regular customers." Ploetz's regular customers do live in Beverly Hills, which isn't the lowest-rent district around, but he doesn't feel that the casual profligacy of the .01 percent caused the shift. "I really think that what people are after is the experience. It's like, 'I know Chave is a great Hermitage producer, and I've never had the wine—for $83, let's give it a go.'" I have to admit, I felt the same tug with that $190 glass of Château Rayas, a wine I rarely, if ever, get to drink.

Paolo Meregalli, owner and wine director of New York City's Mulino a Vino wine bar, calculates that almost 40 percent of his customers are buying wines that are $25 to $50 a glass—Brunellos, Barolos, Amarones. "We have some customers who will come in and have a glass of 1998 Sassicaia with a plate of pasta Bolognese. A couple here on a date shared a glass the other night." A glass of '98 Sassicaia is $145 on Meregalli's list; the pasta Bolognese, $18.

Pouring a single glass of a pricey wine is now financially practical for restaurants thanks to a device called the Coravin, launched three years ago. Created by a medical device inventor named Greg Lambrecht, the Coravin uses technology inspired by tools developed for biopsies. It drives a thin, Teflon-coated needle through the cork in the bottle; then it pumps in argon, a neutral gas that doesn't affect the flavor of wine (as opposed to oxygen, which will). The increased pressure pushes the wine out through the same needle. The result is that a sommelier can extract a glass of an incredibly sought-after wine from a bottle without ever removing the cork or damaging the remaining wine. Over 700 restaurants in the US use the device at this point, and more are adopting it. That said, there's also a small Luddite faction of sommeliers who remain steadfastly anti-Coravin, but I've tested the thing over multiple blind tastings, and as far as I've seen, it works exactly as advertised.

Still, the fact that you can pour a $400 glass of wine without problems doesn't necessarily mean that people will *buy* a $400 glass of wine. Yet, despite what may seem to be the demands of common sense, people do. That, to me, is where this shift becomes truly interesting.

To get a handle on this development, I spoke to Z. John Zhang, the Murrel J. Ades professor of marketing at the Wharton School. As Zhang said, "It's about making the product divisible. The classic example is the Encyclopaedia Britannica. If you bought the whole set at once, it was, like, $1,500. So marketers came up with the idea of allowing you to buy one book per month. You think, *Well, I can afford $50 a month, no problem.* Even though you end up paying the same amount in the end, or more. Time-sharing with vacation houses works the same way."

In other words, if you want that beach view in Boca Raton badly enough but can't afford the whole house, you'll settle for one week a year. Similarly, if you want to try Domaine de la Romanée-Conti but don't relish paying for a whole bottle, a glass might do the trick. The Belvedere offers a six-ounce glass (a fourth of a bottle, essentially) of Domaine de la Romanée-Conti's 2005 Romanée-St-Vivant for $406. The cost of a full bottle there is exactly four times as much. At most restaurants, customers generally pay proportionally more when buying wine by the glass than by the bottle, but Ploetz opted not to follow that rule. "I tried to price the high-end glasses at an advantage to the customer," he told me. "So, weirdly enough, that glass of Romanée-Conti's actually a great value."

A $406 glass of wine is still a rarity almost everywhere; most high-end pours are anywhere from $25 to $50. While that's not exactly cheap, it does offer people the chance to taste wines they might never have the opportunity to buy. At The Village Pub in Woodside, California, a glass of the Aubert Ritchie Vineyard Chardonnay costs $44. Pricey, sure, but the wine is one of California's most prized Chardonnays, and there's a multiyear wait to get on the winery's mailing list. This approach also attracts customers who want to try several high-end wines during a meal, as Thomas Pastuszak of New York City's NoMad restaurant notes.

The NoMad is where my wife and I saw that $190 glass of Château Rayas on the list. I admit I thought about going back later to try it. Why wouldn't I? I mean, it was *Château Rayas*. How often do I get to drink Château Rayas? Almost never! And I'm a wine writer! Surely a glass of Rayas would be a more worthwhile experience than, say, a new pair of shoes? But as my wife pointed out, shoes are a necessity—even very, very expensive shoes. Wine is not. Imagine, she added, if one person were to purchase an expensive glass of wine and thus deprive another person—a *very deserving* other person—of a new pair of shoes. Ridiculous even to think about it.

And because the fundamental rules of journalism demand it, I think I'd better state right here that, as always, she is absolutely right.

Wine Pairing with Jill Mott

BY STEVE HOFFMAN

From Growlermag.com

There's a reason to trust experts, as Twin Cities food writer Steve Hoffman discovered at a dinner set up by website/magazine The Growler, which celebrates craft in food, drink, and the arts. Everyone at the dinner knew the "rules" about what to drink with red meat. A wine guru's picks surprised everyone.

Earlier that afternoon, just outside Jon Wipfli's patio door, an entire boneless leg of lamb had twirled slowly on a string suspended above a hardwood fire for six hours or so, dripping occasional runnels of fat into the coals, and wrapping itself gradually in a cloak of char.

Now, on the cutting board in front of us, through the loose netting that held the roast together, the dark-sheened, coarse-textured crust made promises about smoke, and salt, and rose-colored, fat-rimmed slices of lamb, and because Jon Wipfli may know as much about roasting meat as anyone in the Twin Cities, when his first slice fell sideways onto the board, all of those promises came true.

We were faced with one of those food moments near enough to perfection that you start to examine your own character. "Here I am," says the food moment, eyeing you up and down. "Looks to me like you've got some living up to do." I felt an impulse to tuck in my shirt, and check my fly.

It was also one of those moments when liking wine, if you do, becomes something you are just so damn grateful for. A slice of perfect leg of lamb, just on the rare side of medium rare, is for the most part an unenhanceable thing. There is nothing you can really add or subtract that will make it, or the experience of eating it, any better than itself—with the possible exception of a glass of wine.

We were here to experiment with wine pairing, and that is the simple premise behind it—that what you drink can interact with what you eat, and actually change the experience of eating it, whether by complementing the food, or contrasting instructively with it, or fending off boredom with it, or clearing the sensations in your mouth to taste more of it. At its best, the right pairing can take something merely perfectly crafted, and turn it into a kind of ephemeral art.

But there's a problem, and the problem is precisely that we're talking art, not science. There are a few pairing principles, and a handful of rules, but just as you and I can't paint a Rembrandt, or improvise a jazz riff, we mostly lack the combination of knowledge, practice, and intuition to pair a wine to a particular dish, much less pair an evening of wines to a coursed meal.

Fortunately, tonight, we count Jill Mott among our delicately salivating crew, and Jill is just the wine artist we need.

In fact, she is sort of a wine Renaissance woman—scouting and advocating for natural wines around the world, importing some of her favorites to the Twin Cities, curating and serving the wine selection at GYST Fermentation Bar, and teaching classes to laypeople, restaurant staff, and aspiring sommeliers.

She has paired three wines with our otherworldly lamb.

If there are classic pairings with lamb, they might include a red wine from the southern Rhône valley, or maybe a Provençal rosé. The former to sort of join hands with the lamb in mutual ovine funkiness. The latter to do the opposite—to apply acid and a little dry fruit, as a way of refreshing a mouth coated with salty lamb fat.

The three bottles Jill has set in front of us are a white wine from the country of Georgia, a red wine from an obscure terraced hillside west of Bilbao, Spain, and a sparkling red from coastal Slovenia. Wines that, combined, would be the consensus choice of perhaps zero other sommeliers in the country.

So what is Jill doing? Can we minor leaguers even get a bat on these sophisticated knuckleballs, or is she just toying with us? Well, let me take a few swings.

For one thing, she is introducing us to natural wines, because she believes in them, and they make her happy. "Natural wine," meaning as little intervention by the winemaker as possible—little or no added yeast, sulfur, temperature control, or acidification; it's a little like organic farming—a seemingly recent development that is actually a way of reclaiming very old, pre-industrial methods of growing and making food.

So there's pairing rule number one. Does the wine you're going to serve make you happy? Do you love its story? Did you spend a California afternoon tasting it in a cool cellar beside a vineyard? Did you drink it on your first date with your wife? Serve it. Tell its story. Everyone at the table will love that wine.

What else is Jill doing? Well, despite the rule-bending nature of her choices, she is actually following some basic and reliable guidelines.

There is a red-with-red-meat, white-with-white rule, and if it is simplistic and occasionally sniffed at by sophisticates, it's actually not a bad rule.

She's also following a rule that says if it grows together it goes together. Lamb is particularly popular in Southern Europe, and odds are, a wine from a place where they eat a lot of lamb will probably go with lamb. Jill's Spanish red, for instance. Or her Slovenian sparkler from close to the Italian border. In fact, matching regional food with that region's wine is not just relatively foolproof—hint: Coq au Vin comes from Burgundy—it can lead to a love for certain places on earth that can't be accessed as fully any other way.

She's also matching strong flavor to tannin. All of her wines have a tannic backbone that can stand up to the strong lamb flavor. And she's matching fat to acid. European wines in general are higher in acid because they are meant to be served with food, unlike American wines, which are often made to be drunk, in the American style, as cocktails.

And finally, she is playing with some rules, knowingly. White wine with lamb?

"Yes," she says, and pours the Georgian white—probably the strangest wine any of us has ever tasted. Georgia? Fermented underground in clay qvevri? Colored orange? What?

But bear with her. The orange color comes from extended contact with the skins and stems, and it makes the wine more like a rosé than a white. And rosé happens to be the most forgiving wine to pair with anything. The extended skin contact gives it a huge amount of tannin, to meet the lamb in the middle of the ring and not fold. But because it's a white wine there's still plenty of acid too.

And then she instructs us all to take a mouthful of lamb, and, without swallowing it yet, hold the Georgian wine up to our noses. Natural wines are often described as giving off "barnyard" smells, which its adherents treat as a virtue and its detractors as a vice. In this case, there is very noticeably something animal going on inside my glass. A primal and not unpleasant zoo smell of pelts and hide. It is a lot like the taste of wild game. An intestinal, liverish, guttiness that becomes what you love about eating game if you ever do learn to love it. I do. And the faintly goaty flavor of the lamb in my mouth gets brought out by the smell of the wild and alive wine kicking around in my glass, and I have to say it is a moment worthy of the perfection of Jon Wipfli's work with meat and open fire, and Jill has gotten this one just right for an uncalled for number of reasons.

And see. Now that's just genius.

Fire-Roasted Lamb

1 leg of lamb, either deboned and trussed, or bone-in
Salt and pepper

Method

Cover the lamb generously with salt and pepper, and hang it with butcher twine roughly two feet above and slightly off-center of a smoldering wood pile. Use dry apple wood if available. Oak, maple, or hickory will work as well.

Let it hang for about five to six hours or until it reaches your desired internal temperature (Wipfli prefers about 130 degrees.) The side closer to the fire will cook more quickly, so make sure to hang the larger end facing downward.

The Real Thing

By Matt Bondurant

From *Gravy*

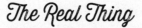

Enough about beer and wine—let's get to the hard stuff. For lapsed son of the South Matt Bondurant that always meant homemade corn liquor, a.k.a. "white lightning." Researching his 2008 novel *The Wettest County in the World,* however, he discovered the depths of his own moonshine heritage.

The liquor store down the street from my house in Oxford, Mississippi, is slowly vanishing, bottle by bottle. When stock is depleted it usually isn't replaced. The land behind the store has been cleared and leveled—like a lot of Oxford recently—and a new mixed-use shopping center is coming soon. There's no more wine to speak of, and all that's left in the vodka section are dusty bottles of expensive European stuff that's quadruple distilled and made with elderberries gathered above the Alpine tree line. Sometimes, just for fun, I peruse the "specialty" whiskies, the new fad of clear corn liquor in mason jars and faux clay jugs, often with names that play on "moon" or "corn" or Southern-hick stereotypes, making claims to authenticity. The real thing, they say. It shouldn't mean anything to me; the people putting this stuff out aren't taking bread from my children or restricting my artistic ambitions. Yet the sight of it on the shelves gives me a jolt of irritation and a lingering hint of something like regret.

The first time I smelled pure corn liquor I was nine years old. A pack of us kids were out in the cornfield that night, racing through the tall rows trying to scare the shit out of each other and herd some unwary loser, usually me, into the high-tensile strands of electric fencing at the perimeter that were nearly invisible in the darkness. This was at my uncle Howard's place in Franklin County, Virginia. The adults were sitting around the television, quietly digesting the evening meal of chicken hash, green beans, and cast-iron skillet cornbread, the crust made from super-heating the lard till it smoked, the inside white and slightly sour. My father and his brothers and sisters would crumble a hunk of it into a glass of fresh buttermilk, spooning it out like ice cream. "I'll have just a light meal," my dad used to say, "a light brown meal."

I was a small child, and that night on a dead run the wire caught me neck high, a 4,000-volt shortcut to my brain. A bit later I stood in the kitchen with my cousin Andrew, holding a rag filled with ice to my neck. I looked like I'd been garroted with a jellyfish. The adults had gone to sleep and the house was quiet enough to hear the roaring cicadas in the trees. Andrew dug around in a bottom cabinet and produced a half-gallon mason jar filled with clear liquid. "White lightning," he said.

He opened the jar and told me to take a sniff. It was like putting my face into a campfire. The heat seared my nostrils and erupted through my skull, the second dose of brain damage I received that evening. He took a sip, then dared me to. For a few minutes we swapped the jar, taking tiny sips and going into exaggerated hacking and coughing fits like some kind of vaudeville act. I thought the sole purpose of it was for a dare—how much miserable suffering could you endure? Why else would you want to drink something like that?

Over the next twenty years, I caught regular glimpses of untaxed, homemade corn liquor. On the day after Christmas in Franklin County, we used to shoot skeet in a sloping pasture that ran down to a muddy creek. The men drank eggnog and white lightning, and as the day went on, things got a bit loose. I remember my father, a teetotaler his whole life, telling me to stand behind the pickup trucks while my cousins tossed clay pigeons like Frisbees, four or five men working their pump shotguns at the same time, the crisp winter air thick with the scent of gunpowder, lead, and whiskey. At family gatherings, men would suddenly disappear, returning an hour later, bleary-eyed and grinning. I remember seeing my grandfather, then well into his eighties, leaning into the trunk of his Oldsmobile in a gravel parking lot, pouring liquid into a plastic cup.

It's the smell that gives it away—pure corn whiskey is an olfactory sledgehammer. You have about a second before the heat of the alcohol burns away any discernable aroma, but in that first instant there is the unmistakable, unadulterated fog of rotting corn mash, the heated stew of fermenting sugars and enzymes. None of my relatives ever called it that. White mule, rotgut, wildcat, stump whiskey, white lightning, or just plain white, but not moonshine. And they ought to know, as the Bondurants of Franklin County remain one of the most notorious moonshining families in Virginia history. The real thing.

We were the branch of the family that left. When the Korean War started, my father and a buddy flipped a coin to see which service they'd join. My father lost and spent the next couple of years at a Navy base in French Morocco, Africa, as a crewman on training aircraft. When he was discharged from the Navy, he hitchhiked from Norfolk across the state to Franklin County in his Navy dress whites, Dixie-cup hat akimbo, wearing the mad grin of the free man. He got a ride with a couple of young women on their way home from college, driving a convertible Chevy. They took him as far as Roanoke, and I imagine that my father, hat in hand, watching those ladies roar away in a cloud of dust, began to think that college seemed like a damn good idea.

He eventually earned a master's degree in engineering and settled in the suburbs of Washington, DC, where I was born and raised. As a child, my dad went barefoot all summer and and worked the fields on the family farm—the endless, backbreaking labor of pulling tobacco. When I was a kid, I spent my summer making mix tapes, going to swim-team practice, and attempting to hack into business mainframes with my Commodore 64 computer via a telephone modem. It would be hard to find a larger generation gap in twentieth-century America, and for this reason I've always considered myself lucky. But the break is about more than just time. We are the branch of the family without a Southern accent. My sensibilities are more East Coast, closer to New England than the South. I prefer chowder to gumbo, Melville to Faulkner.

My wanderlust hasn't helped much. In the last twenty years, I've lived and worked in four different states and two countries. As a professor, I've had teaching jobs at four universities, making me a sort of journeyman academic, a Moses Malone or Bobby Bonilla of English departments. I've published three novels so far, one set in London and

Egypt, one set in Virginia, and one set in Ireland and Vermont. I have a child born in New York, one in Texas, and now one in Mississippi. It is clear to me that I am a man of no place.

All through my childhood, my family made the requisite visits to Franklin County during the holidays and summers, and my cousins took great delight in exposing my naïveté about agricultural practices and rural life. I also heard the stories of how Grandpa Jack was once the moonshine king of the county. This wasn't hard to accept. My Grandpa Jack was a flinty character straight out of a Larry Brown story; stoic, silent as a stone, physically imposing, and with an accent that was nearly impenetrable to my ears. He would stare at me over the breakfast table, slowly masticating a biscuit, his eyes glazed over, then shake his head in a dismissive manner, like I was too pathetic to bother with. He carried a gun for much of his life. A pair of brass knuckles hung on a nail over the toilet in the back bathroom. People from around the county treated him with a palpable deference. He'd been shot at least once, under his left arm on a snowy morning at the Maggodee Creek Bridge in December of 1930, and never told anyone about it. When his own children found out around 1985, he merely acknowledged the story as true and lifted his shirt to show the bullet hole. No explanation, no context. Grandpa Jack was the real thing.

When I visited, my grandfather would roust me in the mornings to feed the cows. I remember the silent truck cab in the darkness before dawn, the wheel wells mucked with red clay, straw, and tobacco. How I stood in the truck bed cutting the twine and pushing out the hay bales as he cruised through the fields, a funnel of cows lumbering in our wake. We didn't talk. This was terrifying, exhilarating stuff for a suburban kid like me, and I have to think that was his way of trying to communicate something to his grandson. He died when I was a teenager, and I regret that I never had an actual conversation with the man.

Instead I pieced together my grandfather's life, in fact and fiction, through rumor and research. He had a rich and violent past, and with his brothers formed the Bondurant Brothers, the infamous crew of moonshiners in Franklin County, Virginia, the "Moonshine Capital of the World." I learned that Bondurants have been living in that little corner of the Appalachian foothills since the early eighteenth century, eking out a subsistence living growing tobacco, raising a bit of cattle and corn, and making untaxed liquor.

I studied basic chemistry, learning the fundamentals of distillation. I toured legitimate distilleries, read all the books, newspapers, letters, memoirs, listened to the music. I rode four-wheelers through the woods to visit old still sites, the rusting remains of cooling coils, thumper kegs, mash boxes. I stood on the remains of Maggodee Creek Bridge, trying to approximate the exact spot where sheriff's deputies shot Grandpa Jack in the chest and my great uncle Forrest in the stomach. Both survived, and my father still remembers the way Uncle Forrest's stomach would bulge unnaturally when he ate, the food leaking through the perforated stomach lining. I sampled product. I holed up in my brother's West Virginia mountain house with a half-gallon jar of Franklin County white for three days, wandering the woods during the day, sitting in a pool of lamplight at night listening to the Carter Family sing murder ballads. I tried to get inside moonshine any way I could.

The result was the novel *The Wettest County in the World*, published in 2008, which became the movie *Lawless* in 2012. My family came to Los Angeles for the premiere, and my dad loved every minute of it, joking with Shia LaBeouf, the actor playing my grandpa Jack, taking selfies with Jessica Chastain, and working the crowd at the afterparty well after midnight. I was having lots of conference calls and meetings in Santa Monica with thirty-year-old guys wearing flannel shirts and flip-flops who wanted me to pitch them ideas for television shows. First-class flights, press junkets, my wife doing the backstroke in the rooftop pool of the W Hotel on Hollywood Boulevard. The world seemed like it was speeding up, and at times I felt a bit sick about it. I had cashed in on my family's past. I took something real, something true, and packaged it into a story. Now, I know enough about the history of moonshine to know that it's always been about money. Was this any different?

I also noticed a growing mainstream interest in moonshine. It began to appear in liquor stores as a sort of boutique whiskey, a way to experience this exotic, outlawed practice. Some say it was the recession that caused a few states, such as Tennessee, to relax their distilling regulations, creating an opening in the market for these faux moonshiners. About 50,000 cases of legal moonshine were sold in 2010, jumping to

250,000 in 2012. And the numbers keep rising. Ole Smoky Tennessee Moonshine, the top-performing brand, sells more than 300,000 cases each year, and the international market is just beginning to catch fire. Now corporate giants like Jim Beam and Jack Daniel's are marketing "white" whiskies. Package the story, feed the legend, make some money.

Last year, my first cousins Robert and Joey Bondurant, buoyed by the press and buzz surrounding the movie made from my book, renovated an old warehouse in Chase City, Virginia. They moved in a couple of stainless-steel stills, got the requisite permits, and started making legal whiskey. Bondurant Brothers Distillery hand grinds Hickory King corn, an heirloom sweet corn, all of it grown in Virginia. This is the same white corn my grandfather used in the 1930s. Their tag line: "Some Moonshine is legendary and some is made by legends, ours is both!" They use an old family recipe, and it's fair to say this is as close to the authentic article as you can get, legally. The real thing. I hope they succeed. I plan to order a bottle or two, if my local liquor store here in Oxford hasn't disappeared.

What does moonshine mean? I'm talking about the actual article, the condensed drops that gather in the coils and coalesce into a stream of clear, hot liquid. Spinning the lid on the jar, the heat on the back of the tongue, the loosening of the joints, the bones of your chest floating apart, watching the clouds race through the trees, the rush of feeling that comes with knowing that anything is possible in this life. Does moonshine have any inherent value or meaning? I've come to the conclusion that it is an existential object; its existence precedes its essence. We as a society have created its value and meaning, bound up in images of mountains and overalls and shotguns and the way a man wears his hat. I played my part in this fiction.

People write me all the time wanting to tell me stories of their family's moonshining past, their Southern roots, even to parse bits of Southern history, culture, recipes. I'm flattered and I try to answer them as best I can, but I am merely feeding an illusion. What I want to say is this: The person you think I am is a façade. I inhabit different worlds for the three to five years that it takes to write a novel. The last four years, I've been living (in my head) in the far northeastern corner of New York, in a fictional town where people work in supermax prisons and run snowmobiles across the frozen Canadian border with a million dollars of ecstasy strapped to their backs. I left that world of southern Virginia, the world of moonshine and dangerous, silent men like my grandfather, ten years ago.

But that's not true either. I was never really there. I was always the outsider, the kid from the suburbs visiting on the holidays, the one who talked differently, the one who didn't hunt. The young boy herded into the wire at midnight.

The Wettest County in the World wasn't about feeding the legend of the Bondurant Boys, or even feeding my growing family. It was a love letter shot into the darkness of the past. I know there will never be a reply.

And yet. The deep red clay of the roadcuts, the ripple of tobacco leaves in the afternoon. A stand of silent corn at night, the winking sliver of taut wire. The way an old woman invites you to come visit, the offer of four different kinds of cake and pie with coffee. The bowl of creamed corn bubbling in the skillet, my grandmother tossing in a heavy pinch of sugar. The sharp tang and burn of corn whiskey going down your gullet like a rusty knife. History reverberates like the tones of church bells in winter; you can't see it or even sense the direction but you can feel something coming back, an answer. The real thing. You're never ready for that. It's everything you were afraid to know, and everything you wanted to say.

Personal Tastes

Wheat Exile

By Paul Graham

From *In Memory of Bread*

Essayist and literature professor Paul Graham and his wife put a lot of effort into eating well. Farm-to-table, locavore, organic, artisanal, mindful—they embraced it all, and food was a major factor in their daily lives. Then a diagnosis of celiac disease came along and upended everything.

I know the very last gluten-based food I ever ate—by which I mean intentionally, not by accident or by "getting glutened" (celiac-speak for poisoned) at the hands of an unknowing or careless person, or even a well-meaning friend. This was my third last meal, the last stop on my farewell tour-du-wheat.

I remember it well because the same day Dr. Song stamped my celiac passport, I drove to our health-food store, Nature's Storehouse. I was filling a basket with yogurt, coconut, aloe vera juice, slippery elm powder, and some other natural remedies that the owner had recommended for ravaged GI tracts,* when the idea occurred to me. I texted Bec and told her I'd be just a little longer. Keeping in touch was part of the deal, in exchange for letting me get back behind the wheel. We both

---

*Did these natural remedies work? It's tough to say for sure, but only the yogurt, which I couldn't tolerate yet, seemed to hurt me. I had entered into a mental space I never thought I'd go, one where scientifically unproven treatments seemed completely legitimate, and no potential cure sounded too strange or unpalatable: a breakfast of rice grits with powdered marshmallow root and slippery elm powder, washed down with a glass of watery cactus pulp (that'd be the aloe juice), for example. It was the meanest, most desperate eating I've ever done.

knew I shouldn't have been driving, but she didn't have the heart to clip my wings, and the store was less than a mile from home.

She should have grounded me, because after my shopping I drove across town to the pub in the Best Western hotel. I walked in and ordered a Reuben sandwich and fries to go. Then I sat down and waited in the lobby while the order was being prepared. As I reclined by the gas fireplace, my head light and buzzing, I considered, distantly and vaguely, what I was about to do to myself.

Well? Why the hell not? What was one more day? How much worse could my gut get?

I had kept craving a Reuben for the several weeks I'd been sick. At odd moments of the day, apropos of nothing, I kept bursting out with "You know what I could really go for? A Reuben!" Bec always looked at me doubtfully; I didn't seem like a man who could handle a child's portion of applesauce. I behaved myself, holding to my bland diet of tea, rice, and toast. But in the midst of the Taste Desert, I had never forgotten about getting salt, fat, sour, and cream, all in one bite.

I should have just eaten the sandwich like I wanted to back in November, I thought. *I should have eaten ten of them.* What had I gained by trying to placate my gut? Nothing.

When the order was ready, I paid and took it to the car. I unzipped my parka, opened the clamshell packaging, and ate the whole thing. I was breaking all the rules I usually worked so hard to honor; the ingredients of this last supper, if that's what it could be called, were processed and from no place that I could even pretend was local. God only knew where the corned beef came from, and how it had come to be "corned." I now also know that the industrial bread had been stabilized with vital wheat gluten, and there was likely additional gluten in the Russian dressing.

I ate without any mindfulness. I ate mechanically. Anyone glancing inside the car would have seen a man whose face was utterly blank except for a few stray crumbs. And very white and sickly-looking, too. I was, I now realize, stress-eating. I'd never done anything like this before, but I was so out of my mind that I didn't even register the strangeness.

And yet, eating the sandwich also felt a little like getting even. A kamikaze valediction, I was going out on my own terms, in a blaze of gluten, not crawling away like some pathetic creature that had been beaten into submission without stealing one last bite. I felt like a ba-dass—until remorse arrived. That took all of fifteen minutes. It was as if I'd swallowed a live grenade.

Though a little crippled, I still had enough foresight to take care of the evidence. I tossed the container into a public trash bin before I pulled away. I drove home with the windows open to disperse the smell of grease and rye toast even though it was twenty degrees and snowing. Thinking about it now, my final encounter with the Reuben even *sounds* shabby, like a food tryst, right down to the meet-up at the hotel bar. I told myself I had no regrets.

But I *did* have regrets. I should have ordered extra rye bread and a beer. Two beers.

I suffered through one more day of GI agony while Bec wondered over the cause. I should have told her, but I kept my secret because, by now, I was ashamed: of my stupidity, of my weakness, of the fact that I couldn't handle what I had just been told by my doctor, *and it wasn't even that bad*. I didn't have cancer; I didn't have Crohn's; nobody was going to have to snip away a piece of my colon. It was just an intolerance to gluten.

And had I enjoyed my Reuben?

Years later, I can't even remember what the sandwich tasted like. All I know is that it's impossible to get enough joy from one meal to sus-tain one's imagination for years. I had eaten takeout, that was all—and middle-of-the-road takeout at that. There are so many better foods that I might have chosen, but I didn't have immediate access to them, and anyway I don't think that desperately stuffing my face with a crusty ba-guette and brie, or homemade ravioli, or a slice of pie would have been any more sustaining.

In the coming years, I would ask almost everyone I know, *You're about to lose everything made of wheat, rye, barley, and oats—all of it, for-ever. What is the last food you eat?* Everyone has an answer. Everyone thinks it's a good one. Everyone is wrong.

Within a few days of that emotional train wreck, the most obvious symptoms of celiac disease abated just as Dr. Song had said they would. I had doubted whether I could really recover even a semblance of well-being simply by cutting out things made of wheat. I hadn't believed these foods could be harmful because nobody else seemed to think they were, and because wheat and gluten surrounded us, and I didn't see other people keeling over.

When I accompanied Bec to the grocery store for the first time since coming home from the hospital, I perceived that not just a few aisles, but complete zones of the food world, had suddenly ceased to apply to us. We walked past the bakery section, with its glass cases full of dough-nuts and cakes, its faux–French market display of wicker baskets tipped on their sides, spilling heaps of not-very-good bread (but bread none-theless), rolls, and muffins. We skipped the aisle with the rows and rows of snack bags stuffed with chips, pretzels, wafers, and puffs; by-passed the mosaic of cereal boxes with colorful panels of inane cartoon toucans, tigers, dinosaurs, cavemen, and bandits; avoided the granola and energy bars, crackers, the wall of pasta in every shape imaginable, prepackaged seasonings and soups, prepared meals, and the endless cookies and snack cakes that contained, collectively, enough sugary energy to propel a rocket into low orbit. And I couldn't even bring my-self to look in the beer cooler. Our store had a gluten-free corner—it would be an exaggeration to call it an aisle—but we didn't investigate its offerings yet. I was still subsisting on clear broth.

None of these foods were, as I would learn to think of it, *for me.* Some of the international aisle still applied, as did the produce and dairy de-partments, but I estimated that well over half the grocery store was lost. And while most of it was processed junk that our great-grandparents would not recognize as food, let alone a Mesopotamian farmer grind-ing wheat flour millennia ago, many of them had formed the tastes of our childhoods: Oreos, Trix cereal, cookie-dough ice cream. They also comprised a garish world of convenience foods and guilty pleasures in the present. The more I thought about it, the more I felt as if I had been suddenly exiled from American food culture. Meanwhile my wife was expatriating herself, willingly turning in her passport to an entire world of food just to come along with me.

In fact, we had rarely eaten most of these processed foods, and hadn't brought them home in a long time. Doritos, SunChips, pre-packaged doughnuts, Mallomars: we'd nearly forgotten they existed. Same thing with imitation crabmeat (which contains gluten, believe it or not), Cheez-Its, and ramen. Not long after Barbara Kingsolver published

Animal, Vegetable, Miracle, Bec and I became invested in community agriculture, shopping mainly at the farmers' market and living off our farm shares. Kingsolver's book, which was so inspirational to many people but tricky to imitate for a variety of reasons—including, most important, access to time and money—nonetheless awakened us to the joys of the agriculture community in our backyard. We were already ripe for conversion because of a cluster of books and authors we read at that time, including Michael Pollan and Wendell Berry. We extended our roots further into the North Country soil, and slowly transitioned to a heavily local diet. The "locavore movement" has its share of doubters with valid criticisms, but despite the long winters, local eating is easier in the North Country than in most places, provided you're fortunate enough to have the resources (money, knowledge, and time) it requires.

In the grocery store, though, I felt keenly that a locavore diet was different from an elimination diet. Philosophical inclination was different from medical mandate. As a locavore, I knew I could at least have a Dorito, or a handful of Nilla wafers, if I wanted to. Did a GF Nilla wafer exist? Did I even want to know?

Baby Foodie

By Eric LeMay

From TheWeeklings.com

Author of *Immortal Milk: Adventures in Cheese* and *Essays on the Essay and Other Essays,* Eric LeMay teaches writing at Ohio University. In this deadpan piece for The Weeklings (a website devoted to the art of the essay), he shares an ingenious plan for the gustatory education of his soon-to-be-born first child.

S ALT is our first taste.

About five weeks into a pregnancy, when we're still embryos, our nervous systems start to form. The cells that will become the brain and spinal cord divide and cluster. At the same time, our taste buds start developing alongside our tongues. A few weeks pass, and our buds eventually link up with our brain through the seventh, ninth, and tenth cranial nerves, at the end of which is our gustatory cortex. It sits in the center of our brain like the pit of an avocado. With this link in place, we still need eight more weeks for our taste buds to develop taste receptors, little pores that allow us to sense the flavors in our food. At that point, we can taste.

And the first taste we experience is salt. It comes from the amniotic fluid that surrounds us and has a flavor similar to sea water. I know because the other day I made a batch.

"It has the brightness of the sea," said my wife, turning over the spoonful of salty water. She was a little over sixteen-weeks pregnant, the moment when a fetus's senses come online, and her belly billowed like the tiny sail on a toy schooner. "But something's missing."

My wife has a good palate. She couldn't have known I'd used a *fleur de sel* to approximate the 98% water and 2% salt that makes up amniotic fluid. Ever since we'd starting reading about fetal development, I'd been curious as to what the baby would be tasting. Concocting amniotic fluid seemed like a good way to find out.

I confess that, when I came out of the kitchen with a pint-sized Mason jar and a spoon, I didn't tell her that the whitish water swirling in the glass was amniotic fluid. For the last few weeks, she'd been repulsed by foods she ordinarily loved. Kale, eggs, and chicken now turned her stomach, so I figured I wouldn't introduce my little experiment with "Hey honey, let's sample the liquid in your womb." Instead, I tasted it first—nothing to fear here—then said, "Try this."

"There's no taste of seaweed," she continued. "No funk. No dead thing floating in it, like you get at the shore."

That's because there's a live thing floating in it—a fetus!

Sometimes what a husband doesn't say shows he cares. I didn't say that. Instead, I calmly listed the ingredients then calmly explained how they calmly approximated amniotic fluid. When I finished, I may have seen her cheeks convulse ("I wish I'd had *some* warning"), but on the whole she was game. No reason to let her know that, in a few more weeks, the amniotic fluid in her belly would include our baby's urine. That funk she was missing would arrive soon enough. I simply focused on my own salty mouthful and saw she was right: the taste was very clean.

"Umami!" she declared, her buds fully recovered, "that's what's missing!"

Umami is a taste identified in 1908 by the Japanese scientist Kikunea Ikeda. He found that glutamate, an amino acid found in salt but not identical to it, was the taste that gave a succulent flavor to broth made out of seaweed. He named it "umami," but non-foodies usually call it "savory." It's the taste in soy sauce, parmesan cheese, and anchovies that imparts their deep, rich flavors.

Baby, it appeared, would not be tasting deep, rich flavors in the womb. Which raised the question: what flavors would baby taste? Would saltiness be the only one? A baby destined for nothing more, gastronomically speaking, than a bag of potato chips? What about sweetness? What about sour and bitter? What, in short, could a father-to-be do to ensure the widest taste experience for his child at the very moment that he, that she (because we'd decided not to find out the baby's sex) is first able to experience the world through taste?

I decided on nothing less—what else do you expect of a first-time father?—than giving our baby the world.

Now, I'll eventually describe this global culinary journey, one that I cooked up for a creature who has yet to develop the ability to swallow, but what I really hope to do is show how we enter into the world of taste. How, that is, we make our journey from fetus to flavor to the foods we'll eat long after we leave our mothers' arms. And to do that, I first need to explain how it feels, as a father, to track the development of your newly conceived baby.

For starters, you don't enter into it until the third week. That's right, the pregnancy clock officially begins when a woman menstruates for the final time *before* conception. It takes two weeks for an egg to bobble from the ovary down the Fallopian tube, where, in week three, it meets up with one of your sperm. This is your big moment. At conception, you contribute half the genetic material that will eventually become a baby. Half baby's gangly limbs and spotty moles, half its bad teeth and moodiness come from you. And then, as far as you're concerned, that's pretty much it. Thanks, Mr. Ejaculate, mom's got it from here.

And what mom does, in all its developmental complexity, is marvelous. In the fourth week, she provides baby with a uterus, so it can burrow and grow. She also starts nourishing baby through her own blood. You, if you're smart, will wave the pregnancy test enthusiastically without flinching at its pee-soaked end.

The following week, mom gives baby blood cells, kidney cells, nerve cells. Here's the beginning of a brain, kid. Here's the start of a heart. How about a spinal cord, would you like one of those? And you, dad, you lovingly dish out a prenatal vitamin that your wife ordered three months before she became pregnant.

Weeks six and seven, mom gives baby arms and legs, eyes and ears, a spinal cord, a heartbeat, bones. Dad gives nothing.

Week eight, mom provides a pair of lungs. Week nine, she follows up with hair follicles, nipples, those tiny toes and fingers that you'll feature in the photos from the hospital. She also gives baby every organ. And don't forget that mom has grown an entirely new organ herself, just for baby. Her placenta is feeding baby, eliminating baby's waste, and protecting baby from disease. You purchase the wrong flavor of ice cream.

On it goes. Mom gives the baby eyelids, nails, facial features, skin. She's the prime mover for all of baby's biological systems—circulatory, muscular, endocrine, nervous, digestive—all while you gain five pounds of sympathy weight.

So, at sixteen weeks, when baby can finally perceive the outside world, when its sense of hearing kicks in and touch becomes possible, when it can finally taste, for the very first time in its existence, of course you, as baby's father, want to make it something special.

The pressing question becomes: what, besides salt, can baby taste? We quickly discovered one answer. My wife had yet to feel the baby move. She might have—maybe, perhaps, she wasn't entirely sure—felt a flutter one night after I had dozed off and she said to the ceiling, "Baby, do something." *Maybe*, at that request, baby moved. She's certain, however, that a few nights later, while we were once again lying in bed, she felt it. She sprang up, and her eyes brightened.

"The baby's moving," she gasped, in a low voice, as though she might spook it.

"What's it feel like?" I asked

She cupped her stomach. "Like that wire brush you use to play the cymbal." She demonstrated, moving her fingers to a soundless tune. "But inside."

"Is it still happening?"

"Yes. No." She hadn't moved. "Maybe."

Neither of us breathed.

"It's gone," she announced, a smile still gripping her cheeks.

Let me pause on this beatific moment and mention that my wife, with her fine palate, had of late not only been rejecting some of her favorite foods. She'd also been gripped by certain cravings. Cravings for pasta. Cravings for cookies and crusty bread and other carb-loaded foods that beckoned to her in the bakery and stalked her in the checkout line. Still worse for a woman who prides herself on her ability to cook up dal makahini from memory, she was craving clichés. Pickles, yes, pickles. And ice cream, in both the wrong and the oh-so-right-just-one-more-bite flavors.

So when I pointed out how baby must have enjoyed the pralines and cream that she'd polished off earlier, I thought I was saying the obvious. I was wrong.

"Oh no," she said, slumping over her belly. "I've given the baby type 2 diabetes."

"You can't give the baby type 2 diabetes with Häagen Dazs."

"You can," she groaned. "I read about it. Gestational diabetes."

"You had three bites. That's like a sip of soda. Most Americans brush their teeth with soda."

"Still," she wavered, unconvinced.

For the rest of the night, we returned to the question of whether a mother could ruin her baby's current health and dietary future by savoring three spoonfuls of Häagen Dazs. Suddenly that hamburger last Tuesday and those enchiladas on Friday and the fact that my wife had eaten only one salad the day before seemed to her like inevitable precursors to baby's insulin shots, EpiPens, and eventual appearance on *The Biggest Loser*. "My mother," baby would sob, "ruined me before I was born."

I hoped a few hours' sleep would shake this worry from us, but the next morning my wife sent me a link to an article informing me that your baby "tastes what you taste—and research has shown that the foods you consume during this time help shape what your baby will enjoy eating, even years later." Her subject heading was "Grilled Cheese Baby, Here We Come."

Our baby was transforming from a belly full of joy into a meal you could buy at a gas station. Mildly concerned, I looked into the research. The upshot, once you click your way from the pregnancy websites to the newspaper reports to the scientific papers themselves, is what you'd expect: baby's diet and health pretty much follows mom's diet and health. Grilled Cheese Mom, Grilled Cheese Baby. Kale Mom, Kale Baby.

This simple dynamic results from a complex mix of biology and culture. We're hardwired to want sugar, salt, and fat—foods once scarce in human existence and now abundant beyond our ability to process them. But how and how much of these foods we eat when we're infants has to do with cultural factors, such as our ethnicity and economic status, factors that show up most immediately in our families' behavior around food. Unsurprisingly, your chances of avoiding gestational diabetes are much better if you're conceived by an educated and healthy mother who has access to wholesome foods and an income to afford them.

The surprise is the sheer power of what researchers call the "cafeteria" or "junk-food" diet to affect a fetus.

As my wife and I learned, if mom spikes her blood sugar with Häagen Dazs, baby will react, so much so that some babies overexposed to sugar in the womb are born "addicted" to it. In certain cases, doctors need to provide newborns with a glucose drip in order to reduce their dangerously high insulin levels. Babies also show a clear preference for bottles that have had their latex nipples dipped in a sugar solution, and sugar can even work as an analgesic on infants. A baby enjoying sugar will endure more pain. Those warnings we're now hearing about the toxic effects of sugar apply all the more to developing babies, who have about as much chance to resisting it as any other addictive drug.

In our Age of the Big Gulp, the sugar baby is the new crack baby.

So, yes, baby liked the taste of sweet. And I soon found myself pausing in the freezer aisle. How much Häagen Dazs is too much Häagen Dazs? Do those little Dixie-cup-size containers really count? The questions nagged at me, but they took a larger toll on my wife.

"Eating anything processed now feels to me like drinking french-fry oil."

"You're doing fine," I assured her. Ever since my wife had found out she was pregnant, our refrigerator had looked like an ad for Whole Foods.

"What if the baby needs magnesium this week, and I'm not tracking my milligrams of magnesium." She spat out the *magnesium* as if it disgusted her. "And one day I'll have to say, 'Sorry, baby, I just didn't care enough about you to track my magnesium! So you don't get whatever you should get that's made of magnesium!'"

I wondered aloud, to no one in particular, if it might be worth having an occasional glass of wine to relieve the stress of worrying about a prenatal diet.

"The pregnancy guide says that experts say that the prenatal research says that expecting mothers should be eating multiple meals a day. Not just three." She was reading the guide, I should probably note, while eating a chocolate chip cookie.

"You have those snacks."

"Maybe I should eat half of my lunch at lunch and then eat the other lunch later."

"Maybe double every meal and eat all day?"

My wife looked up from the guide and released a long breath that began as a hiss and ended as a sigh.

Fortunately, the research out there offers more than information meltdown. The good news is that, if mom eats healthfully, she can not only create a healthier baby but also shape baby's future eating habits for the better.

Take a vegetable like carrots. Researchers at the Monell Chemical Senses Center designed an experiment to find out whether pregnant women and new mothers who drink carrot juice would have babies who also liked it. One group of women was asked to drink carrot juice regularly during their last trimester. Another group was asked to drink it during their first three months of breast feeding. The final group didn't drink it at all. When their babies were six months old, the women in all three groups "exposed" their babies to carrot juice by mixing it in cereal.

The results? Those babies whose mothers had drunk carrot juice, either while they were pregnant or while they were breast feeding, "exhibited fewer negative facial expressions" than the babies whose mothers hadn't had any carrot juice. The flavor of the carrot, in the amniotic fluid and in the mother's milk, had made a difference in the babies' response. Some babies, I suppose, made yuck-yuck faces, while those babies more inclined to carrots made single-yuck faces. I can picture the mothers staring at their babies the way an insecure chef might scrutinize a restaurant critic: how much does this guy hate my dish?

So if, like me, you're thinking that fewer negative facial expressions isn't exactly a triumph when it comes to getting a baby to like certain foods, keep in mind that babies normally need to experience a new taste eight to ten times before they'll start eating it. Everything gets spit on the feeding tray at first. Like fussy critics, getting babies to like certain foods takes time.

And yet the carrot juice shows us this process starts in the womb. Researchers have found that the flavors of fruit, vegetables, and spices show up in amniotic fluid a few hours after a pregnant woman has eaten them. Even perfume and cigarette smoke, when inhaled by mothers-to-be, make it into the womb.

"Dietary learning" is the phrase used by Julie Mennella, one of the researchers behind the carrot experiment, to describe this process. As a fetus, then as an infant, the tastes that we experience as our mothers eat prepare us for the tastes we'll experience once we start eating by ourselves. We learn what our future diets will be like from our mothers and, to a large extent, from what our mothers like.

In light of this research, I devised a plan for baby's dietary learning and, after days of preparation, shared it with my wife.

"Our goal," I said, flashing the first slide of my PowerPoint presentation and displaying a close-up of her rounded belly, "is to take advantage of this moment when baby can finally taste. What we want is to give baby the widest possible range of tastes."

She nodded cautiously.

Next slide: an image of brilliantly colored spices—rusty orange, midnight blue, berry red—piled in grainy heaps.

"The challenge," I said, "is that only the strongest tastes are able to flavor the amniotic fluid." I glanced at my wife. "Garlic, for example."

"Yes," she said, less intrigued than braced.

"So we'll be using the most powerful spices occurring in nature." Another look.

"We?"

Next slide: a map of the world, marked with six red dots. "Our other goal," I continued, "is to 'expose' baby to as many global cuisines as possible." I thought I sounded impressive using the scientific lingo.

"Ambitious," my wife said.

"Think of it as baby's first study-abroad program, *in utero*."

I then clicked through a series of slides, highlighting the six meals that I would cook in the next six days, meals that would take us, culinarily, around the world. We would begin with the street vendors in Vietnam and, from there, travel to the hearths of Northern India. Then onward we'd go, finding our way to a table in Tunisia, and then we'd head north, into the icy Norwegian sea. From there, at last, we'd cross the Atlantic Ocean and land on the shores of the arid Yucatán

Peninsula, all before arriving back home, in Ohio, on what would fortuitously be the Fourth of July.

Our travels would cover approximately 29,000 imaginary miles, more than the circumference of the earth. It would cost more real dollars than I'm going to admit. And it would dirty every dish we had in the house multiple times over. After we were done, I would never want to travel again, and I'd accomplish this culinary feat all without ever leaving the kitchen.

"Are you sure you want to do this? Seems like *a lot* of work." To me, my wife's words sounded more like code for "Please don't feed me more amniotic fluid."

"It'll end with pie," I promised. "Apple pie."

"Have you ever made pie?"

No, I thought, but then I hadn't made any of the dishes I'd planned, but I wasn't going to let that fact deprive baby of an education. Besides, how hard could it be?

An International Prenatal Gastronomical Education in Six Meals (with Travel Notes)

Monday
Location: Vietnam
Meal: Coconut Lemongrass Chicken and Sweet Potato Shrimp Cakes
Major Spices: Lemongrass, ginger, garlic
Notes: The corn starch on the fried shrimp cakes doesn't ring of health. "On my final bite," says wife, "I suddenly ask myself: should a pregnant woman be eating shrimp?" Wife reports no response from baby.

Tuesday
Location: Northern India and Pakistan
Meal: Baked Beef Curry and Saag Paner with an Anise-Almond Lassi
Major Spices: Anise, cardamom, cumin, cinnamon, ginger, cayenne
Notes: I cook for four and a half hours. Wife eats Cheez-Its a half an hour before meal. "Not having had to do the work," says wife, "I can tell you this tastes amazing." Wife reports no response from baby.

Wednesday
Location: Tunisia and Morocco

Meal: Lamb Meatballs in Saffron with Golden-Raisin Couscous

Major Spices: Saffron, turmeric, clove, cayenne, cinnamon, ginger, garlic, cumin

Notes: Tastes amazing, like the spice trade happening in your mouth. "Baby likes this dish so far," says wife. "Are you feeling something?" I ask. "No, but I can tell by how happy my tummy is." Wife reports no response from baby.

Thursday

Location: Norway

Meal: Baked Salmon with a Juniper Berry Rub, Anchovies and Potato Casserole, Sautéed Broccoli, and Bay Leaf and Fresh Berry Custard

Major Spices: Juniper berries, bay leaves

Notes: Norway is the big surprise. Its cuisine has a spiciness rivaling the previous meals, but wholly its own. Wife reports not liking Norway. Wife reports no response from baby.

Friday

Location: Southern Mexico

Meal: Yucatecan Slow-Roasted Pork, Cumin-Pickled Onions, Guacamole, and Hand-Made Tortillas

Major Spices: Habanero, clove, garlic, cumin

Notes: The habanero peppers give the pork the blazing color of a Mayan sunset. "In terms of pure chew experience," says wife, "this one wins." Wife reports no response from baby.

Saturday, the Fourth of July

Location: The Middle of Middle America

Meal: Cheeseburgers, Baked Beans, Coleslaw, Kraft Mac and Cheese, and Apple Pie

Major Spice: Mustard

Notes: I make mac and cheese from a box, predicting that, despite my efforts, it's likely to be baby's favorite. "All the sides are basically condiments," says wife. "The baked beans are ketchup. The coleslaw is mayo. The mac and cheese is cheese." Wife reports no response from baby.

On Sunday, we ordered pizza. We were both ready for something simple, and what's better that a nice slice of fatty, starchy, sweetly saucy goodness served in a cardboard box?

Did baby respond to the pizza? you might be asking. Good question.

I also wondered if that would happen. But no, baby didn't go for pizza either. You might also be asking, as many of our friends did, whether I was disappointed that baby never responded to any of the meals I cooked, no, not to one single spice. *Wasn't that, wouldn't you say, a little frustrating?*

Sort of, but not really. Sure, I'll freely admit that I would have liked it if baby had done its little cymbal dance when my wife sipped her lassi. And I'll admit that, by the time I finished making the apple pie, I felt fried and self-pitying. After all that cooking and baby not responding to any of it, shouldn't the band in the Fourth of July parade have played just for me?

In the end, though, baby's radio silence clarified for me a few of my own expectations about becoming a father, which are, with a nod to Dickens, not all that great. I don't mean I'm not looking forward to being a father. I am. I'm thrilled about it. What I mean is that my expectation is that baby, more often than not, will sidestep, thwart, or frustrate any particular expectations I might have as a father. Baby will probably not like, for example, the books I'd like for baby to like or baby will probably not like books at all. Baby will probably not like the foods I'd like for baby to like, nor will baby likely become the baby foodie I'd like baby to be. No, baby will probably like Elmo and eat paste. That, as a future father, is what I'm expecting.

And I think that's okay. In fact, I think I'll love the baby all the same, maybe all the more, for it. Expectations aren't as great as surprises, and that, as every parent I know is now quick to stress, is what baby will bring to our table and our lives. Indeed, that's what baby has already done.

Case in point: To celebrate the Fourth, my wife and I joined the crowd to watch the fireworks explode over the small river that skirts our town. Kids were running around crazily in the dark, as kids do, and fireflies were flaring up in the nearby trees. We waited with everyone else, looking up, my arms wrapped around my wife's belly and her back pressed against my chest. Finally, the first tester shot launched into the sky with a streak of white light and exploded above us. As its boom echoed against the nearby hills, my wife turned to me and smiled.

"The baby's kicking," she said.

My Father, the YouTube Star

By Kevin Pang

From the *New York Times Magazine*

Food editor at *The Onion*'s entertainment website A.V. Club, Kevin Pang* is a former staff writer for the *Chicago Tribune* and a 2010 winner of the James Beard award. Imagine his surprise, then, to discover that he wasn't the only member of his family with a following in the food world.

The first few emails were marked "Fwd: Jeffrey Pang sent you a video," so I ignored them. Statistics were on my side: In the history of parental email forwards, roughly 0.001 percent have been worth opening.

Later he followed up by phone. I told him I hadn't found time to watch whatever it was he sent. Several seconds of silence hung between us before my dad replied: "Oh."

This is how it had gone for 30-some years—a father-son relationship kept cordial and indifferent through habit and physical distance. I live in Chicago; he's in Seattle. Once a week, we'd talk on the phone for five minutes and exchange the least substantive of pleasantries: "How's the weather?" "Plans this weekend?" Not a meaningful conversation so much as a scripted set of talking points.

Only when my mom nudged did I open the video Dad had sent.

Fade in: the company logo for Creative Production, with the E-A-T in "Creative" highlighted. Cue soft piano melody, the type of royal-ty-free soundtrack that sounds like the hold Muzak when you call your dermatologist. Dissolve to title screen: "Catherine Mom's Shang-hainese Green Onion Pancake," with its translation in Chinese. And then a photo of my mother (Catherine) and my grandma. A shot of our white kitchen island, and my mother's hands, her unmistakable wedding band, digging into and massaging wet dough. My virulently anti-technology Chinese parents were starring in their own internet cooking show.

As a child who immigrated from Hong Kong, I was raised as an American during the day and Chinese after school. I brought home Western ideas that confounded my parents: sarcasm, irony, recalci-trance. My father and I argued all the time. The grievances were usu-ally benign, but they would erupt into battles between two headstrong males, each standing his cultural ground. It didn't help that I stubbornly refused to speak Cantonese at home. Or when, during college, I went home for Thanksgiving with newly bleached blond hair. My dad was apoplectic, screaming the moment he saw me in the driveway, accusing me of being ashamed of my Chinese heritage.

Our differences would burn hot, then smolder, then fizzle to a détente. Eventually we would acknowledge each other, and everything would stay cool until the next flare-up. Our relationship reached a pla-teau of cordial indifference: We lived 2,000 miles apart and talked on the phone once a week about nothing important at all.

But something changed in our relationship the day I switched jobs. I was working as a metro news reporter at *The Chicago Tribune* when I was offered a position on the paper's food writing staff. I had zero expe-rience, but I did have one advantage: I was Cantonese. We Cantonese have a love of eating that borders on mania. Our people eat every part of almost every animal; we were the original snout-to-tail diners, long before hipsters hijacked the term. Hong Kong, where I lived until age 6, is a place where instead of asking "How are you?" we greet one another with "Have you eaten yet?"

Food was my dad's obsession. He had always been a marvelous cook. He dreamed of being one of those Iron Chefs in white toques who en-ter Kitchen Stadium through dramatic fog. Much of the joy of Chinese food for him seemed nostalgic: He always lamented his decision to leave his beloved Hong Kong, to come here, to a foreign land, for the sake of his children.

So when I became a food writer, my father and I shared, for the first time, a mutual interest. I would call to ask about recipes and cooking techniques. He would school me on the world of Cantonese cuisine. The first time he visited me in Chicago, I took him to a dim sum restaurant for brunch, and as we ate shrimp dumplings and barbecued pork buns, he explained—gesticulating with his arms like a conductor—how the *shiu mai*'s wrapper should caress its filling "like a dress on a woman, like petals of a flower, like prongs on a diamond ring." I had never heard him speak with such enthusiasm or eloquence. My father never taught me to swim, or to ride a bike, but he did teach me how to tell a good dim sum restaurant from a great one.

Food became something I could use to engage him and repair our relationship. When we talked on the phone about how to wrap Shanghai water dumplings or braise *dong po rou* pork belly, 30 minutes would fly by. Then, when the subject turned to anything else: "How's the weather? Plans this weekend? O.K., goodbye."

It's not doing "Carpool Karaoke" numbers or landing guest appearances by Michelle Obama, but the relative success of my dad's cooking videos has been, for me, almost unbelievable. Most people would kill to have these viewer metrics. The videos are earnest and adorably cheeseball, bearing the production tropes of '80s VHS: There are spinning wipe effects, gratuitous zooms, saccharine background music.

His most-watched recipe, with nearly a quarter-million views, is for Chinkiang-style pork ribs. I remember eating these when I was growing up. He would use a cleaver to chop spare ribs into two-bite cubes, wokfry them, then sauce them with a viscous glaze of Chinese black vinegar. The result was fatty and sticky and crisp, and I would slurp the meat clean off the bone in one motion. Watching through nearly two dozen more videos, I realized every single dish had been served in my childhood home. Macau-style Portuguese coconut chicken. Pan-fried turnip cake. Sweet-and-sour pork. This time, the wave of nostalgia washed over *me*: I was 12 again, sitting at the kitchen table, my family's mouths too preoccupied to squabble.

My dad makes enough in each month's ad revenues to take my mom out for a nice lunch. Making the clips is a lot of work. The two of them test each recipe a half-dozen times before committing it to film. Dad is behind the camera and editing the footage; it's usually my mom's hands demonstrating. They don't speak in the videos. They say they're embarrassed by their spoken English and feel more comfortable using onscreen text, in Chinese and English, for instruction. Writing and translating this adds several more hours of work.

"Why?" I asked during one of our weekly phone conversations. "Do you want a show on the Food Network or something?"

"You really want to know?" my dad asked in Chinese. "Your mom's great-grandmother used to cook amazing Shanghainese food for her. She would dream about it. But when your mom was finally old enough to ask for the recipes, her great-grandmother had already developed dementia. She couldn't even remember cooking those dishes. The only thing your mom had left was the memory of her taste. We're afraid that if you wanted to eat your childhood dishes, and one day we're both no longer around, you wouldn't know how to cook it."

"You know," he added, "you can be pretty uncommunicative."

Neither of us is likely to have the courage to sit down and hash out years of father-son strife; we're both too stubborn, and verbalizing our emotions would leave us squirming. I even waited until the last minute to send him a draft of this story, and waited nervously for the response. Soon enough, a reply arrived:

Hi Kevin,
This is a good and true story. Thank you. Call me sometime.
Dad

Cooking

By Elissa Altman

From *Treyf: My Life as an Unorthodox Outlaw*

In this memoir, as in her previous book *Poor Man's Feast* (2013), Elissa Altman decodes the mixed messages of her turbulent Queens Jewish upbringing, where temple services were followed by sweet-and-sour pork at a Chinese restaurant. In her family, nothing was more emotionally loaded than food.

During the school year, she makes potato latkes and diaphanous matzo meal pancakes the size of saucers. She makes salty matzo brei egg scrambles with caramelized onion and a shower of black pepper. There are kugels sweet and savory, roast chickens kneaded with vegetable oil and paprika, their metal kosher certification tags dangling from their ankle cartilage like charms from a bracelet. There is stuffed breast of veal sewn up with a carpet needle she bought special from a flooring store on Queens Boulevard, and in the heat, chef salads into which she slices neat triangles of cold cuts: long sheets of Swiss cheese differentiated from American only by virtue of color and hole; bologna; Hebrew National salami; Oscar Mayer boiled ham. There are television snacks of saltines and spray cheese; grilled cheese and bacon at McCrory's on Sixty-Third Drive served to me by a strawberry blonde shiksa wearing a peach-toned, triple-weave polyester apron who Gaga introduces to me as *my lady friend*. There are frozen fish sticks cooked in a smoking toaster oven that always catches fire; doughy French bread pepperoni pizzas; Weaver fried chicken drumsticks; Swanson's

Hungry-Man dinners; blueberry blintzes topped with dollops of sour cream; cold leftover brisket stuffed into soft onion pockets; chopped chicken livers on Russian black bread so dense and dark that it looks like a starless midnight sky.

What shall I make for your return? she writes to me in her letters, when I'm at sleepaway camp and, then, working at the hotel. The question feels formal, asked in the old-fashioned style of a mother writing to her son off fighting at Gettysburg or the Somme. *What would you like me to have waiting for you?* she says, and I believe at that moment my universe is comprised of just the two of us: Gaga, whose daughter's attention has turned toward a new life as a single woman in late–1970s Manhattan, and me, whose world is stitched together by her grandmother— the foul-tempered, unsmiling woman who once loved another woman. After the divorce, Gaga and I spend our days together quietly at the kitchen table while my mother is out with Ben, and my father is living in Brooklyn with his mother, who after sixty years is still trying to feed him the borscht that he has hated since he was a baby. He rails and fights with her as though nothing has changed for them; nothing has.

Gaga and I are heretics, watchers, quick to temper, brokenhearted. Our lives begin and end in the kitchen, connected to each other by love and the fraying cords of domestic madness and disappointment: I am my mother's daughter. My mother is Gaga's daughter. Together, we form a triangulation of anger and disappointment that dissipates only when Gaga and I are alone together. She is my safety net and my world, even with her temper that leaves our apartment door slammed, our drinking glasses broken, my sneakers—when I choose to spend Saturday nights with my father rather than with her after the divorce—once spat upon in a torrent of fury that we both choose, somehow, to forget.

What shall I make for your return? she asks, and I live for this question as much for the food as for the love, because the food is the love. I dream of her goulash—a mosaic of sinewy kosher chuck roast that she cubes by holding large pieces of the meat in her left hand and slicing it with a cheap flexible serrated steak knife held in her right like she's sectioning an apple. More than once she nicks herself, dropping tiny beads of scarlet blood along with the cubes into her lime green plastic mixing bowl. There is a long massage with ancient paprika and the addition of slivered onions and smashed garlic cloves, half a can of Del Monte tomato sauce, and then the dump into a squat, avocado-colored Teflon pot into which she slices unpeeled nuggets of floury potato to thicken the contents into the consistency of slow, meaty sludge.

What shall I make for your return? she asks me in a letter, and I write back and say, *Goulash,* even in the heat of the late summer, and she writes back and says, *All right, my darling, I'll make it for you.*

"She never called *me* 'darling,'" my mother snarls in the car on the way home from meeting the camp bus with my father. She folds down the makeup mirror and glares at me sitting in the backseat while I read Gaga's letters, which I carry in my knapsack, aloud. I never read them out loud again.

Gaga doesn't come with my parents to pick me up from the camp bus. A year later, after the divorce, she won't meet my father's car downstairs as it pulls into The Champs-Élysées Promenade after the long drive home from Sugar Maples. Instead, I find her upstairs at our white Chambers stove, stirring her pot in silence, droplets of sweat dripping down her lined forehead. She folds and turns and mixes and blends and after an unfathomable, shocking hug when I burst through the door—she isn't a hugger—I sit down at the breakfast counter in our narrow galley kitchen with my mother's mostly forgotten, half-empty boxes of Ayds diet candies in front of me, and Gaga reaches over my shoulder and puts down a small melamine bowl and a spoon and I eat in silence with her standing over my shoulder, clacking her false teeth together to keep them from slipping, and my heart bursts open.

There is goulash on toast; goulash on spaetzli; goulash on rice; goulash on challah. There is leftover goulash—goulash that I eat alone in the early morning hours before my mother returns from an evening out with Ben, goulash at midnight, goulash at four in the morning when I wake up and can't sleep. The pot, its contents slowly receding like the ocean, takes up the entire bottom shelf in our fridge, but I never think to decant it into a smaller container. When the silver slashes of the dinged Teflon begin to peek through, I ration the stew, pulling the shards and shreds of meat into strings, adding meager tablespoons of hard New York City tap water to the leftovers in order to lengthen the sauce, and her love. When the pot is nearly empty, its sides and bottom lacquered with the remnants of meat juice and tomato and dried white potato starch, I heat it up to melt them into a final puddle the size of the half dollars I collect, and I use a small piece of stale challah to sponge down the sides and the corners of the pot, like its content was pure gold.

What shall I make for your return? Gaga asks in her letters. Goulash— the food her Hungarian immigrant mother made her—ties us together, grandmother to granddaughter, outlier to outlier.

Make me your heart, I think, and she does.

"She was born with a mean mouth," my mother says about Gaga.

"What's that?" I ask when I'm a young teenager.

"I don't know," she says. "But just look at her."

Instead of a downturn of sad resignation, Gaga's mouth is pulled taut as a wire, rarely smiling or moving. I have a cousin with a mouth curled into a perpetual snarl like a mountain lion. Mine is crooked and unsure, like my father's and his father's. But Gaga's is a tight red line, a boundary so straight that I expect it to creak like an old floorboard when she opens it to speak or to fight with anyone who dares cross her: the grocery store delivery boy, who she accuses of shortchanging her; the sixth-grade teacher who bullies and torments me in front of a classroom of laughing schoolmates; my mother, when she stays overnight at Ben's and skulks back into our apartment just before sunrise.

Gaga came into the world in 1901 on the precipice of a new century, almost a year to the day after Queen Victoria's death: she inherits her mother's love of music and her father's ferocious disposition. A massive, barrel-chested six-foot-four Budapest-born Hungarian hussar turned kosher butcher who wrings the scrawny necks of kosher chickens in the feather-covered back room of his Williamsburg store, he sets six-year-old Gaga on a ladder over an immense cauldron of boiling water and instructs her to submerge the dead birds by their feet, to loosen their feathers. I imagine her holding the creatures, the hot water splattering up onto the dress that her mother, Esther, has sewn for her; she accidentally drops one whole chicken into the water—it slips out of her sweaty baby hands—and her father chases her around the store, taking off a blood-splattered boot and throwing it at his oldest child until she runs out the door and down Broadway, tears of frustration caught in her throat. Every afternoon, she tries to fix her mistake, and to please him, to make things right; she spends her days after school singing to herself while sitting outside the store on an upturned wooden crate, plucking feathers from piles of birds, ankle-deep in viscera and plumage, directly across the street from what will become, a century later, Marlow & Daughters, the greatest pork emporium in New York.

Gaga is the oldest of six—five girls and a boy, Herman, who will die during the 1918 flu epidemic—and their mother, Esther, a tiny small-pox-scarred homemaker with a sweet soprano voice who turned her brownstone into a boardinghouse after her husband died at forty-two. The only way she can keep the family together and keep the roof over her children's heads is to house and feed perfect strangers for five dol-lars a week. Day and night, while World War I rages on the other side of the Atlantic, Esther stands in her kitchen cooking for her family and the German and Austrian and Irish and Italian and Polish boarders who sleep and bathe and eat side by side with her Jewish children, coddling and loving them, and teaching them the languages of their homelands just so that they can hear them spoken by innocent voices: by the time Gaga marries Grandpa Philip in 1934, she is fluent in German and speaks Italian as if she herself came directly off the boat from Palermo.

There is a dusty, dog-eared photograph of Esther that I am shown over and over again, and this is how I imagine her whenever I imag-ine her: her thinning, graying hair pulled back in a loose bun, smudged round Emma Goldman glasses perched on the end of her nose, black bump-toe shoes, and an apron covering a thin cotton dress laden with petunias. Every day, before the boarders come home, she takes an after-noon break and ushers Gaga and her sisters into the parlor and teaches them how to sing *And the Band Played On* in harmony around the mas-sive upright Kranich & Bach piano that stands in the middle of the room.

"She was always working," Gaga told me when I was older, "always working. Always in the kitchen; always feeding people, whoever came by." When one overnight visitor, an opera singer who was performing that night in Manhattan, gave an impromptu recital in the parlor for the other boarders, the man's manager, Gatti-Cazza, found Esther sitting on a stool in the kitchen, taking a break from her day's work, a damp dish-cloth in her hands, her head resting against the doorjamb and listening to the overnight guest sing Puccini.

"Take your apron off, Mrs. Gross, and please come into the parlor—"

Gatti-Cazza said, holding his hand out. She took it and followed him into the long, cavernous room, and quietly sat out of view while Enrico Caruso sang *Vecchia Zimarra*. Gaga said that her mother hummed it sweetly to herself for the rest of her life, even when the asthma was killing her, when she could barely breathe and they had to bring an oxygen tank into the apartment she shared with my mother, Gaga, and Grandpa Philip, thirty years later.

"A religion; it was like her religion," Gaga would say while she cooked for me, telling me this story of her mother, Esther, who died in 1948, and who made it her life's work to feed and provide nourishment and sustenance to perfect strangers, even as the only worlds they knew, thousands of miles away, were imploding.

"Maybe because," Gaga says. She speaks through lips as tight as a cord, putting a bowl of goulash down in front of me one day after school. Chronically soaked with perspiration, even in the dead of winter, Gaga wipes her eyes with a greasy, flowered terrycloth dish towel and goes back into the kitchen.

"But why?" I ask her. "Why would she want to feed people she didn't even know?"

I have been taught over the years, by Aunt Sylvia, by my mother, that cooking for other people is labor, that it's nothing to be proud of or ever to aspire to; the act of providing sustenance is something to be embarrassed by, the downstairs to our upstairs. The need—the desire—for sustenance and nurturing is even worse: it's shameful.

After my family has fallen apart, after my father has left and moved back to Brooklyn and my mother is out every night, the only thing I want or need is Gaga, just the two of us, alone together, sometimes listening to music, sometimes not. She tells me the story of her mother, Esther, and the boardinghouse, and the time that Caruso came to stay and sang Puccini, and she feeds my heart and soul, plate after plate, bowl after bowl. When she is in it, the kitchen is my safe room, the place where I am most secure, protected, sustained.

"Do you know that you were named for her?" she repeats, and I say, "Yes, I do."

"What shall I make for you, Elissala?" Gaga says to me every day, and she stands in the kitchen, and she cooks for me.

Years later, after I leave for college in Boston, after my mother marries Ben and moves into Manhattan, Gaga will step out of the building she moved my mother to in 1960, leaving Grandpa Philip to sleep alone in his furniture store in Williamsburg with nothing but Sister Redempta and his homing pigeons for company; Gaga will stand in the middle of The Champs-Élysées Promenade and look up at our apartment in The Marseilles, occupied, after eighteen years, by strangers.

"No one left to cook for," she says, when she calls me in my dormitory room in Boston. "No one left to eat with. When are you coming home?"

Six months later, at five in the morning, Ben will call my dorm room: "Gaga is gone," he tells me. A massive heart attack in the middle of the night.

"Don't come—don't even try to get home," he says as I stand at the window facing west over Commonwealth Avenue. Enormous snowflakes the size of half dollars flutter past me; the wind blows them up and sideways and down; I can't focus on them. Ben's voice is distant, as if he's calling me from another place and time, and I can barely hear him. On that morning, an early April nor'easter—a freak springtime snowstorm—will blanket and shut down the entire East Coast within hours. The trains will stop running and the airports will shut down and the roads will be abandoned. I will never have the chance to say goodbye.

Why You Should Eat All the Asparagus Right Now

By Bethany Jean Clement

From the *Seattle Times*

Every family has its own food traditions, customs and common memories that bind a clan together. And as *Seattle Times* dining critic Bethany Jean Clement discovered this year, there's a poignant comfort in sharing those foods in a year of loss.

Can a family have a vegetable, the way a state has a bird? Why not? My family's is, incontrovertibly, asparagus.

My father grew up east of the mountains, past Yakima, in Sunnyside. As a kid, he worked springtimes in the early morning fields, cutting asparagus before school. He said, if memory serves, that he made the princely sum of 35 cents an hour. At the end of the season—June, usually—the man who owned the fields would take all the part-time child laborers to town for root-beer floats, a treat of a magnitude that never diminished. "They were *so* good," my dad would say decades later, momentarily far away.

When I was growing up, we went over to Sunnyside often, to help my grandmother with the Angus cattle she raised: feeding, branding, mending fence. Spring was the time when we corralled the herd, loaded them into the truck, and took them out to graze on the sage rangeland; it was also the time of an outburst of lilacs and the glory of asparagus season.

For some years, asparagus grew in the neighbor's field, across the dusty road from grandma's house. It was my job before dinner to "go cut some grass"—to take the long, forked-tongued asparagus knife and walk out into the field in the evening breeze, the land seemingly breathing, the light tending toward golden. My grandmother's collie would stand guard, gazing nobly into the distance.

It is difficult to equal asparagus that is mere minutes and yards from dirt to plate, just boiled briefly in an old farm pan, maybe a little butter melting on top. But Washington asparagus from the farmers market or the grocery store is still a miracle of spring, and this year, there's a bumper crop, with a couple-few more weeks of eating left. My dad eventually started grilling asparagus—just salt and pepper and a little bit of olive oil, turned once or twice on a hot grill until just roasty and a little floppy—but we all felt, quite strongly, that any other preparation besides grandma's and that one would be gilding the spear.

Then, a few years ago, I accidentally hoarded a lot—a *lot*—of asparagus butt ends, adding them serially to a bag in the freezer. (Also, if you need any of those blue or purple rubber bands that asparagus is bundled with, let me know.) Eventually, I thought I should try making asparagus soup. This very natural conclusion was met at the extended-family table with undisguised suspicion, but even my dad had to admit that it was good. (It also essentially conforms to his first rule of cooking: Every good recipe starts with sautéing an onion.) The recipe here is adjusted with chicken or vegetable stock for those who do not have an obsessive amount of asparagus butts on hand, and it achieves its own kind of richness.

My grandmother lived to a vigorously advanced age; she didn't even give up the last of the cattle until she was 78. My father departed this earth prematurely, by all measures, around this time a year ago. I am not sure he had any asparagus last year at all; he, who had always eaten with an inspirationally majestic appetite, was whittled away at the end, his favorite foods suddenly tasting unbearable, one by one. Terminal cancer is nothing but betrayal.

Love your loved ones—the people, the vegetables—as much as you can. You never know if this is the last of them for you. Eat all the asparagus.

Asparagus Soup for Dad

Organic ingredients—especially for the broth, cream, and sour cream—really make a difference here.

Serves 4 to 6

2 pounds asparagus
3 cups chicken or vegetable broth
1 small yellow onion
3 tablespoons butter
¼ cup whipping cream
1 tablespoon lemon juice
Sour cream for dolloping
Salt and fresh-ground pepper

How to prep asparagus: Rinse each stalk well, then chop an inch or so off the butt end; discard those bits. My family then stores the stalks, up to several days, at room temperature standing upright in a bowl of water; this (perhaps apocryphally) is thought to rejuice them. When you're ready to cook, bend each stalk until it snaps partway up from the butt end; magically, the top is the good part to eat, but the bottoms are also used for this soup (or you can hoard them in your freezer for future asparagus stock).

For the soup: Bring the butt ends of the asparagus to a boil in the broth, then reduce heat and simmer for 25 minutes. Strain and reserve broth (you can smush extra liquid out of asparagus butts with a wooden spoon if you're motivated); discard asparagus butts. Sauté onion in butter until soft, sprinkling with a little salt and pepper. Cut the asparagus into about 2-inch pieces; reserve the dozen or so prettiest, smallest tips for garnish. Add the stock and the asparagus pieces to the butter and onion; bring to a boil, then reduce heat and simmer, stirring occasionally, about 5 minutes, until pieces are soft to the bite. Blend in batches or with an immersion blender until fairly smooth. Stir in cream and then lemon juice; taste and season with salt and pepper (it'll want some of both). Garnish each bowl with a dollop of sour cream and asparagus tips, plus a little pepper over the top.

La Serenata

By Floyd Skloot

From *Southwest Review*

Award-winning poet, novelist, memoirist, and essayist Floyd
Skloot has lived in Oregon for decades, but he grew up in
Brooklyn and then Long Beach, New York. In this tender essay,
he takes us back to that boyhood, to a time when all was not right
in his world—and a special restaurant offered him safe haven.

I opened the door of La Serenata around 5:30 as usual. It was a cold
winter evening in early 1959, and the restaurant's thick garlicky
warmth was like a second door to walk through. I waved at Paul Russo,
part-owner and bartender, and smiled at his brother Vince, part-owner
and maître d'.

"Evening, Mr. Skloot. We've got your table ready."

I hung up my overcoat, checked that I had all the papers I needed,
and followed Vince to my booth near the kitchen. I liked the anonym-
ity of its location, and the hubbub when Vince rushed through the
doors releasing the voices of his mother, wife, and sister-in-law as they
cooked.

Vince unfolded the white cloth napkin for me and handed me a
menu. "Mama's cooking tonight," he said. "So you might want to try the
Homemade Ravioli."

"Thank you, Vince. I had the Shrimps fra Diavolo last night."

"Make Mr. Skloot his drink, Paul," he called as he left for the kitchen.

I was still considering my choice of appetizer when Paul brought
over my iced drink, garnished the way I preferred it with lime rather

than a maraschino cherry. It was a Shirley Temple. I was eleven years old.

About fifteen months earlier, my father had been critically injured in a crash during his dawn commute to Manhattan. Waiting for roadside assistance from the AAA, parked just off the edge of Rockaway Boulevard, he went to open the trunk and was hit by a car that hopped the curb and slammed into him, smashing his head and chest against the still-shut trunk, shattering both legs between the bumpers. For a week, it wasn't clear that he would live. Then it wasn't clear that he would walk again.

He'd been hospitalized ever since—first in Queens, not far from the site of the accident, then in Long Beach, a small barrier island off the south shore of Long Island, where we'd been living since 1957. Because children were not permitted to visit, my mother would drop me off at La Serenata each evening on her way to the hospital and pick me up on her way home two or three hours later. I'd never had dinner alone in a restaurant before. I ate and did homework, lingering in my booth, comforted by the warm light, the red flocked wallpaper, the large oil painting of a fantastical Italian castle nestled among snowy mountains. Sometimes Vince would sit with me for a few minutes, sighing as he sank into the red cushioned seat and leaned back, and sometimes he would wink as he rushed past with dishes of hot food riding on his arm and in his hands.

I worked my way through most of the menu, skipping the Steak alla Pizzaiola because at $4.95 it was more than double the price of other entrees, and the Saltimboca alla Romana because Vince said I wouldn't like it. After a month, I knew my favorites, but tried to keep rotating what I ordered so I wouldn't get tired of them. Except for Chicken Cacciatore, with its silky sauce and mushrooms, a dish so delicious I had to have it twice a week. My father had been a Kosher chicken butcher until selling his market in Brooklyn when we moved to Long Beach, so I convinced myself that ordering chicken was a way to honor him. Keep him in mind. On the other evenings, I listened to Vince's suggestions, studied the menu, remembered seeing or smelling various dishes as they passed by me each night or overhearing diners' reactions, and thought seriously for the first time in my life about what I actually wanted to eat, learning the way appetite and mood and daily circumstance interacted. Some evenings were right for heaped, filling plates of Linguini with White Clam Sauce or Lasagna, others for the spicy shock of Sausage and Peppers with Special Marinara Sauce or the solace of Veal Cutlet Parmagiani, the touchstone of Chicken Cacciatore.

When he returned to take my order, Vince brought me a complimentary plate with two Clams Arreganata, two steamed mussels in their shells, chopped carrots, and a small square of Sicilian Pizza. He placed a shellfish fork beside the plate.

"How'd you do on that math test today?" he asked. "I know you studied hard."

"I'll find out tomorrow, but I think I got everything right."

The restaurant had opened in 1957 in a building that once housed the Long Beach Public Library. La Serenata's bathrooms were at the top of a long flight of stairs, the dimly lit space cluttered with extra tables and chairs, stacks of white tablecloths, ice buckets and tongs. The only quiet spot in the place, its hushed air was like a preserved pocket from the original library, and entering its stillness was like slipping back in time, as though I'd stumbled into an episode of the new television show *The Twilight Zone*.

The Russo brothers had grown up working in the family restaurant in Brooklyn. They'd swept floors, washed dishes, stocked the kitchen, bused and waited on tables. After it closed, Paul and his wife, Frances, and Vince and his wife, Lisa, had moved to Long Beach and opened La Serenata. The similar paths and timeframes their family and mine had taken to arrive at that place made them feel like relatives to me.

Paul was the quieter older brother, thirty-six, with thick graying hair, a suave stillness of demeanor, and a slight stoop I imagined he'd developed from bending over to measure precisely the drinks he made. He reminded me of Dean Martin and I kept waiting for him to start singing "Volare." From behind the bar he seemed to keep a close eye on things in the dining area and knew just when to ask if another drink was needed. We shared a July birth date, which added to my feeling that we were related.

At thirty-four, Vince had a receding hairline and a rounder face that seemed a perfect expression of his open, friendly, gregarious nature. He moved quickly, issued loud but friendly directives to the waiters or called orders to his brother from across the restaurant. His clothes were always disheveled, white shirt poufed above the waist of his black slacks, collar unbuttoned. When he stood by a table to take orders and write them in his tiny spiral notepad, he couldn't help taking quick glances around the room. Like Paul, he watched everything that went on so he'd be sure none of his guests felt neglected.

One evening when he sat next to me I asked Vince why they'd named the restaurant La Serenata.

"It means 'Serenade,'" he said, checking the table for crumbs and sweeping a few into his hand. "You know, like the love song for someone special."

The first time I remember eating at La Serenata with my parents, shortly after it opened, my mother made her usual grand entrance, demanding that we be moved to a different table from the one Vince had chosen for us, demanding a different set of utensils from the one on the table, a different napkin, a different ashtray. All throughout her performance, Vince was calm and accommodating, soothing, cheerful. When he spoke to her, his voice was a soft croon. He was neither intimidated nor apologetic, but determined to find a way to make my mother feel welcomed despite her shenanigans. He brought over a plate of fresh bread that radiated warmth and a soft yeasty aroma. He made sure her water glass was full. I liked him and the restaurant instantly.

We were a family that ate dinner out once a week, on Sundays. After we'd moved to Long Beach, the dinners followed a regular monthly routine: Wing Loo's one week for the combination platters with extra fried rice, then Meyer & Kronke's just across the bridge in Island Park for seafood, Lenny's in the west end of town for steak or barbecued ribs, and then La Serenata. Wherever we ate, my mother began with a Brandy Alexander, my father with a Seven and Seven, the drinks consumed slowly with an order of appetizers—egg rolls, shrimp cocktail, oysters on the half-shell. I remember my mother's disgust as my father savored Clams Posillipo at La Serenata, getting tomato sauce splatters on the tablecloth, on his shirt, and eventually on my shirt as I leaned over to eat a clam off his extended fork.

La Serenata provided my first taste of veal scallops, of eggplant, Manicotti Parmagiani, cooked shrimp, Biscuit Tortoni. That's where I learned to like string beans slathered in marinara sauce, and broccoli crisply sautéed rather than boiled until limp. Where I understood the difference between homemade spaghetti and Ronzoni from a box.

By the time my father was injured, we'd eaten at La Serenata often enough for the Russos to know our peculiarities. Vince would greet us by asking my mother where she would like to sit, effectively blocking her standard table-switch maneuver. He would show her the napkin before placing it in her lap and check out the silverware, sometimes frowning and removing it himself and bringing her a new set without being asked. Paul would mix and deliver the drinks unbidden.

"I'll tell Mama you're here," Vince would say, implying that of course my mother would be receiving special attention from the chef.

The restaurant was exactly two miles from our home. Sometimes it felt like another world altogether, a million miles away, so full of family warmth and ease, so different from our way of life, and sometimes when my parents laughed and lingered over coffee and Spumoni it felt like a newly discovered part of our home, no distance at all.

I think I remember that first dinner at La Serenata so clearly (Shrimps Scampi, Veal Pizzaiola, String Beans Marinara at Vince's suggestion) because it was the evening my mother announced she would learn to drive. It was as though she'd needed her Brandy Alexander and anti-pasto before mustering the courage to break this news. My father, bent over his plate, came to a dead stop, threads of fettucine dangling from his mouth, and stared across the table at her for a long time.

"Well, I'm not about to teach you," he mumbled, then looked at me and continued eating.

"I didn't think you would." She paused to light her Chesterfield. "So I'm going to take private lessons. Edith Sills knows a man."

He shrugged and said, "I hope he knows what he's getting into."

It was difficult to imagine my mother driving. As a passenger she had a peculiar relationship with the rules of the road. Sitting beside my father while he drove, she would argue with traffic signs, certain they couldn't apply to a vehicle she was in, insisting that he ignore one-way streets or speed limits and stop signs if we were in a hurry, or that east and west were meaningless pieces of information when she wanted to know where Westbury was. And she loathed being told what to do—I think that was a key element in my father's reaction.

My mother was forty-seven and had never felt the need to drive.

Living in Manhattan or Brooklyn all her life, she'd gotten where she wanted to go by taxi, subway, bus, or trolley, or as a passenger in someone's car. But the public transit options on the small island of Long Beach were limited and less convenient than she liked, and she only knew a few people there she felt comfortable asking for a ride.

After taking lessons and practicing for weeks with Edith, she failed her first road test. "Stupid examiner!" she said. "Made me parallel park and had the nerve to say I was too far from the curb." When she finally passed and began driving a new white Plymouth Fury around town, she seldom ventured off the island, until when my father ended up in Queens General Hospital and she would visit him there daily.

One night my mother dropped me off during a light snowfall. As the evening passed, the snow worsened to a blizzard and I noticed that there was only one other customer in the restaurant. I knew who he was: Mr. Ritacchio, a language teacher at the high school I would be attending in a few years. Usually, his table at the center of the restaurant attracted a steady progression of visitors, students and parents, colleagues. But tonight it was just the two of us and he sat with his back toward me, glancing at the window. Vince kept looking out the window too, checking the weather, shaking his head. The restaurant was eerily quiet.

When Mr. Ritacchio left, Vince exchanged glances with Paul and they both shrugged. Vince went back into the kitchen. I heard him talking to his family but couldn't make out the words. Paul picked up the phone near the bar and made a call, speaking softly. I wasn't used to the subdued atmosphere, but it felt cozy rather than alarming.

After a few minutes, Vince sat next to me. "Your mother," he said. "She's still at the hospital with your father and didn't notice how bad the snow is. She can't drive in this."

I remember feeling a rush of confusion. My mother couldn't come for me? Maybe she'd have to sleep in the hospital and maybe I'd have to sleep in the restaurant. Maybe upstairs in the Twilight Zone there was a secret room with a bed or something. Would the Russos cook me breakfast? That would be all right. All of it would be all right.

"What I'm going to do," Vince said, "is I'm going to close up. Then I'll drive you over to the hospital, we'll pick up your mother, and I'll drive you both home. Don't worry, okay?"

I wasn't worried. I was disappointed not to be staying overnight at La Serenata. Or—I hadn't thought of it till that moment—at Vince or Paul's house. And I was embarrassed that the restaurant had to close, even though they had no customers, because my mother couldn't come to get me. But more than anything else, I felt overwhelmed by the kindness in Vince's voice and in his actions.

A few weeks later I had a mini-breakdown over a plate of Baked Ziti with Meat Sauce. Earlier in the day, I'd gotten home from school and decided the time had come to find out what was inside the carton my mother had stashed in the garage shortly after my father was injured. She'd told me never to touch it, had written DO NOT TOUCH across the top in large red letters, and stashed the carton underneath an old bedsheet against the back wall. All of which drew me until I could no longer resist.

It was too light to contain books or dishes. I felt sure it had something to do with my father. Something he didn't need now but was too important to throw away. I wasn't sure what a will was, but had heard the word mentioned lately. Was a will large enough to justify a carton like the ones we'd used when we moved from Brooklyn?

When I opened it the first thing I saw was a large envelope containing photographs of my father lying on the ground in the immediate aftermath of the crash. He was flat on his back, hands raised as though warding off further assault. Below the envelope were his blood-drenched wingtip shoes and socks, torn pants, shirt and tie. Some kind of sheet or blanket that must have been used to cover him. It would all be evidence for the trial of the man who had crashed into my father, but I didn't grasp that then. I thought my mother was saving it as some kind of ghoulish souvenir. I couldn't stop thinking about it. I couldn't stop smelling it.

At La Serenata, when Vince put the plate of Ziti with Meat Sauce in front of me, all I could see, in its mixture of deep red and bone white and bits of meat, was gore. I was swamped by a kind of sensory overload—the sight before me, the odor rising from it, a feeling as though my entire body had become entangled in the gruesome fabric I'd touched that afternoon.

I pushed the plate aside and tried to stand, but the configuration of booth cushion and table seemed to hold me down. Vince, who hadn't yet left the table, reached for me as I sat back and began to cry. Then he slipped into the booth and settled next to me, moving the plate out of sight. He didn't speak, just stayed with me, waiting with me for the moment to pass.

My father came home from the hospital in late spring and my nightly dinners at La Serenata stopped. A few weeks later I went away to summer camp in Pennsylvania for two months and by the time I returned my father was able to get around in a wheelchair. The hospital bed we'd rented was gone but now there was a set of parallel bars in my parents' bedroom where he would work three or four days a week with his physical therapist.

In the fall of 1959, we resumed our monthly routine of dinners out. I remember how bizarre it felt to return to La Serenata with my parents. The first time, Vince solemnly bowed to my mother, shook my father's hand and asked how he was doing, then looked at me for a moment and opened his arms in greeting. He seated us at a central table my mother requested, not at my booth. Being there began to feel so formal, familiar but unfamiliar, like visiting a house you no longer live in. Vince never stopped to sit down with us or put his hand on my shoulder as he passed by.

My father died two years later. He'd gone from using a wheelchair to using crutches to using a cane to, at last, walking with the aid of a built-up shoe. In November 1961, he and my mother went with a group of friends for a Veterans' Day holiday weekend at a hotel in upstate New York. Despite how much effort it took for him to get around, he must have felt somehow liberated to be there, away from the places that reminded him of his injuries and long recovery, because he spent most of his time either riding horses, playing shuffleboard, throwing horseshoes, and walking on wooded trails. Toward evening, after dozing under a poolside sunlamp, he dove into the water and drowned. Going from the heat to the cold, he might have had a shock-induced heart attack, or he might have found himself too tired to swim after all his activity, might have become disoriented—there was no autopsy to establish cause of death—but he died there beside the pool, having finally been dragged out by friends who at first thought his flailing was meant to be comic.

After his funeral we followed the Jewish seven-day ritual of mourning, *shiva*, sitting in our living room on small hard stools, saying prayers, talking about my father, welcoming visitors and their gifts of food. I remember my aunt calling to ask if there was anything special I'd like them to bring for dinner, something that perhaps reminded me of my father. I hadn't felt like eating since he'd died. But once my aunt asked, I knew exactly what to request. I asked her to stop at La Serenata—124 West Park Avenue, they'd pass right by it on their way to our house—and pick up an appetizer of Clams Posillipo and an order of Chicken Cacciatore.

By the spring of 1982, I'd been gone from Long Beach for seventeen years and was living in Springfield, Illinois. My mother and stepfather, Julius Rosen, whom she'd married the year I left for college, planned to drive the 950 miles for a visit. But they didn't get past the first mile, running a stop sign and smashing into a delivery van.

I received the call from Julius at my office. His voice was tight with pain and his breath rattled. "Broken ribs," he said. "Cuts. And bruises. I'll be. Fine." But my mother was in bad shape, with a leg broken in at least three places. "They had to cut her out of the car," he whispered. "She wants you here."

I was in Long Beach the next day. And that night, after visiting my mother and Julius, after dealing with the towing company and insurance and police, I went to dinner at La Serenata. I hadn't been there in so long I wasn't sure Vince and Paul would recognize me, bearded now, hair close-cropped, eyeglasses with transition lenses that made me look like a Mafioso in the least light.

As soon as I entered, Vince said, "Evening, Mr. Skloot. We've got your table ready." He shook my hand. "I heard about your mother and Mr. Rosen, so I knew you'd be here."

Paul nodded at me from behind the bar. "Not a Shirley Temple, Mr. Skloot, am I right?"

I laughed for the first time that day. When he brought me my martini, Paul whispered, "On the house."

That dinner (Shrimps Scampi, Veal Pizzaiola, String Beans Marinara) and the four others I had there during my five-day stay in Long Beach were the last I ever ate in La Serenata. The restaurant closed in 1984, after a twenty-six-year run. Paul's wife, Frances, recently told me that she and Vince's wife, Lisa, wanted to keep it open. "But the men were done," she said.

In 2014, on the fifty-third anniversary of my father's death—the year in which he'd been dead as long as he'd been alive—images and memories of La Serenata flooded back. I wanted to research what had happened to the place and to the Russo family. I wanted to remember more details about the menu, decor, atmosphere, wanted to pay homage, maybe try to cook their version of Chicken Cacciatore.

I learned that the building is still in use as a restaurant, currently occupied by Sutton Place Great American Bar & Grille. I emailed the owner to ask if he had any old materials—a menu, a photograph, memorabilia—he'd be willing to share with me.

"I am sorry," he wrote, "but we don't have anything from those days. This location has changed hands so many times since then. I am here my whole life since 1969 yet I was too young really for La Serenata. We have been here for 13 years now."

Calls to the Long Beach Public Library and to the Long Beach Historical and Preservation Society yielded no information. Internet searches turned up very little as well, though I did find an obituary for Vince, who died in 2007 at the age of eighty-three.

I suppose it's not unusual for there to be little public notice of a small family restaurant located on a small barrier island nine miles long by one mile wide, an establishment that has been out of business for thirty-two years. But the virtual absence of information made La Serenata seem like a kind of Brigadoon, a mystical place that appears for just a single day every hundred years. If it lives in the present, if there are traces of it in 2016, they exist in the memories of those who knew it.

In 2005 *The New York Times* interviewed my classmate and friend Billy Crystal during the Broadway run of his play *700 Sundays*. The play recalls his Long Beach childhood, and in amplifying details for the interviewer Billy said his family "ate Chinese at Wing Loo's or dined at La Serenata, at Italian restaurant." I think because I'd always felt cocooned in my booth, and isolated within the strangeness and fear and grief over what was happening to my father and my family, I didn't remember seeing people I knew in the restaurant. But Billy was there, and there had to have been kids eating there with their families when I was present, kids I knew. I wondered what they remembered of La Serenata, what they liked to eat. So I wrote emails to a few old friends with whom I was still in touch.

"I loved La Serenata," Murray Schwartz wrote back. As our graduating class reached its fiftieth anniversary, Murray's capacity to recall details from our school years became legendary. "My strongest memory of La Serenata is of their hospitality. You were welcome." He gave me email addresses for some other friends and I learned that many of them ate at La Serenata weekly or biweekly. Donna Selnick wrote, "it was my family's go-to place to eat out and it set the standard for Eggplant Parmagiani and Veal Parmagiani for the rest of my life." Janie Samuels wrote "Stuffed Clams, Veal Parmagiani, and Spaghetti with Clam Sauce were always our favorites." Arlene Krasner loved the Antipasto so much she would order it as her main course. My neighbor and lifelong friend Billy Babiskin wrote that the Veal Parmagiani and the linguine were very good.

One of my friends mentioned a closed Facebook group, "IF YOU GREW UP IN LONG BEACH NEW YORK IN THE 50'S, 60'S & 70'S." I was accepted into the group and posted a query asking for recollections and for the names of their favorite dishes. Never having belonged to a Facebook group and not knowing what to expect, I was astounded by the response: seventy-two people offered comments and a few photographs. Seven had eaten at La Serenata once a week and another remembered eating dinners there three times during a single Christmas week. Many said they ate there "often" or "all the time," three recalled celebrating their elementary or high school graduations, two celebrated their sweet sixteen, and one celebrated his midget football league championship at La Serenata. I'd anticipated that if anyone named a favorite dish, it would likely be the Veal Parmagiani, which my email correspondents had each cited. But instead, the group's members named thirty different dishes as their favorite. From the Antipasto (nine) and Baked Clams Arreganata (eight) to the Veal Francaise (two), Beef Rollatine (one), and Chicken Cacciatore (one—me), this was a menu of greatest hits, consistent, memorable, and apparently much missed.

Among the respondents was Frances Russo, Paul's wife, who told me that Paul had died in March 2016, at ninety-two and after sixty-three years of marriage. She photocopied and mailed me a menu. When I asked her if she could send a recipe for Chicken Cacciatore so I could cook the dish here in Portland for my wife, Frances said, "What recipe? We just cooked."

In a sense, the Russos are still taking care of me. Of course there's no point in my attempting to duplicate La Serenata's Chicken Cacciatore. I've cooked many versions of that dish since 1959 when I first tasted the Russo version. Each time, it brought back memories that, for all their painful associations, were full of warmth, tenderness, and a kind of sanctuary.

Recipe Index

Permissions Acknowledgments

Grateful acknowledgment is made to all those who gave permission for written material to appear in this book. Every effort has been made to trace and contact copyright holders. If an error or omission is brought to our notice, we will be pleased to remedy the situation in subsequent editions of this book. For further information, please contact the publisher

Addison, Bill. "I Want Crab. Pure Maryland Crab." Copyright © 2016 by Vox Media, Inc. Originally published on Eater.com, September 15, 2016. http://www.eater.com/2016/9/15/12929848/baltimore -maryland-where-to-eat-crab-crabcakes

Amster-Burton, Matthew. "Japan's Cult Food Drama *The Lonely Gourmet* Is Essentially Pornography." Copyright © 2016 by Matthew Amster-Burton. Originally published by *AVClub.com* (September 21, 2016). Used by permission of the author.

Arellano, Gustavo. "In Defense of the Mexican-American Chef, Or: No One Hates on Mexicans Like Mexicans." Copyright © 2016 by Gustavo Arellano. Originally published by *OC Weekly* (August 18, 2016). Used by permission of the publisher.

Excerpt(s) from TREYF: MY LIFE AS AN UNORTHODOX OUTLAW by Elissa Altman, copyright © 2016 by Elissa Altman. Used by permission of Berkley, an imprint of Penguin Publishing Group, a division of Penguin Random House LLC. All rights reserved.

Birdsall, John. "The Story of the Mission Burrito" / Bon Appetit; Copyright © Conde Nast.

Black, Jane. "Claus Meyer to Open Brownsville Community Culinary Center & Neighborhood Eatery." Copyright © 2016 by Jane Black. Originally published by GrubStreet.com (October 18, 2016). Used by permission of the publisher.

About the Editor

Holly Hughes is a writer, the former executive editor of Fodor's Travel Publications, and author of *Frommer's 500 Places for Food and Wine Lovers*.

Submissions for Best Food Writing 2017

Submissions and nominations for *Best Food Writing 2018* should be forwarded no later than December 15, 2017, to Holly Hughes at *Best Food Writing 2018*, c/o Da Capo Press, 53 State Street, Ninth Floor, Boston MA 02109, or emailed to bestfood@hbgusa.com. Articles or excerpts published between January 1, 2017 and November 30, 2017 are eligible. We regret that, due to volume, we cannot acknowledge receipt of all submissions.